ADVANCES IN
EXPERIMENTAL
SOCIAL PSYCHOLOGY

VOLUME 1

CONTRIBUTORS TO VOLUME 1

FRED E. FIEDLER

WILLIAM A. GAMSON

WILLIAM J. McGUIRE

WILLIAM A. MASON

ROSS D. PARKE

STANLEY SCHACHTER

MARVIN E. SHAW

HARRY C. TRIANDIS

RICHARD H. WALTERS

ADVANCES IN

Experimental Social Psychology

EDITED BY

Leonard Berkowitz
DEPARTMENT OF PSYCHOLOGY
UNIVERSITY OF WISCONSIN
MADISON, WISCONSIN

VOLUME 1

1964
ACADEMIC PRESS   New York   San Francisco   London
A Subsidiary of Harcourt Brace Jovanovich, Publishers

ACADEMIC PRESS, INC.
111 Fifth Avenue, New York, New York 10003

United Kingdom Edition published by
ACADEMIC PRESS, INC. (LONDON) LTD.
24/28 Oval Road, London NW1

LIBRARY OF CONGRESS CATALOG CARD NUMBER: 64-23452

PRINTED IN THE UNITED STATES OF AMERICA

CONTRIBUTORS

FRED E. FIEDLER, *Department of Psychology, University of Illinois, Urbana, Illinois*

WILLIAM A. GAMSON, *Department of Sociology, University of Michigan, Ann Arbor, Michigan*

WILLIAM J. McGUIRE, *Department of Social Psychology, Columbia University, New York, New York*

WILLIAM A. MASON,* *Delta Regional Primate Research Center, Tulane University, New Orleans, Louisiana*

ROSS D. PARKE, *Department of Psychology, University of Waterloo, Ontario, Canada*

STANLEY SCHACHTER, *Department of Social Psychology, Columbia University, New York, New York*

MARVIN E. SHAW, *Department of Psychology, University of Florida, Gainesville, Florida*

HARRY C. TRIANDIS, *Department of Psychology, University of Illinois, Urbana, Illinois*

RICHARD H. WALTERS, *Department of Psychology, University of Waterloo, Ontario, Canada*

---

* Present address: International Center for Medical Research and Training, Universidad del Valle, Cali, Colombia.

PREFACE

The tremendous growth in the number of articles, journals, and books relevant to social psychology is a testimony to the vitality of the science and the energy of social psychologists. Quick to question—and encouraged by the increasing financial support being given to the behavioral sciences—social psychologists are accumulating observations and research findings at an impressive rate. Thus, as facts multiply, the problems of their storage and integration become even more serious. If scientific research is to be conducted as efficiently as possible, information must be stored and made readily available when needed. The present series attempts to do this along with such well established and effective institutions as *Psychological Abstracts, Sociological Abstracts,* and the *Annual Review of Psychology.* We hope that the many people interested in the behavioral sciences will come to regard the *Advances* as an important repository of information. However, as necessary as information storage is, it is the integration of facts with which we shall be primarily concerned.

There certainly is no paucity of hypotheses in contemporary social psychology. Do we really need any more speculative generalizations? In many ways our theoretical aspirations have outraced our actual attainments. For example, probably no other science abounds with as many unwarranted usages of the term "theory" (e.g., role theory, reference group theory, cognitive theory); instead of leading to fairly specific predictions, these "theories" in actuality are often nothing but conglomerations of imprecisely formulated concepts. (As an illustration, I can think of at least three conceptually quite different ways that the notion "reference group" has been employed. Which of these meanings does a writer have in mind? It is often difficult to say.) But granting that social psychology contains many crudely drawn generalizations, this series is built on the belief that the scientist must do more than accumulate facts. He must also integrate the available data in such a way that the observed events can be shown to be special cases of a more general phenomenon. In his book, "The Art of Scientific Investigation" (revised edition, page

123, W. W. Norton, New York, 1957), W. I. B. Beveridge has pointed out:

". . . facts obtained by observation or experiment usually only gain significance when we use reason to build them into the general body of knowledge. Darwin said: 'Science consists in grouping facts so that general laws or conclusions may be drawn from them.' In research it is not sufficient to collect facts; by interpreting them, by seeing their significance and consequences, we can often go much further . . . "

The papers in this series, then, will do more than report research findings. Interpretations and generalizations will also be offered so that we can see the "significance and consequences" of the data and (hopefully) can go much further.

The last phrase deserves some additional comment. There is no claim (at least as far as the editor is concerned) that the theoretical statements presented in these volumes are the last word and will remain unaltered as additional information is obtained. We can be assured that most of the hypotheses listed in these pages will be found wanting in one way or another as the years go by. By presenting their hypotheses, the writers have contributed to the data collection and theory development that will question their own formulations. Their theoretical statements will help social psychology go further.

As the series title indicates, the papers in these volumes will deal mainly with experimental research. More and more social psychologists are turning to the laboratory for answers to their questions since the development of precise theoretical statements requires tests made with well-designed experimental controls. Nevertheless, social psychology must also conduct field research in naturalistic settings. Some problems obviously cannot be investigated adequately under the restricted and usually short-lived conditions of the laboratory. But more than this, field research can also suggest hypotheses that may be investigated in the laboratory and, in addition, provides a test of the generality of the experimental findings. The present volumes will therefore focus their attention on the laboratory but will not neglect observations of behavior in "real-life" situations.

With these introductory remarks Volume 1 begins.

LEONARD BERKOWITZ

Madison, Wisconsin
April, 1964

CONTENTS

Cultural Influences upon Cognitive Processes

Harry C. Triandis

The Interaction of Cognitive and Physiological Determinants of Emotional State

Stanley Schachter

Experimental Studies of Coalition Formation

William A. Gamson

Communication Networks

Marvin E. Shaw

A Contingency Model of Leadership Effectiveness

Fred E. Fiedler

Inducing Resistance to Persuasion
Some Contemporary Approaches

William J. McGuire

Social Motivation, Dependency, and Susceptibility to Social Influence

Richard H. Walters and Ross D. Parke

Sociability and Social Organization in Monkeys and Apes

William A. Mason

ADVANCES IN

EXPERIMENTAL
SOCIAL PSYCHOLOGY

VOLUME 1

CULTURAL INFLUENCES UPON COGNITIVE PROCESSES[1]

Harry C. Triandis

DEPARTMENT OF PSYCHOLOGY
UNIVERSITY OF ILLINOIS
URBANA, ILLINOIS

[1] Martin Fishbein and Charles E. Osgood read an earlier draft of this chapter and made many valuable suggestions. Donald Campbell, J. B. Carroll, J. Casagrande, Roger Brown, Susan Ervin, R. Jessor, W. W. Lambert, E. Rose, and M. H. Segall provided me with unpublished manuscripts of their work relevant to this chapter, and/or guided me to other unpublished materials.

1

I. Introduction

A. DEFINITIONS

1. Culture

Culture is "the man-made part of the human environment" (Herskovits, 1955, p. 305). This definition subsumes not only the material features of the human environment, but also its "conceptual" features—the beliefs, science, myths, religions, laws, etc., held by a group of people.

Language is one of the important elements of culture, but language and culture cannot be considered as identical (Voegelin, 1949). Animals may be able to learn some significant aspects of human culture, but appear unable to master the syntactical aspects of language (Hebb and Thompson, 1954). The present chapter focuses particularly on comparisons of groups that employ mutually unintelligible languages.

Many variables may cause a group of people to interact more frequently. Among these factors are similarities in values, ideals, attitudes, language, geographic location, race (physical type), social class, occupation, religion, nationality, age, sex, roles, etc. High rates of interaction tend to increase the similarity in the characteristic patterns of behavior and in values, ideals, and attitudes. Thus, similarity in any of the characteristics listed above may produce similarities in culture between two groups.

2. Cognition

Cognition is the subfield of psychology that is concerned with the laws determining how organisms know the world around them. It subsumes perception, recognition, retention, imagination (including dreams and hallucinations), meaning, associations, and attitudes, as well as concept formation and problem solving.

B. OUTLINE OF THE CHAPTER

1. General

The view that certain aspects of cognition depend on language and culture has a history going back to Plato. However, systematic research on this topic is relatively recent. Many of these investigations have been initiated as a test of the so-called Whorfian hypothesis (Whorf, 1956), which states that the world view of individuals in a culture depends on the structure and characteristics of the language they speak. The present chapter will examine a considerable body of data relevant to this issue. It is divided into two main parts. The first part outlines a theoretical framework and provides the concepts that are used in the second part. The second part reviews the empirical evidence that is relevant to the theoretical framework.

2. What Is Excluded

The focus is on the last ten years of research. Older material is excluded or referred to very briefly.

Since cognition is a vast topic, the review focuses on those areas which have not been covered by other surveys. The following topics were excluded because they are reviewed by others: projective techniques (Lindzey, 1961), dreams (D'Andrade, 1961; Eggan, 1961), intelligence (Anastasi and Foley, 1958), national character (Rokkan, 1955; Duijker and Frijda, 1960), and the interaction of cultural and developmental factors in perception (Dennis, 1951). The noncognitive aspects of the culture and personality area will not be discussed, since this would dilute the intended concentration on cognitive materials. Hsu (1961) and Kaplan (1961), as well as Wallace (1962a), have provided useful recent guides to such discussions, and LeVine (1963) has reviewed most of the recent anthropological literature. The focus of the chapter also differs from that employed by French (1963) in his excellent survey of the same area.

Approaches not involving measurements taken directly from subjects, such as Cattell's (1950), or those dealing with cross-cultural contact and its effects (e.g., Smith, 1956; Bjerstedt, 1958) have also been excluded.

C. A NOTE ON METHODOLOGY

The ideal methodology for studying the effect of cultural factors on cognition would involve a representative sample of cultures, with samples of individuals in each culture that are the same age, sex, etc. Cognitive tasks of equivalent meaning would be given to each subject. The subjects' responses would be recorded and analyzed in identical ways. The cultures would differ from each other in specified ways. Some would have the same language and/or religion; others would not.

The subjects in the several cultures would be chosen according to a factorial design, and analyses of variance would permit the determination of the kinds of cultural features (linguistic, religious, etc.) which account for the differences in subject performance to various classes of cognitive tasks. Such a design would permit the determination of the within and between culture variance for the various cognitive tasks, and would thus enable the researcher to focus on only those tasks where the between culture variance is greater than the within.

It is clear that such a design emphasizes the experimenter's concern with what Pike [1954 (reviewed by French, 1963, pp. 398–399)] called the *etic* as opposed to the *emic* approach. The emic approach attempts to describe a phenomenon in terms of its own structure; the etic, in terms of some external yardstick, such as other cultures, or an external set of units. Anthropologists have usually analyzed cultures emically. Through intensive analyses, they have tried to show interrelationships of various aspects of a single culture. Many anthropologists have analyzed such interrelationships in the terms of the particular culture with varying degrees of success. Social psychologists, on the other hand, are usually interested in generalizations that hold for all humans. Such generalizations require an etic approach.

The difficulty with the etic approach, however, is that it imposes universal categories on the data of each culture. Thus, if the categories do not fit the data, it's too bad for the data. Ideally, the experimenter agrees with French (1963, p. 401) that three steps are needed: (a) an initial etic approach using established categories; (b) an emic organization of the data; and (c) a well-considered etic approach (employing a metalanguage) which preserves the insights gained from the emic analysis.

In the review that follows, etic studies that approximate the ideal design described above have been given more room than studies not meeting this criterion. Emic studies have been excluded, except in a few cases where they made a particularly useful point that other kinds of data could not make.

II. Theoretical Framework

A. GENERAL

The present section will define a number of concepts, which will be used as the main building blocks of a theoretical framework. This framework is quite eclectric and is not offered as a theory of cognition, but rather as a map for the guidance of the reader. The map consists of the concepts *categorization, evaluation, behavioral intentions, attitudes,* and *values.* No attempt will be made to tie these concepts to behavior. However, the framework lends itself quite readily to an extension such as that provided by Miller *et al.* (1960). Some of the concepts of the present framework, such as behavioral intentions, have been tied to behavior by Dulany (1962) through a series of theoretical statements supported by excellently conceived and executed experiments. The present framework also contains elements that bear some resemblance to Wallace's (1956, 1961) concept of a *mazeway.* A mazeway is the totality of learned cognitive representations. It is to the individual what culture is to the group.

B. Categorization

1. General

There are potentially an infinite number of just noticeable differences in the human environment. In the area of color discrimination alone, color engineers estimate that there are 7,500,000 discriminable colors (Brown and Lenneberg, 1954). Normal humans, regardless of culture, are capable of making these discriminations. Since that fine a discrimination of the environment is beyond the capacity of human attention and decoding, man typically treats many discriminable stimuli as instances of the same thing. In other words, he categorizes stimuli. All stimuli grouped together within a category are regarded as equivalent. Thus, drivers behave the same in relation to red lights, regardless of the saturation and variation of red hue in the light. By means of categorization man is able to respond selectively to the environment. Categorization has considerable survival value, since it simplifies a person's task of responding to the environment. Allport (1954) and also Bruner (1958) stressed the great loss of information in categorization. Furthermore, misinformation may be added, for when a stimulus is placed in a category, it is assumed to have the same associations with other categories that the typical members of the category have with such other categories. Language has a key function in categorization. The 7,500,000 colors are dealt with by only 4000 English words, of which only 8 are commonly used.

Bruner (1957, p. 123) stated: "Perception involves an act of categorization." What is perceived achieves its "meaning" from the class of percepts with which it is grouped and the relation of the category in which it is classified to other categories. The meaning of a category depends on its relation to other categories. Bruner summarized experiments which suggest that subjects learn the transitional probabilities of "what goes with what."

By *category* Bruner meant "a rule for classification of objects [stimuli] as equivalent." The rule specifies (a) the critical attribute values that must be present in a stimulus so that it may be placed in a particular category; (b) the manner of combination of the attribute values; (c) the weights assigned to various attributes; and (d) the acceptable limits of the attributes.

The above discussion is mainly in terms of the perceptual signs of objects in the human environment, but no significant changes in the argument are necessary if the symbols or signs of the objects are involved instead. Osgood's (1953) mediation theory, in which signs produce a fraction of the responses normally elicited by the objects themselves, suggests that the same theoretical framework may be used for both symbols and objects.

2. Organization of Categories

a. Schemata and lexical fields. Categories are organized in *schemata,* which are super-categories. The words corresponding to categories derive their meaning from their relationships to other words. Dictionaries employ synonyms and antonyms to define the meaning of a word.

The notion that categories are organized into schemata has been elaborated by Bartlett (1932), Piaget (1961), and others. The development of such schemata has been described by Piaget and is well reviewed by Church (1961) and J. McV. Hunt (1961).

Trier (1931) provided one of the best analyses of such schemata in the field of meaning. Words do not exist by themselves, but together with other words that are their conceptual relatives (*Begriffsverwandten*). The meaning of a word depends, in part, on the meaning of its conceptual relatives. For example, the meaning of "warm" depends on the meaning of "cold" and "hot."

3. Stereotypes

Words acquire their meaning not only in relation to other words in their lexical field, but also in contrast with other lexical fields and due to probabilistic associations of the kind: word A goes with B, C, . . . Z. It will be shown that such probabilistic associations are greatly affected by cultural variables in the case where A is a word representing a group of people.

C. EVALUATIONS

Once a category is stabilized, subjects are likely to experience positive or negative reinforcements in connection with this category. As a result, they will learn to experience positive and negative affect states in the presence of the category.

An extensive literature has emerged in the last ten years in which the writers describe the experimental development of attitudes through conditioning. The present writer prefers to employ the term "attitudes" to convey the idea of a "predisposition to respond" (Campbell, 1963). For this reason, studies such as those of Eisman (1955), Solley and Messick (1957), Rhine and Silum (1958), Rhine (1958), Staats *et al.* (1960), Weiss (1962), and Das and Nanda (1963) are considered as studies of the development of judgments and evaluations, rather than attitudes.

Fishbein (1961) showed that the scores obtained from subjects on semantic-differential-type attitude scales when judging a concept A are closely correlated with scores obtained by summing the products of the probabilities of connection of several attributes of A and the evaluations of these attributes. In other words, if the evaluation of each of several attributes of A is multiplied by the subject's subjective probability that A has the particular attribute, and if the sum of these products is computed, the obtained score is highly correlated with the subject's "attitude" toward A. In the language of the present chapter, evaluations may be summated, and the evaluation of a concept depends on the evaluations of its attributes. This theory will be discussed later as an example of a cognitive summation theory.

D. BEHAVIORAL INTENTIONS

Behavioral intentions, as well as content and affect, are associated with categories. These behavioral intentions appear to be most imperfectly related to evaluations. Triandis and Triandis (1962) presented 16 complex stimuli to 100 Greek and 100 Illinois subjects. The stimuli were of the type: "A Portuguese Negro coal miner of the same religion as you are." The subjects judged them on both the evaluative scales of semantic differentials (Osgood *et al.*, 1957) and on social distance scales that were separately standardized in each of the two cultures. The results of analyses of the data from the two scales suggest that there are large discrepancies between the results obtained from the semantic differential (evaluations) and social distance scales (behavioral intentions).

In the present chapter, when a category A is judged on the evaluative factor of semantic differentials, or involves responses of the "I feel . . . ," "I like . . ." type, the measures obtained will be called *evaluations*. Statements of the "I would do . . ." type will be considered measures of *behavioral intentions*. Statements of the "I should do . . ." type correlate quite highly with behavioral intentions [in Bastide and van den Berghe (1957) it was .68] and may be called *behavioral norms*. Statements of the form "I believe X goes with Y" may be called *opinions*. All of the above may then be subsumed under the term *attitude*.

E. ATTITUDES AND VALUES

In the previous section attitudes were described as consisting of both evaluations and behavioral intentions. When the responses of the subject to a variety of stimulus situations are obtained, we are able to study the way in which attitudes are structured. Katz (1960) suggested that when attitudes are organized into hierarchies, they form value systems. Factor analyses of attitudes have suggested broad values such as conservatism, nationalism, etc. An even more abstract conception considers the organization of these values into five basic value orientations (Kluckhohn and Strodtbeck, 1961).

III. Methodology for Operationalization of the Key Variables in the Theoretical Framework

The previous section provided definitions of the key concepts of this chapter, namely, categorization, evaluation, behavioral intentions, attitudes, and values. In the present section, certain procedures that permit the operationalization and measurement of these concepts will be described.

A. CATEGORIES

Among the procedures now available for the study of categories, the most promising appear to be componential analysis (Goodenough, 1956; Lounsbury, 1956) and procedures that derive from Kelly's (1955) psychology of personal constructs.

1. Componential Analysis

This technique is employed in the analysis of the components underlying a particular lexical field in a particular language. It has been widely used in analyses of kinship data. Wallace (1962b) presents an easy and clear introduction. Briefly, the following steps are required. First, it is necessary to collect a large sample of expressions that belong to a particular universe of meaning, e.g., kinship terms. Second, it is necessary to translate the kinship terms into a basic notation which consists of simple elements such as Fa (Father), Mo (Mother), Br (Brother). Now a particular relative may be described in terms of these basic components, e.g., he is the FaMoBr (a great uncle). Third, it is possible to examine the way in which the lexical field is structured. For instance, a kinship term field may employ as basic structural elements (a) the seniority of the generation of the relative, (b) the sex of the relative, (c) the sex of the relative in relation to ego's sex, and (d) the degree of affinal removal.

When a physical continuum is available, the anthropologist may use it as the stimulus and obtain the corresponding linguistic coding. Lenneberg and Roberts (1956) presented color charts to their subjects and asked them to draw the boundaries of a particular color name. They found only a rough correspondence between certain Navaho and supposedly equivalent English color names. For more complex meaning fields a taxonomic hierarchy comprising different sets of contrasting categories at successive levels is appropriate. Such taxonomies have been published for diseases among the Subanun (Frake, 1961), for botanical terms (Conklin, 1954), and for other meaning fields as well. A taxonomy, according to Frake (1961), is structured along two dimensions: a horizontal one of discrimination (poodle, collie, terrier) and a vertical one of generalization (poodle, dog, animal). Such taxonomies may be very ambitious projects. Frake (1962a, b) has contributed two methodological papers. In the first he wrote:

> A successful strategy for writing ethnographies must tap the cognitive world of one's informants. It must discover those features of objects and events which they regard as significant for defining concepts, formulating propositions, and making decisions. This conception of an ethnography requires that the units by which the data of observation are segmented, ordered, and interrelated be delimited and defined according to contrasts inherent in the data themselves and not according to a priori notions of pertinent descriptive categories.

Though componential analysis is a new technique and has not been sufficiently used to permit a definitive evaluation at this time, there appear to be a number of important methodological problems associated with the method (Wallace and Atkins, 1960). One of the major problems is the imposition of an etic approach on essentially emic data (see Section I,C for definitions of terms). Another problem is that the analysis must be repeated for each and every one of the lexical fields in a language. This is a very elaborate process and is unlikely to be adopted for any except the most important lexical fields.

2. Personal Constructs

Another approach to the study of categories utilizes Kelly's (1955) notion of personal constructs. The approach is exemplified by Triandis (1959a) with subcultures of subjects. It requires the presentation of triads of concepts. The subject is asked, "Which one of these three is different from the other two and why?" The obtained responses may be considered as criterial attributes of the concepts being used, but also as categories of thought about concepts in a particular lexical field. Subjects employing a particular set of categories experience difficulties in communicating with subjects employing another set (Triandis, 1960a).

3. Methods for the Study of Stereotypes

The most frequently used method is the checklist. This method, however, has serious methodological limitations in cross-cultural work. Subjects in different cultures have different notions about the number of checks that they "ought" to place. Particular adjectives are often differently correlated with evaluation (e.g., "aggressive" with "good" in some cultures and with "bad" in others). The social desirability of traits is, generally speaking, similar among Norwegian, Arab, and American subjects (Klett and Yaukey, 1959), but there are some significant differences between the cultures. For instance, Diab (1963) showed that the number and kind of national groups used in the elicitation of stereotypes affects the obtained results.

One useful method is to employ checklists with equal numbers of favorable and unfavorable terms and to ask the subjects to judge both favorable and unfavorable groups and themselves. The analysis is then carried out in terms of similarities between the adjectives checked about (a) self and others, and (b) only others (Vinacke, 1956). Ehrlich (1962) used a similar approach. Student subjects were asked to sort statements into four categories, indicating that the statments were in their opinion primarily applicable to Negroes, to Jews, to both, and to neither. The Jews were seen as an economic elite, exclusive, ethnocentric, aggressive, and exploitative. The Negroes were seen as irresponsible, lazy, and ignorant. However, the characteristics assigned to the category "both Negroes and Jews" consitituted a list which reads "more like a precis of dominant American values than sterotyped characterizations of minority groups" (Ehrlich, p. 174).

Sodhi *et al.* (1958) asked German subjects to check a list of more than two hundred characteristics under three sets of instructions. In this manner they obtained (a) the German autostereotype; (b) the stereotype of Americans, English, French, and Russians; and (c) the reflected autostereotype. The latter was obtained by asking the subjects to indicate how the other nationals were likely to check the list with reference to Germans. Correlations of the autostereotype with the reflected autostereotype were interpreted as indices of received social distance or received understanding. The results indicate that the subjects felt that Americans understand them best ($r = .74$), followed by the English ($r = .70$), and Russians ($r = .52$), and the French, who understand them least ($r = .35$).

Dennis (1957a) suggested that associations with common objects may be good indicators of cultural orientations. For instance, the word "mother" is associated with providing food by 16% of the American subjects, 51% of the Lebanese, and only 7% of the Sudanese. Dennis (1957b) observed also that more objects were seen as living in the Near East than in the U.S. More than half the students in a Baghdad sample attributed life to a match, the sun, wind, and a river. Zaidi (1960) found Dennis' list of common objects useful in research with Pakistani children.

B. EVALUATIONS

The evaluative factor scales of the semantic differential (Osgood et al., 1957) provide the most satisfactory method for the simple measurement of evaluation. There is evidence of increased validity of the instrument when scales from other factors and domains—in addition to the evaluative factor—are incorporated. When additional scales are employed, some aspects of the meaning of a category are being measured, rather than its evaluative aspect alone. However, since evaluation is the most powerful factor present, this measurement can be called the "measurement of evaluations."

A procedure used by Triandis (1959b) permits measurement of aspects not present in the usual semantic differential. The procedure was to include three scales from each of Osgood's main factor analyses, and add scales relevant to the particular lexical fields (in this case, jobs and people in industry) to construct special semantic differentials. The factorial structure of such instruments differs from the usual Osgood structure (Triandis, 1960b). Because of the evidence on the interaction between concepts and scales (Osgood, 1962), it is clear that when a large variety of heterogeneous concepts is to be studied, the general type of Osgood semantic differential is the only suitable instrument. However, when more precise lexical fields or one kind of stimuli (Oyama et al., 1962) are to be analyzed, the greater refinement provided by the Triandis procedure is desirable. This is also the conclusion Micko (1962) arrived at in an attempt to study a particular meaning field (textile fibers) by means of the semantic differential. E. E. Ware and C. E. Osgood recently developed a personality differential and are currently working on other kinds of differentials.

Several experimenters have obtained the evaluations of nationals of other countries by means of the semantic differential, employing Swiss subjects (H. Fischer, 1961; Fischer and Trier, 1962; Molnos, 1962), Italian subjects (Rosen, 1959), and American and Greek subjects (Triandis and Triandis, 1962).

C. BEHAVIORAL INTENTIONS

As mentioned in the previous section, behavioral intentions are statements of the form "I would do . . ." which occur in the presence of specific stimulus situations, such as a particular category of objects, persons, or events. A procedure developed by Triandis (1964) permits the quantification of this concept. The procedure first requires content analyses of novels, short stories, or other materials (e.g., association studies and observations) which contain social behaviors typically occurring in a particular culture. The large number of such behaviors obtained from these procedures may then be reduced to a smaller number by means of logical and analytic procedures, such as Guttman's facet analysis. Last, a sample of maximally heterogeneous behaviors may be selected and intercorrelated, and the matrix of intercorrelations may be factored. Thus, a small number of factor pure behaviors may be obtained which constitute a behavioral differential which can be used in determining what behaviors are appropriate in what situations in a particular culture. In the Triandis (1964) study a typical item was:

A 50-year-old Negro physician, woman, Protestant

would__!__!__!__!__!__!__!__!__!__!__!__!__would not

have a cocktail with

Factor analyses of the behaviors resulted in five orthogonal factors: (1) a social acceptance with subordination factor (I would vote for, I would invite to dinner, I would obey); (2) a marital acceptance factor (I would marry, I would fall in love); (3) a friendship acceptance factor (I would eat with, I would be an intimate friend with); (4) a social distance factor (I would exclude from the neighborhood); (5) a subordination factor (I would be commanded by). The data suggested that different subcultures, e.g., Jewish versus Protestant males, employ different social behaviors in relation to the same stimuli.

D. ATTITUDES

Attitudes are conceptualized as consisting of evaluations and behavioral intentions. Their operationalization requires the use of the techniques described in the previous sections. In predicting behavior from attitudes, a multiple regression approach which employs both evaluations and behavioral intentions is likely to be most useful.

IV. Cultural Influences upon Perception

The two previous sections provided a theoretical framework and suggestions about the methods of measurement of its key concepts. It is now possible to explore how cultural factors affect each of the processes described by these concepts. Before doing so, however, it is important to examine whether cultural factors influence perception.

Physical energies impinge on an organism and are processed in such a way as to acquire meaning. The activation of the organism, in response to such energies, is called *sensation;* when meaning is added to sensation, the process is called *perception.* As Gibson (1963) pointed out, "to feel pain is not to feel the prick of a needle." All the evidence presently available suggests that there are no cultural influences upon sensation. However, cultural factors may provide some of the meaning involved in perception and are therefore intimately implicated with that process.

A. RECOGNITION AND RETENTION

The view that cultural factors are important determinants of perceptual responses is sometimes referred to as the "new look" in perception. Dukes (1955) reviewed the early experimental studies of the conditions under which cultural factors become implicated in perception. It appears, however, that many of the experiments which provided positive results (i.e., which showed the influence of such cultural factors) were subject to experimental artifacts, and well-controlled experiments (e.g., Dorfman and Zajonc, 1963) led to negative results. Eriksen (1963), after a review of 15 years of research, concluded that values, needs, and expectations affect only the responses that subjects make. Perceptual responses, according to Eriksen, are modified by both the frequency of occurrence of a particular stimulus (the more frequent stimuli are recognized more easily) and by the kind of previous reinforcements received in the presence of the stimulus. This view agrees with Doob's (1960) analysis of the effect of category codability on perception. The Luganda language compels its speakers to note whether an event occurred within or before the 24-hour period immediately prior to the time at which the event is described. Doob concluded that this has a small effect on what is perceived (what he calls the afferent function of language) but a substantial effect on response (efferent function).

Eriksen's view of perception suggests that members of a culture may perceive object A rather than object B because of: (a) the greater meaning of A than of B (Bartlett, 1932); (b) the higher frequency of occurrence of A relative to B; and (c) the more pleasant associations with A than with B. Thus, previous cultural experience may enhance the availability of a category and depress the availability of another. In Bagby's (1957) study of perceptual predominance in binocular rivalry, Mexican and American subjects were given exposure with binocular vision to bullfight and baseball pictures. The results indicate that at tachistoscopic speeds, the Mexicans saw the bullfight and the Americans the baseball pictures. The relative availability of a category may have important consequences in problem solving (Cofer, 1951) and the regulation of behavior (Luria, 1961).

Retention is another cognitive process affected by category availability. The method of serial reproduction has been used in different cultural settings (Bartlett, 1932; Nadel, 1937; Talland, 1956; Goodman, 1962). Goodman compared the responses of 239 Japanese and 681 urban middle-class children in the fifth and sixth grades. She employed the same story used by Nadel with the Nupe and Yoruba 12- to 18-year-old West African adolescents. The story included the sentence "God will punish him." The Japanese, who were the least religious of the samples, recalled this in only 6% of the cases in contrast to 17% of the Americans, 25% of the Yoruba, and 50% of the Nupe.

B. THE PERCEPTION OF SPACE

In an interesting study by Hudson (1960), pictures constructed to provide self-evident responses of two- or three-dimensional perception were administered to white and African samples of school-going and non-school-going subjects. School-going subjects saw the pictures predominantly as 3D, while the nonschool-going subjects saw them almost entirely two dimensionally. Evidently, it is necessary to learn to see pictures and photographs in three dimensions. Cultural isolation from pictures and photographs was proportionately related to difficulty of seeing three dimensionally.

C. ILLUSIONS

Experimental work with optical illusions has cast considerable light on cross-cultural differences in spatial perception. Allport and Pettigrew (1957) found that urban Zulus report the trapezoid illusion more often than rural Africans. Under optimal conditions (monocularly at twenty feet) no differences were observed between the Zulus and Europeans, but under suboptimal conditions the unacculturated subjects reported the illusion less frequently than did the acculturated. Bonte (1962) also found that the Bashi Africans were less susceptible to the Müller-Lyer illusion than a European sample.

By far the best study on this topic is Segall et al. (1963, 1964). The study is a model for cross-cultural research. The authors employed extremely careful procedures in standardization. A total of 1878 subjects representing 14 non-European cultures and three European were tested. The test materials were versions of the Müller-Lyer, the Sander Parallelo-gram, and the Horizontal-Vertical illusion. The results strongly support the empiricist hypothesis that the perception of space involves, to an important extent, the acquisition of habits of perceptual inference.

Both Rivers (1905) and Segall et al. (1963, 1964) found that Europeans experience the Müller-Lyer and Sander Parallelogram illusions much *more* sharply than non-Europeans; but they experience the Horizontal-Vertical illusion *less* sharply than non-Europeans. The authors argued that subjects living in a highly carpentered world—more typical of Europeans than non-Europeans—will tend to perceive the "shorter" line of the Müller-Lyer as the "front edge" of boxes, while the "longer" line would be seen as the back edge along the inside of the box. Since they "know" that boxes have edges of the same size, they will infer that the "front" is shorter than the "back" edge. The carpentered world hypothesis, then, predicts that subjects living in tropical forests or other noncarpentered environments would be less susceptible to the Müller-Lyer illusion. The data generally support this prediction. They also point out that a short, vertical line in a drawing may represent a relatively long, horizontal line extending away from the observer. Subjects living on flat plains devoid of trees, posts, or poles tend to interpret vertical retinal extensions as greatly foreshortened lines in the horizontal plane extending along the line of regard. Thus, such subjects would be maximally susceptible to the Horizontal-Vertical illusion. The data again are consistent with this view. Segall *et al.* (1964) concluded that ecological and cultural factors operating in the visual environment create differences in visual inference.

D. PHYSIOGNOMIC PERCEPTION

The previous sections suggest that recognition, retention, the perception of space, and illusions depend largely on the physical characteristics of the stimuli being used. However, cultural factors provide significant modifications to the perceptual process, which can be accounted for by ecological determinants. As the ambiguity of the stimulus increases, the effect of the cultural variables increases. Thus, when the perception of aesthetic qualities is considered, cultural factors should control more variance than the characteristics of the stimuli. Nevertheless, there is evidence that even in the area of aesthetic preference some judgments are not influenced by culture.

Physiognomic perception (Ryan, 1938) appears to be free of cultural influences, although more evidence is needed before this can be regarded as definitely established. One technique for studying physiognomic perception employs nonsense words and abstract drawings and asks subjects from different cultures to match them. Davis (1961) showed that children in Tanganyika were similar to English controls in matching nonsense names and abstract drawings. Thus, some characteristics of visual and auditory stimuli suggest similarities among them. Voorhees (1954) found that American subjects could identify the moods intended in Bedouin, Indonesian, and other exotic music. This suggests that some sounds may have universal meaning.

The hypothesis of phonetic symbolism, that the sound of a word suggests its meaning, has interested social psychologists for some time, Klineberg (1954) reviewed several studies on this subject. In a recent review, Taylor (1963) described some of his own experiments, concluding that "people associate certain sounds with certain meanings, but the same sound is associated with different meaning in different languages" (p. 205). The speakers of a language may learn to associate a particular sound with a particular category because many of the words associated with that category utilize the sound. For instance, in English, G is associated with bigness—grand, great, grow, gain, gargantuan, gross. The Taylor position, however, is challenged by Miron (1961), who presented convincing evidence that certain materials have expressive value due to their inherent phonetic content.

Osgood (1960a) studied visual-verbal synesthetic tendencies with 40 Navahos, 10 Mexicans, 27 Anglos, and 20 Japanese. However, all subjects were bilingual to some extent. Concepts such as up, down, heavy, good, and pictorial alternatives depicting up-down, vertical-horizontal, thick-thin, near-far (Osgood, 1960a, Fig. 1) were employed. The experimenter would name one of the concepts and then show the series of cards with the pictorial alternatives. The subjects pointed to which of the alternatives in each card seemed most appropriate to that concept. The results indicated an impressive cross-cultural agreement in synesthetic tendencies. "Happy," for example, goes with colored, up and white; "sad" goes with uncolored, down, and black.

On the question of aesthetic judgments involving visual or auditory materials, there is little doubt that culture is a most powerful determinant (Lawlor, 1955). However, Pratt (1961) correctly observed that "cultural relativism has gone a bit too far." He reviewed a number of studies that suggest similarities in these judgments across cultures. For instance, Morris (1957) obtained judgments of preference for modern paintings from Chinese, Indian, and American subjects. Though many of the responses were culture-specific, there was enough cross-cultural agreement to suggest a panhuman factor in such judgments.

The evidence suggests, then, that panhuman generality can be demonstrated for physiognomic perception, synesthetic tendencies, and to a lesser extent, aesthetic judgments. This suggests that the same basic emotion mechanism is used by all humans, but ecological differences produce differences in conditioning to particular kinds of stimuli. The following section will develop this point.

E. THE PERCEPTION OF EMOTION

Cultural differences seem to be widespread and quite significant in the definition of what situations are appropriate for what emotional expression

(Klineberg, 1954). However, these must be considered in the same class as customs, rather than as fundamental differences in cognitive functioning.

The evidence concerning the judging of emotional expressions among various national groups indicates that there are no important differences among them. Vinacke and Fong (1955) examined three racial groups in Hawaii and found no significant differences among them in the judgment of facial expression. Studies testing Schlosberg's (1954) theory of emotion with Greek (Triandis and Lambert, 1958), Dutch (Frijda, 1953; Frijda and Philipzoon, 1963), and Australian subjects (Gladstones, 1962) appear to agree.

Schlosberg (1944) attempted to reduce the dimensions required to order judgments of pictures that presumably reflect emotional states in the person photographed. He proposed that the classic Woodworth categories could be arranged in a two-dimensional space defined by (a) pleasant-unpleasant, and (b) attention-rejection. Later Schlosberg (1954) extended this theory to include a further dimension, tension-sleep. A recent study (Gladstones, 1962) with Schlosberg's pictures, employed Torgerson's method of complete triads for multidimensional scaling of the pictures. The pleasant-unpleasant dimension was the first factor, the tension-sleep dimension was the second, and a doubtful third factor also emerged. The contributions of these three factors to the observed variance in judgments were in the proportion $3:2:1$. Thus, five sixths of the variance accounted for can be described by the pleasant-unpleasant and tension-sleep factors. The correspondence between these factors and Osgood's evaluative and activity factors was noted by Triandis and Lambert (1958), Osgood (1963), and others. Semantic differential studies involving judgments of pictures of emotional expression (Osgood, 1955, 1962) also agree with these results.

Given, then, that at least two of the three Schlosberg dimensions are well established, what evidence is there about their cross-cultural generality? Triandis and Lambert (1958) tested a number of hypotheses with two samples of Greek subjects. Fifteen subjects were young adults in an isolated village in the north of the island of Corfu, and 15 were sophisticated young adults from Athens. The choice of samples was an attempt to vary the movie attendance of the subjects, which might lead to stereotypic judgments of emotions.

Triandis and Lambert first tested the hypothesis that the Greek subjects would rate emotional expression in much the same way as American subjects (using the Schlosberg norms of Brown University students). The rank-order correlations for the 48 pictures ranged from .67 ($p < .0001$) (for the judgments of the Brown University students and the Corfu villagers on the sleep-tension dimension), to .91 (for the Brown and Athenian subjects on the pleasant-unpleasant dimension). Using the Thurstone successive intervals procedure, Triandis plotted the emotion solid for the Greek and American data (see Triandis and Lambert, 1958, Fig. 1). The two solids look similar, but the American subjects tended to make wider discriminations than the Greeks on the pleasant-unpleasant dimension for pictures that they judged as "tense." Analysis of the data revealed that, on the average, the Greeks (whether urban or village) gave more ratings toward "attention" and "tension" for the unpleasant pictures, while the Americans gave more ratings of this kind for the pleasant pictures ($p < .001$). One possible explanation is that the Americans are more activist and instrumentally oriented than the Greeks.

The same study hypothesized that the position of a picture in the Woodworth categories (love, surprise, fear, anger, disgust, contempt) can be predicted from its ratings on the pleasant-unpleasant and attention-rejection dimensions, in both cultures. The hypothesis was supported. The study further hypothesized that movie attendance makes the judgments of the urban Greeks more similar to judgments of American subjects than to judgments of the villagers. This hypothesis was also supported.

Although the results of the Triandis and Lambert study supported the hypothesis of generality in judgment of emotion, certain differences in the perception of particular pictures were observed. Thus, the villagers saw a picture which Schlosberg described as "intense anger in argument" as significantly more pleasant and less tense than the two urban groups did. In the village studied, verbal aggression is a traditional form of entertainment, with loud and angry debates the favorite pastime of the villagers. Similarly, the villagers judged pictures that depict physical strain as less tense and less pleasant than the urban samples. The villagers undoubtedly associated physical strain with work, whereas the college students associated it with athletics. Thus, while the frame of reference for the judgments remains the same across cultures, the specific judgments about the meaning of particular emotions may be quite different.

V. Cultural Influences upon Categorization

There is considerable evidence that cultural influences in part determine the number of categories employed by members of a culture to describe particular areas of their cognitive domains, as well as the content and the criterial attributes of the categories that they employ. In many cases, such as kinship categories, the categories used by the members of a culture have functional significance for them; in other cases no such significance is apparent.

Hunt (1962) provided a detailed review of the experimental work on the learning of categories. At the present stage of knowledge, it is a reasonable hypothesis that much of this work, though developed by Western psychologists, is generalizable to cognitive development in other cultures. However, further research is urgently needed to establish this.

A. THE NUMBER OF CATEGORIES AND THEIR CODABILITY

Since the nineteenth century, many observers have noted that a language may have one term for an event for which another language has many. For example, the Eskimos have several words for what we call "snow," while the Aztecs have only one word for what we call "cold, ice, and snow" (Whorf, 1940). The Arabs have 6000 words for camel, of which fifty describe various stages of camel pregnancy (Klineberg, 1954). The Navaho use different words for rough ground, rough object, and rough skin; yet they use the same word for what is designated in English as "flint, metal, and knife" (Kluckhohn and Leighton, 1946). The Masai use 17 terms for cattle, the Ifugao use 20 terms for rice, and the Siriono number system is limited to the words "one," "two," "three," and "many" (Sherif and Sherif, 1956).

Brown and Lenneberg (1954) show that category *codability* has important consequences for recognition. High codability categories (a) have a single name; (b) permit subjects of a homogeneous language community to respond quickly to them; and (c) produce high agreement among subjects as to their name, and also consistency by subjects from one occasion to another. The more codable categories are more frequently used in perception and thought (Frijda and Geer, 1961). Frequently used categories have short words corresponding to them (Zipf, 1949). Brown (1956) argued that we do distinguish several kinds of snow—as many kinds as the Eskimos—but that the codability of such categories is very low, and we need to use several words to describe them. Similarly, it might be argued, we are able to see that a camel is pregnant, but an Arab with a vocabulary of 50 words for pregnant camels must be able to detect the stage and general condition of pregnancy more efficiently than we can.

Using American subjects, Gardner (1953) employed an object-sorting test to study conceptual differentiation (number of categories used by the subject to sort 73 objects), and level of abstraction (judgments of experimenter concerning abstraction level of subject definition of the grouping). He considered individual differences in these variables as important differences in cognitive style. Mercado *et al.* (1963) utilized Gardner's test with Mexican and American children. Preliminary results indicated no difference between boys in the two cultures. However, there was a tendency for Mexican girls to employ less abstract categories than those employed by American girls. If cultural influences on cognitive styles are established, an important research field will be created for psychologists and anthropologists. The cultural factors influencing cognitive structuring would need to be further explored. Beyond the obvious functional utility of having many categories to describe a domain that is particularly important for a culture, little is known about the determinants of the number of categories employed to describe the domain.

B. CONTENT OF CATEGORIES

There is overwhelming evidence that different cultures categorize experience differently. Kluckhohn (1961), in his magnificent summary of the Whorfian hypothesis literature, mentioned the following examples. The differentiation of singular-plural in Chinese is optional. Nootka grammar forces its speakers to indicate some physical feature—like left-handedness, astigmatism, short stature, large appetite, or bald-headedness—each time a person is mentioned or spoken to. Some languages have two kinds of first person plural: a "we" that denotes "you and I" and another that denotes "I and some other people, excluding you." In Japanese the status of the speakers in a conversation is very precisely defined, but the substance and the rest of the context are left highly ambiguous. Kluckhohn concluded, "The facts compel agreement that languages differ in their categories and as to what distinctions it is obligatory to make," but he adds that this in itself does not provide a test of the Whorfian hypothesis. The latter point refers to the circulatory of inference from which Whorf appears unable to escape. Whorf begins and ends his argument with linguistic data, and the argument requires behavioral data in order to break the circularity (see also Walker *et al.*, 1954).

Lounsbury (1956) illustrates the intimate tie between category content, social structure, and social norms with kinship terminology. The Pawnee have the same word for the mother's brother's wife, ego's wife, and the sisters of ego's wife. Analysis of the social norms of this group reveals that the adolescent Pawnee is supposed to have his first sexual experience with his mother's brother's wife, and when he marries he may have sexual intercourse with his wife's sisters. The designation of all these women by a single kinship term is consistent with these customs, though such correspondence between category content and social structure is itself arbitrary and may occur in one culture but not in another.

1. The Content of Color Categories

The physical characteristics of the color continuum can be rigorously and objectively defined. For this reason, much research on the content of categories has employed this continuum. A typical technique is to present a group of people with color chips or color charts and ask them to name the color or to indicate on the chart the regions that are designated by a particular color name. One of the best studies in this area is the Landar *et al.* (1960) study of the Navaho color categories in comparison with the categories of English-speaking subjects. Previous work on color categorization by Lenneberg and Roberts (1956) with Zuni Indians, and Hoijer (1953, 1954) with the Navaho developed the methodology and established that there are differences in categorization between nonliterate people and people who speak English. The Landar *et al.* paper is particularly interesting because it provides probability distributions for color responses of monolingual English and Navaho, plotted against a stimulus continuum of Farnsworth-Munsell numbers. Thus, in the range of 25 to 40 F-M, the probability of the response "green" by English monolinguals is higher than .80 and their reaction times are very short. In that same range, the Navaho use four different terms (in other words, employ terms of low codability)—one term corresponds to "browngreen," one to "blue-green," one to "greenyellow" and one to "purplegreen." As expected, the Navaho reaction times were much longer in that range than in other ranges.

2. Content of Categories of Bilinguals

Bilinguals show semantic shifts in the direction of compromises between the two linguistic communities. Landar *et al.* (1960) suggested that in the case of the Navaho, the monolinguals may be shifting in the English direction, due to their contact with Navaho bilinguals. A detailed analysis of semantic shifts by Ervin (1961) showed that the color categories of bilinguals and monolinguals are different.

> In the domain where one language had a single high probability name and the other had none, the high probability term and its translation dominated in bilinguals in both languages. Where the two languages differed in the boundary between two categories, both of which have translational terms, the bilingual's dominant language determined his boundary in both languages. Where a category in one language covered the domain of two categories in the other language, the boundary point in the latter language was variable and reflected the degree of learning of that language.
> A domain divided into two categories in one language was divided into three in the other, with the added category straddling the boundary in the two-category language; bilinguals reduced the size of the middle category when speaking the language with three categories (p. 240).

3. Concluding Comment

From Woodworth's 1904 studies (Woodworth, 1939) to the present, there is no suggestion that the sensations of nonliterate people are different from those of Europeans. Nevertheless, when asked to make discriminations that involve categorization, the frequency distributions of their verbal responses differ from the distributions of Europeans. The responses are, of course, tied to the languages that they are using. Thus, language molds the responses, and from the differences in the distributions of responses, we infer differences in the content of the categories.

C. THE CRITERIAL ATTRIBUTES USED

The carving of experience out of the physical universe, then, is dependent on culture. Furthermore, the criterial attribute values required for categorization appear to differ. Hallowell (1951) states that the male Ojibwa apparently notice first whether a woman is a totemic sister (sexual taboo) or not. Males in certain cultures value particular parts of a woman's anatomy and in other cultures different parts. The categorization into "beautiful woman" is culturally determined. Orientation in space is a focal concept of the Balinese. All instructions of direction are given in terms of the points of the compass. A musician may say, "Hit the key to the East of the one you are hitting" (Kluckhohn, 1954, p. 932). Stimuli that have particular cultural meaning may lead to "perceptions" of monsters (e.g., the windigo among the Ojibwa). Once the perception occurs, panic behavior takes place.

Some anthropologists, e.g., Mathiot (1962), have provided explicit statements of perceptual criteria for the classification of categories. In Papago, they use what Mathiot calls "mass nouns," that is, a grammatical category which includes words like "water," "coffee," "wine," "salt," "sand," "clouds," "rain," etc. The perceptual criterion for classification in this category is *texture*. Mathiot also discusses some of the criteria used for botanical and zoological classifications.

Even subtle stimuli like vowel duration may have important influences in categorizing. Brown and Lenneberg (1958) described an experiment by Brown and Horowits in which the Navaho use of the duration of a vowel to signal different meanings was employed to obtain different categorization responses. Navaho subjects responded to this cue and used four categories to differentiate chips that had previously been associated with long and short duration monosyllables. The English-speaking subjects used fewer categories. When the English subjects were told that their classification was incorrect, they began paying attention to the vowel change. Many of the latter said that they had noticed the variations of vowel length at the start of the experiment, but had assumed they were accidental. Brown and Lenneberg remarked: "We could have no better statement of the cognitive status of this speech variation for the speaker of English" (1958, p. 12).

VI. Cultural Influences upon the Organization of Categories

The previous section presented evidence suggesting that cultural factors affect the process of categorization. The present section will show that cultural factors also influence the organization of categories. However, when the researcher employs sufficiently abstract categories of analysis, some important panhuman tendencies may be detected. The present section begins by examining such panhuman tendencies.

A. THE STRUCTURE OF WORD ASSOCIATIONS

Rosenzweig (1957, 1961) studied word associations in English, French, German, and Italian. For about half the Kent-Rosanoff list, the responses given with high frequency in one language tended to be similar in meaning to the responses given in the other languages. When he examined the primary responses (the most frequent given) to a given word, Rosenzweig found that the greater the frequency of the primary response in one language, the more likely it is to be equivalent in meaning to the corresponding primary response in another language. Such lawfulness in response distributions appears to have considerable generality. Miron and Wolfe (1962) examined the response distributions to frames of the form "The house is . . ." and "The . . . truth," in 12 divergent linguistic communities. They found that the response distributions of such restricted word associations were very similar.

B. STEREOTYPES

1. General

Stereotypes are generalizations about the characteristics of groups of people. They are part of the "what goes with what" process which organizes categories, places them in schemata, and orients the schemata to make them consistent with the person's value orientations.

Stereotypes are thought-savers, but are they valid? Some writers favor the "kernel of truth" hypothesis, which is extensively discussed by Allport (1954). The evidence suggests that there is some truth in a stereotype. Prothro and Melikian (1954) found considerable similarity in the stereotypes held by Arab and American students with reference to Germans, Negroes, and Jews. It is true, of course, that American mass media and books are widely used in the Middle East, but content analyses of these materials do not suggest enough references to stereotypes to create such similarity in judgments.

Furthermore, studies of changes in stereotypes (Prothro and Melikian, 1955) suggest close correspondence to situational changes. The Katz and Braly (1933) technique was used with Arab subjects before and after much contact with Americans (visits of Point Four personnel and the Seventh Fleet). While the stereotypes of other groups remained unchanged, the American stereotype changed by addition of the characteristics sociable, jolly, superficial, and simple. This stereotype did not differ very much from the stereotype obtained from students in East Pakistan (Zaidi and Ahmed, 1958). Roth and Das (1958) studied the stereotypes of college freshmen in Orissa, India, toward themselves and four other nationalities, including the Chinese. During the Sino-Indian border dispute, Sinha and Upadhyaya (1960) obtained the stereotype of the Chinese from a similar sample of subjects. There were marked changes of this stereotype in the unfavorable direction.

Fishman (1956) reviewed studies that demonstrate that stereotypes do not correspond to known facts and also studies which show changes corresponding to real changes in political and social conditions, etc. Thus, though stereotypes are seen by Fishman as "inferior judgmental processes," they are not necessarily rigid or contrary to fact. Their development may reflect characteristics of the stereotyped group, the stereotyping group, and interactions between these characteristics.

One of the most extensive studies of stereotypes was reported by Buchanan and Cantril (1953) in connection with an investigation of public opinion. Friendliness toward other nations appears to depend on the following factors: (a) place of the subject's nation in the bipolar world of Russia-U.S.A.; (b) place of the subject's nation and the nation being stereotyped during World War II; (c) common boundaries; (d) common language; (e) neutrality in war of the nation being stereotyped.

Fischer and Trier (1962), in an investigation which employed about 1500 subjects from the German- and French-speaking parts of Switzerland, examined the autostereotypes and stereotypes of "the other group," as well as stereotypes of the French and Germans. A 24-scale semantic differential was employed. With impressive consistency, the autostereotypes (group A's stereotype of A) agree with the heterostereotype (group B's perception of A), only the heterostereotypes were an exaggerated version of the autostereotypes. For instance, the German-Swiss see themselves as angular, dry, and conservative. The French-Swiss also see the German-Swiss as being angular, dry, and conservative—only more so. When the profile of the Swiss is compared with the profiles for German-Swiss and French-Swiss, for both types of subjects it is closer to the profile of German-Swiss than to French-Swiss. This is presumably realistic, reflecting the fact that 72% of the Swiss are German-speaking and only 21% are French-speaking (the remainder speak Italian and Romanic). The German-Swiss autostereotype and their stereotype of German are very similar, only their stereotype of German is more exaggerated on the activity and potency factors. The French-Swiss autostereotype and their stereotype for French are similar. The German-Swiss autostereotype is most similar in meaning to the words "manly," "work," "father," and "authority." The French-Swiss autostereotype is closest to the words "love," "friend," "mother," and "female."

2. Development and Content of Stereotypes

Children may use a large set of vaguely favorable or unfavorable terms as synonyms, prior to making finer distinctions between attributes (Ervin and Foster, 1960). Thus, when a child feels a vague antipathy for a group of children, any unfavorable term would be suitable to describe the group, regardless of relevance. As the child experiences a transition from egocentricity to reciprocity (Piaget and Weil, 1951), ideas about the self and others are gradually formulated. Vague feelings of "nice" people and "bad" people are likely to guide this development. The kinds of criterial attributes that make the difference between good and bad people may also shift. La Roque (1960) showed that the Jew-non-Jew antagonism of the Diaspora has been replaced in Israel by the East-West dualism. The Jewish ideal now combines the characteristics that belong to the stereotypes of the Sabra and the German Jew.

A recent study of the origin and development of stereotypes was conducted by Lambert and Klineberg (1959) and reported in the 1960 Bonn International Congress of Psychology (Avigdor, 1962; Lambert, 1962; Klineberg, 1962; Sato, 1962; Sodhi, 1962). Six, 10- and 14-year-old children in several countries were asked, "What are you?" "What else are you?" until they made a national reference. The names of other people who are *like* them and *unlike* them were elicited. Incomplete sentences were used to elicit feelings for or against specific national groups. Textbooks that were widely read by the children of each group were content analyzed. Though the final report of this study is not yet available, preliminary results suggest that the study will be an important contribution to the literature on stereotype development.

Exotic characteristics such as dress, differences in skin color, and customs appear to be important criterial attributes for categorization in the "not like us" category. However, the evaluations of both the "like us" and the "not like us" people tend to be generally positive. As a function of age, a decrease was noted in the use of physical-racial descriptions and descriptions of clothing and customs, and an increase was noted in personality descriptions, political, religious, and material possession references.

VII. Cultural Influences upon Judgments and Evaluations

A. THE STRUCTURE OF CONNOTATIVE MEANING

The previous sections suggest that important influences are exerted by cultural factors on the content, number, and criterial attributes of categories and the relationships between categories. However, some similarity in the associations and stereotypes obtained from subjects from different cultures suggests panhuman factors operating on certain aspects of the association process. The work of Osgood and his associates has provided further evidence of the operation of panhuman factors.

In 1956, Osgood and his associates undertook a series of studies which is still in progress to test one aspect of the Whorfian hypothesis. Kumata and Schramm (1956) conducted a pilot study with Japanese and Korean bilingual students and monolingual American students. Kumata (1957) extended this work to monolingual Japanese, Triandis and Osgood (1958) to Greeks, Michon (1960) to Dutch, and Suci (1960) to Southwest Indian cultures. In most of these studies the subjects were given translation-equivalent forms of the semantic differential (Osgood *et al.,* 1957). Typically, 20 or 30 concepts were judged against 30–50 scales, the scales were intercorrelated, and the matrix of intercorrelations was factor analyzed. The factor structures obtained from these samples tended to be very similar. An important evaluative factor, having loadings on scales such as good-bad; a less important potency factor, having high loadings on large-small, strong-weak; and a weak activity factor, having high loadings on active-passive were obtained in most analyses. In some cases a dynamism factor combining the potency and activity factor emerged.

These results tend to limit the generality of the Whorfian hypothesis. However, most of these studies employed materials developed in Illinois which were then translated, through the method of back translation, into other languages. Since this translation procedure has important limitations (cf. Jacobson *et al.,* 1960), Osgood extended the work to 17 distinct linguistic communities which represent most of the major language families of the world, employing procedures not requiring translation. In some of these communities the analysis is still in progress, but Osgood *et al.* provide enough data in their 1962 report to make the results from the remaining analyses fairly predictable.

The subjects in each of these 17 cultures were young, male monolinguals. They were asked to give qualifiers to one hundred "culture fair" and "universal" substantives (e.g., "house," "truth," and "poison"), by completing frames of the type: "The house is . . . " or "The . . . truth." The 10,000 responses obtained from each culture were then analyzed in terms of frequency and diversity (number of times the qualifier was given as an associate to different substantive stimuli by one or more subjects). The qualifiers were then ranked according to an entropy measure that considers both their frequency and diversity. Those qualifiers which had a high entropy value (very frequent and highly diverse) and which were relatively independent in their use (i.e., low correlations in usage across one hundred substantives) were used in the construction of semantic differential scales.

New samples of 200 subjects judged 100 concepts against 50 such scales. Ten subgroups of subjects made approximately one-tenth of the 5000 necessary judgments. The scales were then correlated with each other, and principal axes factor analyses, with orthogonal varimax rotations, were performed.

Comparison of the factor structures obtained from the several cultures revealed considerable similarity. In all of the cultures an *evaluative* factor was present and dominant. In all of the cultures a *potency* and *activity* or a *dynamism* (combination of potency and activity) factor was also observed. These results are considered as clear evidence that at least in one respect the extreme cultural relativity suggested by the Whorfian hypothesis is not supported by the data.

These studies, then, showed that the structure of connotative meaning, in a very broad sense, is similar across cultures. A later section, however, will show that the specific placement of categories on this structure is influenced by culture.

B. SOCIAL DESIRABILITY

Some recent studies have made cross-cultural comparisons of judgments of social desirability. Lövass (1958) and Klett and Yaukey (1959) have generally shown considerable correspondence in judgments of social desirability across Norwegian, Arab, Nisei, and American samples.

Triandis (1963) asked Greek and Illinois personnel directors and students to judge the desirability of hiring employees having certain combinations of characteristics. Complex stimuli, varying in age, sex, race, competence, religion, sociability, and wealth, arranged in factorial designs, were presented to the subjects. Analyses of variance permitted the computation of the relative weights given to these characteristics by the subjects. There was considerable similarity in the judgments of the four samples.

The judgments of the two American samples correlated .95 across samples. The judgments of the two Greek samples correlated .77. The American and Greek students agreed very well ($r = .94$) and the two samples of personnel directors also agreed quite well ($r = .83$). However, within this framework of similarities, there were some cultural differences. The Americans gave the competence of the stimulus person more weight than the Greeks did. The Americans also put greater emphasis on the race and sex of the stimulus, while the Greeks were more concerned with the age of the stimulus.

C. CULTURAL DIFFERENCES IN CONNOTATIVE MEANING

The structure of connotative meaning appears to be invariant across cultures. However, concepts are judged against the three major dimensions of this structure quite differently from culture to culture. The previous section showed that social desirability judgments (evaluations) illustrate both similarities and differences across cultures. In the Triandis (1963) study, sub-culture differences (personnel directors vs. students as subjects) were more important than cultural differences. However, Havighurst (1963) found that nationality was more important than social class in determining the semantic differential judgments of Argentine and American children. In the present section, comparisons between the connotative meanings of key terms in several linguistic communities will be reviewed.

Osgood et al. (1962), in the study previously described, defined eight octants of a meaning space determined by high or low value on the evaluative (E), potency (P), and activity (A) factors. They showed the location of each of the one hundred concepts used' in their research within this meaning space. The meaning of a term can now be described by its location in this space. Thus "progress" is E + P + A + for American, Flemish, and Japanese subjects, but is E + P + A — for Finnish subjects. In other words, the Finns see progress as less active than the other samples. A "girl" is E + P — A — for the Americans and Flemish, but E + P — A + for the Finns and Japanese. "Power" is E + P + A + for the Americans and Flemish, E + P + A — for the Finnish, and E — P — A + for the Japanese.

Differences in meaning across cultures seem well established from other studies too. Rosen (1959), for instance, in a comparison of Italians and Americans, found that the former see "thieves" and "criminals" as more "successful" and less "foolish" than the latter. American subjects seem to be more romantic in their response pattern than Greek subjects (Triandis and Osgood, 1958) and Italian subjects (Rosen, 1959). Important differences between the Eastern Mediterranean and American views of key family concepts such as "mother" and "wife" have been noted by Najarian (1959).

Haire et al. (1963) reported the semantic differential judgments of certain key concepts by managers in 11 countries. For instance, the concept "to reprimand" is judged as good in Spain and bad in Japan. Haire et al. employed the responses obtained from 3500 managers to group countries in terms of similarities. Four groups emerged: the U.S. and Britain; the Latin culture countries, such as Spain, Italy, and France; the Nordic culture countries, such as Scandinavia and Germany; and Japan. They found few relationships between the state of technological development and the managerial judgments obtained from their instrument. It appears, then, that cultural factors are more important than technological development in the determination of these evaluations.

The generalization may be made, then, that the structure of connotative meaning remains invariant from culture to culture, but differences in culture (see above), subculture [e.g., management-workers (Triandis, 1959b)], or social class (Haire and Morrison, 1957) may have important influences on the perceived meaning of key concepts.

D. CONSISTENCY THEORIES

Perhaps the most significant theoretical development in social psychology in the last ten years, is the intensive interest in consistency theories. Heider (1944, 1946, 1958), Newcomb (1953), Osgood and Tannenbaum (1955), and Festinger (1957) have provided theoretical statements of great importance, which have been elaborated, tested, and extensively reviewed (Zajonc, 1960; Osgood, 1960b). Extensive research (Abelson, 1959; Cohen, 1960; Rosenberg, 1960; Rosenberg et al., 1960) and innumerable publications have supported predictions made from such theories. Most of this work, however, was done with American subjects. The only cross-cultural study on this topic known to the experimenter is the study by Triandis and Fishbein (1963).

Triandis and Fishbein began with an attempt to test predictions from Osgood and Tannenbaum's (1955) cognitive congruity theory. Because of its detailed specification of how cognitive interactions occur and its precise quantitative predictions about the resolution of inconsistencies, this theory is more readily testable in other cultures.

Osgood and his associates (1957, pp. 276–284) worked with adjectives such as "artistic," "hairy," "listless," and "treacherous," and nouns such as "nurse," "scientist," "thug," and "prostitute." They obtained judgments of these concepts with the usual semantic differential procedures. Following this, they analyzed the judgments that subjects make of combinations of these components, such as "hairy nurse," "treacherous scientist," etc., with the usual semantic differential procedure. They predicted the semantic differential judgments of the word mixtures from the semantic judgments of the components, by using a precise, mathematical formula. The correlations between the predicted and the obtained scores were between .86 and .90 for the three semantic differential factors.

During the study described in Section VIII, A, Triandis and Triandis (1962) administered to Greek and Illinois subjects semantic differentials with complex stimuli, such as "A Negro, Portuguese physician of the same religion as you are." The components that constituted the stimuli were also presented as concepts, with the same semantic differential. Using an extension of Osgood's formula, which is suitable for four stimulus elements, the judgments that the subjects would make to the complex stimuli were predicted. The average correlations between predicted and observed judgments were .908 for the Greek and .855 for the American subjects. However, the average correlations between the obtained judgments of the complex stimuli and the occupational component of the stimuli alone were .955 for the Greeks and .925 for the American samples. These results remained unaltered, using three ways of analyzing the data. Thus, the congruity principle is not necessarily the best predictor of person perception in all situations. Since the congruity principle proved to be unsatisfactory, a test of other principles was undertaken.

Of those tested, the best was Fishbein's theory of summation of evaluations (Section II, C). Triandis and Fishbein (1963) presented an extensive comparison of summation and congruity theory predictions. Fishbein's cognitive summation theory made better predictions than either the congruity theory or the method which used the occupational component of the complex stimulus.

The issue—whether evaluations of several inconsistent components are averaged, by some kind of principle, or summed—is important theoretically. Summation does not involve an infinite series of components, since only a few components have sufficiently high probabilities of association with a particular concept to make a difference in the total evaluation of that concept. The Triandis and Fishbein publication is an example of one more cross-cultural study where a principle, in this case Fishbein's summation theory, appears to hold for subjects regardless of culture. Consistencies in social perception across Dutch and American samples were also reported by Fiedler and Hoffman (1962).

VIII. Cultural Influences upon Behavioral Intentions

A. STUDIES OF SOCIAL DISTANCE

Banton (1960) discussed the revival of interest in social distance in his report of Mitchell's study which showed that social distance responses of different African tribes towards each other follow a particular law: the more similar the religion and form of social organization between two tribes, the less the social distance between them. An interesting adaptation of the social distance scale is Pauline Mahar's (1960) ritual pollution scale for ranking Hindu castes. The most intimate behaviors ("can touch our earthware vessels," "can come in our cooking area") are not permitted for members of inferior castes. Behavior in the middle of the scale ("can touch our brass vessels," "can accept fried food from him") is permitted for people who are not too low in the caste hierarchy. Behaviors such as "can touch our children" are permitted to members of most castes, except shoemakers, agricultural laborers, and sweepers.

In a fascinating study of a particular step on the social distance scale, Roger Brown (1962) examined the conditions under which a person may use the familiar pronouns "tu" and "du" or must use the polite pronouns "vos," "vous," and "Sie." He designated the former with T and the latter with V. According to Brown, the probability of the use of V increases with the status of the other person and decreases with the degree of solidarity between the other person and the speaker. Under certain conditions the status and solidarity norms are in conflict and then the dyad may employ either form. Brown also explored the conditions of nonreciprocity in the use of this form. He found that Afrikaaners use more nonreciprocal forms than modern Europeans and showed the evolution of the reciprocal and nonreciprocal forms. Examining the conditions of nonreciprocity in several Indian speech communities (Telugu, Bengali, Punjabi, Hindhi, and Tamil) and in French, Brown discovered the Indian responses are quite similar, in spite of linguistic heterogeneity. The data indicated that an Indian is most likely to address his father V and be addressed by his father T; to address his wife T and be addressed by her V. By contrast, the French have few nonreciprocal arrangements (a notable exception is the grand-father), but have a number of mutual V (waiter-customer, distant relatives) and some ambiguous ones (male fellow-student, soldier).

Most of the work with behavioral intentions has been done with versions of the Bogardus social distance scale. The early work by Bogardus (1928) is a classic and need not be described here. However, it did have a serious defect. The use of a single stimulus, such as "Negro" or "Irishman," permitted only ambiguous interpretations of the results. Triandis and Triandis (1960) pointed out that when a stimulus such as "Negro" is judged, the subject may be responding either to the race or to the probable social class (lower) of the stimulus; when "Irishman" is the stimulus, the subject might be responding to either nationality or probable religion (Roman Catholic). Thus, the results obtained with single stimuli cannot help but be ambiguous. Many recent studies of social distance (Ansari, 1956, with Hindus and Muslims; C. L. Hunt, 1956, with Philippinos; Rioux, 1959, with Algerians) also suffer from this defect.

Triandis and Triandis (1960) standardized an equal-interval scale of social distance and employed 16 stimuli in a study of Illinois students. The 16 stimuli were chosen so that they had characteristics consisting of combinations of one of two levels of race, occupation, religion, and nationality. Since the stimuli were chosen according to a factorial design, analyses of variance determined the percentage of variance controlled by race, occupation, religion, and nationality. The results indicated that 77% of the controlled variance in the social distance scores was accounted for by race, about 17% by occupation, 5% by religion, and 1% by the nationality of the stimulus person. The emphasis on race as a determinant of social distance also appeared in the study by van den Berghe (1962) with subjects from Durban, South Africa. Vaughan (1962), noting the Triandis and Triandis findings, hypothesized that New Zealand students show the same effect toward the Maoris, and that the greater the perceived physical dissimilarity between the subjects and another ethnic group, the larger the social distance. The rank order correlation between social distance and perceived dissimilarity in physical characteristics was .92 ($p < .01$).

That race is a very important determinant of social distance was also shown by Triandis (1961) in a disagreement with Rokeach (1961) over the latter's assertion that cognitive dissimilarity is the most significant variable in prejudice. More recently, Triandis and Triandis (1962) repeated their previous study with Greek and Illinois subjects. The new sample of Illinois subjects again responded primarily in terms of race. The Greeks, however, were more concerned with the religion of the stimulus person; for them 55% of the controlled variance of the social distance scores was accounted for by religion, 24% by race; 5% by occupation and the rest by interactions. With Arab subjects, Prothro and Melikian (1952) noted relatively great social distance and an emphasis on nationality. Arabs rarely agree to marry outside of their own religious group (Prothro and Melikian, 1953), so that religion is a particularly important factor in the last social distance step between friendship and family relationship. However, nationality appears to be an important determinant of other steps on the social distance scale.

The non-unidimensionality of social distance scales has been noted by most careful researchers in this area. Lambert (1952) noted that French subjects valued "citizen in my country" much more than American subjects. Thus, Triandis' (1964) factor analytic procedures and the isolation of several behavior differential factors are likely to improve the methodology of this research area. The study shows that for American Protestant male subjects, for instance, the social acceptance with subordination factor (see Section III, C) is mostly controlled by the occupation of the stimulus person; the marital acceptance by the race and age of the stimulus person; the friendship acceptance by the race, sex, age, and religion of the stimulus person (in that order); the social distance factor by the race; and the subordination factor by the occupation of the stimulus person.

Interest in social distance is likely to continue as data from a project by Campbell and LeVine (1961), now in progress, become available.

B. MORAL JUDGMENTS

An interesting study by Biesheuvel (1957) examined the moral judgments of Africans and Europeans. A remarkable overall acceptance of Western ethical and social values characterized this urban, South African, native sample. However, the South African situation did have an important influence: African subjects indicated that since discrimination in legislation and the administration of justice deprives both laws and social conventions of their moral foundations, they would not have to observe normal, civic duties. They argued that Africans are justified in not paying taxes; they rejected the idea that it is a disgrace to go to prison; and they were in favor of *ir*regular working habits (since employers do not pay them enough). Thus, a person's evaluations are made to conform within a broader value system that includes his orientation toward the society in which he lives. Frank (1963) discussed cultural differences in rejection of illegitimate means to desirable goals among Spanish, Anglos, and Indians in a Colorado community.

Rettig and Pasamanick (1962) asked 489 American and 513 Korean subjects to indicate the degree of "wrongness" of fifty morally prohibited behaviors. They factor analyzed the 50 by 50 matrix and obtained very similar factor structures. The only important difference was a "puritanical morality" factor which was only present in the American sample, and a "personal welfare" factor present only in the Korean sample. The position of complete relativism in relation to morality, then, may now be questioned. Rettig and Lee (1963) examined the stability of such moral judgments by comparing the above mentioned judgments obtained from Korean subjects before the 1961 Korean revolution with judgments made after this revolution. The 1962 data showed significantly more disapproval of immoral behavior in the economic sphere (e.g., to falsify child's age to secure reduced fare) and less severe judgments in the religious sphere. It is quite likely that there are certain characteristics of moral codes that are universal. For instance, Gouldner (1960) presented a discussion of the reciprocity norm (people should help and not injure those who have helped them). He argued that the reciprocity norm is one of the universal "principal components" of moral codes.

Christensen and Carpenter (1962) noted important differences between Danish, Midwestern, and Mormon samples regarding values related to premarital coitus. With the Danish sample there was more approval of premarital coitus than was reported as actual practice, whereas with the American samples the reverse was true, with accompanying feelings of guilt.

IX. Cultural Influences upon Attitudes and Values

Gillepsie and Allport (1955) studied students from three American colleges, from four South African groups (Afrikaans-speaking, English-speaking, Bantu, and Indian), from New Zealand, and from Egypt, Mexico, France, Italy, Germany, Japan, and Israel. The subjects prepared an auto-biography of the future—"From now to 2000 A.D."—and answered a

relatively structured questionnaire. The data showed some striking similarities and also some differences in the subjects' responses. For instance,
most of the responses were anchored within the basic family frame of reference: frequent references were made to parents, siblings, future mates, and
offspring. All subjects used themes such as honesty, reliability, decency
and integrity in describing values they will attempt to impart to their children. All had an interest in the future achievements of science and in
travel, and the majority regarded war as "needless and preventable." The
latter opinion was less pronounced among the younger and more national-
istic groups: Egyptians, Afrikaners, Mexicans, and Bantus.

Some of the differences are interesting. American subjects seemed
to value variety more than any other sample. More Americans than other
subjects stated that the worst thing that could happen to them would be
to have a dull, monotonous life. French, Italian, and German students
seemed more concerned with "forming a character," and the new, national-
istic countries supplied themes of personal achievement and social utility.
The American themes indicated little concern with social problems (pov-
erty, delinquency, race relations) while the new nationalist groups mentioned them frequently. Danziger (1958) also found that Bantu and Indian
samples from South Africa were more concerned with political and social
issues and South African whites with private issues.

The Gillespie and Allport procedures have also been employed by
Stoetzel (1954) with Japanese subjects and Hyman et al. (1958) with
Turkish ones. Turkey was found to be similar to Egypt and Mexico in the
pattern of dominant values. Nationalism and an interest in public rather
than private values is the dominant theme.

MacLeod (1959) considers nationalism the dominant theme in the
Middle East. Prothro and Keehn (1956), in an analysis of personality
scale results obtained from Arab students, found a "cynicism" factor which
has loadings on political themes, punitiveness, and authoritarian aggression.

National differences in values and their relation to behavior have also
been noted in recent studies. Milgram (1961), in carefully controlled experiments, found more conformity to Asch-type situations among Norwegian than among French subjects. It appears that the French placed a
particularly high value on "critical judgments" and had norms which approved of disagreement with other people. This was not the case with
the Norwegians.

Jones and Bock (1960) applied multiple discriminant analysis to the
13 "ways of life" listed by Morris. They employed responses collected before 1950 from more than one hundred subjects from each of the following
groups: U.S. white, U.S. Negro, India, Japan, China, Norway. The first

discriminant function accounted for 48% of the variance and contrasted the two American samples with Japan. The high (American) value reflected agreement with the statement, "We should at various times . . . accept something from all other paths of life . . . when any path is carried to extreme we lose something important." The Japanese pole indicated high value placed upon receptivity to nature or other persons, self-containment, and lack of dependence on others. The second discriminant function accounted for 23% of the variance. India is high on this factor and indicated acceptance of values related to dignity, refinement, and self-control. The third discriminant accounted for 14% of the variance and contrasted social action (pre-revolution China) and quiet receptivity to nature (Norway).

Prothro (1958) obtained Arab responses to the Morris ways-of-life questionnaire. The Arabs preferred ways involving activity, group participation, and self-control; they rejected receptivity, contemplation, and carefree enjoyment. Prothro also did a factor analysis and found three of the five factors obtained by Morris and Jones (1955) from American and Indian subjects. One of Prothro's factors was a "simplicity and moderation" factor, which appears to be genuinely Arab.

Perhaps the most important recent study on values is the one published by Kluckhohn and Strodtbeck (1961), considering values at the highest level of abstraction. They assumed that there are a limited number of common human problems for which all peoples at all times must find some solution. While there is variability in these solutions, it is neither limitless nor random, but is definitely variable within a range of possible solutions. All alternatives of all solutions are present in all societies at all times, but are differentially preferred. Kluckhohn and Strodtbeck assumed a priori that five basic value orientations underlie all values at this level of abstraction: man's nature (evil, good, neither); man versus nature (changer or adapter to nature); time (past, present, future); activity (being, being-in-becoming, doing); and the relational (lineality, collaterality, individualism) orientation.

The human nature orientation was further subdivided into mutable and immutable. Furthermore, a category which is a mixture of good-and-evil and is immutable was added.

The man-nature orientation was divided into subjugation to nature, harmony with nature, and mastery over nature.

Of the activity values, the being orientation emphasizes the Dionysian value of intensive experience of the present. The being-in-becoming orientation is also concerned with the human being rather than with what the human can accomplish. The idea of development of all aspects of the self

(self-actualization) as an integrated whole is the key to this value. The doing orientation often involves activity for its own sake and is characteristic of American society.

Of the three relational orientations, the lineal orientation values those activities which emphasize the continuity of the group (e.g., British aristocracy). The collateral orientation emphasizes relations with contemporaries. The individualism orientation permits the dominance of individual rather than collateral or lineal goals.

Five communities in the American Southwest were studied in order to test the value-orientation theory. The five cultures, within fifty miles of each other, were a group of Zuni Indians, a group of Navaho Indians, a Spanish-American community, a Mormon village, and a group of Texas homesteaders. Samples of about twenty subjects from each community were studied intensively with a questionnaire that permitted determination of a subject's orientation. The findings were quite interesting. For example, the Spanish-Americans preferred the present time orientation, the being alternative in the activity orientation, and the subjugated-to-nature position on the man-nature orientation. These differences separated them from the other four cultures. The within culture variance in many cases was larger than the between culture variance, but on a few interesting items, as indicated above, the between culture variance was larger than the within. Another important project, which was directed by Jessor (1962), focused on several studies of values among the Spanish, Anglos, and Indians of Colorado.

An ambitious public opinion survey was reported by Buchanan and Cantril (1953), with subjects representative of the populations of several countries. The subjects were asked questions designed to obtain information about their basic values, such as the question "Do you believe that human nature can be changed?" The answers were reported as percentages of the representative samples answering affirmatively. Thus, the subjects from France, Germany, Norway, and the United States answered the above question in the affirmative, while the subjects from Italy and Mexico tended to be nonaffirmative. In this study, however, it became clear that the horizons of the respondents were often quite limited. The subjects tended to respond quickly and surely to questions about their jobs and their feelings of personal security, and slowly to broad questions such as the one above. This suggests that many respondents probably had not considered such questions prior to having been asked and did not think seriously about the answer, when answering these questions.

Another important work relevant to value orientations is McClelland's (1961) attempt to state the environmental and child-training antecedents of achievement motivation, which may be conceived as an individual orientation. The reliability of the projective instruments used by McClelland and his associates, however, seems quite low in relation to more structured instruments (Christie and Lindauer, 1963).

The influence of language and reference group on the themes evoked from bilinguals appears to be important. To test this, Ervin (1963) gave TAT's to French bilinguals. The subjects told their stories in English and in French on two different occasions, in balanced order. Themes of achievement were more common for women subjects in the English than the French version, and themes of autonomy, withdrawal from others, and verbal aggression against peers appeared more frequently in the French than in the English version.

X. Retrospect and Prospect

A. CRITIQUE OF ACCOMPLISHMENTS

The Whorfian hypothesis (Whorf, 1940, 1956) was the most significant theoretical formulation on the question of the influence of cultural factors upon cognition. The research reviewed here suggests that the hypothesis was stated much too vaguely and too generally. Furthermore, the methods employed to test it often began and ended with linguistic data. This circularity made an adequate test of the hypothesis quite difficult.

Fishman (1960) provided an important reformulation of the hypothesis. He considered four levels along which the hypothesis may be tested: level 1, differences in linguistic codifiability; level 2, the effects of linguistic codifiability on behavior; level 3, linguistic structure and its cultural concomitants; and level 4, the effects of linguistic structure on behavior.

Fishman pointed out that differences in linguistic codifiability do not imply a difference in world view. Though we do not have a word for a particular kind of snow, as the Eskimos do, this does not necessarily imply that we experience snow differently.

Fishman's level 2 deals with linguistic codifiability and its behavioral concomitants. To avoid circularity it is necessary to consider a nonlinguistic response. Here Lehmann's classic study, which showed that when shades of gray were labeled, they could be identified more easily, is relevant, and so is Carroll and Casagrande's study (1958). The latter, noting that Hopi subjects used a linguistic form equivalent to our idea of "closing openings" when they described situations we would call "putting covers on things," did an experiment that tied linguistic and behavioral data. They drew pictures that permitted interpretations on the basis of either "closing openings" or "putting covers on things." Hopi subjects tended to give the

"Hopi response" more often than English-speaking subjects. It is hard to argue, however, that such differences in responses indicate major differences in the world view of Hopi and English-speaking subjects.

Fishman's level 3 dealt with linguistic structure and its cultural concomitants. His review suggested that while there are a number of stimulating papers in the literature, none are experimental. More data are needed on the relationship between grammatical structure and cultural concomitants.

Finally, Fishman's level 4 dealt with linguistic structure and behavioral concomitants. Here, one of Carroll and Casagrande's (1958) experiments is relevant. The results favor Whorf, but they permit alternative interpretations. Doob's (1962) study is also at this level and does not favor the Whorfian hypothesis.

Concluding his excellent review, Fishman (1960) stated:

> . . . linguistic relativity, where it does exist, is not necessarily an awesomely powerful factor in cognitive functioning. Relationships . . . seem to be neither very great nor irreversible . . . . The time might now be ripe for putting aside attempts at grossly "proving" or "disproving" the Whorfian hypothesis and, instead, focusing on attempts to delimit more sharply the types of language structures and the types of non-linguistic behaviors that show the Whorfian effect as well as the degree and the modifiability of this involvement when it does obtain (p. 337).

The above views are representative of the opinions expressed by other reviewers (e.g., Hymes, 1961b). Hoijer (1954), after an excellent summary of the differences between Hopi and Standard Average European (pp. 562–566), concluded that the Whorfian hypothesis needed further testing. Fearing (1954) concluded that sensory phenomena are unaffected by language, and the category of language universals includes kinesthesia, synesthesia, and physiognomic perception. Hockett (1954) thought that:

1. The most precisely definable differences between languages are also the most trivial from the Whorfian point of view. . . .
2. Languages differ not so much as to what *can* be said in them, but rather as to what it is *relatively easy* to say. . . .
3. The impact of inherited linguistic pattern on activities is, in general, least important in the most practical contexts and most important in such going-on as story telling, religion, and philosophizing—which consists largely or exclusively of talking anyway. Scientific discourse can be carried on in any languages the speakers of which have become participants in the world science, and other languages can be properly modified with little trouble; some types of literature, on the other hand, are largely imprevious to translation (p. 123).

According to Carroll (1958): "In a limited sense, then, the Whorfian hypothesis seems to have been verified although it still cannot be said that a language necessarily affects the whole world view and philosophy of the speaker of that language" (p. 85). In partial agreement, Hymes (1961a) wrote:

> It is clear in general that linguistic habits, including those involved in typology of cognitive styles, do influence nonlinguistic behavior, especially habitual behavior. At the same time it is clear that such influence is partial and complex in its manifestations rather than complete and easy to discern (p. 41).

Finally, Kluckhohn (1961) completed his review of the Whorfian hypothesis with this statement:

> The Whorfians have justified a hypothesis, but this hypothesis (or particular derivations of it) requires validation where the reasoning is not circular and where there are genuinely independent variables. No validation can be obtained by pointing on an *ad hoc* basis to correspondences, however actual, between features of language and features of non-linguistic culture (p. 910).

Since these statements were made, the evidence has not been particularly helpful to the Whorfian view. In fact, Osgood *et al.* (1962) employed linguistic data to disprove one aspect of the hypothesis. Briefly, it will be recalled, they obtained evidence which indicated that the structure of connotative meaning in heterogeneous cultures is very similar. As a test of the Whorfian hypothesis, this approach may be criticized on two counts: (1) it is not a fair test; (2) the interpretation given to the factors by Osgood and his associates is not sound.

The first is a very serious objection. Whorf explicitly discussed the influence of the grammatical structure of language on thought. The existence of a common frame of reference in connotative meaning may not be relevant to Whorf's argument. The present writer believes that rather than testing the Whorfian hypothesis, Osgood and his associates simply delineated an area in which the Whorfian hypothesis is not relevant.

The second objection is less important, because only two studies have challenged Osgood's interpretation of his factors and there is reason to believe that the discrepancies are due to differences in procedure. The two studies are by Dietze (1962) and Sagara *et al.* (1961). Dietze worked with Finnish subjects but used a sample of concepts and scales rather different from that of Osgood *et al.* (1962). In view of the concept-scale interaction problem (see Osgood, 1963), the deviation of his results from Osgood's is not surprising and does not appear to challenge Osgood's position.

More significant is a study done by four Japanese social scientists. Sagara *et al.* (1961) had subjects judge 120 concepts against 50 scales. The varimax rotated factors which they obtained were: (1) *moral correctness*—accurate, right, superior, consistent, complete, fine; (2) *magnitude*—heavy, deep, wide, masculine, strong; (3) *sensory pleasure*—soft, free, round, hot, pleasurable, happy; (4) *dynamism*—quick, positive, fast, sharp, active, strong. Differences in names of the factors isolated by factor analysis are not indications of differences in factor structure. Examination of the qualifiers that have high loadings suggests that moral correctness is a version of the evaluative factor, magnitude a version of the potency, and dynamism a previously identified factor (Triandis and Osgood, 1958). The sensory pleasure factor, however, appears to be a genuine Japanese factor. The authors pointed out that the Japanese language contains a very large number of sensory words, which may be responsible for the appearance of this factor.

Now, given that the Japanese results differed from the Osgood results, at least to the extent that they involved a genuinely Japanese factor not obtained in other studies, are they sufficient to accept the Whorfian hypothesis? In view of the differences in procedure employed by Sagara and Osgood, differences that are known to produce artifacts, the present writer is not inclined to accept the Whorfian hypothesis from this data.

B. CONCLUSIONS

The theoretical framework adopted for this chapter began with categories that are organized into schemata in certain lexical fields and are associated with each other with different, subjective probabilities. Positive and negative affects and behavioral intentions are attached to such categories. Attitudes include both evaluation and behavioral intentions and are organized within value systems.

Culture was found to intrude in almost all phases of this structure. Cultural and linguistic conventions determine much of the variance of what is categorized, how an event is categorized, what the relative weights of the criterial attributes used in categorization "ought to be," and the probabilities of "what goes with what." Different emotions and behavioral intentions are attached to these categories and the schemata that include them. Thus, the attitudes, values, images, and plans of persons in different cultures may be quite different, and much of the variance may be traced to the culture.

Tempering this picture of complete cultural relativism are the following considerations. All humans use categories (Kluckhohn, 1954), organize them into schemata, and experience subjective probabilities of connection between the categories. All humans organize the world in terms of its affective impact—evaluation, power, and activity (Osgood's three main factors), or some combination of these factors. In addition, culture-specific factors may influence human experience. All humans operate in terms of behavioral intentions which, together with their evaluations, are organized into attitudes that determine some of the variance in behavior.

Furthermore, though subjects in different cultures use different categories and different organizations of lexical fields, there is considerable similarity in the ways they evaluate key concepts, make judgments of emotion, desirability, and morality. Human life, for instance, is valued in all cultures, and there are no cultures where systematic extermination of other humans, regardless of their characteristics, is a dominant value.

The present chapter attempted to present a coherent view of the influences of culture on categorization, schemata, evaluations, behavioral intentions, attitudes, and values. Due to limitations of space, many important topics that did not fit this schema were omitted. The omitted topics include: the effect of cultural influences on patterns of thought (e.g., Kluckhohn, 1954; Baron, 1961); the influence of child training practices on belief systems (e.g., Lambert *et al.,* 1959; Triandis and Lambert, 1961b); cross-cultural uniformities in beliefs about appropriate ways of raising children (e.g., Triandis and Lambert, 1961a); the relationship between different social systems and different conceptions about the nature of supernaturals (D'Andrade, 1961; Swanson, 1962); and of art (J. L. Fischer, 1961); analysis of the development of languages and the effect of these changes on the conception of the world of those using them (Moscovici, 1961; Rose, 1962); the effect of cultural change on changes in the conception of the world (e.g., Dozier, 1956); the relationship between demographic variables and attitudinal variables (e.g., Herr, 1959; Pettigrew and Cramer, 1959); the effects of different belief systems on social behavior (e.g., Anderson and Anderson, 1962); the possibilities of electronic computer simulations of patterns of thought in various cultures; and many other topics.

The task of systematic description of cultural influences on cognition has only just begun. What is now known, relative to what remains to be known, places us in the position of the ancient Greeks with respect to atomic physics. We may have some of the right hypotheses—much as Empedocles and Democritus hypothesized the existence of the atom—but the ancient and modern views of the atom are very different. Only extensive, systematic, painstaking research will spell out the exact nature of the concepts and interrelationships sketched out in the present chapter.

REFERENCES

Abelson, R. P. (1959). *J. Conflict Resolution* **3**, 343–352.
Allport, G. W. (1954). "The Nature of Prejudice." Addison-Wesley, Cambridge, Massachusetts.
Allport, G. W., and Pettigrew, T. F. (1957). *J. Abnorm. Soc. Psychol.* **55**, 104–113.
Anastasi, A., and Foley, J. P. (1958). "Differential Psychology: Individual and Group Differences in Behavior," 3rd ed. Macmillan, New York.
Anderson, H. H., and Anderson, G. L. (1962). *J. Social Psychol.* **58**, 207–226.

Ansari, A. (1956). *J. Educ. & Psychol. Boroda* **14**, 28–35.
Avigdor-Coryell, R. (1962). *Proc. 16th Intern. Congr. Psychol. Amsterdam, 1960* pp. 586–592.
Bagby, J. W. (1957). *J. Abnorm. Soc. Psychol.* **54**, 331–334.
Banton, M. (1960). *Sociol. Rev.* **8**, 169–183.
Baron, R. (1961). *Rev. Psychol. Peuples* **16**, 179–186.
Bartlett, F. C. (1932). "Remembering." Cambridge Univ. Press, London and New York.
Bastide, R., and Berghe, P. van den. (1957). *Am. Sociol. Rev.* **22**, 689–694.
Berghe, P. L. van den (1962). *J. Social Psychol.* **57**, 55–72.
Biesheuvel, S. (1957). *South African J. Sci.* **53**, 309–314.
Bjerstedt, A. (1958). *Acta Psychol.* **14**, 329–346.
Bogardus, E. S. (1928). "Immigration and Race Attitudes." Heath, Boston.
Bonte, M. (1962). *J. Social Psychol.* **58**, 265–268.
Brown, R. (1956). *In* Appendix to "A Study of Thinking" (J. S. Bruner *et al.*), pp. 247–312. Wiley, New York.
Brown, R. (1962). *In* "Social Psychology." MIT Press, Cambridge, Massachusetts. (Mimeo.)
Brown, R. W., and Lenneberg, E. H. (1954). *J. Abnorm. Soc. Psychol.* **49**, 454–462.
Brown, R. W., and Lenneberg, E. H. (1958). *In* "Readings in Social Psychology" (E. Maccoby, T. M. Newcomb, and E. L. Hartley, eds.), 3rd ed., pp. 9–18. Holt, New York.
Bruner, J. S. (1957). *Psychol. Rev.* **64**, 123–152.
Bruner, J. S. (1958). *In* "Readings in Social Psychology" (E. Maccoby, T. M. Newcomb, and E. L. Hartley, eds.), 3rd ed., pp. 85–94. Holt, New York.
Buchanan, W., and Cantril, H. (1953). "How Nations See Each Other." University of Illinois Press, Urbana, Illinois.
Campbell, D. T. (1963). *In* "Psychology: A Study of a Science" (S. Koch, ed.), pp. 94–172. McGraw-Hill, New York.
Campbell, D. T., and LeVine, R. A. (1961). *J. Conflict Resolution* **5**, 82–108.
Carroll, J. B. (1958). *Rev. Educ. Res.* **28**, 79–88.
Carroll, J. B., and Casagrande, J. B. (1958). *In* "Readings in Social Psychology" (E. Maccoby, T. M. Newcomb, and E. L. Hartley, eds.), 3rd ed., pp. 18–31. Holt, New York.
Cattell, R. B. (1950). *J. Social Psychol.* **32**, 215–253.
Christensen, H. T., and Carpenter, G. R. (1962). *Am. Sociol. Rev.* **27**, 66–74.
Christie, R., and Lindauer, F. (1963). *Ann. Rev. Psychol.* **14**, 201–230.
Church, J. (1961). "Language and the Discovery of Reality." Random House, New York.
Cofer, C. N. (1951). *In* "Groups, Leadership, and Men," (H. Guetzkow, ed.), pp. 206–217. Carnegie Press, Pittsburgh, Pennsylvania.
Cohen, A. R. (1960). *Public Opin. Quart.* **24**, 297–318.
Conklin, H. C. (1954). *Trans. N.Y. Acad. Sci.* [2] **17**, 133–142.
D'Andrade, R. G. (1961). *In* "Psychological Anthropology" (F. L. K. Hsu, ed.), pp. 296–332, Dorsey Press, Homewood, Illinois.
Danziger, K. (1958). *J. Abnorm. Soc. Psychol.* **57**, 339–346.
Das, J. P., and Nanda, P. C. (1963). *J. Abnorm. Soc. Psychol.* **66**, 12–16.
Davis, R. (1961). *Brit. J. Psychol.* **52**, 259–268.
Dennis, W. (1951). *In* "Perception: An Approach to Personality" (R. R. Blake, and G. V. Ramsey, eds.), pp. 148–149. Ronald Press, New York.

Dennis, W. (1957a). *J. Abnorm. Soc. Psychol.* **55**, 21–28.
Dennis, W. (1957b). *J. Educ. Psychol.* **48**, 193–198.
Diab, L. (1963). *J. Social Psychol.* **59**, 29–40.
Dietze, A. G. (1962). *J. Social Psychol.* **57**, 33–48.
Doob, L. W. (1960). *J. Social Psychol.* **52**, 3–15.
Doob, L. (1962). *J. Social Psychol.* **57**, 133–141.
Dorfman, D. D., and Zajonc, R. B. (1963). *J. Abnorm. Soc. Psychol.* **66**, 87–90.
Dozier, E. P. (1956). *Language* **32**, 146–157.
Duijker, H. C. J., and Frijda, N. H. (1960). "National Character and National Stereotypes." North-Holland Publishing Co., Amsterdam.
Dukes, W. F. (1955). *Psychol. Bull.* **51**, 24–50.
Dulany, D. E. (1962). *In* "Behavior and Awareness—A Symposium of Research and Interpretation" (C. W. Eriksen, ed.) pp. 102–129. Duke Univ. Press, Durham, North Carolina.
Eggan, D. (1961). *In* "Studying Personality Cross-Culturally" (B. Kaplan, ed.) pp. 551–577. Harper & Row, New York.
Ehrlich, H. J. (1962). *Social Forces* **41**, 171–176.
Eisman, B. S. (1955). *J. Abnorm. Soc. Psychol.* **50**, 321–326.
Eriksen, C. W. (1963). *In* "Concepts of Personality," pp. 30–60. Apdine Press, Chicago, Illinois.
Ervin, S. M. (1961). *Am. J. Psychol.* **74**, 233–241.
Ervin, S. M. (1963). *J. Abnorm. Soc. Psychol.* **61**, 271–275.
Ervin, S. M., and Foster, G. (1960). *J. Abnorm. Soc. Psychol.* **71**, 261–275.
Fearing, F. (1954). *In* "Language in Culture" (H. Hoijer, ed.) Anthrop. Assn., **56**, 47–81.
Festinger, L. (1957). "Theory of Cognitive Dissonance." Harper & Row, New York.
Fiedler, F. E., and Hoffman, E. L. (1962). *Acta Psychol.* **20**, 185–195.
Fischer, H. (1961). *Rev. Psychol. Peuples.* **16**, 306–318.
Fischer, H., and Trier, U. P. (1962). "Das Verhältnis zwischen Deutschschweizer und Westschweizer: Eine sozialpsychologische Untersuchung." Hans Huber, Bern.
Fischer, J. L. (1961). *Am. Anthropol.* **63**, 79–93.
Fishbein, M. (1961). Tech. Rept. No. 6, Contract Nonr. 233 (54). Univ. of Calif., Los Angeles, California.
Fishman, J. A. (1956). *J. Social Psychol.* **43**, 27–64.
Fishman, J. A. (1960). *Behav. Sci.* **5**, 323–339.
Frake, C. O. (1961). *Am. Anthropol.* **63**, 113–132.
Frake, C. O. (1962a). *Am. Anthropol.* **64**, 53–59.
Frake, C. O. (1962b). *In* "Anthropology and Human Behavior," pp. 72–85. Anthropol. Soc. of Washington, D.C.
Frank, C. (1963). "Acceptance of Illegitimate Means," Research Rept. No. 155 Tri-Ethnic Project, Univ. of Colorado, Boulder, Colorado. (Mimeo.)
French, D. (1963). *In* "Psychology: A Study of a Science" (S. Koch, ed.), Vol. 6, pp. 388–428. McGraw-Hill, New York.
Frijda, N. H. (1953). *Acta Psychol.* **9**, 294–362.
Frijda, N. H., and Geer, J. P. van de. (1961). *Acta Psychol.* **18**, 360–367.
Frijda, N. H., and Philipszoon, E. (1963). *J. Abnorm. Soc. Psychol.* **66**, 45–51.
Gardner, R. W. (1953). *J. Pers.* **22**, 214–233.
Gibson, J. J. (1963). *Am. Psychol.* **18**, 1–15.
Gillespie, J. M., and Allport, G. W. (1955). "Youth's Outlook on the Future: A Cross-National Study." Doubleday, Garden City, New York.

Gladstones, W. H. (1962). *Australian J. Psychol.* **14,** 95–100.

Goodenough, W. H. (1956). *Language* **32,** 195–216.

Goodman, M. E. (1962). *Ethnology* **1,** 374–386.

Gouldner, A. (1960). *Am. Sociol. Rev.* **25,** 161–178.

Haire, M., and Morrison, F. (1957). *J. Social Psychol.* **46,** 179–197.

Haire, M., Ghiselli, E. E., and Porter, L. W. (1963). *Ind. Relat.* **2,** 95–117.

Hallowell, A. I. (1951). *In* "Social Psychology at the Crossroads" (J. H. Rohrer, and M. Sherif, eds.), pp. 164–195. Harper, New York.

Havighurst, R. J. (1963). "Cross National Differences Compared with Age, Sex, and Social Class Differences." Univ. of Chicago, Chicago, Illinois. (Mimeo.)

Hebb, D. O., and Thompson, W. R. (1954). *In* "Handbook of Social Psychology" (G. Lindzey, ed.), pp. 532–561. Addison-Wesley, Cambridge, Massachusetts.

Heider, F. (1944). *Psychol. Rev.* **51,** 358–374.

Heider, F. (1946). *J. Psychol.* **21,** 107–112.

Heider, F. (1958). "The Psychology of Interpersonal Relations." Wiley, New York.

Herr, D. M. (1959). *Am. J. Sociol.* **64,** 592–598.

Herskovits, M. J. (1955). "Cultural Anthropology." Knopf, New York.

Hockett, C. F. (1954). *In* "Language in Culture" (H. Hoijer, ed.), Am. Anthropol. Assoc., Washington, D.C.

Hoijer, H. (1953). *In* "Anthropology Today" (A. L. Kroeber, ed.), pp. 554–573. Univ. of Chicago Press, Chicago, Illinois.

Hoijer, H. (1954). *In* "Language in Culture" (H. Hoijer, ed.), pp. 92–105. Am. Anthropol. Assoc., Washington, D.C.

Hsu, F. L. K. (1961). "Psychological Anthropology." Dorsey Press, Homewood, Illinois.

Hudson, W. (1960). *J. Social Psychol.* **52,** 183–208.

Hunt, C. L. (1956). *Sociol. Soc. Res.* **40,** 253–260.

Hunt, E. B. (1962). "Concept Learning." Wiley, New York.

Hunt, J. McV. (1961). "Intelligence and Experience." Ronald Press, New York.

Hyman, H. H., Payaslioglu, A., and Frey, F. W. (1958). *Publ. Opin. Quart.* **22,** 275–291.

Hymes, D. H. (1961a). *Anthropol. Linguistics* **3,** 22–54.

Hymes, D. H. (1961b). *In* "Studying Personality Cross-Culturally" (B. Kaplan, ed.), pp. 313–359. Harper & Row, New York.

Jacobson, E., Kumata, H., and Gullahorn, J. E. (1960). *Public Opin. Quart.* **24,** 205–223.

Jessor, R. (1962). *In* "Anthropology and Human Behavior" (T. Gladwin and W. C. Sturtevant, eds.), pp. 94–114. Anthropol. Soc. of Washington, D.C.

Jones, L. V., and Bock, R. D. (1960). *Sociometry* **23,** 162–176.

Kaplan, B., ed. (1961). "Studying Personality Cross-Culturally." Harper & Row, New York.

Katz, D. (1960). *Public Opin. Quart.* **24,** 163–204.

Katz, D., and Braly, K. W. (1933). *J. Abnorm. Soc. Psychol.* **28,** 280–290.

Kelly, G. A. (1955). "The Psychology of Personal Constructs." Norton, New York.

Klett, J. C., and Yaukey, D. W. (1959). *J. Social Psychol.* **49,** 19–26.

Klineberg, O. (1954). "Social Psychology." Holt, New York.

Klineberg, O. (1962). *Proc. 16th Intern. Congr. Psychol., Amsterdam, 1960* pp. 592–600. North Holland Publishing Co., Amsterdam.

Kluckhohn, C (1954). *In* "Handbook of Social Psychology" (G. Lindzey, ed.), pp. 921–976. Addison-Wesley, Cambridge, Massachusetts.

Kluckhohn, C. (1961). *Am. Anthropol.* **63,** 895–910.

Kluckhohn, C., and Leighton, D. (1946). "The Navaho." Harvard Univ. Press, Cambridge, Massachusetts.

Kluckhohn, F. R., and Strodtbeck, F. L. (1961). "Variations in Value Orientations." Harper & Row, New York.

Kumata, H. (1957). Unpublished Ph.D. Dissertation. Univ. of Illinois, Urbana, Illinois.

Kumata, H., and Schramm, W. (1956). *Public Opin. Quart.* **20,** 229–237.

Lambert, W. E. (1952). *Social Forces* **31,** 155–160.

Lambert, W. E. (1962). *Proc. 16th Intern. Congr. Psychol., Amsterdam, 1960* pp. 612–619. North-Holland Publishing Co., Amsterdam.

Lambert, W. E., and Klineberg, O. (1959). "A Pilot Study of the Origin and Development of National Stereotypes." (Mimeo.)

Lambert, W. W., Triandis, L. M., and Wolf, M. (1959). *J. Abnorm. Soc. Psychol.* **58,** 162–169.

Landar, H. J., Ervin, S. M., and Horowitz, A. E. (1960). *Language* **36,** 368–382.

La Roque, B. B. de. (1960). *Bull. Centre Etude Rech. Psychotech.* **9,** 363–384.

Lawlor, M. (1955). *J. Abnorm. Soc. Psychol.* **51,** 690–692.

Lenneberg, E. H., and Roberts, J. M. (1956). *Intern. J. Am. Linguistics* **22** (Suppl.) No. 2.

LeVine, R. A. (1963). *Biennial Rev. Anthropol.* **3,** 107–145.

Lindzey, G. (1961). "Projective Technique and Cross-Cultural Research." Appleton-Century-Crofts, New York.

Lövass, O. I. (1958). *J. Abnorm. Soc. Psychol.* **57,** 124–125.

Lounsbury, F. G. (1956). *Language* **32,** 158–194.

Luria, A. R. (1961). "The Role of Speech in the Regulation of Normal and Abnormal Behavior." Liveright, New York.

McClelland, D. C. (1961). "The Achieving Society." Van Nostrand, Princeton, New Jersey.

MacLeod, R. B. (1959). *J. Social Issues* **15,** 69–75.

Mahar, P. M. (1960). *Sociometry* **23,** 292–306.

Mathiot, M. (1962). *Am. Anthropol.* **64,** 340–350.

Mercado, S. J., Diaz-Guerrero, R. D., and Gardner, R. W. (1963). *J. Social Psychol.* **59,** 199–208.

Michon, J. A. (1960). *Acta Psychol.* **17,** 377–391.

Micko, H. C. (1962). *Z. Exptl. Angew. Psychol.* **9,** 242–280.

Milgram, S. (1961). *Sci. Am.* **205,** 45–51.

Miller, G. A., Galanter, E., and Pribram, K. H. (1960). "Plans and the Structure of Behavior." Holt, New York.

Miron, M. S. (1961). *J. Abnorm. Soc. Psychol.* **62,** 623–630.

Miron, M., and Wolfe, S. (1962). "A Cross-Linguistic Analysis of the Response Distributions of Restricted Word Associations." Univ. of Illinois, Urbana, Illinois. (Mimeo.)

Molnos, A. von. (1962). *Rev. Psychol. Peuples* **17,** 314–340.

Morris, C. (1957). *In* "The Language of Value" (R. Lepley, ed.), pp. 58–76 Columbia Univ. Press, New York.

Morris, C., and Jones, L. V. (1955). *J. Abnorm. Soc. Psychol.* **51,** 523–535.

Moscovici, S. (1961). "La Psychanalyse, son Image et son Public." Presses Univ. de France, Paris.

Nadel, S. F. (1937). *Africa* **10,** 421–435.

Najarian, P. (1959). *J. Social Issues* **15**, 28.

Newcomb, T. M. (1953). *Psychol. Rev.* **60**, 393–404.

Osgood, C. E. (1953). "Method and Theory in Experimental Psychology." Oxford Univ. Press, London and New York.

Osgood, C. E. (1955). *In* "Information Theory in Psychology" (H. Quastler, ed.) pp. 374–384. Free Press, Glencoe, Illinois.

Osgood, C. E. (1960a). *Behav. Sci.* **5**, 146–169.

Osgood, C. E. (1960b). *Public Opin. Quart.* **24**, 341–365.

Osgood, C. E. (1962). *Am. Psychol.* **17**, 10–28.

Osgood, C. E. (1963). *In* "Universals of Language" (J. H. Greenberg, ed.), pp. 236–254. MIT Press, Cambridge, Massachusetts.

Osgood, C. E., and Tannenbaum, P. H. (1955). *Psychol. Rev.* **62**, 42–55.

Osgood, C. E., Suci, G. J., and Tannenbaum, P. H. (1957). "The Measurement of Meaning." Univ. of Illinois Press, Urbana, Illinois.

Osgood, C. E., Archer, W. K., and Miron, M. S. (1962). "The Cross-Cultural Generality of Meaning Systems." Institute of Communications Research, Urbana, Illinois. (Mimeo.)

Oyama, T., Tanaka, Y., and Chiba, Y. (1962). *Japan. Psychol. Res.* **4** (in press).

Pettigrew, T. F., and Cramer, M. R. (1959). *J. Social Issues* **15**, 61–71.

Piaget, J. (1961). "Les Mecanismes Perceptifs." Presses Univ. de France, Paris.

Piaget, J., and Weil, A. (1951). *Intern. Social Sci. Bull.* **3**, 561–578.

Pike, K. L. (1954). "Language in Relation to a Unified Theory of the Structure of Human Behavior." Summer Institute of Linguistics, Glendale, California.

Pratt, C. C. (1961). *Ann. Rev. Psychol.* **12**, 71–92.

Prothro, E. T. (1958). *J. Social Psychol.* **47**, 3–7.

Prothro, E. T., and Keehn, J. D. (1956). *J. Abnorm. Soc. Psychol.* **53**, 157–160.

Prothro, E. T., and Melikian, L. (1952). *Sociol. & Social Res.* **37**, 3–11.

Prothro, E. T., and Melikian, L. (1953). *Sociol. & Social Res.* **37**, 375–379.

Prothro, E. T., and Melikian, L. (1954). *J. Social Psychol.* **40**, 237–243.

Prothro, E. T., and Melikian, L. (1955). *J. Social Psychol.* **41**, 3–10.

Rettig, S., and Lee, J. S. (1963). *J. Social Psychol.* **59**, 3–9.

Rettig, S., and Pasamanick, B. (1962). *Sociometry* **25**, 73–84.

Rhine, R. J. (1958). *Psychol. Rev.* **65**, 362–369.

Rhine, R. J., and Silum, B. A. (1958). *J. Exptl. Psychol.* **55**, 524–529.

Rioux, G. (1959). *Enfance* **12**, 509–516.

Rivers, W. H. R. (1905). *Brit. J. Psychol.* **1**, 321–396.

Rokeach, M. (1961). *J. Abnorm. Soc. Psychol.* **62**, 187–188.

Rokkan, S. (1955). *Intern. Social Sci. Bull.* **7**, 622–641.

Rose, E. (1962). *In* "Two Papers on the Use of Words as Cultural Units." Pergamon Press, New York.

Rosen, E. (1959). *J. Social Psychol.* **49**, 137–144.

Rosenberg, M. J. (1960). *Public Opin. Quart.* **24**, 319–340.

Rosenberg, M. J., Hovland, C. I., McGuire, W. J., Abelson, R. P., and Brehm, J. W. (1960). "Attitude Organization and Change." Yale Univ. Press, New Haven, Connecticut.

Rosenzweig, M. R. (1957). *Année Psychol.* **57**, 23–32.

Rosenzweig, M. R. (1961). *Am. J. Psychol.* **74**, 347–360.

Roth, D., and Das, J. P., (1958). *J. Social Psychol.* **47**, 373–385.

Ryan, T. A. (1938). *Am. J. Psychol.* **60**, 629–650.

Sagara, M., Yamamoto, K., Nishimura, H., and Akuto, H. (1961). *Japan. Psychol. Res.* **3**, 146–156.

Sato, K. (1962). *Proc. 16th Intern. Congr. Psychol., Amsterdam, 1960* pp. 610–612. North-Holland Publishing Co., Amsterdam.

Schlosberg, H. (1944). *J. Exptl. Psychol.* **44**, 229–237.

Schlosberg, H. (1954). *Psychol. Rev.* **61**, 81–88.

Segall, M. H., Campbell, D. T., and Herskovits, M. J. (1963). *Science* **139**, 769–771.

Segall, M. H. Campbell, D. T., and Herskovits, M. J. (1964). "The Influence of Culture on Visual Perception." Bobbs-Merrill, Indianapolis, Indiana.

Sherif, M., and Sherif, C. W. (1956). "An Outline of Social Psychology." Harper, New York.

Sinha, A. K. P., and Upadhyaya, O. P. (1960). *J. Social Psychol.* **52**, 31–39.

Smith, M. B., ed. (1956). *J. Social Issues* **12** (entire issue).

Sodhi, K. S. (1962). *Proc. 16th Intern. Congr. Psychol., Amsterdam, 1960* pp. 601–609. North-Holland Publishing Co. Amsterdam.

Sodhi, K. S., Bergius, R., and Holzkamp, K. (1958). *Z. Exptl. Angew. Psychol.* **5**, 547–604.

Solley, C. M., and Messick, S. J. (1957). *Am. J. Psychol.* **70**, 161–173.

Staats, C. K., Staats, A. W., and Heard, W. G. (1960). *Sociometry* **23**, 338–350.

Stoetzel, J. (1954). "Jeunesse sans Chrysantheme ni sabre." Plon. Univ., Paris.

Suci, G. J. (1960). *J. Abnorm. Soc. Psychol.* **61**, 25–30.

Swanson, G. E. (1962). "The Birth of the Gods." Univ. of Michigan Press, Ann Arbor, Michigan.

Talland, G. A. (1956). *J. Social Psychol.* **43**, 75–81.

Taylor, I. K. (1963). *Psychol. Bull.* **60**, 200–209.

Triandis, H. C. (1959a). *J. Appl. Psychol.* **43**, 338–344.

Triandis, H. C. (1959b). *J. Appl. Psychol.* **43**, 221–225.

Triandis, H. C. (1960a). *Human Relat.* **13**, 175–183.

Triandis, H. C. (1960b). *J. Appl. Psychol.* **44**, 297–302.

Triandis, H. C. (1961). *J. Abnorm. Soc. Psychol.* **62**, 184–186.

Triandis, H. C. (1963). *J. Appl. Psychol.* **47**, 89–96.

Triandis, H. C. (1964). *J. Abnorm. Soc. Psychol.* **68**, 420–430.

Triandis, H. C., and Fishbein, M. (1963). *J. Abnorm. Soc. Psychol.* **67**, 446–453.

Triandis, H. C., and Lambert, W. W. (1958). *J. Abnorm. Soc. Psychol.* **56**, 321–328.

Triandis, H. C., and Osgood, C. E. (1958). *J. Abnorm. Soc. Psychol.* **57**, 187–196.

Triandis, H. C., and Triandis, L. M. (1960). *J. Abnorm. Soc. Psychol.* **61**, 110–118.

Triandis, H. C., and Triandis, L. M. (1962). *Psychol. Monogr.* **76**, No. 21.

Triandis, L. M., and Lambert, W. W. (1961a). *J. Abnorm. Soc. Psychol.* **62**, 631–639.

Triandis, L. M., and Lambert, W. W. (1961b). *J. Abnorm. Soc. Psychol.* **62**, 640–648.

Trier, J. (1931). "Der deutsche Wortschatz im Sinnbezirk des Verstandes: Die Geschichte eines Sprachfeldes." Carl Winters, Heidelberg.

Vaughan, G. M. (1962). *J. Social Psychol.* **57**, 85–92.

Vinacke, W. E. (1956). *J. Social Psychol.* **43**, 105–132.

Vinacke, W. E., and Fong, R. W. (1955). *J. Social Psychol.* **41**, 185–195.

Voegelin, C. F. (1949). *Word* **5**, 44–45.

Voorhees, J. M. (1954). "Toward a Cross-Cultural Concept of Music and Emotion." Senior Thesis, Princeton Univ., Princeton, New Jersey. Quoted by Pratt (1961).

Walker, D. E., Jenkins, J. J., and Sebeok, T. A. I. (1954). *J. Abnorm. Soc. Psychol.* **49** (Suppl.), 192–203.

Wallace, A. F., ed. (1956). *Selected Papers 5th Intern. Cong. Anthropol. & Ethnol. Sci., Philadelphia.*

Wallace, A. F. C. (1961). *In* "Studying Personality Cross-Culturally" (B. Kaplan, ed.) pp. 129–163. Harper & Row, New York.

Wallace, A. F. C. (1962a). "Culture and Personality." Random House, New York.

Wallace, A. F. C. (1962b). *Science* **135,** 351–357.

Wallace, A. F. C., and Atkins, J. (1960). *Am. Anthropol.* **62,** 58–80.

Weiss, R. F. (1962). *Psychol. Rept.* **11,** 709–732.

Whorf, B. L. (1940). *Technol. Rev.* **44,** 229–248.

Whorf, B. L. (1956). "Language, Thought and Reality" (J. B. Carroll, ed.). Wiley, New York.

Woodworth, R. S. (1939). "Psychological Issues." Columbia Univ. Press, New York.

Zaidi, S. M. H. (1960). *J. Social Psychol.* **52,** 41–49.

Zaidi, S. M. H., and Ahmed, M. (1958). *J. Social Psychol.* **47,** 387–395.

Zajonc, R. (1960). *Public. Opin. Quart.* **24,** 280–296.

Zipf, G. K. (1949). "Human Behavior and the Principle of Least Effort." Addison-Wesley, Cambridge, Massachusetts.

THE INTERACTION OF COGNITIVE AND PHYSIOLOGICAL DETERMINANTS OF EMOTIONAL STATE[1]

Stanley Schachter

DEPARTMENT OF SOCIAL PSYCHOLOGY
COLUMBIA UNIVERSITY
NEW YORK, NEW YORK

I. Introduction

Many years ago, piqued by the disorderly cataloguing of symptoms which, in his time, characterized the classic works on emotion, William James offered what was probably the first simple, integrating, theoretical

[1] Much of the research described in this paper was supported by Grant MH 05203 from the National Institute of Mental Health, United States Public Health Service, and by Grant G 23758 from the National Science Foundation.

statement on the nature of emotion. This well-known formulation stated that "the bodily changes follow directly the perception of the exciting fact, and that our feeling of the same changes as they occur *is* the emotion" (James, 1890). Since James' proposition directly equates bodily changes and visceral feelings with emotion, it must follow, first, that the different emotions are accompanied by recognizably different bodily states and second, that the direct manipulation of bodily state, by drugs or surgery, also manipulates emotional state. These implications have, directly or indirectly, guided much of the research on emotion since James' day. The results of such research, on the whole, provided little support for a purely visceral formulation of emotion and led Cannon (1927, 1929) to his brilliant and devastating critique of the James-Lange theory—a critique based on the following:

1. Total separation of the viscera from the central nervous system does not alter emotional behavior.

2. The same visceral changes occur in very different emotional states and in nonemotional states.

3. The viscera are relatively insensitive structures.

4. Visceral changes are too slow to be a source of emotional feeling.

5. Artificial induction of the visceral changes typical of strong emotions does not produce them.

Though new data have weakened the cogency of some of these points, on the whole Cannon's logic and findings make it inescapably clear that a completely peripheral or visceral formulation of emotion, such as the James-Lange theory, is inadequate to cope with the facts. In an effort to deal with the obvious inadequacies of a purely visceral or peripheral formulation of emotion, Ruckmick (1936), Hunt *et al.* (1958), Schachter (1959), and others have suggested that cognitive factors may be major determinants of emotional states. It is the purpose of this paper to spell out the implications of a cognitive-physiological formulation of emotion and to describe a series of experiments designed to test these implications.

A. THE INTERACTION OF COGNITIVE AND PHYSIOLOGICAL PROCESSES

To begin, let us grant on the basis of much evidence (see Woodworth and Schlosberg, 1958, for example) that a general pattern of sympathetic discharge is characteristic of emotional states. Given such a state of arousal, it is suggested that one labels, interprets, and identifies this stirred-up state in terms of the characteristics of the precipitating situation and one's apperceptive mass. This suggests, then, that an emotional state may be considered a function of a state of physiological arousal[2] and of a cognition appropriate to this state of arousal. The cognition, in a sense, exerts a steering function. Cognitions arising from the immediate situation as interpreted by past experience provide the framework within which one understands and labels his feelings. It is the cognition which determines whether the state of physiological arousal will be labeled "anger," "joy," or whatever.

In order to examine the implications of this formulation, consider the fashion in which these two elements, a state of physiological arousal and cognitive factors, would interact in a variety of situations. In most emotion inducing situations, of course, the two factors are completely inter-related. Imagine a man walking alone down a dark alley when a figure with a gun suddenly appears. The perception-cognition "figure with a gun" in some fashion initiates a state of physiological arousal; this state of arousal is interpreted in terms of knowledge about dark alleys and guns, and the state of arousal is labeled "fear." Similarly, a student who unexpectedly learns that he has made Phi Beta Kappa may experience a state of arousal which he will label "joy."

1. Physiological Arousal Not Sufficient

Let us now consider circumstances in which these two elements, the physiological and the cognitive, are, to some extent, independent. First, is the state of physiological arousal alone sufficient to induce an emotion? The best evidence indicates that it is not. Marañon (1924), in a fascinating study (replicated by Cantril and Hunt (1932) and Landis and Hunt (1932)), injected 210 of his patients with the sympathomimetic agent adrenaline and then asked them to introspect. Seventy-one % of his subjects reported physical symptoms with no emotional overtone; 29% responded in an apparently emotional fashion. Of these, the great majority described their feelings in a fashion that Marañon labeled "cold" or "as if" emotions; that is, they made statements such as "I feel *as if* I were afraid" or "*as if* I were awaiting a great happiness." This is a sort of emotional *déjà vu* experience; these subjects are neither happy nor afraid, they feel "as if" they were. Finally, a very few cases apparently reported a genuine emotional experience. However, in order to produce this reaction

---

[2] Though the experiments to be described are concerned largely with the physiological changes produced by the injection of adrenaline—which appear to be primarily the result of sympathetic excitation—the term physiological arousal is used in preference to the more specific "excitement of the sympathetic nervous system" because there are indications, discussed later, that this formulation is applicable to a variety of bodily states.

in most of these few cases, Marañon pointed out

> one must suggest a memory with strong affective force but not so strong as
> to produce an emotion in the normal state. For example, in several cases
> we spoke to our patients before the injection of their sick children or dead
> parents and they responded calmly to this topic. The same topic presented
> later, during the adrenal commotion, was sufficient to trigger emotion. This
> adrenal commotion places the subject in a situation of "affective imminence."

Apparently, then, to produce a genuinely emotional reaction to adrenaline, Marañon was forced to provide such subjects with an appropriate cognition.

Though Marañon was not explicit on his procedure, it is clear that his subjects knew that they were receiving an injection, in all likelihood knew that they were receiving adrenaline, and probably had some order of familiarity with its effects. In short, although they underwent the pattern of sympathetic discharge common to strong emotional states, at the same time they had a completely appropriate cognition or explanation as to why they felt this way. This, it is suggested, is the reason so few of Marañon's subjects reported any emotional experience.

2. The Need To Evaluate One's Feelings

Consider next a person in a state of physiological arousal for which no immediately explanatory or appropriate cognitions are available. Such a state could result were one covertly to inject a subject with adrenaline or, unknown to him, feed the subject a sympathomimetic drug such as ephedrine. Under such conditions a subject would be aware of palpitations, tremor, face flushing, and most of the battery of symptoms associated with a discharge of the sympathetic nervous system. In contrast to Marañon's subjects, he would, at the same time, be utterly unaware of why he felt this way. What would be the consequence of such a state?

Schachter (1959) suggested that just such a state would lead to the arousal of "evaluative needs" (Festinger, 1954). That is, pressures would act on an individual in such a state to understand and label his bodily feelings. His bodily state grossly resembles the condition in which it has been at times of emotional excitement. How would he label his present feelings? It is suggested, of course, that he will label his feelings in terms of his knowledge of the immediate situation.[3] Should he at the time be with a beautiful woman, he might decide that he was wildly in love or sexually excited. Should he be at a gay party, he might, by comparing himself to others, decide that he was extremely happy and euphoric. Should he be

---

[3] This suggestion is not new, for several psychologists have suggested that situational factors should be considered the chief differentiators of the emotions. Hunt *et al.* (1958) probably made this point most explicitly in their study distinguishing among fear, anger, and sorrow in terms of situational characteristics.

arguing with his wife, he might explode in fury and hatred. Or, should the situation be completely inappropriate, he could decide that he was excited about something that had recently happened to him or, simply, that he was sick. In any case, it is my basic assumption that emotional states are a function of the interaction of such cognitive factors with a state of physiological arousal.

B. THEORETICAL PROPOSITIONS

This line of thought leads to three propositions. One, given a state of physiological arousal for which an individual has no immediate explanation, he will "label" this state and describe his feelings in terms of the cognitions available to him. To the extent that cognitive factors are potent determiners of emotional states, it could be anticipated that precisely the same state of physiological arousal could be labeled "joy" or "fury" or any of a great diversity of emotional labels, depending on the cognitive aspects of the situation.

Two, given a state of physiological arousal for which an individual has a completely appropriate explanation (e.g., "I feel this way because I have just received an injection of adrenaline"), no evaluative needs will arise, and the individual is unlikely to label his feelings in terms of the alternative cognitions available.

Finally, consider a condition in which emotion inducing cognitions are present but there is no state of physiological arousal; an individual might, for example, be aware that he is in great danger, but for some reason (drug or surgical) remain in a state of physiological quiescence. Does he then experience the emotion "fear"? This formulation of emotion as a joint function of a state of physiological arousal and an appropriate cognition, would, of course, suggest that he does not, which leads to our final proposition. Three, given the same cognitive circumstances, the individual will react emotionally or describe his feelings as emotions only to the extent that he experiences a state of physiological arousal.[4]

II. Cognitive, Social and Physiological Determinants

The experimental test of these propositions requires (1) the experimental manipulation of a state of physiological arousal or sympathetic activation; (2) the manipulation of the extent to which the subject has an appropriate or proper explanation of his bodily state; and (3) the creation of situations from which explanatory cognitions may be derived.

In order to satisfy these experimental requirements, Schachter and

[4] In his critique of the James-Lange theory of emotion, Cannon (1929) made the point that sympathectomized animals and patients do seem to manifest emotional behavior. This criticism is, of course, as applicable to the above proposition as it was to the James-Lange formulation. The issues involved will be discussed later in this chapter.

Singer (1962) designed an experiment cast in the framework of a study of the effects of vitamin supplements on vision. As soon as a subject arrived, he was taken to a private room and told by the experimenter:

> In this experiment we would like to make various tests of your vision. We are particularly interested in how certain vitamin compounds and vitamin supplements affect the visual skills. In particular, we want to find out how the vitamin compound called "Suproxin" affects your vision.
>
> What we would like to do, then, if we can get your permission, is to give you a small injection of Suproxin. The injection itself is mild and harmless; however, since some people do object to being injected we don't want to talk you into anything. Would you mind receiving a Suproxin injection?

If the subject agreed to the injection (and all but one of 185 subjects did), the experimenter continued with instructions described below, then left the room. In a few minutes a doctor entered the room, briefly repeated the experimenter's instructions, took the subject's pulse, and then injected him with Suproxin.

Depending upon condition, the subject received one of two forms of Suproxin—epinephrine or a placebo.

Epinephrine or adrenaline is a sympathomimetic drug whose effects, with minor exceptions, are almost a perfect mimicry of a discharge of the sympathetic nervous system. Shortly after injection systolic blood pressure increases markedly. Heart rate increases somewhat, cutaneous blood flow decreases, muscle and cerebral blood flow increase, blood sugar and lactic acid concentration increase, and respiration rate increases slightly. For the subject, the major subjective symptoms are palpitation, tremor, and sometimes a feeling of flushing and accelerated breathing. With a subcutaneous injection, (in the dosage administered) such effects usually begin within three to five minutes of injection and last anywhere from ten minutes to an hour. For most subjects these effects are dissipated within 15–20 minutes after injection.

Subjects receiving epinephrine received a subcutaneous injection of ½ cc of a 1:1000 solution of Winthrop Laboratory's Suprarenin, a saline solution of epinephrine bitartrate.

Subjects in the placebo condition received a subcutaneous injection of ½ cc of saline solution.

A. MANIPULATING AN APPROPRIATE EXPLANATION

"Appropriate" refers to the extent to which the subject has an authoritative, unequivocal explanation of his bodily condition. Thus, a subject who had been informed by the physician that as a direct consequence of the injection he would feel palpitations, tremor, etc. would be considered to have a completely appropriate explanation. A subject who had been informed only that the injection would have no side effects, would have no appropriate explanation of his state. This dimension of appropriateness was manipulated in three experimental conditions which shall be called: (1) Epinephrine Informed (Epi Inf), (2) Epinephrine Ignorant (Epi Ign), and (3) Epinephrine Misinformed (Epi Mis).

Immediately after the subject had agreed to the injection and before the physician entered the room, the experimenter's presentation in each of these conditions went as follows:

1. Epinephrine Informed

"I should also tell you that some of our subjects have experienced side effects from the Suproxin. These side effects are transitory, that is, they will only last for about 15 or 20 minutes. What will probably happen is that your hand will start to shake, your heart will start to pound, and your face may get warm and flushed. Again these are side effects, lasting about 15 or 20 minutes."

While the physician was giving the injection, she told the subject that the injection was mild and harmless and repeated this description of the symptoms that the subject could expect as a consequence of the shot. In this condition, then, subjects had a completely appropriate explanation of their bodily state. They knew precisely what they would feel and why.

2. Epinephrine Ignorant

In this condition, when the subject agreed to the injection, the experimenter said nothing more about side effects and left the room. While the physician was giving the injection, she told the subject that the injection was mild and harmless and would have no side effects. In this condition, then, the subject had no experimentally provided explanation for his bodily state.

3. Epinephrine Misinformed

"I should also tell you that some of our subjects have experienced side effects from the Suproxin. These side effects are transitory, that is, they will only last for about 15 or 20 minutes. What will probably happen is that your feet will feel numb, you will have an itching sensation over parts of your body, and you may get a slight headache. Again these are side effects lasting 15 or 20 minutes." And again, the physician repeated these symptoms while injecting the subject.

None of these symptoms, of course, are consequences of an injection of epinephrine and, in effect, these instructions provided the subject with a completely inappropriate explanation of his bodily feelings. This condition was introduced as a control condition of sorts. It seemed possible that the description of side effects in the Epi Inf condition might turn the subject introspective, self-examining, possibly slightly troubled. Differences on the dependent variable between the Epi Inf and Epi Ign conditions might, then, be due to such factors rather than to differences in appropriateness. The false symptoms in the Epi Mis condition should similarly turn the subject introspective, etc., but the instructions in this condition do not provide an appropriate explanation of the subject's state.

Subjects in all of the above conditions were injected with epinephrine. Finally, there was a placebo condition in which subjects who were injected with saline solution were given precisely the same treatment as subjects in the Epi Ign condition.

B. PRODUCING AN EMOTION-INDUCING COGNITION

We initially hypothesized that given a state of physiological arousal for which the individual has no adequate explanation, cognitive factors can lead the individual to describe his feelings with any of a variety of emotional labels. In order to test this hypothesis, it was decided to manipulate emotional states which can be considered quite different—euphoria and anger.

There are, of course, many ways to induce such states. In this program of research, we have concentrated on social determinants of emotional states. Other studies have demonstrated that people evaluate their own feelings by comparing themselves with others around them (Wrightsman, 1960; Schachter, 1959). In the experiment described here, an attempt was again made to manipulate emotional state by social means. In one set of conditions, the subject was placed together with a stooge who had been trained to act euphorically. In a second set of conditions, the subject was with a stooge trained to act angrily.

1. Euphoria

Immediately[5] after the subject had been injected, the physician left the room and the experimenter returned with a stooge whom he introduced as another subject. The experimenter then said, "Both of you have had the Suproxin shot and you'll both be taking the same tests of vision. What I ask you to do now is just wait for 20 minutes. The reason for this is simply that we have to allow 20 minutes for the Suproxin to get from the

---

[5] It was, of course, imperative that the sequence with the stooge begin before the subject felt his first symptoms. Otherwise the subject would be virtually forced to interpret his feelings in terms of events preceding the stooge's entrance. Pretests had indicated that, for most subjects, epinephrine caused symptoms began within three to five minutes after injection. A deliberate attempt was made then to bring in the stooge within one minute after the subject's injection.

injection site into the bloodstream. At the end of 20 minutes when we are certain that most of the Suproxin has been absorbed into the bloodstream, we'll begin the tests of vision."

The room in which this was said had been deliberately put into a state of mild disarray. As he was leaving, the experimenter added apologetically, "The only other thing I should do is to apologize for the condition of the room. I just didn't have time to clean it up. So, if you need any scratch paper, or rubber bands, or pencils, help yourself. I'll be back in 20 minutes to begin the vision tests."

As soon as the experimenter left, the stooge introduced himself again, made a series of standard icebreaker comments and then went into his routine. He reached first for a piece of paper, doodled briefly, crumpled the paper, aimed for a wastebasket, threw, and missed. This led him into a game of "basketball" in which he moved about the room crumpling paper, and trying out fancy basketball shots. Finished with basketball, he said, "This is one of my good days. I feel like a kid again. I think I'll make a plane." He made a paper plane, spent a few minutes flying it around the room, and then said, "Even when I was a kid, I was never much good at this." He then tore off the tail of his plane, wadded it up, and making a slingshot of a rubber band, began to shoot the paper. While shooting, he noticed a sloppy pile of manila folders. He built a tower of these folders, then went to the opposite end of the room to shoot at the tower. He knocked down the tower, and while picking up the folders he noticed a pair of hula hoops behind a portable blackboard. He took one of these for himself, put the other within reaching distance of the subject, and began hula hooping. After a few minutes, he replaced the hula hoop and returned to his seat, at which point the experimenter returned to the room.

All through this madness an observer, through a one-way mirror, systematically recorded the subject's behavior and noted the extent to which the subject joined in with the stooge's whirl of activity.

Subjects in each of the three "appropriateness" conditions and in the placebo condition were submitted to this setup. The stooge, of course, never knew in which condition any particular subject fell.

2. Anger

Immediately after the injection, the experimenter brought a stooge into the subject's room, introduced the two, and after explaining the necessity for a 20-minute delay for "the Suproxin to get from the injection site into the bloodstream" he continued, "We would like you to use these 20 minutes to answer these questionnaires." Then handing out the questionnaires, he concluded: "I'll be back in 20 minutes to pick up the questionnaires and begin the tests of vision."

The questionnaires, five pages long, started off innocently, requesting face sheet information and then grew increasingly personal and insulting, asking questions such as:

"With how many men (other than your father) has your mother had extra-marital relationships?"

4 and under_____ : 5–9_____ : 10 and over_____ .

The stooge, sitting directly opposite the subject, paced his own answers so that at all times subject and stooge were working on the same question. At regular points in the questionnaire, the stooge made a series of standardized comments about the questions. His comments started off innocently enough, grew increasingly querulous, and finally he ended up in a rage, ripping up his questionnaire, slamming it to the floor, saying "I'm not wasting any more time. I'm getting my books and leaving," and stomping out of the room.

Again an observer recorded the subject's behavior.

In summary, this was a seven-condition experiment which, for two different emotional states, allowed us (1) to evaluate the effects of "appropriateness" on emotional inducibility, and (2) to begin to evaluate the effects of sympathetic activation on emotional inducibility. In schematic form, the conditions were:

Euphoria	Anger
Epi Inf	Epi Inf
Epi Ign	Epi Ign
Epi Mis	Placebo
Placebo	

The Epi Mis condition was not run in the Anger sequence. This was originally conceived as a control condition, and it was felt that its inclusion in the Euphoria conditions alone would suffice as a means of evaluating the possible artifactual effect of the Epi Inf instructions.

The subjects were all male college students, taking classes in introductory psychology at the University of Minnesota. The records of all potential subjects were reviewed by the Student Health Service in order to insure that no harmful effects would result from the injections.

C. MEASUREMENTS

Two types of measures of emotional state were obtained. Standardized observation through a one-way mirror was used to assess the subject's behavior. To what extent did he join in with the stooge's pattern of behavior and act euphoric or angry? The second type of measure was a self-report questionnaire in which, on a variety of scales, the subject indicated his mood of the moment.

These measures were obtained immediately after the stooge had finished his routine, at which point the experimenter returned saying, "Before we proceed with the vision tests, there is one other kind of information we must have. We have found that there are many things beside Suproxin that affect how well you see in our tests. How hungry you are, how tired you are and even the mood you're in at the moment—whether you feel happy or irritated at the time of testing will affect how well you see. To understand the data we collect on you, then, we must be able to figure out which effects are due to causes such as these and which are caused by Suproxin." He then handed out questionnaires containing a number of questions about bodily and emotional state. To measure mood the following two were the crucial questions:

1. How irritated, angry, or annoyed would you say you feel at present?

I don't feel at all irritated or angry	I feel a little irritated and angry	I feel quite irritated and angry	I feel very irritated and angry	I feel extremely irritated and angry
(0)	(1)	(2)	(3)	(4)

2. How good or happy would you say you feel at present?

I don't feel at all happy or good	I feel a little happy and good	I feel quite happy and good	I feel very happy and good	I feel extremely happy and good
(0)	(1)	(2)	(3)	(4)

D. THE EFFECTS OF THE MANIPULATIONS ON EMOTIONAL STATE

1. Euphoria

The effects of the several manipulations on emotional state in the euphoria conditions are presented in Table I. The scores recorded in this table were derived, for each subject, by subtracting the value of the point he checked on the "irritation" scale from the value of the point he checked on the "happiness" scale. Thus, if a subject were to check the point "I feel a little irritated and angry" on the "irritation" scale and the point "I feel very happy and good" on the "happiness" scale, his score would be +2. The higher the positive value, the happier and better the subject reports himself as feeling. Though an index is employed for expositional simplicity, it should be noted that the two components of the index each yield results completely consistent with those obtained by use of this index.

Let us examine first the effects of the "appropriateness" instructions. Comparison of the scores of the Epi Mis and Epi Inf conditions makes it immediately clear that the experimental differences are not due to artifacts resulting from the "informed" instructions. In both conditions the subject was warned to expect a variety of symptoms as a consequence of the injection. In the Epi Mis condition, where the symptoms were inappropriate to the subject's bodily state, the self-report score is almost twice that in the Epi Inf condition, where the symptoms were completely appropriate to the subject's bodily state. It is reasonable, then, to attribute differences between informed subjects and those in other conditions to differences in manipulated appropriateness, rather than to artifacts such as introspectiveness or self-examination.

TABLE I

SELF-REPORT OF EMOTIONAL STATE IN THE EUPHORIA CONDITIONS

Condition	N	Self-report scales
Epi Inf	25	.98
Epi Ign	25	1.78
Epi Mis	25	1.90
Placebo	26	1.61
Comparison		p values[a]
Epi Inf vs. Epi Mis		$< .01$
Epi Inf vs. Epi Ign		.02
Plac vs. Epi Mis, Ign or Inf		n.s.

[a] All p values reported throughout this paper are two-tailed.

It is clear that, consistent with expectations, subjects were more susceptible to the stooge's mood and consequently more euphoric when they had no explanation of their own bodily states than when they did. The means of both the Epi Ign and Epi Mis conditions were considerably greater than the mean of the Epi Inf condition.

Comparing the placebo to the epinephrine conditions, we note a pattern which repeated itself throughout the data. Placebo subjects were less euphoric than either Epi Mis or Epi Ign subjects, but somewhat more euphoric than Epi Inf subjects. These differences were not, however, statistically significant. The epinephrine-placebo comparisons are considered in detail in a later section of this paper, following the presentation of additional relevant data. For the moment, it is clear that, by self-report, manipulating "appropriateness" had a very strong effect on euphoria.

The analysis of the observational data was reported in detail elsewhere (Schachter and Singer, 1962). Here it is sufficient to note that on all behavioral indices devised—e.g. the amount of time the subject spent on stooge-initiated activity; "creative euphoria" (the extent to which the subject initiated euphoric activities of his own devising)— the same pattern of between-condition relationships held. Subjects in the Epi Mis and Epi Ign conditions behaved more euphorically than subjects in the Epi Inf condition. Placebo subjects again fell between Epi Ign and Epi Inf subjects.

2. Anger

In the anger conditions, we should again expect the subject to catch the stooge's mood only in those conditions where he was injected with epinephrine and had no appropriate explanation for the bodily state thus created. Subjects in the Epi Ign condition should, then, be considerably angrier than those in the Epi Inf or Placebo conditions. Data on behavioral indications of anger are presented in Table II. These figures were derived

TABLE II
BEHAVIORAL INDICATIONS OF EMOTIONAL STATE IN THE ANGER CONDITIONS

Condition	N	Anger index
Epi Inf	22	$-.18$
Epi Ign	23	$+2.28$
Placebo	22	$+.79$
Comparison		p value
Epi Inf vs. Epi Ign		$< .01$
Epi Ign vs. Placebo		$< .05$
Placebo vs. Epi Inf		n.s.

from coding the subject's comments and behavior during the experimental session with the angry stooge. The nature of the index devised is described in detail elsewhere (Schachter and Singer, 1962). For present purposes, we can note that a positive value to this index indicates that the subject agreed with the stooge's comments and was angry. The larger the positive value, the angrier the subject. A negative value indicates that the subject either disagreed with the stooge or ignored him.

It is evident in Table II that expectations were confirmed. The value for the Epi Ign condition is positive and large, indicating that the subjects became angry; while in the Epi Inf condition, the score is slightly negative, indicating that these subjects failed to catch the stooge's mood at all. Placebo subjects fall between Epi Ign and Epi Inf subjects. On the self-report scales of mood, this pattern repeated itself, though on this measure

Placebo subjects do not differ significantly from either Epi Ign or Epi Inf subjects.

E. DISCUSSION OF RESULTS

Having presented the basic data of this study, let us examine closely the extent to which they conform to theoretical expectations. If the hypotheses are correct, and if this experimental design provided a perfect test for these hypotheses, it should be anticipated that in the euphoria conditions, the degree of experimentally produced euphoria should vary in the following fashion:

$$\text{Epi Mis} \geq \text{Epi Ign} > \text{Epi Inf} = \text{Placebo}$$

In the anger conditions, anger should conform to the following pattern:

$$\text{Epi Ign} > \text{Epi Inf} = \text{Placebo}$$

In both sets of conditions, emotional level in the Epi Inf condition was considerably less than that achieved in any of the other Epi conditions. The results for the placebo condition, however, were ambiguous, for consistently the placebo subjects fell between the Epi Ign and the Epi Inf subjects. This is a particularly troubling pattern, making it impossible to evaluate unequivocally the effects of the state of physiological arousal and indeed raising serious questions about the entire theoretical structure. Though the emotional level was consistently greater in the Epi Mis and Epi Ign conditions than in the Placebo condition, this difference was significant at acceptable probability levels only on the behavioral indices in the anger conditions.

In order to explore the problem further, let us examine experimental factors which might have acted to restrain the emotional level in the Epi Ign and Epi Mis conditions. Clearly the ideal test of the first two hypotheses requires an experimental setup in which the subject has no other means of evaluating his state of physiological arousal other than the experimentally provided cognitions. Had it been possible to produce physiologically a state of sympathetic activation by means other than injection, one could have approached this experimental ideal more closely than in the present setup. As it stands, however, there is always a reasonable alternative cognition available to the aroused subject—he feels the way he does because of the injection. To the extent that the subject seizes on such an explanation of his bodily state, we should expect that he will be uninfluenced by the stooge.

It is possible, fortunately, to examine the effect of this artifact. In answers to open-end questions in which subjects described their own mood and physical state, some of the Epi Ign and Epi Mis subjects clearly attributed their physical state to the injection, e.g. "the shot gave me the shivers." In effect, such subjects are self-informed. Comparing such subjects to the remaining subjects in a condition, one finds in the Anger-Epi Ign condition that self-informed subjects are considerably less angry than the remaining subjects. Similarly in the Euphoria-Epi Mis and Ign conditions, self-informed subjects are considerably less euphoric than are their non-self-informed counterparts. If one eliminates such self-informed subjects, the differences between the Placebo and Epi Ign or Epi Mis conditions become highly significant statistically in both the Anger and the Euphoria set of conditions. Clearly, indications are good that this self-informing artifact has attenuated the effects of epinephrine.

Consider next the fact that the emotional level in Placebo conditions was greater than that in the Epi Inf conditions. Theoretically, of course, it should be expected that the two conditions will be equally low, for by assuming that emotional state is a joint function of a state of physiological arousal and of the appropriateness of a cognition we are, in effect, assuming a multiplicative function: if either component is at zero, emotional level is at zero. This expectation should hold, however, only if one can be sure that there is no sympathetic activation in the placebo conditions. This assumption, of course, is completely unrealistic, for the injection of placebo does not prevent sympathetic activation. The experimental situations were fairly dramatic and certainly some of the Placebo subjects must have experienced physiological arousal. If this general line of reasoning is correct, it should be anticipated that the emotional level of subjects who give indications of sympathetic activity will be greater than that of subjects who do not.

Since, in all conditions, a subject's pulse was taken before the injection and again after the session with the stooge, there is one index of sympathetic activation available—change in pulse rate. The predominant pattern in the Placebo conditions was, of course, a decrease in pulse rate. It is assumed, therefore, that in the Placebo conditions, those subjects whose pulses increase or remain the same give indications of sympathetic arousal, while those subjects whose pulses decrease do not. Comparing, within Placebo conditions, such self-aroused subjects with those who give no indication of sympathetic activation, we find in the Anger condition that those subjects whose pulses increase or remain the same are considerably and significantly angrier than those subjects whose pulses decrease. Similarly, in the Euphoria Placebo condition, the self-aroused subjects are considerably and significantly more euphoric than the subjects who give no indication of sympathetic activation. Conforming to expectations, sympathetic activation accompanies an increase in emotional level.

It should be noted, too, on the several indices, that the emotional

level of subjects showing no signs of sympathetic activity is quite close
to the emotional level of subjects in the parallel Epi Inf conditions. The
similarity of these sets of scores and their uniformly low level of indicated
emotionality would certainly make it appear that both factors are essential
to an emotional state. When either the level of sympathetic arousal is low
or a completely appropriate cognition is available, the level of emotionality
is low.

Let us summarize the major findings of this experiment and examine
the extent to which they support the propositions offered in the introduction of this paper. It has been suggested, first, that given a state of physiological arousal for which an individual has no explanation, he will label
this state in terms of the cognitions available to him. This implies, of
course, that by manipulating the cognitions of an individual in such a state,
his feelings can be manipulated in diverse directions. Experimental results
support this proposition, for following the injection of epinephrine, those
subjects who had no explanation for the bodily state thus produced, proved
readily manipulable into the disparate feeling states of euphoria and anger.

From this first proposition, it must follow that given a state of
physiological arousal for which the individual has a completely satisfactory
explanation, he will not label this state in terms of the alternative cognitions available. Experimental evidence strongly supports this expectation.
In those conditions in which subjects were injected with epinephrine and
told precisely what they would feel and why, they proved relatively
immune to any effects of the manipulated cognitions. In the anger condition, such subjects did not become at all angry; in the euphoria condition,
such subjects reported themselves as far less happy than subjects with an
identical bodily state but no adequate knowledge of why they felt the way
they did.

Finally, it has been suggested that given constant cognitive circumstances, an individual will react emotionally only to the extent that he
experiences a state of physiological arousal. Without taking account of
experimental artifacts, the evidence in support of this proposition is consistent but tentative. When the effects of "self-informing" tendencies in
epinephrine subjects and of "self-arousing" tendencies in placebo subjects
are partialed out, the evidence strongly supports the proposition.

III. Physiological Arousal and Emotionality

The pattern of data, then, falls neatly in line with theoretical expectations. However, the fact that it was necessary to some extent to rely on
internal analyses in order to partial out the effects of experimental artifacts
inevitably makes these conclusions somewhat tentative. In order further
to test these propositions on the interaction of cognitive and physiological

determinants of emotional state, a series of additional experiments was designed to rule out or overcome the operation of these artifacts.

The first of these experiments was designed by Schachter and Wheeler (1962) to test the proposition that emotionality is positively related to physiological arousal by extending the range of manipulated sympathetic activation. It seemed clear from the results of the study just described that the self-arousing tendency of placebo subjects tended to obscure the differences between placebo and epinephrine conditions. A test of the proposition at stake, then, would require comparing subjects who have received injections of epinephrine with subjects who, to some extent, were incapable of self-activation of the sympathetic nervous system. A class of drugs known generally as autonomic blocking agents makes such blocking possible to some degree. If it is correct that a state of sympathetic discharge is a necessary component of an emotional experience, it should be anticipated that whatever emotional state is experimentally manipulated should be experienced most strongly by subjects who have received epinephrine, next by placebo subjects, and least of all by subjects who have received injections of an autonomic blocking agent.

A. PROCEDURE

In order to conceal the purposes of the study and the nature of the injection, the experiment was again cast in the framework of a study of the effects of vitamins on vision. As soon as a subject—a male college student —arrived, he was taken to a private room and told by the experimenter:

"I've asked you to come today to take part in an experiment concerning the effects of vitamins on the visual processes. Our experiment is concerned with the effects of Suproxin on vision. Suproxin is a high concentrate vitamin C derivative. If you agree to take part in the experiment, we will give you an injection of Suproxin and then subject your retina to about 15 minutes of continuous black and white stimulation. This is simpler than it sounds: we'll just have you watch a black and white movie. After the movie, we'll give you a series of visual tests.

"The injection itself is harmless and will be administered by our staff doctor. It may sting a little at first, as most injections do, but after this you will feel nothing and will have no side effects. We know that some people dislike getting injections, and if you take part in the experiment, we want it to be your own decision. Would you like to?" (All subjects agreed to take part.)

1. Drugs Used

There were three forms of Suproxin administered—epinephrine, placebo, and chlorpromazine.

1. Epinephrine. Subjects in this condition received a subcutaneous injection of $\frac{1}{2}$ cc of a 1:1000 solution of Winthrop Laboratory's Suprarenin.

2. Placebo. Subjects in this condition received a subcutaneous injection of $\frac{1}{2}$ cc of saline solution.

3. Chlorpromazine. Subjects in this condition received an intramuscular injection of a solution consisting of 1 cc (25 mg) of Smith, Klein and French Thorazine and 1 cc of saline solution.

The choice of chlorpromazine as a blocking agent was dictated by considerations of safety, ease of administration, and known duration of effect. Ideally, one would have wished for a blocking agent whose mechanism and effect were precisely and solely the reverse of those of epinephrine —a peripherally acting agent which would prevent the excitation of sympathetically innervated structures. Though it is certainly possible to approach this ideal more closely with agents other than chlorpromazine, such drugs tend to be dangerous, difficult to administer, or of short duration.

Chlorpromazine is known to act as a sympathetic depressant. It has a moderate hypotensive effect, with a slight compensatory increase in heart rate. It has mild adrenergic blocking activity, for it reverses the pressor effects of small doses of epinephrine and depresses responses of the nictitating membrane to preganglionic stimulation. Killam (1959) summarizes what is known and supposed about the mechanism of action of chlorpromazine as follows: "Autonomic effects in general may be attributed to a mild peripheral adrenergic blocking activity and probably to central depression of sympathetic centers, possibly in the hypothalamus." Popularly, of course, the compound is known as a "tranquilizer."

It is recognized that chlorpromazine has effects other than the sympatholytic effect of interest to us. For purposes of experimental purity this is unfortunate but inevitable in this sort of research. It is clear, however, that the three conditions do differ in the degree of manipulated sympathetic activation.

2. Emotion Induction

Rather than the more complicated devices employed in the previous experiment, an emotion-inducing film was used as a means of manipulating the cognitive component of emotional states. In deciding on the type of film, two extremes seemed possible—a horror, fright or anxiety-provoking film or a comic, amusement-provoking film. Since it is a common stereotype that adrenaline makes one nervous and that the tranquilizer, chlorpromazine, makes one tranquil and mildly euphoric, the predicted pattern of results with a horror film would be subject to alternative interpretation. It was deliberately decided, then, to use a comedy. If the hypothesis is correct, epinephrine subjects should find the film somewhat funnier than placebo subjects who, in turn, would be more amused than chlorpromazine subjects.

The film chosen was a 14-minute excerpt from a Jack Carson movie called "The Good Humor Man." This excerpt is a self-contained, comprehensible episode involving a slapstick chase scene.

Three subjects (one from each of the drug conditions) always watched the film simultaneously. The projection room was deliberately arranged so that the subjects could neither see nor hear one another. Facing the screen were three theatre seats, separated from one another by large, heavy partitions. In a further attempt to maintain the independence of the subjects, the sound volume of the projector was turned up so as to mask any sounds made by the subjects.

3. Measures

The subjects' reactions while watching the film were used as the chief index of amusement. During the showing of the movie an observer, who had been introduced as an assistant who would help administer the visual tests, systematically scanned the subjects and recorded their reactions to the film. He observed each subject once every ten seconds, so that over the course of the film 88 units of each subject's behavior were categorized. The observer simply recorded each subject's reaction to the film according to the following scheme: (a) neutral—straight-faced watching of film with no indication of amusement; (b) smile; (c) grin—a smile with teeth showing; (d) laugh—a smile or grin on face accompanied by bodily movements usually associated with laughter, e.g., shaking shoulders, moving head; (e) big laugh—belly laugh; a laugh accompanied by violent body movement such as doubling up, throwing up hands.

In a minute by minute comparison, two independent observers agreed in their categorization of 90% of the 528 units recorded in six different reliability trials.

The observer, of course, never knew which subject had received which injection.

B. RESULTS

The observation record provides a continuous record of each subject's reaction to the film. As an overall index of amusement, the number of units in which a subject's behavior was recorded in the categories "smile," "grin," "laugh," and "big laugh" are summed together. The means of this amusement index are presented in Table III. The larger the figure, the more amusement was manifest. Differences were in the anticipated direction. Epinephrine subjects gave indications of greater amusement than did

TABLE III
THE EFFECTS OF EPINEPHRINE, PLACEBO, AND CHLORPROMAZINE ON AMUSEMENT

Condition	N	Mean amusement index
Epinephrine	38	17.79
Placebo	42	14.31
Chlorpromazine	46	10.41
Comparison		p value
Epi vs. Plac		n.s.
Epi vs. Chlor		< .01
Plac vs. Chlor		< .05

placebo subjects who, in turn, were more amused than chlorpromazine subjects.

Though the trend is clearly in the predicted direction, epinephrine and placebo subjects do not differ significantly in this overall index. The difference between these two groups, however, becomes apparent when we examine strong ("laugh" and "big laugh") reactions to the film; we find an average of 4.84 such units among the epinephrine subjects and of only 1.83 such units among placebo subjects. This difference is significant at better than the .05 level of significance. Epinephrine subjects tend to be openly amused at the film, placebo subjects to be quietly amused. Some 16% of epinephrine subjects reacted at some point with belly laughs, while not a single placebo subject did so. It should be noted that this is much the state of affairs one would expect from the disguised injection of epinephrine—a manipulation which, as has been suggested, creates a bodily state "in search of" an appropriate cognition. Certainly laughter can be considered a more appropriate accompaniment to the state of sympathetic arousal than quiet smiling.

It would appear, then, that degree of overt amusement is directly related to the degree of manipulated sympathetic activation.

IV. Sympathetic Activity and Emotionality in Rats

A further test of the relationship of emotionality to sympathetic activity was made by Singer (1963) who, in a deliberate attempt to rule out the operation of the self-informing artifact, conducted his study on rats—a species unlikely to attribute an aroused physiological state to an injection. Among other things, Singer examined the effects of injections of epinephrine (an intraperitonial injection of epinephrine suspended in peanut oil in a concentration of .1'0 mg. per kg of body weight) and placebo on the reactions of rats to standard frightening situations. His technique was simple. In fright conditions, he placed his animals in a box containing a doorbell, a door buzzer, and a flashing 150 watt bulb. After a brief interval, a switch was tripped setting off all three devices simultaneously for a one-and-a-half minute interval. In nonfright conditions, of course, the switch was never tripped.

Singer's results are presented in Table IV. The figures presented in

TABLE IV
THE RELATIONSHIP OF EPINEPHRINE TO FRIGHT

Condition[a]	Epinephrine	Placebo	p value of difference
Fright	13.15	11.49	.025
Nonfright	7.47	7.17	n.s.

[a] $N = 12$ in each of the four conditions.

this table represent an index whose components are generally accepted indicators of fright such as defecation, urination and the like. The¨larger the figure, the more frightened the animal. Clearly there is a substantial drug-related difference in the fright condition and no difference at all in the nonfright condition. The drug $\times$ stress interaction is significant at better than the .01 level of significance. It would certainly appear that under these experimental circumstances the state of fear is related to sympathetic activity. Further evidence for this relationship is found in a study conducted by Latané and Schachter (1962) which demonstrated that rats injected with epinephrine were notably more capable of avoidance learning than were rats injected with a placebo. Using a modified Miller-Mowrer shuttlebox, these investigators found that during an experimental period involving two hundred massed trials, 15 rats injected with epinephrine avoided shock an average of 101.2 trials, while 15 placebo-injected rats averaged only 37.3 avoidances.

V. Discussion and Implications

Taken together, this body of studies does give strong support to the propositions which generated these experimental tests. Given a state of sympathetic activation, for which no immediately appropriate explanation is available, human subjects can be readily manipulated into states of euphoria, of anger, and of amusement at a movie. Varying the intensity of sympathetic activation serves to vary the intensity of a variety of emotional states in both rat and human subjects. Clearly the line of thought guiding these experiments is modified Jamesianism, for emotion is viewed as visceral activity in interaction with cognitive or situational factors. Let us examine the extent to which the addition of cognitive elements allows us to cope with the shortcomings of a purely visceral formulation. Since Cannon's critique (1927, 1929) has been the most lucid and influential attack on a visceral view of emotion, I shall focus discussion around Cannon's five criticisms of the James-Lange theory.

A Re-examination of Cannon's Critique of a Visceral Formulation of Emotion

1. Criticisms Overcome by Cognitive Considerations

a. Cannon's criticism that "artificial induction of the visceral changes typical of strong emotions does not produce them" is based on the results of Marañon's (1924) study and its several replications. The fact that the injection of adrenaline produces apparently genuine emotional states in only a tiny minority of subjects is, of course, completely damning for a theory which equates visceral activity with affect. This is, on the other hand, precisely the fact which inspired the series of studies described earlier. Rather than a criticism, the fact that injection of adrenaline, in and of itself, does not lead to an emotional state is one of the strong points of the present formulation; for, with the addition of cognitive propositions, we are able to specify and manipulate the conditions under which such an injection will or will not lead to an emotional state.

b. Cannon's point that "the same visceral changes occur in very different emotional states" is again damning for a purely visceral viewpoint. Since we are aware of a great variety of feeling and emotion states, it must follow from a purely visceral formulation that the variety of emotions will be accompanied by an equal variety of differentiable bodily states. Though the evidence as of today is by no means as one-sided as it appeared in Cannon's day, it does seem that the gist of Cannon's criticism is still correct. Following James' pronouncement, a formidable number of studies were undertaken in search of the physiological differentiators of the emotions. The results, in those early days, were almost uniformly negative. All of the emotional states experimentally manipulated were characterized by a general pattern of activation of the sympathetic nervous system but there appeared to be no clearcut physiological discriminators of the various emotions.

More recent work, however, has given some indication that there may be differentiators. Ax (1953) and Schachter (1957) studied fear and anger. On a large number of indices both of these states were characterized by a similar high level of sympathetic activation, but on several indices they did differ in the degree of activation. Wolf and Wolff (1947) studied a subject with a gastric fistula and were able to distinguish two patterns in the physiological responses of the stomach wall. It should be noted, though, that for many months they studied their subject during and following a great variety of moods and emotions, but were able to distinguish only two patterns.

Whether there are physiological distinctions among the various emotional states must still be considered an open question. Recent work might be taken to indicate that such differences are at best rather subtle, and that the variety of emotion, mood, and feeling states are by no means matched by an equal variety of visceral patterns—a state of affairs hardly compatible with the Jamesian formulation. On the other hand, the question of the physiological differentiability of the various emotions is essentially irrelevant to the present formulation, which maintains simply that cognitive and situational factors determine the labels applied to any of a variety of states of physiological arousal.

The experimental search for the physiological differentiators of emotional states has involved such substantial, long-time effort that the problem merits further comment. Viewed en masse, these experiments have yielded quite inconclusive results. Most, though not all of these studies have indicated no differences among the various emotional states. Since as human beings, rather than as scientists, we have no difficulty identifying, labeling, and distinguishing among our feelings, the results of these studies have long seemed rather puzzling and paradoxical. Perhaps because of this, there has been a persistent tendency to discount such results as due to ignorance or methodological inadequacy and to pay far more attention to the very few studies which demonstrate *some* sort of physiological differences among emotional states than to the very many studies which indicate no differences at all. It is conceivable, however, that these results should be taken at face value and that emotional states may, indeed, be generally characterized by a high level of sympathetic activation with few if any physiological distinguishers among the many emotional states. If this is correct, the cognitive-physiological formulation outlined here and the findings of the studies described may help to resolve the problem.

Obviously these studies do *not* rule out the possibility of differences among the emotional states. It is the case, however, that given precisely the same state of epinephrine-induced sympathetic activation, it has been possible, by means of cognitive manipulations, to produce in subjects the very disparate states of euphoria, anger, and amusement at a movie. It may, indeed, be the case that cognitive factors are major determiners of the emotional "labels" we apply to a common state of sympathetic arousal.

In *"Background to Danger,"* novelist Eric Ambler (1958) describes a fugitive who introspects this way:

Rather to his surprise, he found that being wanted for murder produced in him an effect almost identical to that of a dentist's waiting-room—a sense of discomfort in the intestinal region, a certain constriction in the chest. He supposed that the same glands discharged the same secretions into the blood stream in both cases. Nature could be absurdly parsimonious.

If these speculations are correct, nature may indeed be far more parsimonious than Ambler suggests.

c. Cannon's point that "the viscera are relatively insensitive structures" is again telling for a formulation which virtually requires a richness of visceral sensation in order to be able to match the presumed richness of emotional experience. For the present formulation, of course, the criticism is irrelevant. Just so long as there is *some* visceral or cardiovascular sensation, the cognitive-physiological hypotheses are applicable.

The introduction of cognitive factors does allow us, then, to cope with three of Cannon's criticisms of a purely visceral formulation. Let us turn next to Cannon's remaining two points which are quite as troublesome for the present view of emotion as for the Jamesian view.

2. Visceral Separation and Emotion

a. Effects of sympathectomies. Cannon's remaining criticisms are these: "Visceral changes are too slow to be a source of emotional feeling" (i.e., the latency period of arousal of many visceral structures is longer than the latency of onset of emotional feelings reported in introspective studies); and "total separation of the viscera from the central nervous system does not alter emotional behavior." Both criticisms make essentially the same point, for they identify conditions in which there are apparently emotions unaccompanied by visceral activity. The data with which Cannon buttresses his latter criticism are based on his own studies (Cannon *et al.,* 1927) of sympathectomized cats, and Sherrington's (1900) study of sympathectomized dogs. For both sets of experimental animals "the absence of reverberation from the viscera did not alter in any respect the appropriate emotional display; its only abbreviation was surgical." In the presence of a barking dog, for example, the sympathectomized cats manifested almost all of the signs of feline rage. Finally, Cannon notes the report of Dana (1921) that a patient with a spinal cord lesion and almost totally without visceral sensation still manifested normal emotionality.[6]

---

[6] More recent work supporting Cannon's position is that of Moyer and Bunnell (Moyer, 1958a,b; Moyer and Bunnell, 1959, 1960a,b) who, in an extensive series of studies of bilaterally adrenalectomized rats, have consistently failed to find any indication of differences between experimental and control animals on a variety

b. Prior learning. For either the Jamesian or the present formulation, such data are crucial, for both views demand visceral arousal as a necessary condition for emotional arousal. When faced with this evidence, James' defenders (e.g., Wenger, 1950; Mandler, 1962) have consistently made the point that the apparently emotional behavior manifested by sympathectomized animals and men is well-learned behavior, acquired long before sympathectomy. There is a dual implication in this position: first, that sympathetic arousal facilitates the acquisition of emotional behavior and, second, that sympathectomized subjects act but do not feel emotional. There is a small but growing body of evidence supporting these contentions. Wynne and Solomon (1955) have demonstrated that sympathectomized dogs acquire an avoidance response considerably more slowly than do control dogs. Further, on extinction trials most of their 13 sympathectomized animals extinguished quickly, while not a single one of 30 control dogs gave any indications of extinction over two hundred trials. Of particular interest are two dogs who were sympathectomized after they had acquired the avoidance response. On extinction trials these two animals behaved precisely as did the control dogs—giving no indication of extinction. Thus, when deprived of visceral innervation, animals are quite slow in acquiring emotionally linked avoidance responses and, in general, rapid in extinguishing such responses. When deprived of visceral innervation only after acquisition, the animals behave exactly as do the normal dogs—they fail to extinguish. A true Jamesian would undoubtedly note that these latter animals have learned to act as if they were emotional, but he would ask: Do they feel emotional?

c. Autonomic dysfunctioning in humans. This apparently unanswerable question seems on its way to an answer in a thoroughly fascinating study of the emotional life of paraplegics and quadriplegics conducted by Hohmann (1962). Hohmann studied a sample of 25 patients of the Spinal Cord Injury Service of the Veterans Administration Hospital at Long Beach. The subjects were divided into five groups according to the height of the clinically complete lesions as follows:

Group I, with lesions between the second and eighth cervical segmental level, have only the cranial branch of the parasympathetic nervous system remaining intact.

Group II, with lesions between the first and fourth thoracic seg-

---

of emotionally linked behaviors such as avoidance learning. The effects of adrenalectomy are by no means clearcut, however, for other investigators (Levine and Soliday, 1962) have found distinct differences between operated and control animals.

mental level, have in addition to the above, at least partial innervation of the sympathetically innervated cardiac plexus remaining intact.

Group III, with lesions between the sixth and twelfth thoracic segmental level have, additionally, at least partial innervation of the splanchnic outflow of the sympathetics remaining intact.

Group IV, with lesions between the first and fifth lumbar segmental level, have in addition at least partial sympathetic innervation of the mesenteric ganglia.

Group V, with lesions between the first and fifth sacral segments have, in addition, at least partial innervation of the sacral branch of the parasympathetic nervous system.

These groups then fall along a dimension of visceral innervation and sensation. The higher the lesion, the less the visceral sensation. If the present conception of emotion is correct, one should expect to find decreasing manifestation of emotion as the height of the lesion increases.

With each of his subjects, Hohmann conducted an extensive, structured interview which was "directed to specific feelings in situations of sexual excitement, fear, anger, grief and sentimentality, and the subject's attention was directed toward their feelings rather than to the concomitant ideation." Hohmann asked his subjects to recall an emotion-arousing incident prior to their injury and a comparable incident following the injury. They were then asked to compare the intensity of their emotional experiences before and after injury. Changes in reported affect comprise the body of data. I have adapted Hohmann's data for presentation in Figure 1. Following Hohmann's coding schema a report of no change is scored as 0; a report of mild change (e.g., "I feel it less, I guess") is scored −1 for a decrease and +1 for an increase; a report of strong change (e.g., "I feel it a helluva lot less") is scored as −2 or +2.

Hohmann's data for the states of fear and anger is plotted in Figure 1. It can be immediately seen that the higher the lesion and the less the visceral sensation, the greater the decrease in emotionality. Precisely the same relationship holds for the states of sexual excitement and grief. The sole exception to this consistent trend is "sentimentality," which, I suspect, should be considered a cognitive rather than a "feeling" state. It is clear that for these cases deprivation of visceral sensation has resulted in a marked decrease in emotionality.

If, in an attempt to assess the absolute level of emotionality of these cases, one examines their verbalized introspections, we note again and again that subjects with cervical lesions described themselves as acting emotional but not feeling emotional. A few typical quotes follow:

". . . it's sort of cold anger. Sometimes I act angry when I see some injustice. I yell and cuss and raise hell, because if you don't do it sometimes, I've learned people will take advantage of you, but it just doesn't have the heat to it that it used to. It's a mental kind of anger."

"Seems like I get thinking mad, not shaking mad, and that's a lot different."

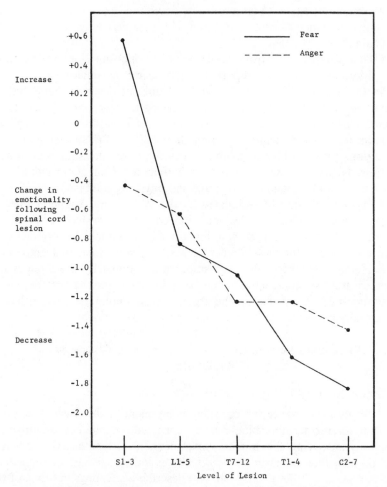

FIG. 1. Changes in emotionality as related to height of spinal cord lesion. (Adapted from Hohmann, 1962.)

"I say I am afraid, like when I'm going into a real stiff exam at school, but I don't really feel afraid, not all tense and shaky, with that hollow feeling in my stomach, like I used to."

In effect, these subjects seemed to be saying that when the situation demands it, they make the proper emotional-appearing responses, but they do not feel emotional. Parenthetically, it should be noted that these quotations bear an almost contrapuntal resemblance to the introspections of Marañon's subjects who, after receiving an injection of adrenaline, described their feelings in a way that led Marañon to label them "cold" or "as if" emotions. Many of these subjects described their physical symptoms and added statements such as, "I feel as if I were very frightened; however, I am calm."

The two sets of introspections are like opposite sides of the same coin. Marañon's subjects reported the visceral correlates of emotion, but in the absence of veridical cognitions did not describe themselves as feeling emotion. Hohmann's subjects described the appropriate reaction to an emotion-inducing situation but in the absence of visceral arousal did not seem to describe themselves as emotional. It is as if they were labeling a situation, not describing a feeling. Obviously, this contrasting set of introspections is precisely what should be anticipated from a formulation of emotion as a joint function of cognitive and physiological factors.

The line of thought stimulated by the Wynne and Solomon (1955) and Hohmann (1962) studies may indeed be the answer to Cannon's observation that there can be emotional behavior without visceral activity. From the evidence of these studies, it would appear, first, that autonomic arousal greatly facilitates the acquisition of emotional behavior but is not necessary for its maintenance if the behavior is acquired prior to sympathectomy; and, second, that in the absence of autonomic arousal, behavior that appears emotional will not be experienced as emotional.

VI. Some Effects of Cognitive Factors on the Appraisal of Bodily States

A. COGNITIONS AND RESPONSE TO MARIHUANA

Let us turn now to the cognitive component of this view of emotion and examine further implications of the formulation. The key cognitive assumption underlying the human experiments described is that "given a state of physiological arousal for which an individual has no immediate explanation, he will label this state and describe his feelings in terms of the cognitions available to him." Obviously, this proposition implies that a drive exists to evaluate, understand, and label ambiguous body states. It is suggested that Festinger's (1954) theoretical invention—the "evaluative need," which he employs as the conceptual underpinning of his theory of social comparison processes—is as necessary and useful for an understanding of emotion and the perception of bodily states as it has proven for understanding of the opinions. Given a new, strange, or ambiguous bodily state, pressures will act on the individual to decide exactly what it is that he feels and to decide how he will label these feelings. In the Schachter and Singer (1962) study the differences between the Epi Ign and Epi Inf conditions would certainly indicate that it is useful to apply this notion of evaluative needs to bodily states.

These cognitive assumptions as worded clearly imply applicability to bodily states other than the epinephrine induced state of sympathetic activation. If these ideas are correct, it should be expected that any novel bodily state will give rise to pressures to decide what is felt, to decide how these feelings are to be labeled, and, perhaps, to decide whether these feelings are pleasant or unpleasant ones. Though I know of no experiments directly designed to test these ideas for states other than that induced by epinephrine, the extensive literature on the effects of drugs provides constant hints and bits of data which suggest that these ideas do have wide applicability.

As an example, consider the effects of smoking marihuana. Following the pharmacological texts, marihuana or cannabis produces the following physiological effects:

> Marihuana usually causes an increase in pulse rate, a slight rise in blood pressure, and conjunctival vascular congestion; the cardiovascular system is otherwise unaffected. The blood sugar and basal metabolic rate are elevated, but usually not beyond the upper limits of normal. Urinary frequency without diuresis occurs. A marked increase in appetite (especially for sweets) and hunger are characteristic, and hypergeusia may occasionally be prominent. Dryness of the mouth and throat is frequent. Nausea, vomiting, and occasionally diarrhea may be noted.
>
> Tremor, ataxia, vertigo, tinnitus, hyper-reflexia, increased sensitivity to touch, pressure, and pain stimuli, pupillary dilatation with sluggish light reflexes, and a sensation of floating are also observed. . . . Tremulousness of the eyelids, lips, and tongue and nystagamus on lateral gaze are common. (Goodman and Gilman, 1958, pp. 172–173.)

These are the measured physiological changes caused by smoking marihuana. In and of themselves, are such bodily feelings pleasant or unpleasant? Given such symptoms, should the smoker describe himself as "high" or as "sick"?

In an absorbing study of fifty marihuana users, the sociologist Becker (1953) reports an invariable sequence in learning to use marihuana for pleasure. Once he has learned the techniques of smoking, the smoker must learn to label his physiological symptoms as being "high." In Becker's words,

> . . . being high consists of two elements: the presence of symptoms caused by marihuana use and the recognition of these symptoms and their connection by the user with his use of the drug. It is not enough, that is, that the effects

be present; they alone do not automatically provide the experience of being high. The user must be able to point them out to himself and consciously connect them with his having smoked marihuana before he can have this experience. Otherwise, regardless of the actual effects produced, he considers that the drug has had no effect on him.

An example of learning that he is high is provided by this quotation from a novice who gets high for the first time only after he learned that intense hunger is one consequence of smoking marihuana:

> They were just laughing the hell out of me because like I was eating so much. I just scoffed (ate) so much food, and they were just laughing at me, you know. Sometimes I'd be looking at them, you know, wondering why they're laughing, you know, not knowing what I was doing. (Well, did they eventually tell you why they were laughing?) Yeah, yeah, I come back, "Hey, man, what's happening?" and all of a sudden I feel weird, you know. "Man, you're on you know. You're on pot (high on marihuana)." I said, "No, am I?" Like I don't know what's happening.

An instance of more indirect learning is the following: "I heard little remarks that were made by people. Somebody said, 'My legs are rubbery,' and I can't remember all the remarks that were made because I was very attentively listening for all these cues for what I was supposed to feel like."

Obviously, these are instances where the novice must literally learn to notice his feelings. Given that a user is made aware of his symptoms and has learned that what he is feeling is being "high," Becker notes that one further step is necessary for continued use of the drug:

> He must learn to enjoy the effects he has just learned to experience. Marihuana-produced sensations are not automatically or necessarily pleasurable. The taste for such experience is a socially acquired one, not different in kind from acquired tastes for oysters or dry martinis. The user feels dizzy, thirsty; his scalp tingles; he misjudges time and distances, and so on. Are these things pleasurable? He isn't sure. If he is to continue marihuana use, he must decide that they are. Otherwise, getting high, while a real enough experience, will be an unpleasant one he would rather avoid.

Becker supports this analysis with numerous instances of novice smokers being taught, in social interaction, that their feelings were pleasant.

This study, then, indicates that new marihuana users must be taught to notice and identify what they feel, must be taught to label the state as "high" and must be taught that the state is "pleasant." The marihuana induced state of feelings appears to be another instance of a bodily state which takes its meaning and labels in good part from cognitive and social factors.

I would guess that the labels and hedonic valuation attached to an amazing variety of bodily conditions are cognitively determined.

Obviously, there are limits. It is unlikely that anyone with undiagnosed peritonitis could ever be convinced that he was euphoric, high, or anything but deathly ill. I suspect, though, that the limits are astonishingly wide. Vomiting to us may seem unpleasant, but to a banqueting Roman gourmet, it may have been one of the exquisite pleasures.

B. LABELING OF BODILY STATES IN OBESITY

As a final point, if it is correct that the labels attached to feeling states are cognitively, situationally, or socially determined, it becomes a distinct possibility that an uncommon or inappropriate label can be attached to a feeling state. Where such is the case, we may anticipate bizarre and pathological behavior. As an example of this póssibility, consider the state of hunger. We are so accustomed to think of hunger as a primary motive, innate and wired into the animal, unmistakable in its cues, that even the possibility that an organism would be incapable of correctly labeling the state seems too far fetched to credit. The physiological changes accompanying food deprivation seem distinct, identifiable, and invariant. Yet even a moment's consideration will make it clear that attaching the label "hunger" to this set of bodily feelings and behaving accordingly, is a learned, socially determined, cognitive act.

Consider the neonate. Wholly at the mercy of its feelings, when uncomfortable, in pain, frightened, hungry, or thirsty, it screams. Whether it is comforted, soothed, clucked at, fondled, or fed has little to do with the state of its own feelings, but depends entirely on the ability and willingness of its mother or nurse to recognize the proper cues. If she is experienced, she will comfort when the baby is frightened, soothe him when he is chafed, feed him when he is hungry, and so on. If inexperienced, her behavior may be completely inappropriate to the child's state. Most commonly, perhaps, the compassionate but bewildered mother will feed her child at any sign of distress.

It is precisely this state of affairs that the analyst Hilde Bruch (1961) suggests is at the heart of chronic obesity. She describes such cases as characterized by a confusion between intense emotional states and hunger. During childhood these patients have not been taught to discriminate between hunger and such states as fear, anger, and anxiety. If correct, these people are, in effect, labeling a state of sympathetic activation as hunger. Small wonder that they are both fat and jolly.

REFERENCES

Ambler, E. (1958). "Background to Danger." Dell, New York.
Ax, A. F. (1953). *Psychosomat. Med.* **15**, 433–442.
Becker, H. S. (1953). *Am. J. Sociol.* **59**, 235–242.

Bruch, H. (1961). *Psychiat. Quart.* **35**, 458–481.

Cannon, W. B. (1927). *Am. J. Psychol.* **39**, 106–124.

Cannon, W. B. (1929). "Bodily Changes in Pain, Hunger, Fear and Rage." 2nd ed. Appleton, New York.

Cannon, W. B., Lewis, J. T., and Britton, S. W. (1927). *Boston Med. and Surg. J.* **197**, 514.

Cantril, H., and Hunt, W. A. (1932). *Am. J. Psychol.* **44**, 300–307.

Dana, C. L. (1921). *Arch. Neurol. Psychiat.* **6**, 634–639.

Festinger, L. (1954). *Human Relat.,* **7**, 114–140.

Goodman, L. S., and Gilman, A. (1958). "The Pharmacological Basis of Therapeutics." Macmillan, New York.

Hohmann, G. W. (1962). The effect of dysfunctions of the autonomic nervous system on experienced feelings and emotions. Paper read at Conference on Emotions and Feelings at New School for Social Research, New York.

Hunt, J. McV., Cole, M. W., and Reis, E. C. (1958). *Am. J. Psychol.* **71**, 136–151.

James, W. (1890). "The Principles of Psychology." Holt, New York.

Killam, E. K. (1959). *Natl. Acad. Sci.—Natl. Res. Council Publ.* 583.

Landis, C., and Hunt, W. A. (1932). *Psychol. Rev.* **39**, 467–485.

Latané, B., and Schachter, S. (1962). *J. Comp. Physiol. Psychol.* **55**, 369–372.

Levine, S., and Soliday, S. (1962). *J. Comp. Physiol. Psychol.* **55**, 214–216.

Mandler, G. (1962). *In* "New Directions in Psychology" (R. Brown *et al.*, eds.), pp. 267–343. Holt, Rinehart and Winston, New York.

Marañon, G. (1924). *Rev. Franc. Endocrinol.* **2**, 301–325.

Moyer, K. E. (1958a). *J. Genet. Psychol.* **92**, 17–21.

Moyer, K. E. (1958b). *J. Genet. Psychol.* **92**, 11–16.

Moyer, K. E., and Bunnell, B. N. (1959). *J. Comp. Physiol.* **52**, 215–216.

Moyer, K. E., and Bunnell, B. N. (1960a). *J. Genet. Psychol.* **96**, 375–382.

Moyer, K. E., and Bunnell, B. N. (1960b). *J. Genet. Psychol.* **97**, 341–344.

Ruckmick, C. A. (1936). "The Psychology of Feeling and Emotion." McGraw-Hill, New York.

Schachter, J. (1957). *Psychosom. Med.* **19**, 17–29.

Schachter, S. (1959). "The Psychology of Affiliation." Stanford Univ. Press, Stanford, California.

Schachter, S., and Wheeler, L. (1962). *J. Abnorm. Soc. Psychol.* **65**, 121–128.

Schachter, S., and Singer, J. (1962). *Psychol. Rev.* **69**, 379–399.

Sherrington, C. S. (1900). *Proc. Roy. Soc.* **66**, 390–403.

Singer, J. E. (1963). *J. Comp. Physiol. Psychol.* **56**, 612–615.

Wenger, M. A. (1950). *In* "Feelings and Emotions" (M. L. Reymert, ed.), pp. 3–10. McGraw-Hill, New York.

Wolf, S., and Wolff, H. G. (1947). "Human Gastric Function." Oxford Univ. Press, London and New York.

Woodworth, R. S., and Schlosberg, H. (1958). "Experimental Psychology." Holt, New York.

Wrightsman, L. S. (1960). *J. Abnorm. Soc. Psychol.* **61**, 216–222.

Wynne, L. C., and Solomon, R. L. (1955). *Genet. Psychol. Monogr.* **52**, 241–284.

EXPERIMENTAL STUDIES OF COALITION FORMATION

William A. Gamson
DEPARTMENT OF SOCIOLOGY
UNIVERSITY OF MICHIGAN
ANN ARBOR, MICHIGAN

The study of coalitions abounds with paradoxes. "Strength is weakness" and "Playing to win is playing to lose," are fair samples of the conclusions one might legitimately draw from studies on this subject. These are not false paradoxes that can be easily removed by semantic clarification; they embody some of the most enduring and fascinating features of coalition situations. To unravel them takes some of the strangeness from political bedfellows.

I. What Is a Coalition Situation?

"The meaning of the term coalition is ambiguous," Marie Borgatta (1961) suggested, "until it is specified whether it is . . . defined in terms of activity, solidarity, or influence." It is sometimes used to mean no more than joint activity. Thus, a brother and sister playing together while their mother cooks dinner might be said to have a coalition. Another usage centers around the mutuality of affective support. If the brother and sister are sharing the pleasure of a fantasy from which the mother is excluded, they might be said to have a temporary coalition against the mother.

If such uses seem farfetched, witness the interpretations that have been made of Simmel's observations on the triad. "No matter how close a triad may be," Simmel (1950) wrote, "there is always the occasion when two of the three members regard the third as an intruder. . . . Sensitive union of two is always irritated by the spectator." Interestingly enough, Simmel's analysis centered mainly on those triadic situations in which there is no coalition of two against one—even in the sense of shared feelings. He was concerned with situations in which one party acts as a mediator in conflicts between the other two, and in those in which one acts as "tertius gaudens"—that is, situations in which one party draws advantage from the conflict of the other two. Despite his emphasis, several writers (see, for example, Mills, 1953) have drawn from the above quotation a proposition which asserts that triads will tend to segregate into a pair and an other.

The truth or falsity of such a proposition is less an issue than its meaningfulness for coalition formation. It is undoubtedly true that three is sometimes a crowd but apparently it was not with the Three Musketeers. The development of cliques within a larger group is an important problem in its own right, but it adds nothing except confusion to see such cliques as coalitions. Under such usage, any partitioning of a group into subparts on whatever basis could be viewed as a "coalition structure." In this paper, the word *coalition* is reserved for a considerably narrower kind of differentiation.

A. COALITION DEFINED

The term *coalition,* it is suggested, should be used to mean the *joint use of resources to determine the outcome of a decision* in certain specified situations. Thibaut and Kelley (1959) suggested a very similar definition. "By coalition, we mean two or more persons who act jointly to affect the outcomes of one or more other persons." Coalitions, then, are tied to influence. A *resource* is some weight controlled by the participants such that some critical quantity of these weights is necessary and sufficient to determine the decision. Two or more participants will be said to be using their resources jointly if they coordinate their deployment of resources with respect to some decision. Only then can they be said to have formed a coalition.

Studies by Mills (1953, 1954), Strodtbeck (1954), and Borgatta and Borgatta (1963), which are cast in terms of coalition formation, do not meet the above criteria. Mills' approach, as the Borgattas point out, "centers around rate of supportive acts. That is, two people who have a high ratio of supportive acts to each other in an interaction situation involving [more than two] are considered to have a coalition."

In Mills (1953), the decision involved was the creation of a single dramatic story about a TAT picture by each set of three subjects. In a second experiment (Mills, 1954), subjects were asked to come to a decision (not necessarily unanimous) about what should be done in the trial of Melville's hero, Billy Budd. In each of these situations, as in Strodtbeck (1954) and Borgatta and Borgatta (1963), interaction was coded according to the Bales' categories, and various indices of support between each pair of participants were calculated.

If we are to regard such experiments as dealing with coalition formation, we must be able to specify the resources that are being used jointly. In this case, we might consider "persuasion attempts" as the resource, with magnitude being determined by frequency. Two individuals who present reasons for the same decision outcome would then be using their resources jointly. Thus, they could be said to have formed a coalition under the above definition. However, the fact that various positive feelings may develop between coalition partners is a by-product which lies outside the realm of coalitions.

Similar considerations apply to Strodtbeck's (1954) study of family decision-making. In this experiment, Strodtbeck asked triads composed of a father, mother, and son to reconcile a series of previously established disagreements which pitted each pair against the other member an equal number of times. Thus, by the interpretation suggested above, a coalition may be assumed to have formed at the outset. The subsequent discussion simply pits the resources of the coalition against the other in a battle of influence. If the frequency of persuasion attempts is in fact a measure of amount of resources as suggested above, then the side with the highest frequency should necessarily be the winner. As the data were presented, the number of such attempts was not analyzed separately from total participation, but Strodtbeck drew some conclusions which suggest that this is probably an inadequate statement of the resource involved. He wrote that, "We do not find in families the regularities and distribution of support which Mills reported. *Nor do we confirm the tendency for solidary high participating members to dominate the decision-making* which Mills anticipated would materialize. We do find in families, as in many other groups, decision-making power is associated with high participation." It would appear that some independent, prior measure of persuasive skill is necessary as a measure of amount of resource. Nevertheless, even without knowing the magnitude of the resources involved, participation on the same side of an argument is sufficient justification for asserting that a coalition has been formed. It enables us to establish the direction in which resources are used. Thus, joint participation tells us the existence but not the strength of a coalition.

B. THE MIXED-MOTIVE SITUATION

Even if we are successful in identifying a joint use of resources in the experimental situations described by Mills, Strodtbeck, and the Borgattas, their relevance for coalition formation is problematic on other grounds. Schelling's (1958) classification of two-person games of strategy suggests a convenient way of stating the requirements for a coalition situation. Schelling divided such games into (1) pure coordination games, (2) pure conflict (or zero-sum) games, and (3) mixed-motive games. The "game" between a single set of partners in bridge is a good example of a pure coordination game. The interests of the two are identical and the necessity of achieving coordination is the only problem. The game between the two teams in bridge is a good example of a pure conflict situation—whatever one team wins the other must lose. The so-called "prisoner's dilemma" game is the prototype of the mixed-motive category in the two-person situation. In this game, if each player tries for his maximum gain, both will do worse than if they agree to play a joint strategy that will bring both less than their maximum. Thus, there are elements of both conflict and coordination.

Such a classification can be easily enough translated for situations involving more than two participants. Pure coordination games are characterized by the fact that there exists a solution which maximizes the return for all players. There is no reason to exclude any participant in this situation, since in pursuing his interests he is aiding others to achieve their own. The problem is one of coordination and mobilization of all available resources for the most efficient achievement of the goal. To call such joint action a coalition of the whole debases the word, since any group which coordinates resources toward some collective goal would then be considered a coalition. It seems more useful to exclude from the definition of a coalition situation those decisions in which no conflict of interest exists among the participants.

Pure conflict situations, on the other hand, are characterized by a pursuit of some scarce thing of value in which no player can gain more in a coalition than he can gain singly. This definition departs some what from the two-person analogy where the zero-sum condition defines pure conflict. Some n-person, zero-sum games are *not* pure conflict games, since it is possible for a subset of players to combine and gain at the expense of those who are excluded. In pure conflict games, coalitions are excluded either because there is no incentive for them, or because the joint use of resources is prohibited by the rules.

A coalition situation is defined by mixed-motive, n-person games. In such games, there is an element of conflict, since there exists no outcome which maximizes the payoff to everybody. There is an element of coordination, since there exists for at least two of the players the possibility that they can do better by coordinating their resources than by acting alone.

The experimental situations designed by Mills and Strodtbeck seem to be predominantly coordination games. When three subjects have the task of creating a story about a TAT picture, there is no reason why an outcome which maximizes the return for all participants is excluded. Similarly, when the task is deciding on the proper fate for Billy Budd, there is no inherent conflict in the situation, even though in this case, the experimental design guaranteed disagreement through the use of two stooges in each triad. Similarly, in Strodtbeck's experiment, a disagreement between the participants is built into the design, but there is no reason why the three could not get all that they want (by someone changing his mind or by all agreeing to disagree).

One might, perhaps, be able to include such situations by the assumption that each participant wishes to maximize his or her relative influence over the outcome of the decision. Since this can only be done at the expense of others, the reconciliation of disagreements could be considered a mixed-motive situation. However, in the father-mother-son triads studied by Strodtbeck, it is particularly doubtful that maximizing relative influence rather than achieving a mutually satisfactory consensus is the predominating motive of the participants.

The definition of a coalition given earlier can now be given more precise statement. A coalition is the joint use of resources to determine the outcome of a decision in a mixed-motive situation involving more than two units. Studies by Mills (1953, 1954), Strodtbeck (1954), and the Borgattas (1963) are of doubtful relevance even though they have been cast in coalition terms. This, of course, does not detract from the contributions these studies may make to our understanding of stability and change in interaction patterns in three-person groups.

II. Some Theoretical Alternatives

There has been an encouraging convergence of theoretical explanations of coalition formation' in recent years. Yet, it is impossible to look closely at the available, experimental evidence without the feeling that a few, judicious changes in the conditions of the experiments could produce positive or negative support for any existing explanation. The implication here is not theoretical chaos, but a limited number of sometimes complementary, sometimes conflicting theories—each true under a particular set of conditions. Our object, then, in reviewing the relevant data, is not to find out which theories can be discarded, but to identify the optimal conditions for each.

A theory of coalition formation should tell us who will join with whom and how they will divide the rewards. Only those theories which are descriptive, or can be interpreted as such, will be considered here; prescriptions to the participants on how they *should* behave will be treated only through the addition of assumptions which translate them into predictions of how participants actually will behave. Each theory is based on a series of specific assumptions about norms operating in coalition situations, the motives of the participants, and various other aspects of the situation which will be made explicit below.

The exposition and comparison of the different theories will be helped by having available a standard coalition situation as an example. Toward this end, imagine the following: There are three leading candidates at a nominating convention, each with absolute control over the votes of his followers. Candidate A controls 48% of the votes, Candidate B controls 30%, and Candidate C controls 22%. A simple majority is needed for nomination.

A. MINIMUM RESOURCE THEORY

This theory emphasizes the initial resources which the players bring to the situation rather than their strategic bargaining position. For reasons discussed below, the following proposition emerges as the central hypothesis of the theory: a coalition will form in which the total resources are as small as possible while still being sufficient. Applied to the convention example, the prediction is clear and unequivocal. The coalition *48–30*[1] has 78% of the votes, *48–22* has 70%, while *30–22* has only 52%. The coalition *30–22* is clearly the winning coalition with the smallest total resources.

It is this theory which points to the paradox, "Strength is weakness." If by strength we mean the amount of initial resources one possesess, then the strongest player will, according to the prediction, be excluded in many situations. In the convention example, the strongest candidate, A,

[1] Frequent use is made of the convention of referring to a given coalition situation by the initial distribution of resources among the players ordered from highest to lowest. Thus, the convention example will be labeled 48–30–22 to represent the votes of candidates A, B, and C. Similarly, a coalition will be referred to by the player's resources and is italicized. Thus, *48–30* refers to a coalition between candidates A and B.

with 48%, will be the loser, since he is not included in the predicted coalition.

The minimum resource principle is applicable to groups of any size and it does not always predict defeat for the player strongest in initial resources. For example, if Candidate A's votes were split equally between Candidates D and E, then B with 30% would be the strongest candidate in a four-man game with an initial vote distribution of 30–24–24–22. He is also a member of the smallest winning coalition. Thus, in this situation, strength in resources would be converted into strength in rewards. Strength is weakness only sometimes—and "the sometimes" is clearly specified by minimum resource theory.

While hints of this theory are contained in Caplow (1956, 1959), Gamson (1961a) and Riker (1962) developed it explicitly. Caplow's analysis focused on several different types of resource distribution among three-person groups. He put his emphasis on maximizing the number of people over whom one has a resource advantage. Thus, his crucial assumption was that "each member of the triad seeks control over the others. Control over two others is preferred to control over one other. Control over one other is preferred to control over none" (Caplow, 1956). While this leads to the same predictions as minimum resource theory in many instances, it does not always do so. In situations like our convention example, Candidate A with 48% would control one other player in either the *48–30* or *48–22* coalition. Candidate B with 30% would control no one in the coalition *48–30,* but would control one player in the *30–22* coalition. He will, therefore, prefer the latter. Candidate C with 22% would not control anyone in either the *48–22* or *30–22* coalitions; under Caplow's assumptions he is indifferent between these possibilities. Thus, in the convention example, Caplow's analysis allowed either the coalition *48–22* or *30–22* as equally likely. "Whether the differential strength of A and B will make them differentially attractive to C lies outside the scope of our present assumptions," Caplow (1956) admitted.

Gamson (1961a) and Riker (1962) made the connection between the relative strength of members of a coalition and the distribution of rewards more explicit. Gamson suggested that "any participant will expect others to demand from a coalition a share of the payoff proportional to the amount of resources which they contribute to a coalition." Riker developed a similar notion which he called the "size principle." Building his analysis on the concepts of game theory, he suggested that "in social situations similar to n-person, zero-sum games with side-payments, participants create coalitions just as large as they believe will insure winning and no larger."

Why, we must ask, should a winning coalition with smaller resources be preferred to one which has more? The most convincing answer to this question is based on the existence in many situations of what may be called the parity norm. This is the belief by the participants that a person ought to get from an agreement an amount proportional to what he brings into it. It is important to note that this is *not* an assessment of relative power in the situation, but a statement of what the players feel they deserve. It is a normative belief, not a perception of bargaining advantage.

The parity norm is no more than distributive justice applied to coalition situations. "A man in an exchange relation . . . with another," Homans (1961) wrote, "will expect that . . . the net rewards, or profits, of each man be proportional to his investments." The existence of this norm works against coalitions which are larger than necessary. If a player gets from a coalition his parity price, i.e., an amount proportional to his resources, he gets the most by maximizing the ratio of his resources to the total resources of the coalition. Since his initial resources are the same regardless of which coalition he joins, the lower the total resources, the greater will be his share.

Players may be able to gain a larger than proportional share by skillful bargaining. However, this will involve a violation of the parity norm; such a victimization of the other players will be regarded as wrong and will not occur. The division of the payoff among the partners in a coalition will follow their parity prices. In the convention example, Candidate B will get 30/52 of the rewards while Candidate C will get 22/52.

Some psychologists have suggested that in situations such as the convention example, participants pay attention to the distribution of resources only through a *misperception* of the real power situation. Thus, Thibaut and Kelley (1959) maintained that Player A

> might believe that because of the high weight he brings to the coalition, he deserves a larger share of the prize (and others might share this belief). But this belief would have no correspondence with the objective facts concerning his power. . . . Each of the three must take zero points if the other two form an alliance. Hence, logically speaking, in cases such as the one described, the initial weights do not coincide with the power the person has alternately in a three-way bargaining situation . . . One wonders, then, why persons with smaller (though sufficient) initial weight are preferred as coalition mates.

Similarly, Vinacke and Arkoff (1957) and Stryker and Psathas (1960) cast the issue in terms of perception or power versus actual power. Under this interpretation, players may be said to misperceive the real power situation and, consequently, their resultant coalition behavior is irrational.

By basing minimum resource theory on the *norm* of parity, any onus of irrationality is completely removed from those players who observe it. Resources do not necessarily correspond to *pivotal power* (see discussion below), but they are not irrelevant if they suggest to players what they *ought* to get. Not being a perception of power, this belief can not be shown to be more or less accurate. A player who takes less than he can get in order to be closer to what he feels he should get, can not be said to be making an error.

B. Minimum Power Theory

This theoretical emphasis is an outgrowth of work in the mathematical theory of games. Game Theory is not a descriptive theory and the particular interpretation made here should not be taken as an intrinsic part of the mathematical theory. To quote Luce and Raiffa (1957), Game Theory "states neither how people do behave nor how they should behave in an absolute sense, but how they should behave if they wish to achieve certain ends."

The formation of coalitions is the main feature of a subclass of games which Rapoport and Orwant (1962) referred to as negotiable, *n*-person games. With respect to these games, the theory is frequently not even prescriptive. For example, Rapoport and Orwant pointed out that the von Neumann-Morgenstern "solution" for *n*-person games "is in no way a prescription to any player or even to any set of players collectively concerning what coalitions they should form and what the [distribution of rewards] should be." Solution theory offers no answer to the question of who will join with whom; at best, it may be interpreted as suggesting what the division of spoils will be. Luce (1954) suggested an alternative concept, psi-stability, in which a game is described by both a division of rewards (called an imputation) and a coalition structure. A pair—that is, an imputation and a given coalition structure—is stable when no admissible change in the coalition structure is immediately profitable. Psi-stable pairs, like solutions, are not generally unique, and the problem of how to select just one still exists. In the convention situation, for example, any two-man coalition will meet the conditions of psi-stability.

Perhaps the most immediately relevant contribution here is Shapley's (1953) method for evaluating the worth of an *n*-person game for any player. This Shapley value can be interpreted as a measure of a priori bargaining power. He arrives at an explicit formula for calculating the value for a player, *i*. "It amounts," to quote Luce and Raiffa (1957), "to a weighted sum of the incremental additions made by *i* to all the coalitions of which he is a member." This idea of power is clearly not identical with the amount of initial resources. When applied to certain simple games,[2] a player's pivotal power is the proportion of times his resources can change

[2] In a simple game, every coalition has as its payoff either one or zero, i.e., it is either winning or losing. See Shapley and Shubik (1954).

a losing coalition into a winning one. It is given by the index P/N where N is the total number of permutations among the players and P is the number of permutations in which his resources are pivotal (Shapley and Shubik, 1954). In the three-man convention situation there are 3! or six permutations and each candidate will be pivotal twice. Thus, the relative power of the candidates is equal even though their initial resources differ.

Harsanyi (1963) suggested a generalized solution of negotiable, n-person games which utilizes a modified version of the Shapley value. Harsanyi pointed out that under specified conditions, "the final payoffs defined by our solution will be simply the modified Shapley values." To translate the concept of pivotal power into a descriptive theory, we can simply assume that all participants will demand a share of the payoff proportional to their pivotal power rather than to their resources. The implication of this pivotal power assumption is, again, the formation of the minimum winning coalition, but size is now defined by the total of the pivotal power of the participants, rather than their total resources. Thus, in the convention situation, each two-man coalition is the same size and is, therefore, equally likely. Rewards will be divided evenly since partners have the same power.

C. Anticompetitive Theory

The stimulus for this theory was a series of experiments by Vinacke and his students in which female subjects were frequently used. The girls, as shown in Section III, frequently behaved differently from their male counterparts. If players in minimum power theory are trying to get as much as they can and players in minimum resource theory are trying to get as much as they deserve, players in anticompetitive theory are focused on maintaining the social relationships in the group. An anticompetitive norm exists, the theory suggests, against efforts to strike the most advantageous deal possible. Coalitions will form along the lines of least resistance.

If players are really intent on avoiding conflict, will they not find the very act of forming a coalition which excludes others a disruptive and conflict producing act? Are not coalitions of the whole, with all players sharing equally, the ultimate implication of the anticompetitive norm? This is, certainly, one solution which fits the anticompetitive norm, but it is excluded by definition in the situations which we are considering. A coalition situation, remember, is a mixed-motive game. If players are interested only in minimizing conflict, then we are dealing with a pure co-ordination game. Although anticompetitive theory would, in general, predict attempts by the players to transform mixed strategy games into pure coordination games, coalition behavior must be predicted in situations where this is inherently impossible. Thus, as a coalition theory, anticompetitive theory emphasizes the minimization of disruptive aspects of bargaining rather than the removal of conflict in the total situation.

Coalitions will form, then, along the path of least resistance in bargaining. This path of least resistance will be between those partners for whom there exists the most obvious and unambiguous solution to the problem of dividing the relative share of the payoff. This will occur among players who are equal in resources, because according to either the parity norm or the pivotal power principle, players with equal resources will share equally.

It is true that if all players followed the parity norm only, or the pivotal power principle only, there would be no need for any bargaining even where players are unequal. However, there is always the danger that the players may invoke rival standards. Where unequal resources exist, the potential for bargaining is always greater.

The standards of the parity norm and pivotal power are always identical where equal resources exist between members of a prospective coalition. Since there is no apparent justification for differential rewards, they can anticipate an agreement on an equal basis which can be concluded rapidly and with a minimum of haggling, unpleasantness, and subsequent resentment. Simmel's (1950) description of ancient Peru is interesting in this regard.

> It was the general custom of the Incas to divide a newly-conquered tribe in two approximately equal halves and to place a supervisor over each of them but to give these two supervisors slightly different ranks. This indeed was the most suitable means of provoking rivalry between the two heads [and] prevented any united action against the ruler on the part of the subjected territories.

It is under the anticompetitive norm that "playing to win is playing to lose." Where participants are interested in keeping the disruptive effects of bargaining to a minimum, a player who exhibits the characteristics of a hard and skillful bargainer will be avoided. The more openly he seeks to get as much as he can, the less likely it is that he will get it, because others will prefer to deal with less competitive participants. It is one of the ironies of coalition formation that those players sometimes do best who make the least effort.

In our convention example where each candidate has different resources, it is not clear what the prediction would be from anticompetitive theory. Some bargaining seems inevitable, since there are conflicting standards for dividing the rewards. If some standard such as the parity norm is particularly salient, it might offer an opportunity to resolve the bargaining problem easily. In this case, minimum resource theory would be applicable.

If Candidate A has acquired his initial advantage in resources by his ability as a tough bargainer, he might well find himself the victim of both the "Strength is weakness" and the "Playing to win is playing to lose" paradoxes. Being initially strong, the parity norm militates against him; being known as a hard bargainer, the anticompetitive norm works against him as well.

D. UTTER CONFUSION THEORY

This last theory (or more accurately, antitheory) is not included simply because of some desire for logical completeness. There are some experimental results, as we shall see, for which it is probably the most convincing explanation. Many coalition situations are conducted under conditions which are not at all conducive to rational calculation and analysis. It is well known that political conventions, for example, are frequently scenes of bedlam. Thus, according to this theory, coalition formation is best understood as an essentially random choice process. The coalition which forms will be the result of such fortuitous events as a chance encounter or a missed telephone call.

This explanation is important because, in a number of situations, it makes the same predictions as other theories above. In the convention example, the result of confusion is that any two-man coalition is equally likely. Pivotal power theory also predicts that any two-man coalition is equally probable. Should we find, then, that participants in this type of situation do form each coalition with about the same frequency, we would not know which of two possibilities was correct. Was this the result of an acute analysis by the participants which led them to the conclusion that they all have equal power, or was it the result of the bewildered, random actions of thoroughly confused participants? There are, of course, many other coalition situations in which pivotal power theory and utter confusion theory make different predictions. The prediction from the latter is tantamount to the null hypothesis. When some other theory makes the same prediction for any particular situation, it can not be tested at that point.

III. Experimental Evidence

There are now some dozen or more experiments with an explicit focus on coalitions as defined here. The partisans of any one of the theories presented above can find comfort in at least some of the results, but none will find complete support. This does not suggest, of course, that all of the theories do equally well; some clearly find more supporting evidence than others. It is clear, however, that certain kinds of subjects and certain kinds of experimental conditions are more frequently employed. With a different set of experiments, the weight of evidence might look quite different.

In reviewing experimental results, we will focus on the positive support which each theory finds. In many cases the theories make different predictions, so that positive evidence for one must be read as negative evidence for others. Since only favorable evidence is reported under the heading for such theory, a complete evaluation of any of them requires an examination of the material discussed under the other theories as well.

A. EVIDENCE FOR MINIMUM RESOURCE THEORY

There are three different kinds of evidence for this theory: (1) the coalitions predicted by the theory do in fact form in a number of experiments; (2) the distribution of rewards does tend to be correlated with the player's parity price; and (3) subjects sometimes state their belief in the parity norm quite directly.

1. Predicted Coalitions

Vinacke and Arkoff (1957) designed an experiment to test Caplow's (1956) predictions on coalitions in the triad. The experimenters had subjects play a parchesi game in which each player's moves were weighted by a numbered counter which he drew from a hopper at the beginning of the game. The weights on these counters represented the initial distribution of resources in the game. Table I reproduces the Vinacke and Arkoff results and the minimum resource prediction for those three situations studied which provide a test.

The results supported the prediction very strongly. In each situation, the minimum resources coalition forms even though the three players are equal in pivotal power. Furthermore, this finding held up under a wide variety of conditions in later experiments by Vinacke and his colleagues (Vinacke, 1959; Chaney and Vinacke, 1960; Vinacke, 1962).

Vinacke and Arkoff interpreted this result as indicating *misperceptions* of the power situation. "It is harder," they wrote, "for an initially stronger member to reach the conclusion that the relative strengths are irrelevant than for the other one or two to arrive at this interpretation. In effect, the weaker members can immediately understand the necessity for forming a coalition whereas the stronger member must go through more complex reasoning to do so."

TABLE I
RESULTS OF VINACKE–ARKOFF EXPERIMENT

Distribution of resources	Predicted coalition	Actual coalitions[a]		
		Predicted	Other	None
3–2–2	2–2	64	25	1
1–2–2	1–2[b]	64	15	11
4–3–2	3–2	59	29	2

[a] $N = 90$.
[b] Note that this includes two of the three possible coalitions.

Under the parity norm, it is not necessary to assume misperceptions of power on the part of the players. The stronger player might well perceive very quickly that it is necessary that he form a coalition, but still feel that he ought to get more than his partner gets since he contributes more in resources. The other players may grant this even if they accurately perceive the equal pivotal power of the members. However, they will then choose to join with someone else whose parity price is not so high.

Gamson (1961b) provided additional evidence with a study of five-person groups. Subjects were told that they were participating in an experimental study of "how political conventions operate" and that each was to play the role of delegation chairman at a series of political conventions. At the beginning of a convention, each subject was given a sheet with the number of votes which he and each of the other players controlled. The object of the game was to "win" political patronage or "jobs." To do this, a subject had to put together a simple majority of the votes by combining with others. To form a coalition, he had to decide with the other chairman or chairmen how to divide up the jobs to which their coalition was entitled.

One convention is of particular interest here. In it, three players had 17 votes while two had 25 votes. Minimum resource theory predicts that the coalition 17–17–17 will form. This is only one of the ten possible winning three-man coalitions. Gamson found, however, that in 24 groups, it occurred not 10% but 33% of the time ($p < .002$).

An experiment with three-person groups by Lieberman (1962) is less of a direct test, but is still very suggestive for minimum resource theory. Subjects had no initial resources but instead were presented with a list of different payoffs to the three possible two-man coalitions that might form. In the language of game theory, the subjects were presented with the characteristic function. In one game, the coalition AB received ten cents from Player C, AC received eight cents from Player B, and BC received six cents from Player A. The winning players had to decide by written communications how to divide the winnings.

It is particularly interesting that the coalition with the lowest payoff, BC, occurred most frequently. Lieberman (1962) writes that "we may speculate a bit about such a result . . . if Player A was seen as the strongest and most exploitative individual, this may have led Players B and C to unite against him to form their coalition quite frequently."

2. Distribution of Rewards

In the experiments discussed above and in many others, players with unequal resources did not typically share equally in the distribution of rewards, even when they had equal pivotal power. On the other hand, the distribution seemed to be generally less extreme than the differences in parity price would suggest, although there is clearly a correlation between initial resources and share of the payoff.

Willis's (1962) results on coalition formation in four-man groups were typical in this regard even though they generally do not support minimum resource theory. He found that "the more powerful member [in resources] in a two-way coalition typically receives a share of the winnings which was more than that received by his partner but which was less than proportionate to the difference in [resources]." Where resources differed by *1*, "the mean of splits agreed upon was (56–44) in favor of the more powerful member. For a [resource] difference of *2*, the mean split was (58–42), while for a difference of *3*, it was (61–39)." Among partners of equal strength, the split was (50.1–49.9).

Gamson (1961b), presented evidence on the distribution of rewards among the players in the five-man coalition situation, 25–25–17–17–17, described above. Players with only 17 votes averaged only 31% of the payoff in those coalitions in which they were included against 38% for players with 25 votes.

One might test rather directly for the effect of initial resources on the distribution of rewards by allowing one of the player's resources to vary while his pivotal power and all other conditions of the game remain constant. Stryker and Psathas (1960) did exactly this by comparing triads in which the initial resources were, respectively, (a) 6–6–5, (b) 6–6–3, and (3) 6–6–1. Unfortunately for our purposes here, they complicated their experimental design by prohibiting certain coalitions. Consequently, the results were less definitive than they might otherwise have been. They still found, however, that "while the evidence is not clearcut, there is considerable support . . . that when the weak man is involved in the coalition he tends to receive larger proportions of the prize as his weight increases" (Stryker and Psathas, 1960).

3. Direct Testimonials

In Gamson (1961b), verbatim transcriptions were made of the subjects' bargaining sessions. These have not previously been published, but they contain much informal evidence for the validity of the parity norm. It is worth noting that the experimenter's instructions contained no suggestions about the strategy of play. The following quotations are illustrative:

(Two of the players with 17 votes have already formed a coalition which now has 34 votes. They are bargaining with the third player with 17 votes. 34 has made an offer to 17 of 20% of the payoff):

17: All right. I'll take 38%.
34: No . . . The maximum we would give you would be 30%.
17: I'm sorry.
34: I think that's a pretty good deal myself. Let's go the other way. If you were to go with a man with 25, you would get screwed. This is the maximum amount of jobs you would get being 17. You get the three 17's together, you're going to naturally get the most because each would normally get 33%, but now we're going to give you 30%. We're only dropping 3% of that because we first formed a delegation. I think that's a pretty fair offer.

(The same situation arises in a second group):
34: 40–40–20?
17: Nope.
34: Don't want it, huh?
17: Nope. Because we got an equal number of votes. If you have my 17, it will give us a majority of the votes. If you take one of these guys with 25, you'll have a larger number of votes and he will be in a better position to deal with [you] to get a large number of jobs.
34: I don't follow you.
17: Well, if I've got 17, I can't ask for any more than my share of the jobs which will be one-third.
34: Right.
17: Now, you have 34. This guy comes in because you haven't made an agreement with me because you wanted to give me less than I'm entitled to. Then he can hold out for more . . .

Other experimenters have pointed to similar reactions on the part of their subjects. Kelley and Arrowood (1960) gave their subjects a questionnaire and found that some of them felt that the player with higher resources is "*justified* in demanding the majority share of the coalition reward, because he contributes more to the coalition. One might guess that this interpretation figures more prominently in the early reaction to the situation than the overall figures would indicate" (italics added). The authors do find that this belief weakens in the course of repeated plays of the experimental game.

B. Evidence for Minimum Power Theory

The evidence for minimum resource theory presented above must be taken as evidence against minimum power theory. In the Vinacke and Arkoff (1957) and Gamson (1961b) experiments previously cited, all players were equal in pivotal power. There was reason to expect, according to this theory, that the coalitions would occur with equal frequency, but this was not the case.

Kelley and Arrowood (1960) suggested that it is the complexity of the procedure that prevents subjects from acquiring an adequate understanding of the true power relations. They conducted an experiment in which the initial resource distribution was 4–3–2. Their results showed that "from the first to the last trials, there is not a significant change in the incidence of the three coalitions. Hence we cannot be sure that further experience increased their understanding of the situation." However, they did not find a very sharp initial departure from the minimum power prediction. They suggest that "upon examination of the data on a trial-by-trial basis, it is clear that the learning is very rapid, so that after the first three or four trials, there is little more than chance exclusion of [Player 4] from coalitions."

In the questionnaire which Kelley and Arrowood gave subjects at the conclusion of the experiment, they asked whether the participants thought that Player 4 was "more to be feared, [had] greater potential, etc." They report that the vast majority of the subjects admitted that they had believed this at some time, but that they generally realized by the end of the experiment that Player 4 was not in the most advantageous position. Ironically, the belief that Player 4 is strongest makes him weak, but as the subjects learned in the process of repeated plays that he is more to be pitied than feared, his original disadvantage disappeared somewhat. It is clearly in the long-run interest of the strong player in this situation to attack and destroy the parity norm which would benefit him if he were only able to get into a coalition in the first place.

The experiment by Willis (1962) on four-man groups gave some additional slight evidence in favor of minimum power theory and against minimum resource theory. One situation studied was characterized by a 5–3–3–2 distribution of initial resources. If we consider only internally essential coalitions (that is, coalitions in which the defection of any member makes the coalition no longer winning), we find that there are four such in this game: two 5–3 coalitions, 5–2, and 3–3–2. The smallest resource coalition, 5–2, occurred almost exactly 25% of the time, or just about what one would expect by chance.

Pivotal power in the 5–3–3–2 situation is not at all obvious. It turns out that Player 5 is pivotal in half of the coalitions, while the other three players are each equally pivotal in one sixth of the possible coalitions. If players are to share in coalitions proportionally to their pivotal power, in any coalition with Player 5, the others will receive only one fourth of the payoff. However, in the three-way coalition, *3–3–2,* they will each receive one third. This coalition, then, would be predicted by minimum power theory, and in fact it occurs more frequently than any of the internally essential coalitions which include Player 5. About 31% of them are of the *3–3–2* type; in other words, this coalition occurs about 25% more frequently than the smaller coalition in resources, *5–2.*

The Willis experiment added an important new element which may account for the discrepancy between this and other results. A coalition with a weight of seven could not be absolutely certain of determining the decision against a counter-coalition with a weight of six. The subjects played a game in which the outcome was partly determined by a random element. While a coalition with seven had a definite probability of defeating a coalition with six, a coalition with eight had an additional advantage through a more certain victory.

This introduced a new variable which may explain the lack of support in this experiment for smallest resource theory. As Thibaut and Kelley (1959) suggested, "a person may find it desirable on one occasion to choose a less effective coalition in which he is more powerful, and on another occasion, a highly effective one in which he is less powerful." Gamson (1961a) maintained that this variable might be handled if we assume that a player estimates the payoff to himself as his share of the coalition (figured as his parity price) multiplied by the total payoff to that prospective coalition.

Where the probabilities of success of different coalitions vary, the total payoff may be conceived of as the expected value of that coalition. To take an example, suppose that in the four-man game designed by Willis (1962), any winning coalition received one hundred dollars, but a coalition with resources of eight has a .9 probability of defeating the counter-coalition, while a coalition with resources of seven had only a .6 probability of winning against the opposition. The payoff to coalition, *3–3–2,* is .9 × $100 = $90, while the coalition, *5–2,* is worth only .6 × $100 = $60. If player 2 expects to get his parity price, then he will prefer the coalition *3–3–2,* in which his expectation is .25 × $90 = $22.50 to coalition *5–2* in which his expectation is .29 × $60 = $17.40.

C. EVIDENCE FOR ANTICOMPETITIVE THEORY

The experimenter in studies of coalition formation presents his subjects with an "object of the game." This goal is generally the accumulation for each individual of as much of the monetary or symbolic payoff as possible. When subjects are American male undergraduates, reared on such parlor games as Monopoly, they generally find such a competitive situation natural enough and enthusiastically try to win as many points as possible. However, other kinds of subjects, and even the undergraduate males themselves, sometimes smuggle in additional objectives.

1. The Existence of Anticompetitive Behavior

Uesugi and Vinacke (1963) gave their impressions of their own earlier experiments as follows:

> The men had gratifyingly manifested the sort of behavior that "male" experimenters had expected. Thus, they seemed to enter with gusto into the game, bargaining competitively, making the best "deals" they could, and in short, striving to win. The behavior of the females was puzzlingly different. For them the situation appeared to provide an opportunity for social interaction.

The females in the Vinacke experiments repeatedly attempted to transform the mixed-motive situation into a pure coordination game. Thus, they adopted procedures which made competition unnecessary, using such devices as rotation systems between plays of the game and alliances which included everybody. By using a task designed to enhance feminine interest, Uesugi and Vinacke (1963) were able to increase such anticompetitive behavior even more.

The contrasting behavior of male and female subjects led Vinacke to characterize a typical "masculine" and "feminine" strategy. Feminine strategy is called "accommodative"; it is oriented toward the social relationships of the game, "toward the end of arriving at an equitable or fair outcome of maximum satisfaction (or at least justice) to all concerned" (Bond and Vinacke, 1961). Lest there be any doubt about where their sympathies lie, Vinacke and his colleagues label masculine strategy with the epithet "exploitative"; it is directed toward maximizing one's individual share of the payoff.

In Bond and Vinacke (1961), the experimenters used triads composed of two members of one sex and one of the other. The subjects played the same, modified parchesi game described earlier. It is interesting to ask whether the competitive males or the anticompetitive females are more successful in the manifest objective of gaining the most points. "In terms of which style produces a better outcome," Bond and Vinacke comment, "it is quite clear that the female arrives at a relatively more favorable position than does the male (most striking when she forms the minority)." It is especially typical of females to ally when weak and of males to ally when strong.

An experiment by Chaney and Vinacke (1960) which explored the connection between achievement motivation and coalition strategy suggested some additional support. As in other experiments in this series, the actual alliances which formed tended to support minimum resource theory. "From this standpoint, motivational differences among the players had very little effect upon the play" (Chaney and Vinacke, 1960). However, they did find that, where all subjects have equal initial resources, subjects high in achievement motivation are significantly less often involved in alliances. Perhaps, by a more aggressive style of play, they are driving the others into an alliance with a less competitive participant.

Vinacke is not the only experimenter who found his subjects adopting anticompetitive strategies. Kalisch *et al.* (1954) found in their series of experiments that

> despite the exhortation contained in the general instructions to instill a completely selfish and competitive attitude in the players, they frequently took a fairly cooperative attitude. Of course, this was quite functional in that it heightened their chances of getting into a coalition. One player told the experimenters in an interview after the game that she appreciated the fact "that the favored player did not strike the best deal." When she was in the position of the favored player, she felt that to demand her *due* [would seem] unreasonable to the others. . . . When she was not the favored player, it was not to her advantage to say anything about it.

Kalisch *et al.* also found a tendency to prevent consistent losers. They reported that "it was the feeling among some of the players that no individual should lose twice in a row. So perhaps a rotation system would have developed if there had been more plays (this was also indicated in subsequent interviews)."

Stryker and Psathas (1960) reported instances in which players advised their opponents on their best strategy, even though this could, and sometimes did, result in the exclusion of the person making the suggestion. "The actual altruism, consideration, and empathy which existed in the situation would have been overlooked . . . if outcome data alone were examined," they commented. Vinacke (1959) made such altruistic offers one of the defining characteristics of "accommodative" strategy.

2. The Benefits of Anticompetitive Behavior

While the results above seem to document a considerable range of genuinely altruistic behavior by subjects in coalition experiments, it is important to recognize that anticompetitive behavior may also serve the individual's long-run interest. Thus, Bond and Vinacke (1961) and Kalisch *et al.* (1954) in the experiments discussed above found altruism beneficial to its practitioners. The benefits of competitive restraint are particularly apparent in experiments in which subjects take part in a prolonged sequence of plays of a coalition game. Under such circumstances, and many of the experiments are of this type, the entire, experimental session rather than the individual play of the game is frequently the focus of the subject's coalition strategy. With such a focus, the most selfish and exploitative player might well find that his best, long-run strategy involves deliberate restraint in seeking immediate advantage. While the motivation in such situations may be far from altruistic, the resultant anticompetitive behavior is the same.

Lieberman (1962) made just such observations about his subjects.

> It became obvious that in a number of games, the players came to realize that a maximum return on one or two plays was not important. It was far more profitable to enter into a stable continuing agreement with one other player. Since defection was not an infrequent occurrence, the intuitive notion of trust was significant in determining which coalitions formed and held together. The subjects stated that they would enter into a coalition with a player that they trusted, one they believed would not be tempted to defect from their coalition for a more attractive offer.

In line with this, Lieberman (1963) suggested the notion of i-trust (for "interest" trust) which he defines as "the belief that the parties involved in an agreement will actually do what they have agreed to do. They will fulfill their commitment not only when it is obviously advantageous for them to do so, but even when it may be disadvantageous, when the person must sacrifice some immediate gain. However, the belief does not require that the person take an action that is clearly contrary to an important self-interest. The person who sacrifices some immediate gain to fulfill a commitment believes he is acting in his own interest . . . His interests lie in preserving his alliance which is what yields him his maximum gain."

Another long-run advantage for anticompetitive behavior lies in avoiding the pitfalls of the player who does too well, too soon. Hoffman *et al.* (1954) found that where cumulative score is made salient for the players, one who achieves an early lead is likely to stimulate others to form a coalition against him. They demonstrated that this tendency was greatest when (1) players believe that more is at stake, i.e., the task is regarded as important, and (2) when the early advantage was not seen as a sign of unavoidable superiority on the part of the leader. Vinacke (1962) reported similar tendencies for alignments against the early leaders in triads in which cumulative score is publicized.

3. Coalitions among Equals

It seems clear that subjects often act with competitive restraint and, under the proper circumstances, do better because of such restraint. The above discussion focuses on style of play. Anticompetitive theory also has a content prediction about which coalitions will form. Is it true that coalitions form among those with equal resources?

Some experimenters have noted such a tendency. Willis (1962) remarked that "an even distribution of (resources) between potential (coalition partners) quite clearly favors the formation of . . . coalitions." Gamson (1961b) found that in the 25–25–17–17–17 game described earlier, coalitions among the two players with 25 votes were quite frequent, even though this went directly against their minimum resource strategy. In a second experimental situation where the initial distribution of resources was 35–35–15–10–6, he found that the largest coalition in resources, *35–35,* occurred most frequently (although not statistically more significantly than the others). While this may be due to its being the only winning coalition that could be formed on a single step (all others required at least two bargaining sessions), the equality of resources among the partners may also have been an important factor in its promise of a simple and conflict-free bargaining session.

D. EVIDENCE FOR UTTER CONFUSION THEORY

In the experiments discussed above, there were times when at least some of the subjects appeared to be quite bewildered about their proper coalition strategy. This seemed particularly true in those games involving more than three players. In such games, subjects were frequently, and with good reason, more worried about the danger of being left out of a coalition altogether than about the small differences in terms that one might get by joining with one player rather than another. It is a luxury to worry about the "best" strategy; while one is involved in such analysis, he may find that others have combined, leaving him to his musings.

Pivotal power or resources may not be as relevant to the players as the accidents of propinquity or loudness of voice. Kalisch *et al.* (1954) observed that "in many cases, aggressiveness played a role. . . . Who yelled first and loudest after the umpire said 'go' made a difference in the outcome. . . . In the five-person game, and especially in the seven-person game [geometric arrangement of the players around the table] became quite important. . . . In general, as the number of players increased, the atmosphere became more confused, more hectic, more competitive, and less pleasant to the subjects. The plays of the seven-person game were simply explosions of coalition formation."

When some of the subjects are 7- and 8-year-old children as in Vinacke and Gullickson (1963), they are probably too bewildered much of the time to do anything other than form alliances at random. Vinacke and Gullickson found that in the 4–3–2 game, for example, all coalitions occur with about equal frequency. While this is the prediction that one would make from an analysis of pivotal power, it seems unlikely that the children are more sensitive to this highly sophisticated notion than their elders, who pay more attention to the differences in resources.

Many of the results of Willis (1962) are better "explained" by this theory than by any alternative. It is true that with a 5–3–3–2 distribution, the coalition with the smallest total pivotal power, 3–3–2, occurs slightly more frequently than the others. Willis also experimented with a 4–4–3–2 distribution and here the results were particularly interesting since each of the four theories predicted something different. The minimum resource coalition is either of the two 4–3 coalitions. In terms of pivotal power, the three players with weights of 4 and 3 have equal pivotal power but Player 2 has no pivotal power at all (that is, the player with weight of 2 can never transform a losing coalition into a winning one by the addition of his resources). Anticompetitive theory would suggest the coalition 4–4 between the two players with equal resources.

The fact that chance as well as resources determined the outcome of play in Willis' experimental game is an important limitation on the interpretation one can make of the results. Nevertheless, it is striking that Player 2, who by all theories other than utter confusion should be excluded, is in fact included in initial coalitions only slightly less frequently than the others. The distribution of two-man coalitions in Willis' experiment is quite close to what one would expect if players were choosing at random. He did find that when coalitions of three players form, they are quite likely to be those with the smallest amount of resources.

One final argument for utter confusion theory is in order. The experimenter who finds no clear pattern in his results is, as we all know, not likely to write them up and rush them to the nearest journal. Thus, there is every reason to suspect a systematic bias in reported results which neglects those that best fit this antitheory.

IV. Ideal Conditions for the Theories

One is tempted to conclude from the above pattern of results that, given the proper set of conditions, each of the theories would be supported. This section attempts to specify these ideal conditions by considering the following hypothetical problem. Suppose that we are confronted with a partisan of each of the theories. Each man wishes to produce an experimental *demonstration* (not a test) of his respective theory. How should we advise each in turn that he might best accomplish this purpose?

A. Advice to a Minimum Resource Theorist

First of all, it is important to build a good deal of conflict into the situation. The players must be competing for something that they really value, not something merely symbolic. Only those who value competition for its own sake (as many males do) can be expected to compete for something which has no value to them. If course grades in school or large sums of money are involved, the competition may be made a more intrinsic part of the game instead of something which the players must bring in from outside.

Place some limitation on the freedom of communication in the bargaining situation. If players are allowed to bargain in a face-to-face situation without restriction, two possibilities are more likely to occur: (1) confusion and pressure to form any coalition at all will be enhanced; or (2) pivotal power is more likely to be understood and to operate as a competitor to the parity norm. If, on the other hand, players are allowed to communicate with each other sequentially and in an order of their choosing, they will seek those with whom they can expect their most favorable offer. The parity norm suggests who this will be. Where others have an immediate opportunity to interject a better offer, the parity norm is more prone to break down. Of course, the situation must be kept simple enough that subjects can identify the smallest resource coalition with relative ease.

It helps if subjects are comfortable with competitive situations and even enjoy winning for its own sake without any extrinsic reward. American male undergraduates seem quite suitable in this regard; there is no point in taking risks with females who may concern themselves with such extraneous factors as the feelings of the participants or the strain of bargaining.

It might help to start by enhancing the saliency of the parity norm. This could be accomplished by giving the subjects an initial task in which the parity norm is particularly appropriate. For example, one might have the subjects start by playing a gambling game as a team against the experimenter. They might be given different amounts of money to contribute to a collective bet (while being told that these advantages would even themselves out in the course of the experiment). They would then have to decide how they should allocate any winnings from this bet. Hopefully, they will decide that those who risk the most should get a share that is proportional to their contribution to the bet. Once the parity norm has been made salient in this way, the coalition portion of the experiment which follows should have increased likelihood of demonstrating minimum resource theory.

B. ADVICE TO A MINIMUM POWER THEORIST

Here, the element of conflict should be made as great as it possibly can. Players must be competing for something which is so important to them that it outweighs considerations of what one ought to get (the parity norm) or any delicacy that they might have about ruthless competition (the anticompetitive norm).

Place subjects in a situation in which any offer can immediately be met by a better offer. Give the subjects ample opportunity for learning in a situation which is simple enough for them eventually to perceive the pivotal power of the players. Perhaps it is best to include a stooge who will always make better offers whenever he is not included in a winning coalition and will always accept better offers by a participant who is excluded.

Take precautions to keep subjects from developing trust relationships which extend over several plays. This can be done by simultaneously running several groups and rotating subjects so that they do not know with whom they will be included in the next play. Keep cumulative scores a secret and emphasize the independence and importance of each play. If possible, prohibit agreements which extend beyond a single play. By rotating subjects in many different groups, such a rule will probably be unnecessary.

Use subjects who have no established social relationships with each other and no prospects of a continuing relationship after the experiment. Subjects should be indifferent to each other or even mildly hostile so that they are not bothered if some players consistently lose. Ideally, they should believe that people deserve whatever they can get; if this is more than their resources would indicate, then more power to them. With such subjects, minimum power theory should be substantiated.

C. Advice to an Anticompetitive Theorist

The element of conflict in the situation should be kept to a minimum. The stakes should be little more than symbolic. Participants should feel that they are in a polite game where sportsmanship and how the game is played is regarded as more important than the outcome.

Subjects should be used who already have a friendly relationship with each other and who will continue their association after the experiment is over. They should not, however, be so close that they feel comfortable with the open expression of conflict; their relationships should be fragile enough that the tension created by vigorous bargaining is a threat. Polite acquaintances who value each other's good opinion and propriety in the conduct of social relationships should support anticompetitive theory in their coalition behavior.

D. Advice to an Utter Confusion Theorist

Advice here is easy for there are many alternative ways of confusing subjects. One way is to introduce a large number of complex variables so that subjects are so preoccupied with following the rules and assimilating the information about resources, coalition payoffs, time limits, and so forth that they have little time to consider any strategy at all.

A second method is to use a very short time limit so that the pressure to form any coalition quickly is great. Keep the differences in resources and pivotal power moderate. The object here should be to minimize the differences between alternative coalitions while the contrast between *a* coalition and *no* coalition is maximized.

Use unsophisticated subjects such as children. Make sure, by keeping resources unequal, that no simple formula such as coalitions between equals can be adopted. Make sure that subjects do not know each other previously and are unlikely to encounter each other in the future. Do not allow stable relationships to develop in the course of the experiment lest this provide a focus for coalition strategy. The rotation of subjects in many groups is probably advisable toward this end.

In general, make accurate communication difficult so that the terms of offers and their acceptance or rejection is subject to considerable distortion. Eight or ten subjects standing in a group, with a hazy understanding of the rules and with a good deal of information on resources and payoffs to assimilate, and forced to bargain by shouting at each other under extreme time pressure, should provide strong support for utter confusion theory.

V. Summary and Conclusion

A *coalition,* it is suggested, should be used to refer to influence in a decision-making process, rather than to other bases of differentiation within a larger group. More specifically, it should be used to mean the joint use of resources to determine the outcome of a decision. A number of experiments involving primarily verbal expressions of support between certain members have been cast in terms of coalitions; they are of doubtful relevance by this definition except through considerable reinterpretation.

To be considered a coalition, the joint use of resources must take place in a situation which has elements of both coordination and conflict, i.e., a mixed-motive situation. Joint use of resources in a pure-coordination situation is simply collective activity toward a common goal. On the other hand, there are no coalitions in pure-conflict situations, since there is either no incentive to coordinate resources or such action is prohibited by the rules.

A number of different theories, each with a specific set of assumptions about norms and motives, are available to explain experimental results. Minimum resource theory emphasizes the initial resources which the players bring to the situation. Its basis is the parity norm: the belief that a person ought to get from an agreement an amount proportional to what he brings into it. It follows from adherence to this norm that the coalition which forms will have total resources as small as possible while still being sufficient.

Minimum power theory focuses on strategic position in bargaining. Shapley has suggested a value for n-person games which can be interpreted as a measure of a priori bargaining power. A player's pivotal power in certain simple games is calculated as the proportion of times his resources can change a losing coalition into a winning one. If we assume that all participants will demand a share of the payoff proportional to their pivotal power, then each will get the most by maximizing his relative power within the coalition. This implies that the coalition which forms will be the winning one with the smallest total pivotal power.

Anticompetitive theory focuses on the potentially disruptive aspects of bargaining. It is based on the assumption that players are very much concerned with maintaining smooth social relations in the group and find the conflict involved in vigorous bargaining a threat to such relations. The prediction here is that coalitions will form along the path of least resistance. Where unequal resources exist, the potentiality for competitive bargaining exists, since players may invoke rival standards of pivotal power and parity price. With equal resources, there is no apparent justification for any agreement other than an equal division. Such a coalition promises an agreement with a minimum of haggling and unpleasantness. Under anticompetitive theory, players may also be expected to make whatever efforts are possible to transform the mixed-motive situation into one of pure coordination.

Utter confusion theory emphasizes the importance of a large number of fortuitous factors which have nothing to do with the resources, pivotal power, or stable social relationships of the players. It may be viewed as an interpretation of the null hypothesis which predicts that players are joining randomly. Its inclusion as a separate theory is a reminder that in some situations it makes the same predictions as other theories. Furthermore, confusion may indeed be the most accurate way of describing the psychological state which accompanies coalition formation in many situations.

Each theory finds some support in experimental evidence. The coalitions predicted by minimum resource theory are confirmed in a number of experiments, and the distribution of rewards tends to be correlated with parity price. Players sometimes explicitly state their belief in the parity norm in the course of bargaining.

The evidence for minimum resource theory is generally evidence against minimum power theory. However, in one experiment where players were allowed repeated plays of the same, simple game, there was some indication of increased saliency for pivotal power as opposed to resources. There is some, very slight, additional support in another experiment as well, but this must be qualified by the fact that chance as well as resources influenced the outcome in the experimental game.

A number of experimenters have reported that their subjects behave altruistically, or at least with the kind of restraint that anticompetitive theory suggests. Interestingly enough, there are some benefits for those who do not seek them too aggressively. An accommodating attitude apparently facilitates inclusion in coalitions. Furthermore, where the whole experimental session rather than an individual play of the game becomes the focus of coalition strategy, trust between the players takes on importance. The pursuit of maximum advantage on each play works against a long-run interest which is realized through a stable alliance. Besides this evidence of anticompetitive *style* in play, the *content* prediction that coalitions among equals will form also finds some moderate support.

In some experiments, subjects seem to pay no attention to the variables specified by any of the above theories. Instead, a large number of extraneous factors such as propinquity and loudness of voice seem critical. This seems particularly likely to occur when subjects are confused by the information, rules, and other conditions of the experiment. Such experimental results are likely to appear meaningless and thus, go unreported; they undoubtedly occur more often than an examination of the experiments discussed here would suggest.

It appears that, although there is some support for each theory, one could, if so inclined, create experimental conditions that would support any of them. For minimum resource theory, one would set the stakes moderately high. Players would be allowed to bargain with each other sequentially in an order of their own choosing. Subjects who value competition would be recruited, and the saliency of the parity norm would be increased by an experimental task which precedes the coalition games.

For minimum power theory, the stakes would be made as high as possible. Subjects would be placed in a situation where all players can communicate freely with each other but in an orderly fashion and without time pressure. Subjects would not know each other before, nor be likely to have contact after the experiment. They would be kept from forming stable relationships during the experiment by rotating them in different groups.

For anticompetitive theory, the stakes would be minimal. Decorum would be emphasized in the experimenter's conduct. Subjects who are already acquainted with each other and have prospects for future contact would be used. Subjects would also be those more likely to find competitive bargaining threatening to social relationships, for example, girls rather than boys.

For utter-confusion theory, the stakes would be kept small between alternative coalitions. The difference between being included in some coalition and being excluded entirely would be made large. Subjects would be unsophisticated and the rules and information presented complicated. They would not know each other nor be allowed to form relationships in the course of the experiment. Communication between them would be difficult and time pressure to form coalitions would be great.

This review, like any other, raises rather than answers questions. The "advice" to coalition theorists given here should be regarded as hypotheses concerning the condition under which various assumptions will hold. These assumptions are social-psychological ones, they suggest expectations and motives which the participants will have. But these characteristics are clearly not constant ones; they vary from situation to situation. We have suggested some conditions for some assumptions; these are the ones made salient by the experiments reviewed. Future experiments will reveal many others.

REFERENCES

Bond, J. R., and Vinacke, W. E. (1961). *Sociometry* **24**, 61–75.
Borgatta, E. F., and Borgatta, M. L. (1962). *Social Forces* **41**, 68–77.
Borgatta, M. L. (1961). *J. Social Psychol.* **55**, 287–300.
Borgatta, M. L., and Borgatta, E. F. (1963). *J. Social Psychol.* **60**, 319–326.
Caplow, T. (1956). *Am. Social Rev.* **21**, 489–493.
Caplow, T. (1959). *Am. J. Social.* **64**, 488–493.
Chaney, M. V., and Vinacke, W. E. (1960). *J. Abnormal Soc. Psychol.* **60**, 175–181.
Gamson, W. A. (1961a). *Am. Social Rev.* **26**, 373–382.
Gamson, W. A. (1961b). *Am. Social Rev.* **26**, 565–573.
Harsanyi, J. C. (1963). *Intern. Econ. Rev.* **4**, 194–220.
Hoffman, P. J., Festinger, L., and Lawrence, D. (1954). *In* "Decision Processes" (R. M. Thrall, C. H. Coombs, and R. L. Davis, eds.), Wiley, New York.
Homans, G. C. (1961). "Social Behavior: Its Elementary Forms." Harcourt, Brace and World, New York.
Kalisch, G. K., Milnor, J. W., Nash, J. F., and Nering, E. D. (1954). *In* "Decision Processes" (R. M. Thrall, C. H. Coombs, and R. L. Davis, eds.), Wiley, New York.
Kelley, H. H., and Arrowood, A. J. (1960). *Sociometry* **23**, 231–244.
Lieberman, B. (1962). *In* "Mathematical Methods in Small-Group Processes," (J. H. Criswell, H. Solomon, and P. Suppes, eds.), Stanford Univ. Press, Stanford.
Lieberman, B. (1963). Research Memorandum, S.P. 105 Dept. of Psychol. State Univ. of N.Y. at Stony Brook.
Luce, R. D. (1954). *Ann. Math.* **59**, 357–366.
Luce, R. D., and Raiffa, H. (1957). "Games and Decisions," Wiley, New York.
Mills, T. M. (1953). *Am. Social. Rev.* **18**, 351–357.

Mills, T. M. (1954). *Am. Social Rev.* **19,** 657–667.
Rapoport, A., and Orwant, C. (1962). *Behav. Sci.* **7,** 1–37.
Riker, W. (1962). "The Theory of Political Coalitions," Yale Univ. Press, New Haven, Connecticut.
Schelling, T. C. (1958). *J. Conflict Resolution* **2,** 203–264.
Shapley, L. S. (1953). *Ann. Math. Studies* **28,** 307–317.
Shapley, L. S., and Shubik, M. (1954). *Am. Pol. Sci. Rev.* **48,** 787–792.
Simmel, G. (1950). "The Sociology of George Simmel" (Kurt H. Wolff, Translator), The Free Press, Glencoe, Illinois.
Strodtbeck, F. L. (1954). *Am. Social Rev.* **19,** 23–29.
Stryker, S., and Psathas, G. (1960). *Sociometry* **23,** 217–230.
Thibaut, J. W., and Kelley, H. H. (1959). "The Social Psychology of Groups," Wiley, New York.
Uesugi, T. K., and Vinacke, W. E. (1963). *Sociometry* **26,** 75–88.
Vinacke, W. E. (1959). *Sociometry* **22,** 343–360.
Vinacke, W. E. (1962). Power, Strategy, and the Formation of Coalitions in Triads Under Four Incentive Conditions. Tech. Rept. 1, University of Hawaii.
Vinacke, W. E. (1963). Intra-Group Power Relations, Strategy, and Decisions in Inter-Triad Competition, Tech. Rept. 4, University of Hawaii.
Vinacke, W. E., and Arkoff, A. (1957). *Am. Sociol. Rev.* **22,** 406–414.
Vinacke, W. E., and Gullickson, G. R. (1963). Age and Sex Differences in the Formation of Coalitions, Tech. Rept. 3, University of Hawaii.
Vinacke, W. E., and Stanley, S. (1962). Strategy in a Masculine Quiz Game, Tech. Rept. 2, University of Hawaii.
Willis, R. H. (1962). *Sociometry* **25,** 358–376.

COMMUNICATION NETWORKS

Marvin E. Shaw

DEPARTMENT OF PSYCHOLOGY
UNIVERSITY OF FLORIDA
GAINESVILLE, FLORIDA

I. Introduction

Communication lies at the heart of the group interaction process. No group, whether an informal or formal organization such as an industrial unit, governmental body, or military group, can function effectively unless its members can communicate with facility. One major function of a chain of command is to provide channels of communication extending from the top downward throughout the group structure. The free flow of information (factual knowledge, ideas, technical know-how, feelings) among various members of a group determines to a large extent the efficiency of the group and the satisfaction of its members.

Administrative personnel often assume that the optimum pattern of communication for a given group or organization can be derived from the requirements of the task. Bavelas (1948, 1950) noted this assumption and raised several questions about the effects of fixed communication patterns upon group process. Do some communication networks have structural properties that limit group efficiency? What effects can such structural properties have upon problem-solving effectiveness, organizational development, leadership emergence, the ability of the group to adapt successfully to sudden changes in the environment? Bavelas also suggested a technique for investigating these questions in the laboratory. As a consequence of his work, extensive research has been carried out to analyze the relationships among structural properties of groups (communication networks) and group process variables.

This chapter reviews several of these studies and attempts an integration by means of certain theoretical constructs. Section II reviews the methodology employed in the research on communication networks and considers some of the structural properties of these networks. Section III summarizes the major findings of experimental investigations of the effects of networks on group process. Section IV explicates theoretical constructs advanced to explain network effects. In Section V an attempt is made to relate these theoretical constructs to specific experimental results and to concepts that have been proposed by other experimenters. Section VI summarizes the present state of knowledge and suggests some areas where further research is badly needed.

II. Research Methodology

A. METHODS OF IMPOSING COMMUNICATION PATTERNS

Although the experimental method suggested by Bavelas is simple, it allows for maximum control of the communication structure. Group members are placed in cubicles which are interconnected by means of slots in the walls through which written messages can be passed. Slots may be closed to create any selected communication structure. Each cubicle is fitted with a silent switch which controls a signal light and a timer located at the experimenter's desk. The most common procedure has been to permit free (continuous) communication within limits imposed by the network. However, some investigators (Christie *et al.*, 1952; Schein, 1958) have used an "action quantization" procedure that restricted each subject to single, addressed messages transmitted at specified times. Also, some investigators substituted an intercom system for the slots—written messages system (Heise and Miller, 1951).

B. NETWORK CHARACTERISTICS

Figure 1 shows communication networks that have been studied experimentally. The dots represent persons or positions in the network, and the lines represent communication channels (slots) between positions. Most channels are symmetrical (two-way); asymmetrical (one-way) channels are indicated by arrows. The labels are arbitrary designations, intended only to facilitate identification. It will be noted that the same label is used for similar networks for groups of different sizes, although there has been some criticism that networks of different sizes are not comparable. For

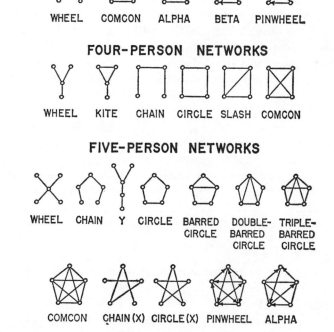

FIG. 1. Communication networks used in experimental investigations. Dots represent positions, lines represent communication channels, and arrows indicate one-way channels.

example, Glanzer and Glaser (1961) asked why the three-person "wheel" could not be called "chain" and compared to the four- and five-person chains. They apparently could see no difference between the three-person wheel and the larger chains. Actually, there is good reason to label it "wheel" and compare it with the larger wheels rather than chains. The essential characteristic of a wheel network is that one person communicates with all others, whereas all other members communicate only with this central person.

The three-person wheel in Fig. 1 clearly fits this description. In a chain, on the other hand, there are two isolates (end-persons) who communicate with only one other (but different) person in the group and two or more persons in the group must serve as message relayers in order to disseminate information throughout the group. The three-person wheel does not have these features and, therefore, is clearly more comparable to the larger wheels than to the larger chains. Similar considerations are involved in the labeling of other networks. When the group size is decreased, different networks do not necessarily coalesce into a single pattern, as Glanzer and Glaser suppose; rather, certain networks found with larger groups cannot be formed with smaller groups.

One further comment regarding the networks shown in Fig. 1. According to the Bavelas analysis, the spatial arrangement of positions is of no consequence; it is the relationships among positions that is important. Two of the networks shown in Fig. 1 depart from this conception: the chain (X) and the circle (X) used by Christie *et al.* (1952).

C. STRUCTURAL INDICES

It has seemed desirable to quantify the structural properties of networks to facilitate the analysis of their effects on group behavior. Bavelas (1950) suggested a "centrality index" as a measure of the differences between networks and positions within networks, based upon the distance, in communication links, between any two positions in the network. Other suggested indices include "relative peripherality" (Leavitt, 1951) and "independence" (Shaw, 1954b). Each of these indices merits consideration.

1. Centrality Indices

In formulating the centrality measures, Bavelas (1950) first defined the *sum of distances* $(d_{x,y})$ for a given position as the minimum number of communication links that must be crossed in order for that position to communicate with all other positions in the group. The individual sums of distances in a network may be summed to obtain a sum of distances for the network $(\Sigma d_{x,y})$. Comparisons among networks may then be made on the basis of $\Sigma d_{x,y}$. However, to make comparisons among positions within a network, a relative measure (called relative centrality) was suggested. This measure is computed as the ratio of the network sum of distances to the sum of distances for the given position. Thus,

$$\text{Relative centrality} = \frac{\Sigma d_{x,y}}{d_{x,y}}$$

Leavitt (1951), working with Bavelas, computed a centrality index for the group by summing the relative centralities of all positions in the network.

In general, total centrality for networks has been found to correlate poorly with group performance and satisfaction (Shaw, 1954a,b), although relative centrality has been found to account moderately well for positional differences in performance and satisfaction (Leavitt, 1951; Shaw, 1954a). However, relative centrality does not reflect differences among positions in similar networks of different sizes, nor does it permit easy comparisons among positions in different networks. Leavitt (1951) noted the first inadequacy and proposed an index of relative peripherality as an alternate to relative centrality; Shaw (1954b) pointed to the second difficulty and attempted to overcome it by an independence index. These indices are described below.

2. Peripherality Indices

The relative peripherality of any position in a network is the difference between the relative centrality of that position and the relative centrality of the most central position in that network. A total peripherality index for the network may be computed by adding all the individual peripheralities in the network.

Leavitt believed peripherality is related to group behavior variables via differences among positions in answer-getting potentials which structure group members' perceptions of their roles in the group. The relative peripherality index reflects differences in position independence, which in turn determine behavioral differences.

Since relative peripherality and relative centrality are perfectly correlated (negatively) within a given network, the two indices relate equally well to positional differences in performance and satisfaction. The advantage of peripherality over centrality lies in the greater comparability among positions in networks of different sizes. However, two positions in different networks having the same relative peripherality index do not necessarily produce the same behavior. Nor do two positions having different peripherality indices necessarily give rise to different behaviors. Likewise, the total peripherality index does not adequately reflect differences among networks. (The same statements hold, of course, for the centrality indices.) The independence index was developed in an attempt to overcome some of these shortcomings.

3. The Independence Index

Since the centrality-peripherality indices are imperfectly correlated with behavioral measures, there clearly are some important characteristics of networks and positions that are not reflected by these measures. Shaw (1954b) proposed that it is necessary to determine what characteristics do contribute to position independence. On a logical basis these features seemed to be (a) the number of channels available to a given position, (b) the total number of channels in the network, and (c) the number of positions for which a given position must relay information. The independence index (I index) for any one position was designed to reflect the weighted contributions of these various characteristics, as shown by the formula:

$$I = n + \left[n \left(1 - \frac{n}{N} \right) \right] + \log R_d + \log R_i$$

where

$n =$ number of channels available to the given position

$N =$ number of channels in a completely interconnected network of the same size

$R_d =$ number of positions for which the particular position must serve as a direct relayer (i.e., directly connected to the position served)

$R_i =$ number of positions for which the position must serve as an indirect relayer (i.e., one or more links removed from the position served)

The I index has been shown to be better than either the centrality or the peripherality index in the sense that it makes possible direct comparisons among positions in different networks (Shaw, 1954b, 1955a). However, no satisfactory method of computing the total independence in a network has been found, since the mere summation of positional values does not correlate highly with behavioral differences among networks.

In summary, the various structural indices described thus far have some explanatory value with regard to differences among positions within networks, but are inadequate to predict or explain differences among different networks.[1] Consequently, more general processes have been invoked as explanatory concepts. Although several such concepts have been described by various writers, this chapter will attempt to explain group behavior in communication networks in terms of two underlying processes

---

[1] For other mathematical analyses, see Flament (1958c), Glanzer and Glaser (1959), and Luce *et al.* (1953).

which have been labeled "independence" and "saturation." Before describing these concepts, however, a consideration of the effects of networks upon group process is helpful.

III. Effects of Networks upon Group Process

This section reviews the initial studies conducted in the Group Networks Laboratory at MIT and selected follow-up experiments to demonstrate that communication networks are related to group behavior in systematic ways.

A. THE MIT EXPERIMENTS

The initial studies are reported in articles by Bavelas (1950), Bavelas and Barrett (1951), Leavitt (1951), and Christie et al. (1952). The experiment reported by Leavitt is representative of the approach described in the first three articles. He carried out his investigation in order to explore the relationship between the behavior of small groups and the patterns of communication in which the groups operate. Leavitt examined the effects of the five-man circle, chain, Y, and wheel (Fig. 1) on problem-solving effectiveness, satisfaction, and organization characteristics of the group. The tasks were extremely simple symbol-identification problems. Each member in the group was given a card containing a number of symbols such as a square, a diamond, an asterisk, etc. Only one symbol appeared on each and every member's card. The task was to identify this commonly held symbol. Measures of performance were time taken to solve the problem, errors, and number of messages sent. Networks did not differ in average time to solve, but the circle was slower than the other patterns when the measure was the single, fastest, correct trial. The circle groups made the greatest number of errors (16.6), the Y the smallest number (2.6), and the chain and wheel an intermediate number (9.8 in each case). The circle required considerably more messages than did the other networks.

Satisfaction of members was determined by means of a questionnaire. Circle members reported greatest satisfaction, wheel members least, with chain and Y members intermediate. Leadership emergence was also measured by questionnaire. The total frequency of persons named as leaders and the unanimity of opinion as to who was the leader, increased in the order: circle, chain, Y, wheel. For example, 23 of the 25 persons in the wheel named a leader and all agreed that he was the person in the most central position, whereas only 13 of the 25 persons in the circle named a leader, and those named were scattered among all positions in the circle.

Operational methods (i.e., organizational patterns) used by the wheel, Y, and chain were such that the information was funneled to the central position, where the decision was made and sent out to the peripheral positions. (Hereafter this organizational pattern will be referred to as a centralized organization.) The circle showed no consistent, operational organization.

With regard to individual positions in the network, persons in the more central positions generally required less time to solve the problem, sent more messages, made fewer errors, were better satisfied, and were named leader more often than persons in the more peripheral positions.

Leavitt's findings clearly demonstrated a systematic relationship between the communication network imposed upon the group and the behavior of the group members. The experiments reported by Bavelas (1950) and by Bavelas and Barrett (1951) were carried out for essentially the same purpose, and their findings generally agree with those obtained by Leavitt. The experiments conducted by Christie et al. (1952, 1956), however, had a rather different purpose. They were concerned with the effects of networks upon the information-handling process, learning in networks, and the testing of mathematical models.

Christie and associates (1952) investigated the effects of five-person networks: circle, circle (X), chain, chain (X), pinwheel, barred circle, wheel, comcon, and alpha (see Fig. 1). The tasks assigned to the groups were number-identification problems, similar to the symbol-identification task used by Leavitt. An action-quantized procedure was used; that is, all subjects prepared messages simultaneously and transmitted them at specified times. On a given exchange, each group member was permitted to send a single message to one other group member. In this experiment, the investigators were interested primarily in testing certain mathematical models; hence, not all data were presented. However, it is clear that the geometrical arrangement of the circle and chain networks had little or no effect on the group process; no differences in time scores and other behavioral measures between the circle and circle (X) or between the chain and chain (X) were observed. With regard to time, networks were ordered (from fastest to slowest) as follows: chain, pinwheel, circle, comcon. The probability of minimum solution (task completion with the smallest number of message exchanges possible in a given network) was found to be greatest in the chain and smallest in the pinwheel. The alpha, barred circle, and wheel networks were about the same on this measure, while the circle was somewhat better and the comcon worse than this group of networks.

In a separate publication, Christie (1954) reported data concerned with the effects of learning in the comcon, circle, chain, and pinwheel networks. The task was reconstruction of a number list, and the performance criterion was number of communication acts (i.e., message exchanges) required for solution. All networks did better than chance from the beginning, but only the chain and the circle showed significant learning. Since task solution required a minimum of five message exchanges in the chain, its absolute performance was poor in comparison with each of the other networks. The circle groups, on the other hand, achieved a high level of efficiency in comparison with other networks.[2]

These early experiments demonstrated quite clearly that the pattern of communication imposed upon a group is an important determinant of the behavior of that group. However, the findings also indicated that the particular relationship between communication pattern and group behavior depends in part upon other variables. The MIT studies stimulated a considerable amount of research designed to examine the effects of these other variables upon network-group behavior relationships, and to test various theoretical interpretations of the underlying processes. A review of selected experiments will reveal the general conclusions that may be drawn from these follow-up investigations.

B. SELECTED FOLLOW-UP INVESTIGATIONS

The experiments described in this section were selected to demonstrate two general conclusions that can be drawn from the many communication network studies: (a) the major differences in group performance and satisfaction are between the centralized (wheel, Y, chain) and decentralized (comcon, circle) networks; and (b) the direction of these differences in group performance depends upon the kind of task assigned to the group.

Leavitt's experiment demonstrated differences among networks on the completion of one kind of task (symbol identification) under noise-free conditions. Heise and Miller (1951) extended this design by varying the intelligibility of the message and the type of problem given the group. They studied the three-person networks shown in Fig. 1, using as tasks word-construction problems, sentence-construction problems, and anagrams. Each problem was attempted in each network under three conditions of intelligibility. Speech, instead of written messages, was the method of communication. Intelligibility of the message was manipulated by controlling the relative intensities of speech and noise. Their results showed that for the word-construction problems the comcon was the most efficient, the wheel was intermediate, and the pinwheel was by far the least efficient network. For the sentence-construction problems, the results were similar except that the wheel replaced the comcon as the most efficient network. There were no marked differences in efficiency for the anagram problems. Noise generally accentuated differences for the first two kinds of tasks but not for the anagram problems.

Unfortunately, Heise and Miller used only three undergraduate sub-

[2] It is interesting to note that Leavitt and Knight (1963) recently concluded, on purely theoretical grounds, that the circle should be the most efficient network.

jects who went through all conditions for the word problem. Two of these subjects continued through the sentence problem with a new recruit as the third member, while the subjects for the anagram problems consisted of two groups of three graduate students each. Therefore, no statistical tests of the reliability of the obtained differences was possible. Since there are individual differences in group performance, we do not know to what extent the observed differences were due to the experimental variables or to individual differences. The large differences in the relationship between networks and group-effectiveness measures (time and errors) as a function of the task, however, suggest strongly that the kind of network that is most efficient depends upon the kind of task faced by the group.

This conclusion is also indicated by the findings in two experiments by Shaw (1954a,b). Leavitt, it will be recalled, interpreted his results in terms of centrality-peripherality indices which were supposed to reflect each position's accessibility to information. The first experiment reported by Shaw was designed to test this interpretation. On the basis of Leavitt's argument, it seemed reasonable to suppose that increasing the information input from external sources (i.e., the experimenter) should have the same effect upon a position as increasing the centrality of that position. For this purpose, the effects of four-person wheel, slash, and circle networks (see Fig. 1) on group effectiveness in solving arithmetic problems were examined. Although quite simple, these problems required more than the mere collation of information required by the symbol-identification task used by Leavitt. For half of the groups in each network the necessary information was distributed equally among group members (as Leavitt did), whereas for the other groups, the information was distributed unequally. In the unequal distribution condition, one of the most peripheral positions in each network was given five units of information, whereas all other positions were given one unit of information each.

Leavitt's measure of performance, the single fastest correct trial, indicated no differences among networks. However, the total time required to complete the task did reveal significant differences, although in a complicated manner. Analysis of variance revealed a significant trials $\times$ networks $\times$ distribution interaction; analysis of the interaction means showed that significant differences among networks occurred only on the third (and last) trial. The circle was fastest, the slash next fastest, and the wheel the slowest of the three patterns, with the difference between the circle and the other patterns being greatest with unequal distribution of information. For overall situational conditions the order was circle, slash, wheel—just the opposite of that expected from Leavitt's results. There were no differences among networks in number of errors, although the ability to correct errors (corrective power of the network) was greatest for the circle, next for slash, and least for the wheel network—again contrary to expectations.

Findings with respect to number of messages, satisfaction, and leadership emergence were in general agreement with Leavitt's results.

All groups used either the centralized organization or "each-to-all" organization (all information sent to all group members and then each member solved the problem independently). Centralized organization was used by 73% of the wheel, 7% of the slash, 'and 7% of the circle groups. Each-to-all organization was used by 27% of the wheel, 93% of the slash, and 93% of the circle groups.

The most striking result of the unequal-distribution-of-information experiment was the reversal of effectiveness of the wheel and circle networks as compared with Leavitt's results. The most obvious difference in the two experiments was the greater complexity of the problems employed in the later study. Two observations suggested that task differences probably accounted for the reversal. First, the central person in the wheel was overloaded by the many communication demands of the situation, and second, persons in the peripheral positions were unwilling merely to accept a solution offered by the central person. Both of these effects presumably were more likely to occur with complex than with simple tasks. However, since there were several other differences between the Shaw and Leavitt experiments, an experiment (Shaw, 1954c) was carried out to demonstrate the effects of the task variable in which the three-person wheel and comcon (Fig. 1) were compared using symbol-identification and arithmetic problems as tasks. Although the difference was not statistically reliable, the wheel groups required less time than did the comcon with the relatively easy symbol identification problems, whereas the comcon required less time than did the wheel with the more complex arithmetic problems. There were no differences in number of errors on the identification problems, but the wheel made more errors than did the comcon on the arithmetic problems.

Numerous other investigators have reported results which support the general conclusions that the major differences are between the centralized and decentralized networks, and that the direction of such differences is contingent upon the kind of task. First, let us consider studies employing fairly simple group tasks. Using symbol identification problems, Guetzkow and Simon (1955) investigated the five-person wheel, circle, and comcon networks shown in Fig. 1. They were interested primarily in the effects of free communication between trials for organizational purposes (discussed later), but they also reported that the wheel was faster than the circle, with the comcon intermediate in speed.

Many other investigations using the symbol identification task might also be mentioned. Cohen et al. (1961) found that five-person wheel groups took less time to solve identification problems, made fewer answer changes and fewer final errors, sent fewer messages, and recognized a leader more frequently than did circle groups. Both groups improved with practice, but wheel groups improved more than circle groups did. Networks did not produce overall differences in satisfaction, but central positions were better satisfied than peripheral positions. Hirota (1953) repeated Leavitt's experiment using Japanese subjects. The wheel required less time to solve, followed by the Y, circle, and chain, in that order; however, differences were not statistically reliable. Hirota also reported positional differences in frequency of communication and leadership emergence which agreed with Leavitt's findings. In a cross-cultural study, Mohanna and Argyle (1960) repeated the portion of Leavitt's experiment that made use the wheel and circle networks. Leavitt's results were confirmed in that the wheel was found to be superior to the circle in time required, number of messages required, and errors made.

Studies using more complex problems usually found the decentralized networks more effective. In Holland, Mulder (1960) examined the effects of four-person wheel and circle networks on the solution of arithmetic problems. Overall, but especially in their early trials, the circle groups required less time per problem than the wheel groups. However, contrary to findings reported in this country (Shaw and Rothschild, 1956), with practice the wheel groups became relatively more efficient than the circle networks. The studies using sentence- and word-construction tasks (Heise and Miller, 1951) and those using noisy marbles (Macy *et al.*, 1953) also showed that more decentralized networks are more efficient than centralized networks when solving even moderately complex problems (Flament, 1956, 1958b; Shaw *et al.*, 1957).

C. Some General Conclusions Concerning the Effects of Networks upon Group Process

The evidence strongly supports the generalization that the major network difference is between centralized (e.g., wheel, chain, Y) and decentralized (e.g., circle, comcon) networks, and that the direction of this difference is determined in part by the degree of complexity of the task. It is instructive to tabulate the number of comparisons showing specified differences between centralized and decentralized networks with simple and with more complex problems. The results of one such tabulation are shown in Table I. The "simple problems" classification includes tasks that require the mere collation of information (symbol-, letter-, color-identification tasks). The "complex problems" classification includes tasks that require some data operation procedures after the information has been collected in one place (arithmetic, word arrangement, sentence construc-

TABLE I
NUMBER OF COMPARISONS SHOWING DIFFERENCES BETWEEN CENTRALIZED
(WHEEL, CHAIN, Y) AND DECENTRALIZED (CIRCLE, COMCON)
NETWORKS AS A FUNCTION OF TASK COMPLEXITY

	Simple problems[a]	Complex problems[b]	Total
Time			
Centralized faster	14	0	14
Decentralized faster	4	18	22
Messages			
Centralized sent more	0	1	1
Decentralized sent more	18	17	35
Errors			
Centralized made more	0	6	6
Decentralized made more	9	1	10
No difference	1	3	4
Satisfaction			
Centralized higher	1	1	2
Decentralized higher	7	10	17

[a] Simple problems: symbol- , letter- , number- , and color-identification tasks.
[b] Complex problems: arithmetic, word arrangement, sentence construction, and discussion problems.

tion, and discussion problems).[3] A comparison is a single difference in means (as reported in the literature) between a centralized and a decentralized network, without regard to level of significance. For example, if an experiment involved three centralized and one decentralized network (as did Leavitt's study), three comparisons were made.

Examination of Table I shows that with simple problems the more centralized network required less time than the decentralized network on 14 of the 18 comparisons, whereas, with more complex problems, the decentralized required less time than the centralized network on every comparison made.[4] Errors show the same pattern, but differences are less

[3] This is a rough classificaion, and admittedly does not do justice to the complexity variable. The categorical grouping of tasks is not intended to deny the essential continuity of the complexity dimension.

[4] Eighteen different experiments were involved in this tabulation. Since a single experiment sometimes contributed more than one comparison, there is some lack of independence among scores in Table I. To overcome this, one comparison was drawn from each experiment. The results of this procedure showed the centralized network faster than the decentralized in 6 of 8 experiments using simple problems, whereas the decentralized network was faster in 10 of 10 experiments using complex problems. This difference is highly reliable ($\chi^2 = 11.26$, $p < .001$).

consistent than for time scores. With very few exceptions, individuals in decentralized networks are more active (send more messages) and are better satisfied than are persons in centralized networks, regardless of kind of task. Differences in activity are probably due merely to the fact that centralized have fewer channels than decentralized networks, as suggested by Glanzer and Glaser (1961). Organizational differences were not included in Table I because relatively few investigators examined this aspect in any systematic way. In most instances, however, centralized networks develop centralized organizations (i.e., all members send their information to one member who solves the problem and sends the answer to other members). Decentralized networks develop either each-to-all or centralized organizations about equally.

Numerous other variables have been examined in relation to group behavior in communication networks. The effects of these other variables generally raised or lowered the behavioral level of groups across all networks, either equally or in a manner which increased the differences among networks. For this reason, it is believed that these effects can be interpreted in terms of the same explanatory concepts used to explain the results presented thus far. Therefore, the independence and saturation constructs will be explained more fully before considering the effects of additional variables.

IV. Explanatory Concepts

It has been suggested (see Section II, C, 3) that the various effects of communication networks upon group behavior can be accounted for by two general processes labeled "independence" (Leavitt, 1951; Shaw, 1954b) and "saturation" (Gilchrist et al., 1954).[5] Further, it is believed that the various explanations advanced by other investigators can be subsumed under one of these two more general processes.

A. INDEPENDENCE

The concept of independence was introduced by Leavitt (1951) to account for differences among network positions. He pointed to the differences in answer-getting potential among positions and suggested that the group members' perceptions of these differences structure their perceptions of their own roles in the group. In the wheel, for example, group members readily perceive the degree of information accessibility and the nature of their own roles. The central person is autonomous and controls the group.

[5] The labels applied to these two classes of intervening processes are unimportant. Independence and saturation were chosen because of the author's familiarity with them; however, "autonomy" or "self-realization" would be just as acceptable as independence, and "vulnerability" or "demands" as acceptable as saturation.

In the circle, on the other hand, any given group member is not exclusively dependent upon anyone else in the net, and his role is not clearly different from anyone else's role. Thus, his action is not as greatly controlled by others. Morale is higher with greater independence because independence permits the gratification of the culturally supported needs for autonomy, recognition, and achievement. Independence bears a more direct relationship to group performance via its organizational influences upon the group. Leavitt concluded, "In summary, then, it is our feeling that centrality determines behavior by limiting independence of action, thus producing differences in activity, accuracy, satisfaction, leadership, recognition of pattern, and other behavioral characteristics" (Leavitt, 1951, p. 49).

While the general notion of independence of action is useful, it has become clear that the original formulation is too limited. As stated earlier, structural indices such as centrality, relative peripherality, and the I index do not appear to be highly valid measures of independence as reflected by measures of performance and satisfaction. As a consequence of the experimental results obtained from many studies, it is now clear that the concept of independence must be expanded to include freedom from all restrictions on action. We shall use the term "independence," then, to refer to the degree of freedom with which an individual may function in the group. A person's independence of action may be influenced not only by accessibility of information but also by the actions of others in the group, by situational factors (such as communication "noise," reinforcement, kind of task), and by the person's own perceptions and cognitions regarding the overall situation. The concepts of "autonomy" (Trow, 1957) and "exercise of power" (Mulder, 1958, 1959a) are similar to independence.

The author's own view is that independence, as defined above, is related to both performance and satisfaction; however, independence probably has a greater effect on satisfaction than on performance. We agree with Leavitt (1951) that its effect on member satisfaction probably is due to the fulfillment of culturally approved needs for autonomy, recognition, and achievement. This chapter will try to show, however, that the effect of independence upon performance is due, not to its organizational influences, but to the individual's willingness and ability to perform under the more autonomous conditions. That is, lowered independence not only directly limits the possibilities for action (hence performance), but also reduces the person's willingness to perform at his optimum level.

B. SATURATION

In addition to independence, a second process operates in group situations to influence group performance and satisfaction. This process, called "saturation," was first described by Gilchrist *et al.* (1954). They observed that when the number of required messages for a given position passed a certain optimal level, communication requirements began to counteract the effects of position centrality. Two kinds of saturation were distinguished: "channel saturation," which refers to the number of channels with which a position must deal, and "message unit saturation," which refers to the number of messages the position must handle. These two kinds of saturation, of course, are correlated. Each of these main classes may be broken down further into "input" and "output" saturation. Total saturation experienced by a position is the sum of all the input and output requirements placed upon that position.

Like the original formulation of independence, this notion of saturation is too limited. The requirements placed upon the position, from whatever source, call for action by the individual who occupies that position. Therefore, the total saturation of a position is the result not only of the communication requirements, but also of the other requirements in the situation, such as data manipulation procedures that are necessary for task completion. Requirements of this sort are essentially those referred to as "task demands" by Lanzetta and Roby (1956a,b, 1957). Saturation, then, refers to the total requirements placed upon an individual in a given position in the network. It varies with communication demands and task demands. Communication demands are determined by the number of channels available to the position, the task information to be transmitted, and the demands imposed by the vagaries of the other members who have access to that position's channels. Task demands are determined by the requirements of the task, per se, and by interferences that must be overcome in the process of task solution.

Several explanatory concepts have been suggested by other investigators that are similar to saturation. The notion of "vulnerability" (Mulder, 1959b, 1960) is essentially the same as saturation; organizational arrangements (Guetzkow and Simon, 1955; Guetzkow and Dill, 1957), task demands (Lanzetta and Roby, 1956a,b, 1957; Roby and Lanzetta, 1956), and "inadequation" (Flament, 1958a,b) may be regarded as special cases of saturation.

Group effectiveness varies inversely with saturation. The greater the saturation the less efficient the group's performance.

C. NETWORK AND TASK EFFECTS IN TERMS OF INDEPENDENCE AND SATURATION

It is proposed, then, that independence and saturation processes jointly determine group behavior; variables such as the communication network and kind of task influence group performance and satisfaction through their effects upon these two underlying processes. In Section III, C, evidence was presented indicating that centralized networks are more effective for simple problems, whereas decentralized networks are more effective for complex problems. To what extent can the concepts of independence and saturation help explain these results?

The effects of networks on independence have already been discussed. Persons in peripheral positions in centralized networks have limited freedom of action (hence low independence), while persons in central positions have relatively great freedom (hence high independence). In decentralized networks, by contrast, all positions have approximately equal freedom of action (hence moderate to high independence). Generally speaking, independence is greater in decentralized than in centralized networks. Task complexity has relatively little effect upon independence.

Saturation is determined in part by the communication channels available to a position. Therefore, the central position of a centralized network is more vulnerable to saturation than any position in the decentralized network. Whether this potential saturation occurs, however, depends upon task demands and member demands. When the task is a complex one, the demands upon the central person are greater than when the task is less complex, not only because the communication demands are increased by complexity, but also because data manipulation procedures are more demanding with the more complex tasks. Therefore, the probability that the network will become saturated is greater with complex than with simple tasks, and greater for the centralized than for the decentralized network.

Further, if our assumptions about the effects of independence are correct, this difference in saturation as a function of task complexity should be enhanced by the unwillingness of group members to accept the dictates of the central person when the task is a complex one. With simple identification problems, needs for achievement and recognition can hardly be satisfied by the simple act of noting that the same symbol appears on each of several cards; hence, subjects in a centralized network are typically willing to accept the report of the central person. This should actually reduce saturation in centralized networks relative to decentralized networks because of decreased message requirements. When the task requires data manipulation, however, needs for achievement and recognition can attain some degree of satisfaction through the problem solution process; members therefore are less likely to accept the solution arrived at by the central person. For example, they ask for the information upon which his solution was based. This increases communication demands and, hence, saturation. In decentralized networks the willingness or unwillingness of members to accept the solution of another has relatively little effect on saturation, since each person typically has all the information for solution and often achieves the solution through his own efforts.

In summary, independence is greater in the decentralized than in the centralized network, regardless of the kind of task. Saturation should be less in the centralized than in the decentralized network with simple tasks, but greater in the centralized network with complex tasks. Therefore, member satisfaction should be greater in more centralized positions, but overall satisfaction should be higher in decentralized networks. With simple tasks, the centralized should be more effective than the decentralized networks; whereas with complex tasks, the decentralized should be more efficient than the centralized networks. As we have seen, the experimental data generally agree with these expectations.

The author's feeling is that the effects of network and task variables upon group behavior are adequately accounted for by independence and saturation processes. Section V attempts to interpret the effects of other variables upon group behavior in different networks, again using the concepts of independence and saturation.

V. Independence and Saturation in Relation to Other Experimental Variables

Since it was well known from theoretical analyses and experimental observations that group behavior is influenced by many other variables, in addition to the communication network and kind of task, the question naturally arose whether these other variables influenced behavior differentially in different networks.[6] The numerous studies concerning this general problem may be classified under three broad headings, in terms of whether they deal with: (1) network-related variables, (2) information-input variables, or (3) group-composition variables.

Network-related variables are those that cannot be manipulated without simultaneous modification of some aspect of the communication network. These include size of the group, change of network, and organizational arrangements. Information-input variables are variables relating to amount and kind of information that is available to group members. This class includes noise, information distribution, and reinforcement variables. Group composition variables are concerned with variations in the personality and behavior characteristics of group members. Ascendance, authoritarianism, popularity, and leadership style are group composition variables

---

[6] Contrary to the conclusion drawn by Glanzer and Glaser (1961), the extension of communication network studies to include other (often nonstructural) variables indicates the vitality of this research; few variables produce a monotonic effect upon group process, regardless of variations in other known determinants of group behavior.

that have been studied in communication networks. These investigations will now be reviewed and the findings interpreted in terms of independence and saturation.

A. NETWORK-RELATED VARIABLES

1. Group Size

Most investigators have compared communication networks having similar topological characteristics without regard to the size of the group. For example, it seemed reasonable to assume that a network in which one person can communicate with everyone else in the group, who are themselves unable to communicate directly with each other (the wheel), would have similar effects upon group process regardless of whether three, four, or five persons are in the group. But what do the notions of independence and saturation lead us to expect with regard to differences in group size?

For a given network increased size of the group should decrease the independence of each member, since the mere presence of additional positions would limit, to some extent, each person's freedom of action. On the other hand, the larger the group the greater the saturation, since a larger group means more channels, more messages, and greater member demands. There is no apparent reason to suppose, however, that group size will affect independence and saturation differentially in different networks. Therefore, we would expect that increasing the size of the group would, within a given network, decrease satisfaction and efficiency (as measured by time and error scores). However, these effects should be the same for all networks.

The experimental evidence concerning the effects of group size is limited but consistent. Walker (1954) compared three-, four-, and five-person wheel networks with comcon networks of the same size. Arithmetic problems were assigned as group tasks. The results showed that as size increased: (a) group efficiency, as measured by problem solution times and errors, decreased; (b) group morale, as measured by ratings of satisfaction and by members' sociometric rejections of their own positions, decreased; (c) number of messages increased; and (d) unanimous selection of a leader decreased. Efficiency, satisfaction, and messages transmitted tended to be higher in the comcon than in the wheel, but there was no significant interaction between network and group size.

The findings are similar if we compare the results of several experiments that differed primarily in the size of the groups employed. Lawson (1963a) examined four-person wheel, comcon, and circle networks using the symbol-identification task. He found that the wheels were fastest in time and made fewer errors than the other networks. Circles were slowest and had the highest member satisfaction. These results agreed with those reported by Leavitt (1951) for five-person networks solving symbol-identification problems, and with those reported by Shaw (1954c) for three-person networks with symbol-identification tasks.

It seems clear that size of the group does have an effect on group problem-solving, but this variable does not interact with the communication network variable (at least, this is true for three-, four-, and five-person groups). It is also clear that the findings are in accord with expectations derived from independence and saturation.

2. Change of Network

Randomly assembled groups are composed of individuals with widely different past experiences in naturally occurring communication networks. Variations in behavior due to this factor are usually treated as errors of measurement. For theoretical as well as practical reasons, however, a number of researchers have thought it worthwhile to study the effects of past experience upon group behavior in communication networks.

It is difficult to make specific predictions about the consequences of changing from one network to another in terms of independence and saturation, since the expected effects vary with the particular change introduced. In general, independence and saturation should be unaltered if the new network permits the group to continue operating in the same manner as it did in the old network. However, if the new network requires a change in operational procedure, independence should be decreased and saturation increased by the network change.

This general principle was well demonstrated by Flament (1956) in an experiment designed to study the effects of imposed networks that were either congruent or incongruent with emergent structures. In the first part of the experiment, five-person groups solved seven symbol-identification problems in the comcon network. Those groups that developed a centralized organization (only two did not) were selected for the second part and assigned to one of four conditions: (1) imposed wheel network with emergent leader in the central position; (2) imposed wheel with the emergent leader in a peripheral position; (3) imposed chain with emergent leader in the most central position; and (4) imposed chain with emergent leader in one of the most peripheral positions. Groups were required to solve seven more symbol-identification problems under the new conditions. On the first problem after the new networks were imposed, the wheel groups required less time and fewer messages than the chain groups, and groups with emergent leaders in the central position required less time and fewer messages than groups with the emergent leader in a peripheral position. These differences tended to disappear with practice in the new situation. Satisfaction was higher in both the wheel and the chain when the emergent leader was in the central position than when he was in a peripheral position. In short, when the new network prevented the group from functioning as it had in the previous network, independence presumably was decreased (leading to lowered satisfaction). Saturation apparently was increased (leading to reduced efficiency).

The results of several other studies also supported this interpretation. Lawson (1961) evaluated the effects of training a group in one network, shifting to a different network, and returning to the original network. Four experimental and two control conditions were established: wheel-comcon-wheel-wheel (WCWW), wheel-wheel-comcon-wheel (WWCW), comcon-comcon-wheel-comcon (CCWC), comcon-wheel-comcon-comcon (CWCC), wheel-wheel-wheel-wheel (WWWW), and comcon-comcon-comcon-comcon (CCCC). In the WCWW condition, for example, groups worked in the wheel on day 1, in the comcon on day 2, and in the wheel on days 3 and 4. The problems to be solved were arithmetic problems. In general, we would expect that changes in networks would be accompanied by changes in independence and saturation, thus producing variations in satisfaction and efficiency. The present analysis suggests, further, that the change from the comcon to the wheel would have greater effects on these intervening processes than changing from the wheel to the comcon network. (The comcon would permit the group to continue functioning as before, whereas the wheel would not necessarily allow this.) The results generally supported these expectations. Group performance and satisfaction improved when the group was changed from the wheel to the comcon, and dropped when the change was from comcon to wheel. It is interesting to note that satisfaction dropped to its lowest point in the WCWW groups on day 3. Presumably, perceived independence in the wheel was reduced by contrast to the relative freedom experienced in the comcon on day 2.

The extensive work of Cohen and associates (summarized by Cohen, 1961, 1962) also lends credence to the independence-saturation hypothesis. These experiments demonstrated that when groups are changed from one network to another they continue the same operational procedures developed in the old network if the new network makes this possible. In one experiment, Cohen and Bennis (1961) explored the effects of changes in networks upon leader continuity. Five-person groups were assigned to one of the following conditions: wheel-circle, circle-wheel, wheel-wheel, and circle-circle. Each group attempted 30 symbol-identification problems in the first network, followed by 30 in the second network. After network change, groups in the wheel-circle condition developed chain problem-solving systems; groups in the circle-wheel and wheel-wheel conditions developed centralized problem-solving systems; and circle-circle groups developed each-to-all problem-solving systems. In the wheel-circle groups, the central person in the wheel remained in the central position in the emergent chain in only one of eight groups. This latter finding led to a second experiment in which groups in the wheel-circle condition were permitted to choose the person to occupy the central position in the wheel after having completed 15 symbol-identification problems. Organizational development after network change was the same as in the first experiment; however, the elected center of the wheel continued in the central position in the emergent chain in eight of the ten groups tested.

In another study using the same general design, Cohen and associates (1962) found similar results with regard to organization and leadership continuity. They reported, in addition, that circle groups with prior experience in wheel networks were better satisfied than those groups that had been in circle networks throughout the experiment. Groups that had been in the wheel throughout the experiment were better satisfied than groups that were changed from circle to wheel networks. Cohen et al. were surprised by these findings, since they had supposed that groups in a changed network would show greater similarities in satisfactions to those of prior networks. A consideration of independence as perceived by group members would have eliminated this surprise. When a group is changed from a restrictive network like the wheel to a less restrictive network like the circle, the amount of experienced freedom of action is undoubtedly greater (by contrast with the previous situation) than when the group has been in the less restrictive network throughout the experiment. Their perceived independence is therefore greater, and higher satisfaction is expected. The reverse is true for the circle to wheel groups. This interpretation is essentially the same as that offered by Cohen et al. to account for their findings, although they used the term "relative deprivation" rather than "perceived independence."

In a final report, Cohen and Bennis (1962) described an experiment comparing five-person groups working in the comcon network throughout the experiment with groups that were changed to the comcon after thirty trials in the wheel network. Symbol-identification problems were used. The results revealed that the groups that had had prior experience in the wheel developed centralized problem-solving systems when changed to the comcon, whereas groups working only in the comcon network developed each-to-all problem-solving systems. They concluded that the problem-solving systems that are adopted in antecedent networks are continued after network change if they are the more efficient systems, and if the new network permits the adaptation of the old system to the new situation.

The author cannot agree that only efficient problem-solving systems will be continued after network change. However, the saturation concept assumes only that continuation of a prior problem-solving system will not affect saturation, whereas forced change to a new system will increase saturation. The Cohen studies are important in demonstrating that a prior problem-solving system will be continued after network change if the new network permits.

In summary, when changes in the network suggest changes in independence and saturation, the expected variations in group satisfaction and performance are observed. This further demonstrates the explanatory value of these concepts.

3. Organizational Opportunity

The variable labeled "organizational opportunity" might be considered one aspect of network change. However, it differs from that variable in that all problem solving takes place in one network. Differential opportunity for organization is provided by varying the opportunity to organize between problem-solving trials. This technique was developed by Guetzkow and associates (Guetzkow and Simon, 1955; Guetzkow and Dill, 1957) to test their hypothesis that network patterns effect the efficiency of groups only indirectly by governing the members' ability to organize themselves for efficient task performance. They assumed that circle and comcon networks are less efficient than the wheel for symbol-identification problems because the people in the former communication nets have greater difficulty developing a hierarchical organization. Theoretically, then, added opportunity for organizational activity should eliminate differences among networks.

Again we might ask, what would be predicted from a consideration of the effects of organizational opportunity upon saturation? The writer thinks agreement among group members regarding organizational procedures would reduce saturation, regardless of the kind of organizational procedure agreed upon. With simple tasks, this reduction should be greater in the circle and comcon than in the wheel where agreement is already evident (see Section IV, C). In other words, the saturation concept would lead to the same prediction as the Guetzkow hypothesis, although the effect would not be expected to be as great as his hypothesis suggests. Let us examine the evidence.

In order to test their hypothesis, Guetzkow and Simon (1955) tested five-person groups in the wheel, circle, and comcon networks, using symbol identification tasks. Groups were given periods of not more than two minutes between successive task trials to provide an opportunity to solve the organizational problem. The results showed clearcut differences among nets, in agreement with previous findings; i.e., the intertrial periods did *not* eliminate network effects as expected. However, Guetzkow and Simon examined the organizational arrangements actually used by their groups, and compared networks using only those groups that developed hierarchical organizations. Since the different networks did not differ when only the selected groups were compared, they argued that their hypothesis was correct.

In a second report, Guetzkow and Dill (1957) tested twenty five-person groups in the circle network, again using the symbol identification task. This time, all communication restrictions were removed during the intertrial planning periods. These groups were then compared with the circle groups in the first experiment. The circle groups with complete freedom of communication during the intertrial periods did *not* perform any better than did the circle groups in the initial experiment. Once again, groups were divided into organized and unorganized, and the organized groups were found to be more efficient than the unorganized groups.

Similar findings are reported by Mulder (1959b, 1960), who proposed that groups with more centralized "decision-structures" (defined as "who makes decisions for whom") will perform better than groups with more decentralized decision structures. He required four-person groups to solve arithmetic problems in the wheel and circle networks. Groups were divided into more-and-less-centralized structures for the wheel and circle considered separately. Within each network, groups with the more centralized decision-structures required less time and fewer messages than the less centralized groups.

At first thought, it appears that all of these results support the Guetzkow hypothesis. Such a conclusion would also be consistent with the saturation hypothesis, since the predictions are the same. Further, it might be argued that saturation is the preferred interpretation, since it accounts for other findings as well as those presented above. Unfortunately, there are some serious questions about the soundness of the methodology employed in these studies. It is clear that opportunity to plan for problem-solution improves performance, as demonstrated by an excellent study by Shure *et al.* (1962). But it is not at all clear that degree of organization accounts for the obtained network differences. The evidence presented by Guetzkow *et al.* and by Mulder merely shows that efficiency and organization are correlated; it does not show that organization *causes* the efficiency. In a series of experiments dealing with this question, Schein (1958) traced the achievement of organization and efficiency across trials. Although he found efficiency and organization perfectly correlated at the end of the experiment, the achievement of efficiency developed *earlier* than organization. Thus it is evident that organization is not a prerequisite of efficiency. It could be just the opposite: more efficient groups tend to become organized, perhaps because the same abilities are required for both efficiency and organization development.

In conclusion, the evidence concerning organizational development is consistent with the saturation hypothesis (and the Guetzkow-Mulder hypothesis), but this evidence rests upon a comparison of selected groups. We have seen that the soundness of this approach is questionable.

B. INFORMATION INPUT VARIABLES

Group behavior may be influenced either positively or negatively by the amount and kind of information that is available to the group. If the information is noise free, for example, the demands upon the group are not great, and the performance should be better than under noisy conditions. Several aspects of this problem have been investigated, including the effects of noise, distribution of information, and reinforcement.

1. Noise

Noise may be introduced into the information available to the group in several ways. Some common types of noise include *channel noise* (transmission of messages is interfered with), *coding noise* (encoding and decoding processes are ambiguous), and *information noise* (apparently task-relevant information is interspersed among task-irrelevant information). Noise, regardless of type, increases saturation relative to noise-free conditions, and, therefore, should decrease performance and, to some extent, satisfaction. Centralized networks should be affected to a greater extent than decentralized networks because the burden of handling the noise falls upon the central positions.

Channel noise was studied by Heise and Miller (1951) in the experiment described in Section III, B. The five three-person networks shown in Fig. 1 were created by means of an intercom system. White noise was introduced into the system at three speech-to-noise ratios: +6 db, —2 db, and —10 db. For those problems requiring communication (word arrangement and sentence construction) lowering the signal-to-noise ratio increased errors, time, and messages required to complete the task, and accentuated the superiority of decentralized over centralized networks.

Coding noise was studied by Macy *et al.* (1953). Coding processes were made ambiguous by requiring group members to write and interpret descriptions of colors that are not easy to describe, in this case mottled and streaked marbles. Varying degrees of coding ambiguity were compared in five-person wheel, chain, circle, and pinwheel networks. Coding noise greatly increased the errors made by all networks. However, certain networks learned to reduce their errors to a previously determined noise-free level, while others did not. The circle showed rapid learning and a good error reduction; the wheel and chain showed no learning and no error reduction; and the pinwheel showed some initial learning and poor error reduction. In general, the results were consistent with predictions from the saturation hypothesis.

The effects of noisy information were studied by Shaw (1958) in the four-person wheel and comcon. The group tasks were arithmetic problems, each requiring twelve items of information for solution. Each group member was given three of these items. Half of the groups in each network were given only this task-relevant information (noise-free condition) and for the other half, each member was given two additional items that appeared relevant but were actually irrelevant to the task (noisy condition). The comcon required significantly less time than did the wheel under both conditions. Noise increased time for both networks, and more in the wheel than in the comcon, but this latter finding was not statistically reliable. Noise significantly increased the number of messages required by the wheel, but not by the comcon. (Incidentally, this finding supports the view that noise increases saturation more in centralized than in decentralized networks.) Noise significantly reduced satisfaction in both the wheel and the comcon. The direction of the findings are consistent with the saturation interpretation, but not all differences are significant.

The results of the studies of the various kinds of noise upon performance in communication networks are unusual in that all agree in showing that noise tends to reduce the effectiveness of groups in centralized, restrictive networks more than groups in decentralized networks, in agreement with expectations based upon the saturation process.

2. Information Distribution

Several investigators have suggested that the way in which the information is distributed among network positions will influence the performance of the group, and that the distributional effects will be different for different networks. These expectations are based upon the undisputed fact that information availability and number of communication channels are positively correlated; hence the conclusion that at least part of the differential effects among network positions can be accounted for by differences in availability of information. It is also obvious that independence and saturation are influenced by variations in information distribution, although the precise effects will depend upon the particular distributional variable under consideration. The distributional variables that have been studied include uniformity of distribution, organization of distributed information, and the temporal aspects of distribution.

Uniformity of information distribution refers to the degree to which available information is distributed equally among group members. Relative to equal distribution, unequal distribution of information should decrease saturation when a peripheral position has the most information and increase saturation when the most central person has the most information. Independence should be increased for the person who has the most information and decreased for those that have the least information, since additional information reduces an individual's dependence on others in the group.

The initial study of distribution uniformity (Shaw, 1954a) compared equal and unequal distribution of task-relevant information in four-person wheel, slash, and circle networks. In the equal distribution condition, the eight items of information needed to solve the assigned arithmetic problems were randomly, but uniformly, distributed among group members; whereas in the unequal condition, one group member (one of the most peripheral positions) in each group was given five items and the other three members only one item of information. Information distribution had no effect upon group time scores in any of the networks. However, in all networks the position having five units of information required less time to solve than the corresponding position in the equal condition. Unequal distribution reduced errors in all networks. Satisfaction was not influenced by the distribution variable, but the position having the most information was valued more highly than other positions in all networks. Messages varied with information distribution only in the wheel and the slash; the position having the most information in the unequal condition sent more messages than the corresponding position in the equal condition. These findings only partially supported the independence-saturation analysis.

In a follow-up study, Gilchrist et al. (1954) compared three information distribution conditions in the four-person wheel network: task-relevant items were distributed equally (four items to each person), unequally peripheral (five items to a peripheral position, one item to all others), or unequally central (five items to the most central position, one item to all others). Additional information to the peripheral position significantly decreased the time taken and increased messages and satisfaction for that position relative to comparable positions in the equal condition; whereas, additional information to the central position increased time, messages, and satisfaction as compared with the central position in the equal condition. It was this finding that led to the formulation of the saturation concept.

The uniformity of distribution studies cited above varied the amounts of information input to each position, but information input may also vary in content. In most network studies, the items of information were distributed randomly among positions, so that the content of the items given a position was matter of chance. In most extant groups, however, the information content available to a given position is determined by the particular functions of the position. For example, the sales manager has information about markets, demands, composition, etc. that derives from the activities associated with his position. This systematic distribution of information should increase independence (hence raise satisfaction) and decrease saturation (hence improve performance), relative to the random distribution situation.

This problem was attacked by Shaw (1956), who suggested that systematic distribution should allow for selective communication and that this effect should be increased by prior knowledge of the distribution. Systematic versus random distribution of information was studied in the four-person wheel and comcon networks. For half of the groups in each network, the information needed to solve arithmetic problems was distributed so that a given position had all the information concerning one particular aspect of the problem, whereas for the other half, the relevant information was randomly distributed. Similarly, half of the groups in each condition were told the nature of the distribution and half were not. Knowledge of distribution did not significantly influence the group process. Systematic distribution, as compared with random distribution, decreased time and errors and increased satisfaction scores.

For time and error scores, this effect was stronger in the wheel than in the comcon. These findings were interpreted as not supporting the selective communication hypothesis; rather, systematic distribution appeared to impose a useful kind of organization upon the content of transmitted messages. That is, each person transmitted all his information on a single message card so that related information was grouped at the time it was received. This led to a reduction in saturation, since the task demands were not as great as when the information had to be grouped before the problem could be solved.

An experiment by Shelly and Gilchrist (1958) represents the third approach to information distribution. They were concerned with the effects produced by variations in the amount of information the group must deal with at any given time when the group must handle a given amount of total information. Eight arithmetic problems, each requiring four items of information for solution, were formulated, so that it was possible to combine some or all of these problems into larger problems which also would have a single answer. These eight problems were given to all groups, but were presented in four different ways: singly in sequential order, sequentially in groups of two as a single problem, sequentially in groups of four as a single problem, and all eight as a single problem. Groups of four persons each were run in the wheel and comcon networks. Under these conditions, saturation effects would be expected to increase and independence to decrease with increasing work load per unit time. The effects of increased work load should of course be greater in the wheel than in the comcon. The results generally supported these expectations.

Although not statistically reliable, the comcon was faster than the wheel under all information conditions, and there was some indication of an increasing divergence with increased communication demands. Questionnaire results indicated that as the number of items to be handled simultaneously increased, group members became less satisfied, and perceived levels of performance and cooperation dropped off. Group members in the wheel were significantly less satisfied with the way they had to operate, whereas those in the comcon were less satisfied with the performance of the group. This suggests that wheel group members blamed the structure for their information-handling difficulties, whereas those in the comcon blamed themselves.

In general, it appears that performance and satisfaction are depressed when information is distributed so that the central person's work load is increased, when the input information is randomly distributed, or when the total work load must be handled at one time. Although the results are not always significant, it appears that the detrimental effects of such adverse information distributions are greater in the more centralized and restricted networks than in the more decentralized and unrestricted networks. Similarly, persons in favorable positions for information accessibility and processing (for example, a position that has most of the information needed to solve the problem, or a position that has many channels to persons who have such information) are more efficient and better satisfied than are persons in less favorable positions. These findings are consistent with the independence-saturation hypothesis.

3. Reinforcement

In addition to information that may be needed to complete the task, other kinds of information may be available to the group. Information about the group's performance, for example, may affect the group's behavior in systematic ways. This information may be knowledge of results, or it may only be information that the performance was good or bad (i.e., positive or negative reinforcement). Only this latter form of information has been studied systematically.

The effects of reinforcement on independence and saturation are not easy to predict. Based on findings by Berkowitz and Levy (1956) that evaluations given to the group as a whole promoted feelings of group interdependence, perceived independence might be supposed to decrease by group reinforcement. Further, Lawson's (1963a,b) conclusions that reinforcement imposes additional pressure upon group members would suggest that reinforcement increases saturation. Evidence on the effects of reinforcement was provided by two experiments. The first experiment (Lawson,

1963a) examined the effects of reinforcement in four-person groups in wheel, circle, and comcon networks. Symbol identification tasks were used. Reinforced groups received randomly positive reinforcement (a chime) at the end of 50% of the trials, and randomly negative reinforcement (a raucous buzzer) at the end of the remaining 50% of the trials. The meaning of the two types of reinforcement was explained to the subjects before the first trial. Reinforcement had a significant effect on group performance only with respect to time scores in the circle. Reinforced circle groups required less time to solve problems than nonreinforced groups. Reinforcement effects were in the same direction in the wheel and in the opposite direction in the comcon, but neither difference was significant. There were no differences in satisfaction of reinforced and nonreinforced groups.

The second experiment (Lawson, 1963b) was similar to the first one except that groups were assigned arithmetic problems. The results showed that under nonreinforced conditions the comcon was fastest, the wheel slowest, and the circle intermediate in speed. Reinforcement exaggerated these differences: the reinforced comcon groups were faster, but the reinforced wheel groups were slower than their controls. Circle groups showed the least change as a consequence of reinforcement. Morale scores tended to be higher in the nonreinforced than in the reinforced groups.

The effects of reinforcement upon performance and morale are consistent with the independence-saturation interpretation except for the improved performance of the comcon groups under reinforcement.

C. Group Composition Variables

Group composition, defined as the individual characteristics of group members, has long been considered one of the major variables in group behavior. Cattell (1948) and Carter (1954) suggested that member personality is one of three broad classes of variables needed to understand group behavior, and Schutz (1958) built an entire theory of group behavior based upon member characteristics. It is obvious that an adequate analysis of network effects must include a consideration of the kinds of individuals who compose the group. The characteristics of group members surely affect independence and saturation, but the direction of these effects will of course depend upon the particular characteristics under consideration. The characteristics that have been studied in networks are ascendance, authoritarianism, popularity, and leadership style.

1. Ascendance

Ascendance may be defined as the tendency to dominate others (i.e., to speak, resist opinion change, interrupt, etc., more often than others). Ascendant persons in groups may be expected to elicit negative attitudes and uncooperative behavior in other group members; especially if they do not have legitimate authority over other group members. Therefore, we would expect ascendant persons to decrease independence and increase saturation effects in networks. Only one study relative to the effects of ascendance has been reported.

Berkowitz (1956) selected high, moderate, and low ascendant persons on the basis of their scores on the Guilford-Zimmerman Ascendance scale and certain measures obtained from their participation in a group mechanical assembly task. Four-person groups, each composed of one high, one low, and two moderates, solved arithmetic problems in the wheel network. In one conditions, the high ascendant person was in the central position, while in another condition the low ascendant person was in the central position. Highs in the central position were faster and more active than lows in the central position on the first trial, but these differences did not persist. Highs in the periphery had faster rates of communication than lows on all trials; however, highs in the periphery tended to become more passive with practice. Both highs and lows rated satisfaction higher than did moderates, even when in a peripheral position. Although Berkowitz did not make group comparisons, analysis of his data revealed that groups with a high ascendant person in the central position required more time (59.2 vs. 51.6) and rated satisfaction lower (4.1 vs. 4.5) than did groups with low ascendant persons in the central position. These findings are in accord with the assumption that ascendant behavior decreases independence and increases saturation. When the ascendant person is in the periphery he is unable to affect the group to the same extent that he can in the central position.

2. Authoritarianism

Authoritarianism is in some ways similar to ascendance. However, the high authoritarian may be either dominant or submissive, depending upon the position in which he finds himself. When he is in an authority (or power) position, he tends to use his authority to control others; when he is in a subordinate position, he accepts this status and submits to the person or persons in superior positions. When in a leadership position, for example, he issues orders to others in the group, and tries to have things done according to the accepted rules, but otherwise he presumably communicates very little. The other group members probably learn fairly quickly what to expect of him. Unlike the high ascendant who communicates a great deal to others, his actions should reduce communication demands. Therefore, we would expect that a high authoritarian assigned to a leadership position in the center of a centralized network would decrease both saturation and independence. Similar effects should occur when a high authoritarian is assigned a leadership position in a decentralized network, but the magnitude of these effects should be attenuated because the communication structure does not permit the leader to exert tight control over the group.

The effects of member authoritarianism upon group behavior was examined by Shaw (1959). The degree to which an individual accepts authority, as measured by the Bales Acceptance of Authority (AA) scale (Bales, 1956), was varied for members of the four-person groups in wheel and comcon networks. Group members were selected to have either high or low scores on the AA scale. One-fourth of the groups in each network was assigned to each of the following conditions: high scoring leader, high scoring followers (HH); high leader, low followers (HL); low leaders, high followers (LH); and low leader, low followers (LL). The leader was always assigned to one of the most central positions in the network.

The fact that assigning a high authoritarian leader to a central position reduces saturation relative to the low leader condition is demonstrated by the results of an analysis of messages transmitted. In the wheel, the mean number of messages by H-leader groups was 15.6 as compared with 25.6 for the L-leader groups; in the comcon, the means were 25.7 and 24.7, respectively. The results also suggested that this reduction in saturation improved performance. Leader AA scores and time scores correlated —.29 in the wheel and +.38 in the comcon, with the effects of intelligence partialled out. The results are not so clear with regard to independence, since ratings of satisfaction were a function of the follower AA score. With H-followers, satisfaction varied only with the network; with L-followers, satisfaction was greater in the comcon than in the wheel, and greater with L-leaders than with H-leaders.

In summary, authoritarian leaders appear to decrease saturation in the centralized network, but not in the decentralized network, and these effects are reflected in performance scores. Authoritarian leaders also tend to reduce independence, but this effect is reflected only in the satisfaction ratings of nonauthoritarian followers. Again, the results are generally consistent with the independence-saturation hypothesis.

3. Leadership Style

The study of leadership styles in communication networks may be regarded as simply another way of investigating the effects of authoritarianism, since leaders of laboratory groups are often asked to behave in either an autocratic, authoritarian manner, or a democratic, nonauthoritarian manner. The difference is that the laboratory variations in leader behavior are produced by instructions rather than by differences in personality characteristics. Since the outward behavior is the important variable, however, the effects on independence and saturation should be similar.

A study by Shaw (1955a) was designed specifically to test predictions based on the independence and saturation concepts. It was hypothesized that authoritarian leadership should decrease independence for followers (and hence decrease satisfaction) and should decrease saturation for all group members (and hence improve performance). Nonauthoritarian leadership should increase both independence (hence increase satisfaction) and saturation (hence lower performance). Leaders were assigned to four-person groups in wheel, kite, and comcon networks. For half of the groups in each network, the leader was instructed to behave in an autocratic manner; for the other half, he was instructed to behave in a democratic manner. Autocratic leadership improved group efficiency (shorter times and fewer messages) relative to democratic leadership in all networks, but differences in the kite were not significant. Similarly, groups were better satisfied under democratic, nonauthoritarian leadership in all networks. Thus, predictions were generally verified.

4. Popularity

Popularity might be viewed as the manifestation of certain personality attributes. But generally, popularity refers to the acceptance of the individual by fellow group members rather than to his behavioral characteristics. A popular group member should be better able to elicit the cooperation of others than an unpopular person, and this should reduce the demands on the group. Thus, a popular person in the central position of a centralized network should decrease saturation relative to an unpopular person in this position. Independence, on the other hand, should be increased since members should feel that they are free to act in other ways if they wish. A study by Mohanna and Argyle (1960) throws some light on this question. The central person in a five-person wheel network was selected sociometrically to be either popular or unpopular. Solving symbol identification problems, wheel groups with a popular center were more efficient (in time taken and messages used) than were groups with unpopular centers. This finding is in agreement with the expected effects on saturation, but no evidence was obtained relative to independence and satisfaction.

In summary, studies of group composition involving the ascendance, authoritarianism, leadership style, and popularity of group members demonstrated the importance of considering the composition of the group. The findings generally supported the independence-saturation hypothesis in that characteristics which may reasonably be expected to influence independence and saturation are related to satisfaction and performance in the predicted direction. However, knowledge of the effects of group composition is woefully limited, and much additional research is badly needed.

VI. Summary and Conclusions

This section summarizes what is known about the effects of communication networks upon group process, and indicates some areas where further research is needed.

A. THE PRESENT STATE OF KNOWLEDGE

The experimental evidence reviewed in this paper clearly demonstrates that the communication network imposed on the group influences its problem-solving efficiency, communication activity, organizational development, and member satisfaction. The major network difference is between centralized (e.g., wheel, chain, Y) and decentralized (e.g., circle, comcon) networks. The direction and magnitude of these effects are modified by the following variables: kind of task, noise, information distribution, member personality, reinforcement, and the kind of prior experience the members have had in networks. Of all those reviewed here, the variable having the most pronounced effect is the kind of task the group must perform. Centralized networks are generally more efficient when the task requires merely the collection of information in one place. Decentralized networks are more efficient when the task requires, in addition to the information collection process, that further operations must be performed on the information before the task can be completed. Decentralized networks are more satisfying to group members regardless of the kind of task.

The experimenter has tried to show that these several effects can be interpreted using the concepts of independence and saturation. The hypothesis that independence is positively related to satisfaction and saturation is negatively related to efficiency is generally supported by the experimental evidence.

B. UNFINISHED BUSINESS

The experiments conducted to date have taught us a great deal about the effects of communication networks, but the precise nature of many of the relationships among variables still remains unclear. In particular, the following variables need much clarification.

1. Network Characteristics

The several attempts to develop quantitative measures of network characteristics (centrality, peripherality, independence) have met with only partial success. Many measures appear adequate for positional differences, but fail to represent network differences adequately. In general, these measures seem to reflect extreme differences, such as differences between the highly centralized networks (wheel, chain, Y) and the highly decentralized networks (circle, comcon). They do not, however, distinguish between networks having smaller pattern differences, such as the Y and chain or the circle and comcon. Perhaps such quantification must await more extensive theoretical developments, or perhaps greater differences than, for example, those between the wheel and chain are necessary to produce consistent effects on group behavior.

2. Kind of Task

The evidence shows unequivocally that network differences vary with the kind of task. So far, the analysis has involved only a crude, dichotomous classification of tasks. Even so, the evidence is strikingly consistent in showing directional differences in favor of centralized networks for simple problems, but in favor of decentralized networks for complex problems. A more careful analysis of tasks is called for. At this stage the hypothesis may be ventured that the magnitude of differences in effectiveness between centralized and decentralized networks will be a positive, increasing function of the differences in task complexity.

3. Group Composition

Despite the obvious relevance of member characteristics for the functioning of groups, the relationship between such characteristics and network performance has been much neglected. Only a few studies have considered this variable, and these have varied only one "trait" of the group members. How effective will a network be when the critical member (e.g., the central person in the wheel) is the least intelligent group member? Can other characteristics of members, such as cooperativeness, need for affiliation, etc., compensate for lack of ability? Are "compatible" or "cohesive" groups relatively more effective in some networks than in others? Many other questions might be asked, but perhaps these will suffice to indicate the problems yet to be solved with reference to group composition variables.

4. Reinforcement

Lawson's (1963a,b) experiments showed that random reinforcement produces differential effects in networks which vary with the task. This is only a beginning. Still to be investigated are the effects of contingent reinforcement, schedules of reinforcements, magnitude of reinforcement, kind of reinforcement, and so on.

5. Network Embeddedness

Experimentation has been limited to isolated networks; however, small groups generally function as subgroups—parts of larger organizations. It may be that the most efficient network in isolation is quite different from the most efficient network embedded in a larger group. Furthermore, a given network may function differently depending upon the structure of the larger organization. These and other related problems demand attention, although no experimental techniques are readily available for their solution.

This brief resume lists only some of the more obvious research needs. Many more problems might be listed and many additional ones no doubt will arise in the course of future experimentation. The communication network studies have provided a great deal of information regarding structural effects upon group behavior. Much more remains to be done.

REFERENCES

Bales, R. F. (1956). "Factor Analysis of the Domain of Values in the Value Profile Test," Mimeo. Rept., Laboratory of Social Relations. Harvard Univ., Cambridge, Massachusetts.

Bavelas, A. (1948). *Appl. Anthropol.* **7**, 16–30.

Bavelas, A. (1950). *J. Acoust. Soc. Am.* **22**, 725–730.

Bavelas, A., and Barrett, D. (1951). *Personnel* **27**, 366–371.

Berkowitz, L. (1956). *Sociometry* **19**, 210–222.

Berkowitz, L., and Levy, B. I. (1956). *J. Abnorm. Soc. Psychol.* **53**, 300–306.

Carter, L. F. (1954). *Personnel Psychol.* **7**, 477–484.

Cattell, R. B. (1948). *Psychol. Rev.* **55**, 48–63.

Christie, L. S. (1954). *J. Operat. Res. Soc. Am.* **2**, 188–196.

Christie, L. S., Luce, R. D., and Macy, J., Jr. (1952). "Communication and Learning in Task-Oriented Groups," Tech. Rept. No. 231, Research Laboratory of Electronics. MIT.

Christie, L. S., Luce, R. D., and Macy, J., Jr. (1956). *In* "Operations Research for Management" (J. F. McCloskey and J. M. Coppinger, eds.), Vol. II, pp. 417–537. Johns Hopkins Press, Baltimore, Maryland.

Cohen, A. M. (1961). *J. Communication* **11**, 116–124 and 128.

Cohen, A. M. (1962). *Admin. Sci. Quart.* **6**, 443–462.

Cohen, A. M., and Bennis, W. G. (1961). *Human Relat.* **14**, 351–367.

Cohen, A. M., and Bennis, W. G. (1962). *J. Psychol.* **54**, 391–416.

Cohen, A. M., Bennis, W. G., and Wolkon, G. H. (1961). *Sociometry* **24**, 416–431.

Cohen, A. M., Bennis, W. B., and Wolkon, G. H. (1962). *Sociometry* **25**, 177–196.

Flament, C. (1956). *Annee Psychol.* **56**, 411–431.

Flament, C. (1958a). *Bull. Centre Etudes Rech. Psychotechn.* **7**, 97–106.

Flament, C. (1958b). *Annee Psychol.* **57**, 71–89.

Flament, C. (1958c). *Annee Psychol.* **58**, 119–131.

Gilchrist, J. C., Shaw, M. E., and Walker, L. C. (1954). *J. Abnorm. Soc. Psychol.* **49**, 554–556.

Glanzer, M., and Glaser, R. (1959). *Psychol. Bull.* **56**, 317–332.

Glanzer, M., and Glaser, R. (1961). *Psychol. Bull.* **58**, 1–27.

Guetzkow, H., and Dill, W. R. (1957). *Sociometry* **20**, 175–204.

Guetzkow, H., and Simon, H. (1955). *Mgmt. Sci.* **1**, 233–250.

Heise, G. A., and Miller, G. A. (1951). *J. Abnorm. Soc. Psychol.* **46**, 327–335.

Hirota, K. (1953). *Japan J. Psychol.* **24**, 105–113.

Lanzetta, J. T., and Roby, T. B. (1956a). *J. Abnorm. Soc. Psychol.* **53**, 307–314.

Lanzetta, J. T., and Roby, T. B. (1956b). *Sociometry* **19**, 95–104.

Lanzetta, J. T., and Roby, T. B. (1957). *J. Abnorm. Soc. Psychol.* **55**, 121–131.

Lawson, E. D. (1961). "Change in Communication Nets and Performance." (Paper read at the 1961 Eastern Psychological Association convention.)

Lawson, E. D. (1963a). "Reinforced and Non-Reinforced Four-Man Communication Nets." (Paper read at the 1963 Eastern Psychological Association convention.)

Lawson, E. D. (1963b). "Reinforcement in Group Problem-Solving with Complex Problems." (Paper read at the 1963 Canadian Psychological Association convention.)

Leavitt, H. J. (1951). *J. Abnorm. Soc. Psychol.* **46**, 38–50.

Leavitt, H. J., and Knight, K. E. (1963). *Sociometry* **26**, 260–267.

Luce, R. D., Macy, J., Jr., Christie, L. S., and Hay, H. D. (1953). "Information Flow in Task-Oriented Groups," Tech. Rept. No. 264, Research Laboratory of Electronics. MIT, Cambridge, Massachusetts.

Macy, J., Jr., Christie, L. S., and Luce, R. D. (1953). *J. Abnorm. Soc. Psychol.* **48**, 401–409.

Mohanna, A. I., and Argyle, M. (1960). *J. Abnorm. Soc. Psychol.* **60**, 139–140.

Mulder, M. (1958). "Groepsstructuur, Motivatie en Prestatie." Nederlands Instituut veer Praeventieve Geneeskunde, Leiden.

Mulder, M. (1959a). *Acta Psychol.* **16**, 178–225.

Mulder, M. (1959b). *Acta Psychol.* **16**, 356–402.

Mulder, M. (1960). *Sociometry* **23**, 1–14.

Roby, T. B., and Lanzetta, J. T. (1956). *Sociometry* **19**, 105–113.

Schein, E. H. (1958). "The Development of Organization in Small Problem-Solving Groups," Final Rept. on Sloan Project No. 134. MIT, Cambridge, Massachusetts.

Schutz, W. C. (1958). "FIRO: A Three-Dimensional Theory of Interpersonal Behavior." Rinehart, New York.

Shaw, M. E. (1954a). *J. Abnorm. Soc. Psychol.* **49**, 547–553.

Shaw, M. E. (1954b). *J. Psychol.* **38**, 139–149.

Shaw, M. E. (1954c). *J. Exptl. Psychol.* **48**, 211–217.

Shaw, M. E. (1955a). *J. Abnorm. Soc. Psychol.* **50**, 127–134.

Shaw, M. E. (1956). *J. Pers.* **25**, 59–69.

Shaw, M. E. (1958). *J. Soc. Psychol.* **47**, 33–37.

Shaw, M. E. (1959). *J. Pers.* **27**, 196–210.

Shaw, M. E., and Rothschild, G. H. (1956). *J. Appl. Psychol.* **40**, 281–286.

Shaw, M. E., Rothschild, G. H., and Strickland, J. C. (1957). *J. Abnorm. Soc. Psychol.* **54**, 323–330.

Shelly, M. W., and Gilchrist, J. C. (1958). *J. Soc. Psychol.* **48**, 37–44.

Shure, G. H., Rogers, M. S., Larsen, I. M., and Tassone, J. (1962). *Sociometry* **25**, 263–282.

Trow, D. B. (1957). *J. Abnorm. Soc. Psychol.* **54**, 204–209.

Walker, L. C. (1954). "The Effects of Group Size and Group Structure on Problem Solving Behavior in Small Groups." Unpublished doctoral dissertation, University of Wisconsin, Madison, Wisconsin.

A CONTINGENCY MODEL OF LEADERSHIP EFFECTIVENESS[1]

Fred E. Fiedler

DEPARTMENT OF PSYCHOLOGY
UNIVERSITY OF ILLINOIS
URBANA, ILLINOIS

[1] The present paper is based on Technical Report No. 10, ONR Project "Group and Organizational Factors Influencing Creativity" (NR 177-472, Nonr 1834(36), Fred E. Fiedler, C. E. Osgood, L. M. Stolurow, and H. C. Triandis, Principal Investigators. The writer is especially indebted to his colleagues A. R. Bass, L. J. Cronbach, M. Fishbein, J. E. McGrath, W. A. T. Meuwese, C. E. Osgood, I. D. Steiner, H. C. Triandis, and L. R. Tucker, who offered suggestions and criticisms at various stages of this paper.

I. Introduction

Leadership research has primarily been concerned with two major questions: What personality factors determine whether a particular individual will become a leader? and What personality traits or attributes determine whether a leader will become effective? The first question was treated extensively in the excellent reviews by Stogdill (1948) and Mann (1959), as well as in discussions by Gibb (1954), Bass (1960), and Hare (1962). It will not be dealt with further at this time.

The second question concerns the identification of personality attributes which characterize the *effective* leader. This problem did not receive much attention until the 1950's, when substantial support of programmatic research became available. Empirical research in this area is notoriously difficult and expensive, especially if the leader's effectiveness is defined in terms of the group's performance. It requires access to a large number of teams having comparable tasks, and it is frequently if not always difficult to develop reliable and meaningful criteria of group output, especially under "real-life" conditions. Most reviewers (e.g., Browne and Cohn, 1958; Hare, 1962; McGrath, 1962; Steiner, 1964) have also taken pains to point out that we have yet to produce a generally acceptable theory of leadership. No major development in recent years requires a basic change in this statement and our understanding of effective leadership is, therefore, at a fairly primitive stage.

It is hoped that this chapter will contribute to the theoretical integration of the area by proposing a framework for the understanding of factors which determine how a leader's personality attributes affect group performance. While a number of programs have demonstrated the influence of various leader attributes on team effectiveness, the results have not been generalizable from one group situation to another. This is true despite the fact that a large number of studies have converged on two major clusters of leadership, beginning with the classical experiments by Lewin and Lippitt, 1938; Lippitt and White, 1952).

These clusters have been variously labeled autocratic vs. democratic; authoritarian vs. equalitarian; task-oriented vs. human-relations-oriented; self-oriented vs. group-oriented; psychologically close, permissive vs. distant, controlling, managing; or "initiation of structure" vs. "consideration." While these concepts are by no means synonymous, they do have certain features in common. There is little doubt at this time that the attitudes and behaviors involved in these clusters play a crucial part in affect ing group performance.

In a summary of relevant research, Hare (1962) noted that autocratic leadership seems to promote greater quantitative productivity, while democratic leadership tends to result in higher morale and qualitative productivity. Autocratic leaders appear, therefore, to be most effective in industrial work situations or the armed forces, in which the task requires strong, centralized control.

However, the data are not as consistent as one might wish. The apparent convergence in selecting relevant leader attitudes or behaviors has not been matched by a corresponding convergence in the results of various investigations. On the one hand, a number of important studies, for example, Katz and Kahn (1953) showed that human-relations-oriented, supervisory attitudes tend to promote increased morale and productivity in a work situation; Argyle *et al.* (1957) found that foremen of highly productive work groups were more democratic and nonpunitive in their supervisory behavior than foremen of low-producing groups (although democratic supervision itself was not related to productivity); Comrey *et al.* (1954) showed that the personal interest of supervisors in their subordinates was positively related to effectiveness of forest management; and McGregor (1960) reported that democratically led organizations function more effectively and creatively.

On the other hand, Spector and Suttell (1956) found no relationship between authoritarianism of the leader and effectiveness of groups in problem-solving situations, and neither did Haythorn (1956) in studies of a leader's authoritarian attitudes and discussion behavior. Hawkins (1962) reported that task-oriented, punitive leaders tend to be more effective in sales display teams and gasoline service station management. Maier and Solem (1952) showed that groups with an active discussion leader were more effective on a problem-solving task than they were with permissive, passive, observing leaders. Halpin (1955) found a positive correlation between rated efficiency of the air crew and the aircraft commander's tendency to manifest friendly, mutually trusting relations defined by the term "consideration." Shaw's (1955) study showed that authoritarian leadership attitudes produced better performance and required less time for correct solution than nonauthoritarian leadership attitudes in communication nets.

While these examples do not represent an exhaustive review of the literature, they indicate clearly that the problem is not simple. Factors other than the strong, centralized control, or the quantitative vs. qualitative nature of task performance are likely to play an important role in determining the type of leader attitude or behavior which is most appropriate in a particular situation.

There are several noteworthy reasons for the low degree of systematization in this field. First, as Mann (1959), McGrath (1962), Steiner (1964), and others have pointed out, most investigators used measures tailored to fit their own research interests and predilections, but which, at the same, time precluded direct comparisons with other studies. Second, definitions of leadership, groups, and even of effectiveness, vary widely from study to study (Janda, 1960). Third, there has been little attempt to systematize the information necessary for identifying the social context within which the groups operate. As a result, it is frequently impossible to tell whether the findings of one investigation do or do not confirm those of a purportedly similar study. In his *Summary of small group research studies,* McGrath (1962) remarked that

> there has been relatively little research which could properly be called systematic, in the sense that it was explicitly designed to explore a wide range of variables drawn from different aspects of the small group field. . . . Nor has much effort been devoted to development and application of a standard battery of measures which sampled the broad aspects of group research and which could provide a direct basis for comparing results from one study to another. Such a procedure seems to represent a first step in the development of something equivalent to standard conditions as utilized in the physical and biological sciences. In the absence of such systematic programming of research, the rate of progress in understanding small group phenomena is likely to remain relatively slow, even though the rate of production of small group research seems to be increasing without abatement.

In light of the existing reviews by Bass (1960), George (1962), McGrath (1962), and others, another attempt to review the literature would not appear profitable. An intensive study of one, unified, programmatic effort is more likely to lead to the development of principles from which to build a general theory. The program directed by the writer and his associates during the last twelve years has involved over 25 major studies with reasonably large numbers of comparable groups and reliable criteria of performance. These studies were based on a unified, if partial, rationale, and are linked together in a cumulative fashion. An intensive examination of this programmatic effort may provide new insights into the problem and it may enable us to integrate other major programs of research on leadership effectiveness.

Before going further it would help to define a few key terms which will be used in this discussion. For the purpose of this analysis, a *group* is defined as a set of individuals who, in Campbell's (1958) terms, have proximity, similarity, and share a "common fate" on task-relevant events. The specific concern is with groups in which the members are, and also perceive each other to be, interdependent in achieving a common goal. It should be noted that this definition explicitly excludes "coacting" groups in which members work individually on a task, even though their performance might later be summed to yield a "group score," and even though coacting group members may indirectly affect each other's performance. According to this definition, a basketball team is a good example of an interacting group, and a track team exemplifies a coacting group.

The *leader* is defined as the individual in the group who directs and coordinates task-relevant group activities, or who, in the absence of a designated leader, automatically performs these functions in the group. It is recognized that leadership functions are frequently shared (Berkowitz, 1953; Cattell, 1951), but only the single individual who meets one of the following criteria is dealt with here: (a) he was appointed by a representative of the larger organization of which the group is a part; (b) he was elected by the group; (c) if there is neither an elected nor an appointed leader, he is the individual who can be identified as most influential on task-relevant questions of a sociometric preference questionnaire.

The leader's *effectiveness* will be defined in terms of his group's performance on its assigned task. This assumes that task-relevant skills and abilities of group members are reasonably similar, or that they were experimentally or statistically controlled.

II. History of the Program

The research program which is the focus of this chapter was initiated in 1951. It hypothesized that the leader's perceptions of his co-workers reflect important, task-relevant attitudes, and that these would materially influence group interaction and performance. This hypothesis was substantiated in a general sense. However, correlations between the leader's interpersonal perception score and his group's performance which were statistically significant and positive in one set of studies were often statistically significant and negative in another. The present theoretical position grew out of the attempt to make psychological sense from the conflicting but highly significant findings obtained in our own research, as well as in related investigations by others.

The interpersonal perception measures which served as predictor variables were first developed in research on psychotherapeutic relations (Fiedler, 1951). The data showed that reputedly effective psychotherapists tended to see their patients as more similar to themselves than did reputedly poor therapists. These results suggested that the individual who perceives another person as similar tends to feel psychologically close, accepting, and permissive toward him. It was, therefore, anticipated that liked persons would be seen as more similar to oneself, and more favorable, than would disliked persons. This hypothesis was clearly supported in an investigation of a college fraternity in which each man was asked to describe his most and his least liked fellow group member (Fiedler *et al.*, 1952), and since then has been substantiated by other studies (e.g., Davitz, 1955; Bieri, 1953). The question remained whether these interpersonal attitudes were also related to team performance.

Early research by Likert (1961) and his associates indicated that human-relations-oriented, supervisory attitudes increased productivity. It was expected, therefore, that our measures of close, interpersonal relations, permissive, and accepting attitudes, would be related to good teamwork. Subsequent research on this problem showed, however, that the prediction of group performance on the basis of these leader attributes is contingent upon the specific, situational context in which the leader operates. The major purpose of this paper is to integrate and explain the currently available findings by developing a generalized model of the relationship between these leader attributes and group performance.

A. PREDICTORS OF LEADERSHIP EFFECTIVENESS

Two main personality measures were used for predicting leadership effectiveness: the "assumed similarity between opposites" (ASo), and the esteem for the least preferred coworker (LPC) scores. ASo and LPC are highly correlated (.70 to .93), and will be used here interchangeably. Because of their importance to the theoretical model, these measures will be discussed in some detail.

The ASo score is obtained by asking a person to think of all the individuals with whom he has ever worked. He then describes: (a) the person whom he considers his most preferred co-worker (MPC), and (b) the person whom he considers his least preferred co-worker (LPC). The descriptions are made on eight-point, bi-polar adjective checklists similar in form to Osgood's (Osgood et al., 1957) Semantic Differential, using items descriptive of personality attributes. For example,

```
Pleasant  :—8—:—7—:—6—:—5—:—4—:—3—:—2—:—1—:Unpleasant
Friendly  :—8—:—7—:—6—:—5—:—4—:—3—:—2—:—1—:Unfriendly
Rejecting:—1—:—2—:—3—:—4—:—5—:—6—:—7—:—8—:Accepting[2]
```

ASo scores are derived by scoring each of the items from most to least favorable (8 to 1) and computing a measure of profile similarity, D (Cronbach and Gleser, 1953). A person who perceives his most and least preferred co-workers as very similar will, therefore, have a high assumed similarity score (or, in operational terms, a small discrepancy score), while a person who strongly differentiates between these two "opposites" on his co-worker continuum, will have a low ASo (and thus a large discrepancy)

[2] Other items in a recent scale were: helpful–frustrating; unenthusiastic–enthusiastic; lots of fun–serious; tense–relaxed; supportive–hostile; distant–close; cold–warm; cooperative–uncooperative; boring–interesting; quarrelsome–harmonious; self-assured–hesitant; efficient–inefficient; gloomy–cheerful; open–guarded.

score. The LPC score is one component of ASo and is obtained by simply summing the item scores on the least preferred co-worker scale sheet.

A person with a high LPC score tends to see even a poor co-worker in a relatively favorable manner (i.e., "Even if I can't work with him, he may still be a very nice and valuable person"). A low LPC person perceives his least preferred co-worker in a highly unfavorable, rejecting manner ("If I cannot work with him, he is probably just no good"). LPC scores have a high internal consistency, with split-half co-efficients of over .90. The scores are reasonably stable over time, although changes do take place depending upon intervening training and experience. In this respect, the scores resemble other attitude measures.

Since LPC and ASo do not correlate consistently with commonly used personality tests, there has been considerable difficulty in deriving an adequate interpretation of these scores. Earlier investigations treated ASo as a measure of psychological distance. This interpretation now appears to be an oversimplification. A recent investigation by Hawkins (1962) showed that individuals who differentiate sharply between their most and least preferred co-workers (low ASo) tend to be more oriented toward the task than toward relationships with others. They also tend to be more punitive, although not necessarily more distant. Studies of group interactions, based on tape-recorded transcripts, support this interpretation. High LPC (or ASo) leaders behave in a manner which promotes member satisfaction and lowers member anxiety; they are more compliant, more nondirective, and generally more relaxed, especially under pleasant and nonthreatening conditions. They are described by their groups as being higher on the Ohio State "Consideration" dimension (Meuwese, 1964).

Low LPC leaders, on the other hand, give and ask for more suggestions, are less inclined to tolerate or to make irrelevant comments, demand and get more participation from members, and are more controlling and managing in their conduct of the group interaction (Fiedler *et. al.*, 1961b). Low LPC leaders also interrupt group members more often, contribute more statements to the discussion, and make and receive more negatively toned statements, again indicating less concern with having pleasant relationships with others in their group. As with all attitude measures, the corresponding behavioral manifestations of high and low LPC leaders appear only under conditions which permit the individuals to behave in either of these ways with equal propriety.

B. PREVIOUS FINDINGS

The problems posed by the prediction of leadership effectiveness might be most readily understood in terms of the specific difficulties which arose in the course of research. The first group effectiveness study investigated 14 high school basketball teams which competed in leagues of matched schools. Team performance was defined as the percentage of games won by mid-season. The leader of the team was identified by means of sociometric preference questions. As mentioned above, it was anticipated that psychologically close teams would be more effective than teams characterized by task-oriented, psychologically distant, and less accepting relations. Contrary to expectation, team performance correlated negatively (—.69) with the leader's ASo score. Thus, better teams apparently had active, controlling, psychologically distant leaders. A similar result was obtained in a validation study at the end of the season by comparing seven teams from the upper and five from the lower third of the Illinois high school team standings ($r_{p.b.}$ —.58).

A study of 22 student surveying parties cross-validated these findings. These three-to-four-man teams were engaged in measuring predetermined parcels of land. The criterion was the accuracy of surveying, as judged by the course instructors. Again it was found that the effective teams had low ASo leaders (—.51) (Fiedler, 1954). Thus, the ASo score—and the personality attribute which it reflected—was clearly an important variable in the prediction of group performance.

However, did the effective teams choose low ASo leaders, or did low ASo leaders make their teams effective? This question could be partly answered in studies of groups in which the leaders were appointed by higher authority.

The first two investigations in this series dealt with B-29 bomber crews and Army tank crews. The criteria consisted of two uncorrelated bomber-crew tasks (radar and visual bombing accuracy) and two uncorrelated tank-crew tasks, time to hit a target and time to travel to a new target). In these studies, significant relations between the leader's ASo score and crew performance measures occurred only if the leader was sociometrically the most chosen member of the crew. Under these conditions, the correlation was *negative* (—.81, —.52, —.60, —.33) for crews in which the leader sociometrically endorsed his keyman (e.g., the gunner on a tank gunnery task), and *positive* (.42, .27, .60, .43) for crews in which the leader sociometrically rejected his keyman (Fiedler, 1955).

The relationship between ASo and crew effectiveness thus seemed to be contingent upon the sociometric choice pattern within the crew. This interpretation was later supported in studies of anti-aircraft artillery crews (Hutchins and Fiedler, 1960) and infantry squads (Havron et al., 1954).

The importance of sociometric acceptance as a moderator variable became even more apparent in a study of 32 farm-supply service companies (Godfrey et al., 1959). The criterion of success was the percentage of a company's net income compared to total sales over a three-year period.

The formal leader of the executive group was the general manager, and the chairman or most influential member of the board of directors was the leader of the policy- and decision-making body.

This investigation, from a theoretical point of view, demonstrated: (a) that ASo or LPC scores predicted leadership effectiveness to the degree to which the leader had good interpersonal relations in the group; and (b) that the direction of the relationship was contingent upon the leader's relations with key group members, as well as upon the nature of the task. In other words, the effective executive group performed better under an accepted, low ASo leader, while the policy- and decision-making groups operated more effectively under permissive, nondirective, and considerate, high ASo leaders (Table I).

TABLE I

CORRELATIONS BETWEEN COMPANY EFFECTIVENESS CRITERIA AND ASo SCORES OF BOARD OF DIRECTORS' INFORMAL LEADER AND COMPANY'S GENERAL MANAGER

| | | Correlations between net income and ASo of | |
| | | | |
Sample	N	Informal leader of board	Company's general manager
All companies	32	−.06	−.14
Informal leader endorses general manager	23	−.08	−.39
Informal leader endorses sociometrically accepted general manager	13	.20	−.′0[a]
Informal leader endorses accepted general manager, who endorses his keyman	8	.62	−.74[a]

[a] Significant at the .05 level of confidence for one-tailed tests.

The results obtained in the study of the board of directors led to an extension of the research to groups having creative tasks. A series of four studies was conducted which showed that the permissive, accepting, high LPC leaders had better group performance on creative tasks under relatively stress-free conditions; the managing, controlling, low LPC leaders had better performance under relatively less pleasant, more tension-arousing group climates (Fiedler, 1962). Thus, the direction of the relationship between the leader's attitude toward co-workers and group performance was again contingent upon his relations with the members of his group.

The nature of the task and the leader's relationship with group members are, however, not the only factors which determine the nature of the optimal leader attitudes. Recent studies have also indicated that the power of the leadership position also plays an important role in determining the type of leadership attitude and behavior which will contribute to group effectiveness. Gerard (1957), and Anderson and Fiedler (1962) have shown that the leader who has a powerful position will behave differently from one who holds a very tenuous position.

In brief, the data, taken as a whole, presented an extremely complex picture. The main problem became one of developing an integrative model which would account for the variations in the relationships which had been obtained.

III. Development of an Integrative Model

A. A System for Classifying Group Situations

The findings in this field made it abundantly clear that different group situations require different leadership styles. Progress in predicting group effectiveness thus seemed to require a meaningful system for classifying groups in terms of relevant situational factors.

Leadership is generally thought of as an interpersonal situation in which one individual in the group wields influence over others for the purpose of performing an assigned task. It will, therefore, be very important to know whether the group environment will make it relatively easy or difficult for the leader to influence the members of his group. A "good" system of classification would then be based on the crucial factors which determine whether a given situation is favorable or unfavorable for the leader.[3]

1. Situational Components

Three, critical, situational components which are likely to affect the leader's influence are postulated: (a) his personal relations with members of his group, (b) the power and authority which his position provides (the legitimate power, in French's term, 1956), and (c) the degree of structure in the task which the group has been assigned to perform.

It is recognized that a variety of other factors may affect the leader's ability to exert his influence. Among these are the relative abilities of the leader and his members, the members' motivation, and the extent to which the group is operating under conditions of external stress. To a large degree, these situational aspects are intercorrelated. A very able

---

[3] A considerable number of excellent papers (e.g., French, 1956; French and Raven, 1958) are available which deal with various influence processes. However, as Janda (1960) pointed out, there has been little effort to relate these influence processes to leadership effectiveness.

leader tends to be highly respected, and a highly respected and liked task leader is able to motivate his group members.

Only the three situational components listed above will be dealt with here. The elaboration and necessary corrections of the model are left to future research. The three specific measures which define the three, major, situational components are presented below.

a. *Affective leader-group relations.* The personal relationship between the leader and key members of his group is probably the most important, single determinant of group processes which affect team performance. The liked and respected leader does not need formal power, and he can obtain compliance from his group under circumstances which, in the case of a disliked or distrusted leader, would result in open revolt. As has been shown (e.g., Godfrey et al., 1959; Fiedler, 1961), the liked and accepted leader's interpersonal attitudes influence group performance to a significantly greater degree than similar attitudes of a leader who is sociometrically not accepted by his group.

A number of indices have been used to tap this particular dimension. Although the various measures are by no means identical, they seem to reflect relatively similar relations. The writer's early studies employed an index which reflected the sociometric acceptance of the leader by his co-workers. Later investigations obtained the leader's rating of the group's atmosphere (GA) on simple scales similar or identical to those used for measuring LPC. The leader was asked to describe the group on 10- to 20-item scales consisting of eight-point continua such as:

> Pleasant:—8—:—7—:—6—:—5—:—4—:—3—:—2—:—1—:Unpleasant
> Bad   :—1—:—2—:—3—:—4—:—5—:—6—:—7—:—8—:Good[4]

The leader who feels (and is) accepted by his group members is obviously able to act more decisively and with more confidence than the leader who feels rejected or distrusted by the members of his group. For purposes of the present analyses, groups in the upper and lower thirds of the group atmosphere or sociometric preference distribution have been chosen. This seems necessary here since only sociometric scores were available for some groups, and only group atmosphere scores for others. Moreover, the dimension is highly subject to shifting frames of reference. What appears relatively pleasant in a stressful situation may seem very unpleasant in a normally relaxed group discussion.

It should also be noted that the group climate and leader-group relations in laboratory studies tend to range from very pleasant to, at worst, moderately unpleasant situations. The most stressful laboratory con-

---

[4] Other items were: worthless–valuable; distant–close; cold–warm; quarrelsome–harmonious; self-assured–hesitant; efficient–inefficient; gloomy–cheerful.

dition we could devise produced a leader-group atmosphere score of only 5.0 (expressed as an item average) on a scale which ranged from a low score of 1.0 to a high of 8.0, and hence fell above the midpoint of the group atmosphere scale.

On the other hand, real-life groups occasionally express strong rejection of the leader, which places him in a very unfavorable position that might well outweigh other factors ordinarily compensating for poor leader-member relations.

b. Task structure. The second important dimension describes the nature of the task in terms of its clarity or ambiguity. Although it is generally not thought of in this manner, the assigned task in effect constitutes an order "from above." This order might be highly programmed, such as drilling "by the numbers," assembling a rifle, or operating a simple machine; or, it may be a very unstructured, vague order, such as to develop a policy which will maximize the profits of a company. The leader's job will be considerably easier if the job is highly structured than if it is vague and unspecific. This can be readily seen by noting, for example, that enlisted men frequently serve as instructors in officer training courses in which the material can be programmed, viz., in assembling and handling of weapons, in map reading, or in close order drill. The authority of the higher command is implicit in such highly structured tasks and the leader serves primarily to supervise the implementation of the task order.

In contrast, when a committee is given an unprogrammed task such as planning an annual picnic, the leader knows no more than do his members, and he cannot readily order anyone to execute such a task in a specific manner. This holds even in situations in which the leader has considerable formal power, e.g., a professor working with his assistants on a research plan, or an army officer working with enlisted specialists who are experts in their fields.

The task structure dimension is operationally defined here by four of the scales developed by Shaw (1962). It was reliably assessed by four, independent judges who rated 35 tasks on eight-point scales with a resulting interrater agreement of .80 to .88 The four dimensions are: *decision verifiability*—the degree to which the "correctness" of the solution or decision can be demonstrated, either by appeal to authority (e.g., the census of 1960), by logical procedures (e.g., mathematical demonstration), or by feedback (e.g., examination of consequences of decision, as in action tasks); *goal clarity*—the degree to which the requirements of the task are clearly stated or known to the group members; *goal path multiplicity*—the degree to which the task can be solved by a variety of procedures (number of different paths to the goal, number of alternative for solution, number of different ways that the task can be completed) (reversed scoring); *solution specificity*—the degree to which there is more than one "correct" solution. (Some tasks, e.g., arithmetic problems, have only one solution that is acceptable; others have two or more, e.g., a sorting task where items to be sorted have several dimensions; and still others have almost an infinite number of possible solutions, e.g., human-relations problems or matters of opinion.).

    c. Position power. A third major dimension is defined by the power inherent in the leadership position. This includes the rewards and sanctions which are officially or traditionally at the leader's disposal, his authority over his men, and the degree to which this authority is supported by the organization within which the group operates. The leader's power is, generally speaking, inversely related to the power of his members.

    The man who occupies a powerful leadership position may be able to obtain compliance even though he is personally resented by his group members. The chairman of a volunteer committee generally has to influence the group by persuasion or other indirect means suggested by Hemphill's term "consideration."

    The dimension of "leader position power" is defined by a checklist in which all items are given one point, except for 4a, b, c, which are weighted $+5$, $+3$, and -5, respectively.

1a. Compliments from the leader are appreciated more than compliments from other group members.
  b. Compliments are highly valued, criticisms are considered damaging.
  c. Leader can recommend punishments and rewards.
  d. Leader can punish or reward members on his own accord.
  e. Leader can effect (or can recommend) promotion or demotion.

2a. Leader chairs or coordinates group but may or may not have other advantages, i.e., is appointed or acknowledged chairman or leader.
  b. Leader's opinion is accorded considerable respect and attention.
  c. Leader's special knowledge or information (and members' lack of it) permits leader to decide how task is to be done, or how group is to proceed.
  d. Leader cues members or instructs them on what to do.
  e. Leader tells or directs members on what to do or what to say.

3a. Leader is expected to motivate group.
  b. Leader is expected to suggest and evaluate the members' work.
  c. Leader has superior, or special, knowledge about the job, or has special instructions, but requires members to do job.

d. Leader can supervise member's job and evaluate it or correct it.
e. Leader knows own as well as members' job and could finish the work himself if necessary (e.g., writing a report for which all information is available).

4a. Leader enjoys special or official rank and status in real life which sets him apart from (or above) group members, e.g., military rank, or elected office in a company or organization. (+5 points)

b. Leader is given special or official rank by experimenter to simulate for role playing purposes, e.g., "you are a general," or, "the manager." This simulated rank must be clearly superior to members' rank, and must not be just that of "chairman" or "group leader" of the group during its work period. (+3 points.)

c. Leader's position is dependent on members. Members can replace or depose leader. (—5 points.)

The position power in 35 group situations was rated by four independent judges, who reached interrater agreement of .95.

2. Interrelations of the Task-situation Dimensions

In the sample of 35 tasks (which contains most of the tasks described in Table II), leader-group relations correlated with task structure .03 and with position power —.09; task structure and position power correlated .75. The last two appeared to measure very closely related aspects of the group-task situation. This reflected the commonly observed fact that leaders of groups which perform highly structured or programmed tasks are generally given relatively higher power than their members. Most industrial and military situations are of this nature. Unstructured tasks, such as research and development, or planning and policy-making, tend to be performed under a chairmanship system in which the leader has relatively low position power.

Although this cannot be inferred from the available data, it also seems likely that certain tasks are naturally more conducive to good leader-member relations than are others. Good interpersonal relations tend to develop in group games or party planning, while work under highly competitive conditions or in a stressful environment frequently leads to unpleasant or hostile relations (Sherif and Sherif, 1953; Deutsch, 1949; Myers, 1962; Sells, 1962).

The three dimensions which are postulated here have previously been described in somewhat similar terms by others in the small group area. Cartwright and Zander (1960) spoke of task structure, labor division, power structure (closely related to position power), and sociometric or friendship structure. The Ohio State studies discussed structure-in-inter-action and consideration (Halpin and Winer, 1957), and Schutz (1953) suggested the dimensions of control (related to position power) and affection and inclusion (related to leader-member relations).

B. DIMENSIONALIZING GROUP SITUATIONS

A rough categorization leads to an eight-celled cube (Fig. 1). According to hypothesis, a group located in one cell or "octant" of this three-dimensional space may require a different leadership style than a group located in an adjacent cell. It is possible to develop a partial order of the various group situations in terms of their favorableness or the degree to which the leader's job of influencing his group will be easy or difficult.

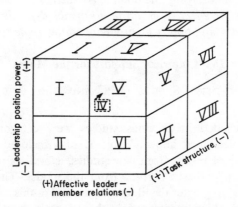

FIG. 1. A model for the classification of group task situations.

As mentioned before, the leader-member relations dimension depicted in this figure extends only from "good" to "moderately good," since very poor leader-member relations are almost never found in laboratory groups. An Octant V-A, which deals with real-life groups having presumably very poor leader-member relations, was later added. This will be described in the section on validation evidence.

There is no difficulty in identifying the extreme points on this dimension of ease of influencing the group (favorableness-to-leader dimension). A leader who is liked by his group, who knows exactly what to do and how to proceed, and who holds a relatively powerful position will find it easier to do his job than one who is disliked by his group, has a vague, unstructured task, and has no power. Difficulty arises because any ordering of intermediate points is to some degree arbitrary. To order these octants, the leader's relationship with his members was postulated to be the most important of the three dimensions. A highly trusted and liked leader usually does not need to rely on the power of his position; he can define the job in the way he sees fit.

The task structure is considered to be next in importance, since it embodies the demands of higher authority, such as a standard operating procedure. Position power is considered third in importance in this model.

The resulting dimensionalization is thus obtained by first ordering the group-task situation on the basis of the leader's relations with his group, then on the basis of task structure, and finally on the basis of position power. An additional "octant" (V-A) includes real-life groups in which the leader's relationship with group members is very poor. This octant was classified as least favorable for the leader, since, it seems reasonable to assume that the strongly disliked leader will have a very difficult job. The basic hypothesis underlying the model is, then, that *the type of leader attitude required for effective group performance depends upon the degree to which the group situation is favorable or unfavorable to the leader.*

IV. Empirical Support for the Model

A. LEADER PERCEPTION SCORES (LPC AND ASo) AND GROUP PERFORMANCE

Groups included in previous studies were categorized by octants (Table II), as described above. Table II also includes "validation evidence," consisting of results from new studies, as well as re-analyses of old data that tested hypotheses derived from the model. The validation evidence is described in greater detail toward the end of this section.

Figure 2 graphically summarizes the information contained in Table II. The correlations between leader LPC/ASo scores and group performance were plotted by octants to indicate the range and dispersion of these correlation coefficients. The validation evidence is indicated by triangles. As can be seen, the correlations between leader scores and group performance measures within each octant are quite similar in size and direction. Even granting the post hoc nature of the classification, the consistency of the relations within octants is highly nonrandom in distribution.

The median correlations between LPC/ASo and group effectiveness can now be plotted against a hypothesized "advantage-for-the-leader" continuum which is obtained by collapsing the three dimensions. This leads to a bow-shaped curve showing that controlling, managing, and directive (low LPC) leaders perform best in group conditions which are either very favorable or very unfavorable to the leader, and that permissive, considerate, passive (high LPC) leaders perform best under moderately favorable or unfavorable conditions (i.e., in Octants IV, V, and VI). This is shown on Fig. 3 and Table III.

In very favorable conditions, where the leader has power, informal backing, and a relatively well-structured task, the group is ready to be directed on how to go about its task. Under a very unfavorable condition, however, the group will fall apart unless the leader's active intervention and control can keep the members on the job. In moderately unfavorable conditions, the accepted leader faces an ambiguous task, or his relations with group members are tenuous. Under these circumstances, a relationship-oriented, nondirective, permissive attitude may reduce member anxiety or intra-group conflict, and this enables the group to operate more effectively (i.e., the members would not feel threatened by the leader, and considerate, diplomatic leader behavior under these conditions may induce group members to cooperate).

The pattern of relations which determine the leader attitudes a group requires is also shown in Fig. 4. This graph presents the correlations between leader LPC/ASo and group performance, plotted against the two dimensions of the leader's position power and task structure for good and for moderately poor leader-member relations. The most important result indicated by this figure is again the remarkable reversal in the direction of the correlation coefficients in Octants IV and VIII, as well as in Octants I and V. While many of the interpretations are still highly speculative, it seems quite obvious that the dimensions of leader-member relations and task structure act as very powerful moderator variables in determining the type of leader attitude which maximizes group performance.

B. QUANTITATIVE INDICATIONS OF RELATIONS WITH COMPONENTS

In order to obtain a quantitative indication of the extent and nature of these relationships, a configural multiple regression technique was employed (Horst, 1954; Lubin and Osborn, 1957). The predictors in this multiple regression equation were the three group dimensions (PP, TS, and leader-member relations, R), and the four interactions of these dimensions with one another (PP $\times$ TS, PP $\times$ R, TS $\times$ R, and PP $\times$ TS $\times$ R). The latter terms were obtained from standard scores on the original dimensions and are thus nonlinear functions of these dimensions. A multiple regression was then computed for these seven predictors, the criterion being the correlation between the leader's LPC score and his group's performance. The number of cases for this multiple regression was 68, which is the number of individual correlations between LPC and performance reported in Table II. The validation data were not included in these analyses.

Table IV shows the correlation among the predictors and their validities. This table also presents the beta weights for the predictors and the multiple correlation between the seven predictors and the criterion. The three dimensions taken alone are unrelated to the LPC-performance

TABLE II

SUMMARY TABLE OF RELATIONS OBTAINED IN RESEARCH WITH LPC AND ASo SCORES

Octants I and V

High leader position power—high task structure
Good/moderately poor leader-member relations

Study			Leader-member relations			
			Good Octant I	Mod. poor Octant V	N_I	N_V
B-29 bomber crews. Military commander in Oct. I is sociometrically most preferred crew member and endorses keyman; is sociometrically most preferred crew member in Oct. V, but rejects keyman.	PP[a]	18.5				
Criterion 1: radar bomb score–circular error average (radar observer or navigator are keyman)	TS[b]	8.0	−.81	.42	11	7
Criterion 2: % satisfactory visual bomb runs (bombardier is keyman) (Fiedler, 1955)	TS	8.0	−.52	.27	6	7
Army tank crews. Tank commander in Oct. I is sociometrically most preferred crew member; in Oct. V is sociometrically most preferred crew member, but does not endorse his keyman.	PP	18.5				
Criterion 1: time to hit target (gunner is keyman)	TS	8.0	−.60	.60	6	5
Criterion 2: time to travel to target (driver is keyman) (Fiedler, 1955)	TS	8.0	−.33	.43		
Antiaircraft artillery crews. Commander in Oct. I is sociometrically most preferred crew member; in Oct. V is among 10 sociometrically least preferred crew members.	PP	18.5				
Criterion: location & acquisition of unidentified aircraft. (Hutchins and Fiedler, 1960)	TS	7.3	−.34	.49	10	10

[a] PP-Leader's Position Power.
[b] TS-Task structure.

Infantry squads. Squad leader is sociometrically most preferred crew member (no data available for sociometrically not chosen men).
Criterion: umpire ratings of field tests
(Havron et al., 1951)

PP	18.8			
TS	7.5	−.36		26

Open hearth steel shops. Foremen accepted by crew.
Criterion: tap-to-tap time (tonnage per unit of time) (no rejected foremen identified)
(Cleven and Fiedler, 1956)

PP	18.5			
TS	7.2	−.52		15

Company management. Gen. mgr. in Oct. I is sociometrically accepted by board and staff; in Oct. V is sociometrically accepted either by board or staff.
Criterion: % of company net income over 3 yrs.
(Godfrey et al., 1959)

PP	18.0			
TS	5.6	−.67	.23	10

Median correlation −.52 .42

Validation evidence

Sales display teams. Teams with detailed instructions for setting up sales displays and preparing merchandise. Only Oct. I data available.
Criterion: ratings by higher supervisors on conformity to performance standards. Tested by analysis of variance; low ASo leaders performed better than high ASo leaders.
(Hawkins, 1962)

PP	17.0		
TS	5.8	−($F < .10$)	76

Service station management. Managers of gas stations in various communities. Company has detailed operating procedure for servicing, stock control, and reporting. (Only Oct. I data available).
Criterion: stock control, sales, monthly audit, and checks by inspectors
Tested by chi-square. Low ASo managers performed better than high ASo managers.
(Hawkins, 1962)

PP	17.0		
TS	5.8	−($X^2 < .05$)	60

TABLE II (*Continued*)

Octants II and VI

Low leader position power—highly structured task
Good/moderately poor leader-member relations

Study			Leader-member relations			
			Good Octant II	Mod. poor Octant VI[c]	N_{II}	N_{VI}
High school basketball teams. "Leader" is sociometrically the most chosen team member, but is not appointed or elected, although wielding considerable influence.						
Study I criterion: % of games won by mid-season	PP	3.8				
	TS	7.2	−.69		14	
Study II criterion: 7 good, 5 poor teams tested at end of season (Pt.bis.r) (Fiedler, 1954)	TS	7.2	−.58		12	
Student surveying parties. "Leader" is sociometrically most preferred team member.						
Criterion: accuracy of surveying pre-selected parcels of land as rated by instructors. (Fiedler, 1954)	PP	3.2				
	TS	7.3	−.51		22	
Median correlation			−.58			
Validation evidence						
Team judgments. Two students were paired to judge which answers are best for *How Supervise Test.* Leader was designated by experimenter, but had no special function.	PP	2.0				
Criterion: # of items completed. Tested by Analysis of Variance, low ASo leaders were better than high ASo leaders (Hawkins, 1962)	TS	8.0	$-(F < .05)$		67	

[c] No groups were classified as belonging into Octant VI.

Octants III and VII

High leader position power—unstructured task
Good/moderately poor leader-member relations

Study			Leader-member relations			
			Good Octant III	Mod. poor Octant VII	N_{III}	N_{VII}
ROTC creativity study. Three-man ROTC groups with leader officially appointed. Study was part of ROTC training course. Highest ranked cadet chosen as leader. Leader-member relations measured by group atmosphere scores from upper and lower third of distribution.	PP	9.0				
Criterion 1: propose new pay scale for all ROTC services which will equalize pay scales (creativity rated by judges)	TS	3.4	−.43	.04	6	6
Criterion 2: tell fable on need for peacetime army (creativity rated by judges)	TS	2.2	−.72	.24	6	6
ROTC creativity study—high stress condition. Same as above, but groups worked under close supervision of senior army officers.	PP	9.0				
Criterion 1: pay scale proposal	TS	3.4	−.14	.11	6	6
Criterion 2: fable	TS	2.2	−.60	.57	6	6
(Meuwese, 1964)						
Navy ROTC Creativity Study. Four-man NROTC groups participated as part of NROTC leadership class problem. Senior midshipmen were appointed leaders, freshmen and sophomores served as members. Leaders chaired and *participated* in session.	PP	9.0				
Criterion 1: tell 2 stories based on TAT card 11 (creativity rated by judges)	TS	2.4	−.26	−.14	6	6
Criterion 2: develop arguments pro & con tough military training (rated by judges)	TS	4.2	−.07	.07	6	6
Criterion 3: suggest how average person can win fame and immortality (rated in terms of originality and uniqueness of solutions)	TS	4.7	−.44	−.07	6	6

169

TABLE II (Continued)

Octants III and VII

High leader position power—unstructured task
Good/moderately poor leader-member relations

Study		Leader-member relations			
		Good Octant III	Mod. poor Octant VII	N_{III}	N_{VII}
Navy ROTC creativity study. Same as above but leaders *supervised*—were not permitted to contribute to task solutions, but could suggest procedures and veto ideas.	PP 11.8				
Criterion 1: TAT stories	TS 2.4	−.39	.47	6	6
Criterion 2: arguments	TS 4.2	−.43	.01	6	6
Criterion 3: fame and immortality	TS 4.7	.84	−.10	6	6
(Anderson and Fiedler, 1962)					
Median correlation		−.41	.05		

Octants IV and VIII

Low leader position power—unstructured task
Good/moderately poor leader-member relations

Study	Leader-member relations			
	Good Octant IV	Mod. poor Octant VIII	N_{IV}	N_{VIII}

"*Dutch*" *creativity study.* Four-man groups consisting of Dutch university students. Leader-member relations inferred from tension indicators in content analysis and group composition, viz., homogeneity vs. heterogeneity, and formal or informal leadership.

Criterion task: tell 3 stories about TAT picture; find alternative uses or invent plot titles (creativity rated by judges)	TS	1.7				
Composition: homogeneous religious membership and formal leaders appointed by experimenter.	PP	5.8	.75	− .72	7	8
Composition: heterogeneous groups, appointed leaders	PP	5.5		− .64		6
Composition: homogeneous, informal leaders	PP	2.0		− .23		8
Composition: heterogeneous, informal leaders	PP	2.0				
(Fiedler *et al.*, 1961b)						
Hypnosis study. Three-person groups, leader selected by experimenter's confederates. Leader-member relations based on group atmosphere scores.	PP	5.0				
Criterion: tell 3 stories about same TAT card (creativity rated by judges)	TS	1.7	.64	− .72	8	8
(Fiedler *et al.*, 1961c)						
Church leadership study. Four-person groups participating in leadership workshop. Leaders selected by experimenter, groups changed each day. Leader-member relations measured by group atmosphere.						
Criterion 1: justify minister's position on mercy killing (creativity in this and other tasks rated by all participants)	PP	4.8	.28	.03	6	6
	TS	2.7				
Criterion 2: tell fable about separation of church and state	PP	4.5	.89	− .03	6	6
	TS	2.2				
Criterion 3: devise campaign to raise funds for young student minister	PP	4.8	.49	− .40	6	6
	TS	3.2				
Criterion 4: plan and perform skit on music for the worship service	PP	4.5	.37	− .60	6	6
	TS	2.2				
(Fiedler *et al.*, 1961a)						
Mental health leadership study. Three-person groups, with chairman selected by experimenter. Leader-member relations measured by group atmosphere score.	PP	4.5				
Criterion task: justify use of elementary schools for approved research (creativity rated by judges)	TS	2.8	.44	− .76	7	7

TABLE II (*Continued*)

Octants IV and VIII

Low leader position power—unstructured task
Good/moderately poor leader-member relations

		Leader-member relations			
		Good Octant IV	Mod. poor Octant VIII	N$_{IV}$	N$_{VIII}$
Study					
ROTC creativity study—internal stress condition. Three-man groups, two army and one navy cadets. Leader was lowest ranking army man.					
Criterion task 1: develop new pay schedule	PP 4.5 / TS 3.4	.49	−.04	6	6
Criterion task 2: tell fable about peacetime army (creativity rated by judges)	TS 2.2	−.03	−.47	6	6
(Meuwese, 1964)					
Chairman, board of directors. Boards of directors of small cooperatively owned corporations. Leader-member relations estimated on basis of board chairman-gen. mgr. relations as indicated by sociometric ratings.					
Criterion: company net income over 3 years	PP 7.0 / TS 4.1	.21	−.60	10	10
(Godfrey *et al.*, 1959)					
Median correlations		.47	−.43		
Validation evidence					
Church leadership study II. Three-person groups assembled ad hoc, with leader designated by experimenter. Leader-group member relations assessed by leader's GA scores and post-meeting questionnaires.					
Criterion task: justify your position to children on reading prayers in school	PP 4.5 / TS 2.2	.27	−.04	19	19

Octant V-A

Very poor leader-group member relations
High leader position power, structured task

Study			Leader-member relations Very poor Octant V-A	N_{V-A}
B-29 bomber crews. As in Octants I and V, except that crew commander is sociometrically rejected and does not sociometrically choose his keygroup members. Validation evidence	PP TS	18.5 8.0	−.67	7
Antiaircraft artillery crews. As in Octants I and V, but crew commanders are sociometrically most rejected (re-analysis)	PP TS	18.5 7.3	−.42	10
Company management. As in Octants I and V, but general manager is sociometrically rejected by *both*, board of directors and staff (re-analysis)	PP TS	18.0 5.6	−.75	7
Median correlation			−.67	

173

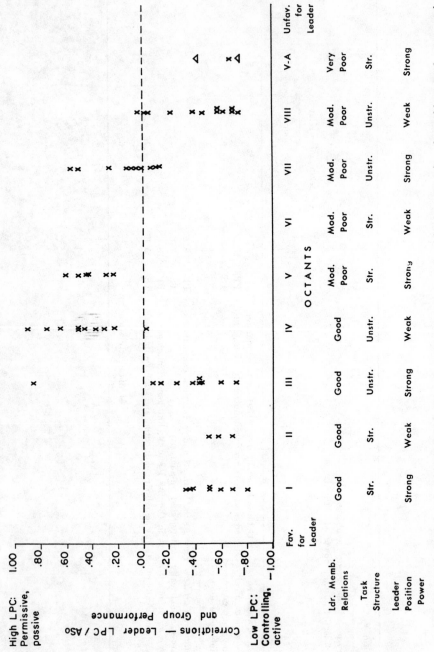

FIG. 2. Correlations of leader LPC and group performance plotted against octants, i.e., favorableness of group task situation for leader.

criterion. However, the two double interaction terms involving leader-member relations (PP $\times$ R and TS $\times$ R) are both significantly related to the criterion. Further, the triple interaction (PP $\times$ TS $\times$ R), while having zero validity for the criterion, has the largest and only significant beta

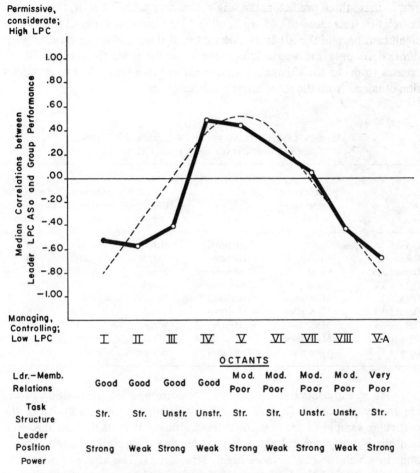

FIG. 3. Curve indicating optimal leader attitudes and behavior (permissive, considerate vs. managing, controlling) required by various group task situations, and median correlations obtained for conditions.

weight. This variable is a suppressor, having relatively high correlations with several other predictors which are components of it. It would appear, however, that this triple interaction is not a particularly important determinant of the LPC-performance correlations. Rather, its relatively large beta weight is a function of its necessarily large relationship with several of the other predictors.

The multiple correlation of all seven predictors and the criterion is .58 ($p < .01$). If we use only the three dimensions as predictors (PP, TS, and R), the multiple R is negligible, namely, .15 (NS). However, if we add to these three predictors the single nonlinear term TS $\times$ R, the multiple correlation increases to .45 ($p < .05$). This increase from .15 to .45 is significant beyond the .01 level. Alternatively, if we add to the three original dimensions only the single interaction term PP $\times$ R, the multiple R increases from .15 to .42, again a significant increase ($p < .01$) over prediction obtained from the three linear predictors alone.

TABLE III

MEDIAN CORRELATIONS BETWEEN LEADER LPC AND
GROUP PERFORMANCE IN VARIOUS OCTANTS

	Leader-member relations	Task structure	Position power	Median corre-lation	Number of relations included in median-
Octant I	Good	Structured	Strong	− .52	8
Octant II	Good	Structured	Weak	− .58	3
Octant III	Good	Unstructured	Strong	− .41	4
Octant IV	Good	Unstructured	Weak	.47	10
Octant V	Mod. poor	Structured	Strong	.42	6
Octant VI	Mod. poor	Structured	Weak		0
Octant VII	Mod. poor	Unstructured	Strong	.05	10
Octant VIII	Mod. poor	Unstructured	Weak	− .43	12
Octant V-A	Very poor	Structured	Strong	− .67	1

As already mentioned, the task structure and leader position power are highly correlated ($r = .75$). While this may be a peculiarity of the particular sample of tasks used in these studies, it is likely that this relationship is fairly general (i.e., that leader power is higher in those situations in which the task is more highly structured). The above findings may then indicate that the leader who is low in LPC has more effective work groups when either his position power or task structure is high *and* leader-member relationships are favorable. When leader power or task structure is low *and* leader-member relations are poor, then the high LPC leader has a more effective group.

However, the multiple correlation tells only part of the story. As Fig. 4 shows, several areas in this three-dimensional space remain empty, suggesting new hypotheses for further investigations. Thus, the correlations between leader LPC and group performance in the upper left-hand

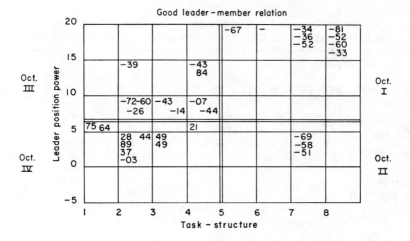

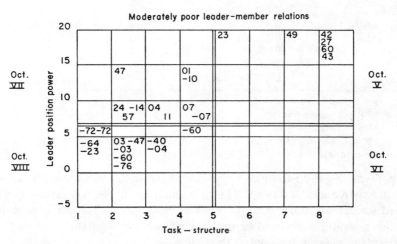

FIG. 4. Correlations between leader LPC/ASo and group performance plotted against leader position power and task structure under good and poor leader-member relations.

corner of Octant III should probably be positive, since an accepted leader with extremely high position power might need to be very permissive and accepting in order to work effectively with a group on a highly ambiguous task. An example might be a general working with two enlisted men on a creative task, or a cardinal with two laymen on a planning committee. The hypothesis is that a large difference in position power would awe low-ranking members and stifle their creativity, unless the leader were extremely permissive and equalitarian in his attitude and behavior. Another

TABLE IV

MULTIPLE CORRELATION ANALYSIS OF GROUP DIMENSION VARIABLES
AS PREDICTORS OF THE LPC/ASo-GROUP EFFECTIVENESS CORRELATION

	(1) PP	(2) TS	(3) R	(4) PP × TS	(5) PP × R	(6) TS × R	(7) PP × TS × R	(Criterion) $r_{LPC-perf.}$
PP[a]		$.75^d$	$-.09$	$.60^d$	$-.08$	$-.17$	$.02$	$-.09$
TS[b]			$.03$	$.43^d$	$-.16$	$-.01$	$-.10$	$-.14$
R[c]				$-.17$	$.16$	$.15$	$.64^d$	$.04$
PP × TS					$.08$	$-.15$	$.01$	$.08$
PP × R						$.78^d$	$.60^d$	$-.34^d$
TS × R							$.49^d$	$-.41^d$
PP × TS × R								$.01$

STANDARDIZED REGRESSION COEFFICIENTS

	$r_{LPC-perf.}$
PP	$-.39$
TS	$.05$
R	$-.22$
PP × TS	$.22$
PP × R	$-.40$
TS × R	$-.39$
PP × TS × R	$.59^d$

NOTE: Multiple r = .58.
[a] PP = Position power.
[b] TS = Task structure.
[c] R = Leader-member relationship.
[d] $p < .01$ (N = 68).

hypothesis based on the plot suggests that the leader in Octant VI should be permissive and accepting. This is a situation in which a relatively disliked leader has little formal power. The most appropriate leader behavior in this situation is likely to be one of guidance and suggestion, rather than attempts to manage and control the group.

V. Validation Evidence

In addition to recent investigations which provide partial tests of the model, appropriate data from previously conducted studies were re-analyzed in light of the new hypotheses.

A. RE-ANALYSES OF DATA FROM REAL-LIFE GROUPS

Previous data suggested that managing, controlling leader attitudes appear most effective under group situations which are either *very* favorable or *very* unfavorable to the leader; permissive, accepting leader attitudes are most appropriate under conditions which are only moderately unfavorable. As indicated before, it was hypothesized that the leader-member relations were the most important factor in determining the favorableness of the group situation. It should then be possible to test this hypothesis on real-life groups, which vary widely in leader-member relations while task structure and position power remain constant. This should result in negative correlations between LPC or ASo of the leader and group performance, in which the leader-member relationship is either very good or very poor, and positive correlations when the leader-member relationship is moderately poor.

Such data were obtained earlier in a study of B-29 bomber crews. The leader-member relations were inferred from sociometric preference ratings obtained from all crew members. The groups ranged from highly cohesive crews with a large proportion of mutual choices, to very uncohesive groups in which the leader was strongly rejected and, in turn, expressed low opinions of his ranking crew members. The relationship in these crews was assessed by (a) whether or not the leader was the most chosen member of his crew, and (b) his acceptance or rejection of his key crew members (i.e., the men who performed criterion relevant tasks). Evaluation of crew performance was based on radar bomb scores, which require the aircraft commander to cooperate closely with the radar observer or navigator, who are the keymen in this instance. (Some of these crews were included in Octant I and IV of Table II).

It was assumed that a very favorable situation existed if a crew leader was sociometrically the most chosen crew member and, in turn, endorsed his keymen, while a less favorable condition obtained if a sociometrically endorsed leader did not endorse his keymen (or if an unchosen leader endorsed his keymen), and a very unfavorable condition existed if a rejected leader also rejected his keymen.

Correlations have been made between the leader's ASo score and his crew's radar bomb scores under six conditions of increasingly poorer leader-member relations (Fiedler, 1955). At the time of the original study, these relations could not be properly interpreted, and only recently was there an opportunity to cross-validate the findings.

As Table V shows, the expected curvilinear relationship was obtained between ASo and group performance and the degree to which the leader-member relationship was good. The problem remained to find similar results in other real-life groups in which leader-member relations varied from very good to very poor.

The hypothesis could be tested on data obtained in a study of anti-aircraft artillery crews (Hutchins and Fiedler, 1960). Effectiveness scores were based on rated crew performance in the "location and acquisition" of unidentified aircraft. These data were re-analyzed by separately analyzing the ten crews which fell most nearly in the middle of the distribution and the ten crews which gave their commanders the lowest sociometric ratings. As Table VI shows, the correlations between leader LPC and the crew performance scores again ranged from negative to positive to negative, thus supporting the findings obtained in the study of B-29 crews.

TABLE V

CORRELATIONS BETWEEN AIRCRAFT COMMANDER'S ASo SCORE AND
RADAR BOMB SCORE UNDER DIFFERENT CONDITIONS OF
SOCIOMETRIC CREW CHOICE PATTERNS[a]

Sociometric choice pattern	Rho	N
AC = MPC → VO/N[b]	−.81	10
AC = MPC --VO/N	−.14	6
AC = MPC ∸ VO/N	.43	6
AC ≠ MPC → VO/N	−.03	18
AC ≠ MPC--VO/N	−.80	5
AC ≠ MPC ∸ VO/N	−.67	7

[a] Table adapted from Fiedler (1955).

[b] Aircraft commander is (=), or is not (≠) most preferred crew member and sociometrically accepts (→). is neutral to (--), or rejects (∸) keyman (radar observer and navigator).

TABLE VI

CORRELATIONS BETWEEN LEADER LPC SCORES AND
ANTIAIRCRAFT ARTILLERY CREW PERFORMANCE

	Rho	N
Most highly chosen crew commanders	−.34	10
Middle range in sociometric choices	.49	10
Lowest chosen crew commanders	−.42	10

A second validation analysis was based on a study of 32 farm-supply cooperative organizations (Godfrey et al., 1959). Each of these companies had its own board of directors which, in turn, hired a general manager. The company managers worked closely with the board of directors, as well as with their staff of assistant managers. The criterion of performance was the percentage of net income of the company over the preceding three-year period.

The groups were again divided according to sociometric choice patterns. It was assumed that a general manager who was chosen both by his board of directors and by his staff had a better relationship and hence a more favorable group situation than one chosen only by the board or only by his staff. It was also assumed that his position would be least favorable when both his board of directors and his own staff of assistant managers sociometrically rejected him. As before, the data supported the hypothesis (Table VII).

TABLE VII
CORRELATIONS BETWEEN GENERAL MANAGER'S LPC SCORE
AND COMPANY NET INCOME

	Rho	N
GM most chosen by board and staff	−.67	10
GM chosen by board, but rejected by staff	.20	6
GM rejected by board, but chosen by staff	.26	6
GM rejected by board and staff	−.75	7

It is not yet known what might happen under even less favorable situations in which the leader is not only rejected by his group, but also has an unstructured task and little power. Groups under these conditions might simply disintegrate, or the leader might lose control. It is hoped that studies testing performance under these specific conditions can be conducted in the near future.

B. RESEARCH BY HAWKINS

Three studies were recently conducted by Hawkins (1962) at the University of Minnesota. The first of these involved two-person teams with one individual appointed as leader. These teams were asked to agree on the "right responses" for the *How Supervise?* test. The team's performance was scored on the basis of items completed within a given time. These teams, which obviously had a highly structured task and a leader with low position power, fell into Octant II. Hawkins found that pairs with low ASo leaders completed a larger number of items than did pairs with high ASo leaders. The results thus supported the hypothesis.

A second study utilized sales display teams from a large company. A detailed operating procedure is provided, thus making the task highly structured. The leader, as in most supervisory situations of this type, had fairly high power. He was in charge of the team and could recommend personnel actions. The groups were evaluated by higher supervisors within the district. Although no sociometric measures were obtained in this study, it seems reasonable to assume that most teams fell into Octant I. In line with the model's predictions, Hawkins found a significant difference between teams, with the more controlling, managing, low ASo leaders rated as being more effective.

The third study dealt with a chain of service stations. These stations were also expected to operate in accordance with detailed instructions under the supervision of the station manager. The effectiveness of the stations was evaluated by spot checks of supervisors as well as stock control, accounting, and sales records. Here again, task structure, as well as position power, appeared to be high. We must again assume that personnel in most stations sociometrically accepted their managers. If this assumption is correct, the group situations fall into Octant I, and Hawkins' findings, that low ASo managers were more effective, support the model.

C. RELAXED VS. STRESSFUL CONDITIONS

It will be recalled that groups in which the leader rated the group atmosphere as pleasant performed better on creative tasks under high LPC leaders, while groups rated as having low group atmosphere performed better under low LPC leaders (Fiedler, 1962). These groups were categorized as having low task structure and low position power and as falling into Octants IV or VIII, depending on the leader's GA score.

A study was recently conducted to test this effect experimentally by making the group situation pleasant under one condition and less pleasant under a second condition. This study was conducted within the context of a leadership training conference in which 57 persons participated. The participants were mature men and women who held responsible positions in the Unitarian-Universalist church. The Conference members were assigned to three-person groups which were given two successive tasks. The first required them to write a statement for their children to justify the parents' opposition to the reading of prayers in public schools. This was presented as a relatively easy task, given as a "warm-up" exercise for which the groups had more than sufficient time (35 minutes). The second task required the group to prepare a statement which would explain the Unitarian-Universalist creed to children of another church. This task was presented as a "real test of leadership" which was quite difficult, and which required the groups to operate under considerable time pressure (20 minutes).

LPC and intelligence test scores had been obtained on a previous day. Sociometric preference ratings, group atmosphere scores, and behavior descriptions of fellow group members were collected after each of the tasks. Group task products were evaluated by all conference participants.

This group situation was rated as having low task structure and low position power. As for leader-member relations, they were less strained for the leader in the first than in the second session. Thus the groups were classified as falling into Octant IV during the first task and Octant VIII during the second task.

In line with this expectation, groups of high LPC leaders performed significantly better under the more pleasant, relaxed condition of the first task, while low LPC leaders performed more effectively on the second, less pleasant and more stressful task (Fiedler *et al.*, 1964).

VI. Discussion

This chapter attempts to reconcile the apparent inconsistencies in our work by showing that the prediction of leading effectiveness by means of LPC scores (and perhaps other leader attributes as well) is contingent upon an adequate classification of the group situation. The data raise several questions which merit further discussion. Specifically, how good is the classification system which has been suggested? What does this model say about the effect of leader and member abilities on task performance? What are the implications of this model for leadership strategy? What is the role of quasi-therapeutic leader attitudes in task groups? Finally, how well does this model serve to integrate the findings of other investigators in this field?

A. Classification of Group Situations

The notion that different types of groups require different types of leaders is, of course, not new. The present model attempts to spell out the specific conditions under which certain leadership attitudes result in effective performance. The first question concerns the adequacy of the proposed classification system.

The underlying basis for categorizing group situations is the degree to which they facilitate the leader's job of influencing his group. This classification system appears to work for the type and range of group situations which have been covered. It remains to be seen whether this classification, based on the three dimensions of leader-member relations, task structure, and leader position power, represents the best solution. Other dimensions, such as group stress or member motivation, may later need to be substituted or added as further data become available.

Several shortcomings of the categorization are readily apparent. One of these is the problem of scaling and ordering the dimensions. Under normal conditions all three dimensions of the group-task situation seem to play an important role. However, some groups dislike the leader enough to sabotage the task. Under these conditions, a leader could not be very effective, even under otherwise favorable circumstances. Such an intense negative feeling by group members toward their leader obviously must be given additional weight. This was done on a rule-of-thumb basis by considering Octant V-A the most unfavorable point on the continuum (cf. Figs. 2 and 3). Similarly, a task might be so highly structured that any permissiveness on the part of the leader would result in degrading the group's performance. Count-downs of space probes or the maintenance of rigid, quality control criteria, are cases in point. These two examples indicate that a better method is needed for weighting the dimensions so as to allow for extreme cases.

B. LEADER AND MEMBER ABILITIES

It is well established that leader and member abilities are among the most important predictors of group performance (Mann, 1959; McGrath, 1962). Teams composed of intellectually inferior and technically unskilled persons will naturally perform worse on almost any task than will groups composed of able and qualified individuals. Fiedler and Meuwese (1963), using commonly accepted intelligence and ability tests, have shown in four different studies that the leader's ability scores correlate highly with performance of military units and laboratory groups *only if the leader is sociometrically accepted.* That is, in groups falling into Octants I and IV, the median correlation between the leader's ability scores and his group's performance was .74 (which is considerably above the comparable median correlation of .25 reported in Mann's 1959 review). In contrast, the corresponding median for uncohesive groups, or those which sociometrically rejected their leader (Octants V and VIII), was only —.22. The difference between these two medians is highly significant.

A high correlation between the leader's ability score and the group's performance presumably reflects the degree of leader influence over the task itself (i.e., either the group followed the leader's suggestions or it permitted the leader to do the job in his own way). The negative correlations found in uncohesive groups suggest that the leader's influence, or his own contribution to the task, is minimal, and that the leader may have to attend primarily to the performance of maintenance functions in these groups.

C. STRATEGIES OF LEADERSHIP

Inasmuch as LPC or ASo are measures of interpersonal attitudes, a leader can, of course, be trained to modify these attitudes. He will probably be able to do so to the same extent to which he can modify other strongly entrenched attitudes. Changes in perceptions of co-workers seem, therefore, possible, but considerable effort might be required on the part of many individuals to make them.

A more practical alternative would involve the training of leaders in diagnosing their group-task situation and in adopting strategies which capitalize on their particular leadership style. For example, a controlling, managing, and directive (low LPC) leader might find himself faced with a relatively unstructured task. According to our contingency model, he should first attempt to structure and clarify the group's problem in order to move his group from Octant IV to Octant I, in which he could operate more effectively. A high LPC leader with poor group-member relations, an unstructured task, and low position power (Octant VIII) should first improve his interpersonal relations to move his group into Octant IV, in which his leadership attitude would be more appropriate.

A different strategy might be desirable for tasks which increase their structure over time. This is well illustrated by research projects which are tentative and unstructured during the planning phases, but become highly structured and programmed once the design is frozen and the experiment is in progress. It is often quite apparent that the group situation changes in other respects as well. While the leader of the project generally plays a very permissive, democratic role during the initial phase of the project, he tends to become managing and autocratic as the experiment gets under way and the need for strict control increases.

D. QUASI-THERAPEUTIC LEADER ATTITUDES AND EFFECTIVENESS

There has been considerable speculation whether the effective leader —or someone in his place—must always perform "quasi-therapeutic" functions which assist the group members to adjust (e.g., Berkowitz, 1953; Clark, 1955; Haernqvist, 1956; Gordon, 1955). The writer's data may throw some light on this question. Studies show that the high LPC leader, who is permissive, non-directive, and considerate in his approach to the group, does tend to promote better group relations and more member satisfaction (Fiedler et al., 1961c; Meuwese, 1964; Hutchins and Fiedler, 1960). It seems likely on the basis of presently available evidence that these quasi-therapeutic attitudes may be especially important in groups which have interpersonal conflict, strained leader-member relations, or an ambiguous, unstructured task. As Neel (1955), Seashore (1955), and others have shown, these conditions tend to arouse anxiety among group members. A quasi-therapeutic leader may then alleviate insecurity and anxiety which might otherwise interfere with efficient performance. Such person-oriented attitudes may be especially desirable in certain co-acting groups in which several individuals independently pursue a common goal with minimal interaction (e.g., a rifle team or a track team). In such coacting groups, the leader has very few directive and controlling functions, and his contribution to effective task performance may consist primarily of providing psychological support and encouragement to the individual team member.

Studies have been conducted on a number of these groups. One investigation dealt with team training of naval aviation cadets. This tends to be an anxiety arousing experience, since it involves not only a demanding ground school program, but also relatively dangerous formation flying. Each "flight" typically consisted of eight trainees who were under the tutelage of a flight instructor team. An informal leader of each flight (who had no power or official status) was identified by means of sociometric indices. The formal leader was the senior instructor in charge of training the flight.

The correlation between the ASo score of the sociometrically preferred member of the flight and the flight's performance was .42 ($N = 36$, $p < .05$). The senior flight instructor's ASo score and the group performance correlated .31 ($N = 14$). These results suggested that the informal leader of the group or the flight's senior instructor promoted effectiveness by his ability to lessen the anxiety of the group's members.

A study by DeZonia (1958) investigated the relationship between the teacher's assumed similarity score and his rated efficiency as a teacher. DeZonia found a correlation of −.55 for English teachers, but +.57 for teachers of speech. The teaching of grammar and English literature probably requires the teacher to keep the student focused on the task. The ability to teach public speaking may, however, also require that the teacher alleviate the anxiety which is associated with stage fright and pre-speaking jitters. This latter quasi-therapeutic function would be more effectively performed by the permissive, nondirective person.

A coacting group situation was also contained in a laboratory study by Anderson and Fiedler (1962). This investigation utilized naval ROTC midshipmen who were asked to devise unusual uses for two objects, namely, a coathanger and a ruler. The leader of the group under the "supervisory" condition could approve or reject suggestions from his group, but he was not permitted to contribute ideas. Under a "participatory" condition, the leader worked with the group as its chairman.

The task was scored in terms of the uniqueness, i.e., infrequency of the suggested uses by various members. This placed them in a coacting relationship, since the productivity of one member was relatively unaffected by that of his colleagues. Here again, the correlation between the leader's LPC score and his group's performance was positive, i.e., .55 and .31 ($N = 15$) under the supervisory and participatory conditions, respectively.

It can readily be seen why the permissive, accepting leader would promote greater productivity under these conditions. Unique solutions, which are often silly and by definition off-beat, are more likely to occur when the leader is permissive and accepting than when he is critical and threatening.[5]

[5] This might also account for the "out-of-place" correlation of .84 between leader LPC and group performance which occurred under the supervisory condition of the Triandis *et al.* (1963) "fame and immortality" problem used in the Navy

We must recognize, of course, that these attempts to relate the leader's task functions and his therapeutic attitudes are highly speculative at this time. Extensive future research will be required to elucidate the role which these therapeutic attitudes play in the group process.

E. GENERALIZABILITY OF THE MODEL

Ideally it should be possible to integrate all other studies of leadership effectiveness traits into the contingency model which has been described here. This is impossible for a number of compelling reasons. Above all, the literature is difficult to interpret, because the profusion of variables does not permit one to infer with any assurance that a particular study fits into one octant rather than another.

However, the model summarized here is consistent with other research. Halpin's finding of negative correlations between the aircraft commander's "consideration" score, and a positive correlation between his "initiation-of-structure" score and crew performance, fit well within the framework outlined here. Likewise, the conclusion is supported that "in an authoritarian setting the most productive group will tend to be authoritarian, whereas in a more democratic situation the equalitarian group will be more productive" (Hare, 1962). Shaw's (1955) finding that authoritarian leadership attitudes led to better performance than did nonauthoritarian leader attitudes is also applicable. Shaw used highly structured tasks and, provided the leaders in his groups were accepted, the groups would then normally fall into Octants I or II.

Permissive, democratic, equalitarian leadership was more effective in Comrey's (1954) study of forest management, and McGregor's (1960) and Likert's (1961) experience with management groups. These, if interpreted correctly, represented situations in which the task was considerably less structured and the leaders tended to be more equal in power to their group members. Given accepted leaders, situations of this nature should fall into Octant IV, which favors the equalitarian, permissive attitudes which McGregor and Likert advocate. Other studies cannot be readily considered as fitting the model (e.g., Argyle et al., 1957; Kahn and Katz, 1960). It is, however, obvious that any attempt to integrate these and similar studies in the absence of specific information about leader-member relations, task structure, and position power becomes speculative to the point of uselessness. If the model is to have any meaning at all, it must be

---

ROTC study (Octant III). In this task, the group members were to suggest ways in which a person of average means and talent could achieve fame and immortality. Each individual contribution was relatively independent of other members' ideas, even though the group later had to agree on the one best solution. The most unusual solution received the highest score.

ι able to predict a reasonably high proportion of appropriate cases. Where such appropriate data are available, as in the Havron *et al.* (1954) investigation of infantry squads, or the studies by Hawkins (1962), the evidence clearly supports the model's requirements. But we do not know in most other studies how well the leader was accepted, how highly structured his task was, or how much position power was at his disposal. It is hoped that such information will be available in the future, as we learn to identify the specific information about group situations which is crucial for the understanding and prediction of leadership effectiveness.

REFERENCES

Anderson, L. R., and Fiedler, F. E. (1962). The Effect of Participatory and Supervisory Leadership on Group Creativity. Group Effectiveness Research Laboratory, Univ. of Illinois, Urbana, Illinois.

Argyle, M., Gardner, G., and Cioffi, R. (1957). *Human Relat.* **10**, 295–313.

Bass, B. M. (1960). "Leadership, Psychology, and Organizational Behavior." Harper, New York.

Berkowitz, L. (1953). *J. Abnorm. Soc. Psychol.* **48**, 231–238.

Bieri, J. (1953). *J. Abnorm. Soc. Psychol.* **48**, 61–66.

Browne, C. G., and Cohn, T. S., eds. (1958). "The Study of Leadership." Interstate Printers and Publishers, Danville, Illinois.

Campbell, D. T. (1958). *Behav. Sci.* **3**, 14–25.

Cartwright, D., and Zander, A., 1960. *Group Dynamics,* (2nd ed.) Row Peterson, Evanston, Ill.

Cattell, R. B. (1951). *Human Relat.* **4**, 161–184.

Clark, R. A. (1955). Leadership in Rifle Squads on the Korean Front Line. Human Resources Research Unit No. 2, CONARC, Fort Ord, California.

Cleven, W. A., and Fiedler, F. E. (1956). *J. Appl. Psychol.* **40**, 312–314.

Comrey, A. L. (1954). *Personnel Psychol.* **7**, 533–547.

Comrey, A. L., Pfiffner, J. M., and High, W. S. (1954). Factors Influencing Organizational Effectiveness. Univ. of Southern California, Los Angeles, California.

Cronbach, L. J., and Gleser, G. C. (1953). *Psychol. Bull.* **50**, 456–473.

Davitz, J. (1955). *J. Abnorm. Soc. Psychol.* **50**, 173–176.

Deutsch, M. (1949). *Human Relat.* **2**, 199–232.

DeZonia, R. H. (1958). Unpublished Ph.D. Dissertation, University of Illinois, Urbana, Illinois.

Fiedler, F. E. (1951). *J. Clin. Psychol.* **7**, 101–107.

Fiedler, F. E. (1954). *J. Abnorm. Soc. Psychol.* **49**, 381–388.

Fiedler, F. E. (1955). *J. Abnorm. Soc. Psychol.* **51**, 277–235.

Fiedler, F. E. (1961). *In* "Leadership and Interpersonal Behavior" (L. Petrullo and B. M. Bass, eds.). Holt, New York.

Fiedler, F. E. (1962). *J. Abnorm. Soc. Psychol.* **65**, 308–318.

Fiedler, F. E., and Meuwese, W. A. T. (1963). *J. Abnorm. Soc. Psychol.* **67**, 83–87.

Fiedler, F. E., Warrington, W. G., and Blaisdell, F. J. (1952). *J. Abnorm. Soc. Psychol.* **47**, 790–796.

Fiedler, F. E., Bass, A. R., and Fiedler, J. M. (1961a). Tech. Rep. No. 1, Group Effectiveness Research Laboratory, Univ. of Illinois, Urbana, Illinois.

Fiedler, F. E., Meuwese, W. A. T., and Oonk, S. (1961b). *Acta Psychol.* **18**, 100–119.

Fiedler, F. E., London, P., and Nemo, R. S. (1961c). Hypnotically Induced Leader Attitudes and Group Creativity. Group Effectiveness Research Laboratory, University of Illinois, Urbana, Illinois.

Fiedler, F. E., Hackman, R. R., and Meuwese, W. A. T. (1964). Group Effectiveness Research Laboratory, University of Illinois, Urbana, Illinois (in preparation).

French, J. R. P., Jr. (1956). Psychol. Rev. 63, 181–194.

French, J. R. P., Jr., and Raven, B. H. (1958). Sociometry 21, 83–97.

George, C. E. (1962). Research Memorandum #26, U.S. Army Infantry Human Research Unit, Fort Benning, Georgia.

Gerard, H. B. (1957). J. Pers. 25, 475–488.

Gibb, C. A. (1954). In "Handbook of Social Psychology" (G. Lindzey, ed.), Vol. II. Addison-Wesley, Cambridge, Massachusetts.

Godfrey, E. P., Fiedler, F. E., and Hall, D. M. (1959). "Boards, Managers, and Company Success." Interstate Press and Publishers, Danville, Illinois.

Gordon, T. (1955). "Group Centered Leadership: A Way of Releasing the Creative Power of the Group. Houghton-Mifflin, Boston.

Haernqvist, K. (1956). "Adjustment: Leadership and Group Relations." Almqvist and Wiksell, Stockholm, Sweden.

Halpin, A. W. (1955). Harvard Educ. Rev. 25, 18–22.

Halpin, A. W., and Winer, B. J. (1957). In "Leader Behavior: Its Description and Measurement" (R. M. Stogdill and A. E. Coons, eds.), Bur. Bus. Res Monograph 88. Ohio State Univ., Columbus, Ohio.

Hare, A. P. (1962). "Handbook of Small Group Research." Free Press, Glencoe, New York.

Havron, M. D., Fay, R. J., and Goodacre, D. M., III. (1951). Research on the Effectiveness of Small Military Units. Adjutant General's Department PRS Report 885. Washington, D. C.

Havron, M. D., Lybrand, W. A., Cohen, E., Kassebaum, R. G., and McGrath, J. E. (1954). Tech. Research Note 31, The Adjutant General's Office, Personnel Research Branch, Washington, D. C.

Hawkins, C. (1962). Ph.D. Dissertation, Univ. of Minnesota.

Haythorn, W. W. (1956). J. Soc. Abnorm. Psychol. 53, 210–219.

Horst, P. (1954). J. Clin. Psychol. 10, 3–11.

Hutchins, E. B., and Fiedler, F. E. (1960). Sociometry 23, 393–406.

Janda, K. F. (1960). Human Relat. 13, 345–363.

Kahn, R. L., and Katz, D. (1960). In "Group Dynamics" (D. Cartwright and A. Zander, eds.), 2nd ed. Row Peterson, Evanston, Illinois.

Katz, E., and Kahn, R. L. (1953). In "Readings in Social Psychology," (G. E. Swanson, T. M. Newcomb, and E. L. Hartley, eds.) Holt, New York.

Lewin, K., and Lippitt, R. (1938). Sociometry 1, 292–300.

Likert, R. (1961). "New Patterns of Management." McGraw-Hill, New York.

Lippitt, R., and White, R. K. (1952). In "Readings in Social Psychology," (G. E. Swanson, T. M. Newcomb, and E. L. Hartley, eds.) Holt, New York.

Lubin, A., and Osborn, H. G. (1957). Psychometrica 22, 63–73.

McGrath, J. E. (1962). HSR-TN-62/3-Gn, Human Sciences Research, Inc., Arlington, Virginia.

McGregor, D. M. (1960). "The Human Side of Enterprise." McGraw-Hill, New York.

Maier, N. R. F., and Solem, A. R. (1952). Human Relat. 5, 277–288.

Mann, R. D. (1959). Psychol. Bull. 56, 241–270.

Meuwese, W. A. T. (1964). The Effect of the Leader's Ability and Interpersonal Attitudes on group creativity under varying conditions of stress.

Myers, A. E. (1962). *J. Abnorm. Soc. Psychol.* **65,** 325–332.

Neel, R. (1955). *Personnel Psychol.* **8,** 409–416.

Osgood, C. E., Suci, G. J., and Tannenbaum, P. H. (1957). "The Measurement of Meaning." Univ. of Illinois Press, Urbana, Illinois.

Schutz, W. C. (1953). Studies in Group Behavior. I. Construction of High Productivity Groups. Department of Systems Analysis, Tufts College, Medford, Massachusetts.

Schutz, W. C. (1958). "FIRO: A Three Dimensional Theory of Interpersonal Behavior." Holt, Rinehart and Winston, New York.

Seashore, S. E. (1955). Institute for Social Research, Ann Arbor, Michigan.

Sells, S. B. (1962). "Military Small Group Performance under Isolation and Stress— a Critical Review." Office of Technical Services, U.S. Dept. of Commerce, Washington, D. C.

Shaw, M. E. (1955). *J. Abnorm. Soc. Psychol.* **50,** 127–134.

Shaw, M. E. (1962). Ann. Tech. Rept. University of Florida, Gainesville, Florida.

Sherif, M., and Sherif, C. W. (1953). "Groups in Harmony and Tension." Harper, New York.

Spector, P., and Suttell, B. J. (1956). American Institute for Research, Washington, D. C.

Steiner, I. D. (1964). *Ann. Rev. psychol.*

Stogdill, R. (1948). *J. Psychol.* **25,** 35–71.

Triandis, H. C., Bass, A. R., Ewen, R. B., and Mikesell, E. H. (1963). *J. Appl. Psychol.* **47,** 104–110.

INDUCING RESISTANCE TO PERSUASION

Some Contemporary Approaches[1]

William J. McGuire
DEPARTMENT OF SOCIAL PSYCHOLOGY
COLUMBIA UNIVERSITY
NEW YORK, NEW YORK

[1] The research by the author which is reported in this chapter was greatly facilitated by two successive grants from the National Science Foundation, Division of Social Sciences. He wishes to acknowledge the aid itself and the enlightened manner in which it was administered by the Foundation.

I. Introduction

Several years ago I thought of doing research on ways of inducing resistance to persuasion, under the impression that while much experimental work was being done on factors that increased persuasive effectiveness, little was being done on ways of producing resistance to persuasion. As I considered the problem further, however, I realized that there are many people investigating resistance to persuasion, only they—like M. Jourdain speaking prose—haven't always been aware of it. The first part of this chapter briefly sketches a dozen or so approaches to producing resistance to persuasion currently under active study; the balance of the chapter presents a more detailed résumé of my own work in the area. The disproportionate coverage of my own work does not (necessarily) mean I believe it merits this much space relative to the others, but simply that it is my own, and hence what I know best and can most competently describe.

Before we review the theories and findings regarding inducing resistance to persuasion, it would be useful to make explicit several points regarding our conceptualization of the process, since this conceptualization has determined the range of coverage. The scope of this inquiry is the uncovering of pretreatments which, when applied to the person, make him less susceptible to persuasive messages than he is found to be without these pretreatments. Hence, studying resistance to persuasion is not simply the inverse of studying persuasion itself. Suppose, for example, persuasive messages are known to be more effective if they are presented with their conclusions explicitly drawn, rather than left to be drawn by the recipient. This fact would not imply that resistance to persuasion—in the sense used here—could be enhanced by presenting messages whose conclusions are left to the recipient to draw. Rather, our interest is in pretreatments which would lessen the effectiveness of any given persuasive message (with or without its conclusion explicitly drawn).

A second preliminary point concerns the "healthiness" of resistance to persuasion. In our society we are inclined to accept the romantic notion that the autonomous man is admirable, while the man easily swayed by argument is weak and deplorable. Such a view suggests that we should look for resisfance-conferring treatment among healthy processes. How-

ever, a consideration of the close psychological relation between susceptibility to persuasion and ability to learn, a closeness that makes it difficult
to distinguish (at least on the basis of the psychological processes involved)
between propaganda and education, shows that this resistance is not
always "healthy." Anyone can be made impervious to the most skillful
propaganda if we reduce him to catatonic schizophrenia and anyone can,
with a bare bodkin, be made forever free from influence. The best of both
worlds would be to discover pretreatments that would make the person
receptive to the true and resistant to the false. But since the distinction
between truth and falsity is not strictly germane to the psychological processes under discussion, such a consideration will be ignored here. Hence,
as ways of inducing resistance to persuasion some possibly "unhealthy"
pretreatments—like enhancing the person's tendency to use perceptual
distortion in the defense of his preconceptions—are included.

A final preliminary point deals with the generality of the induced
resistance to persuasion. The most general type would involve making the
person resistant to the change toward any side of all issues, regardless of
the variables (source, channel, message, etc.) involved. The technique involving enhancing self-esteem comes the nearest to such a panacea against
persuasion, and even this procedure tends to have limitations. A more
specific type of conferred resistance is restricted to a certain type of issue,
or to only one of the two sides of an issue. For example, inducing aggressiveness tends to make the person less susceptible to benevolent appeals
but, if anything, more vulnerable to malevolent ones.

Other resistance-inducing techniques tend to be specific to certain
sources, for example, pairing that source in advance with unpopular stands
on other issues. Another form of specificity involves conferring resistance
to any argument on either side from any source but restricted to a given
issue. An example of a technique which does this is sensitizing the person
in advance of the persuasive attack to how closely his belief on the given
issue is tied with his beliefs on other issues. This chapter concentrates on
techniques that are general to the extent that the resistance they induce is
not specific to certain sources or to just one side of the issue. At least on a
given issue, these treatments make the subject more resistant to any kind
of a persuasive attempt.

The next section briefly reviews four general approaches to the problem of inducing resistance to persuasion, and mentions a number of variations on each approach. The limited space available permits little more
than a statement of the main points involved, along with a few illustrative
experiments. The succeeding sections of the chapter will describe my own
experiments on this problem in somewhat greater detail.

II. Some Contemporary Approaches to the Problem

A. THE BEHAVIORAL COMMITMENT APPROACH

The "behavioral commitment" approaches to inducing resistance to persuasion all involve the believer's taking some more or less irrevocable step on the basis of his belief, thereby committing himself to it. Insofar as commitment makes changing the belief dangerous, costly, awkward, or at least harmful to self-esteem, it strengthens the believer's tendency to resist social influence attempts aimed at this belief. The approaches that fall under this rubric can be grouped into several classes differing among themselves with respect to the nature of the committing behavior or the way of eliciting it. Below are four subclasses, listed in order of increasing externality of the commitment.

1. Private Decision

The most tenuous kind of commitment to the belief is created simply by having the person come to a private decision that he does indeed hold the belief. Edith Bennett (1955) found a significant tendency for subjects who are asked to come to a private (or at least anonymous) decision to persist longer in their intention than those not so requested. Such enhanced persistence may readily be interpreted as an increased resistance to the contrary pressures occurring in the interim. Lewin (1951, 1958) felt that decision-making, even of this anonymous sort, would have a "freezing" effect which could result in the belief's being maintained more firmly in the face of subsequent events. However, it appears that such private decision-making fails to confer any resistance under some conditions. Studies on the primacy-recency effect have generally yielded negative results (Hovland and Mandell, 1957; N. H. Anderson, 1959). Likewise, studies comparing the before-after vs. the after-only designs have failed to show any such freezing effects of the prior decision (Lana, 1959; Hicks and Spaner, 1962).

2. Public Announcement of One's Belief

It has also been suggested (e.g., Lewin, 1958) that public identification of one's belief should constitute a firmer commitment than that established by private decision-making. To the extent this is so, more resistance to subsequent persuasive attempts should follow a public rather than private statement of one's beliefs. Confirmatory evidence has been reported by a number of experimenters (Deutsch and Gerard, 1955; Hovland et al., 1957; Cohen et al., 1959). On the other hand, Bennett (1955) found private decision-making to be at least as effective as publicly identified decisions. Fisher and associates (1956) found that the public decisions did confer resistance to peer conformity pressures on the specific point decided upon, but that accommodations of a basic sort were made so that subsequently the person tended to anticipate and submit in advance to the expected, disparate judgment of the group.

3. Active Participation on the Basis of the Belief

Still more committing, it would seem, than simply stating one's belief is to take some further action on the basis of this belief. A typical action of this type which has been widely studied is the overt defense of one's belief by writing an essay or delivering a speech in support of it. McGuire's studies on the efficacy of active participation reported later in this chapter are examples. Another somewhat relevant set of experiments are the studies dealing with "overt compliance" (Kelman, 1953; King and Janis, 1956; Festinger, 1957; Cohen et al., 1958). These latter studies suggest some conditions under which such compliance has the greatest committing effect (e.g., when elicited with the least pressure; when many alternatives were available).

The use of belief-defensive essays as the form of active participation is somewhat unfortunate for it leaves a theoretical ambiguity: Is the increased resistance resulting from such behavior due simply to acting overtly on the basis of the belief, or is it due to the self-indoctrination and rehearsal of one's defenses involved in this particular type of activity? Fortunately, there have been a number of "forced compliance" studies in which the active participation did take other forms, forms that did not involve this rehearsal of one's defenses (Brehm, 1960; Smith, 1961; Raven and Fishbein, 1961). These studies yield the same implications as did the rehearsal ones just considered.

4. External Commitment

The final type of commitment, and by far the most tenuous of those considered here, is that called "external commitment." Rosenbaum (see Rosenbaum and Franc, 1960; Rosenbaum and Zimmerman, 1959) has shown that if the person is committed to a belief "externally," by being told someone else thinks the person holds that belief, the person does indeed show an increased adherence to the belief. It seems rather surprising that so mild a commitment could have a detectable effect; and yet, when confronted by the data, the phenomenon seems provocative rather than inexplicable.

B. Anchoring the Belief to Other Cognitions

A second family of approaches to inducing resistance to persuasion can be classified as "anchoring the belief to other cognitions." They have in common the notion of somehow linking the belief in question to other cognitions, or at least sensitizing the believer to the fact that such links exist. This procedure makes it more difficult for the person to change his belief because such a change would require his changing all the linked beliefs correspondingly. Otherwise, he would have to endure the discomfort of cognitive inconsistency. It will be recognized that this analysis accepts the basic assumption of the many current balance theories. Three such anchoring approaches, which differ regarding the type of cognitions to which a given belief is to be linked, are considered below.

1. Linking to Accepted Values

A number of theorists have suggested that a belief is held firmly to the extent that it is perceived as instrumental to the attainment of positively valenced goals, and/or as facilitating avoidance of negatively valenced goals (Carlson, 1956; Rosenberg, 1956; Zajonc, 1960). According to this approach, any pretreatment that would strengthen the believer's perception that his opinion did have such linkage to valenced goals (or, alternatively, made him increase the valence of the goals involved in the perceived instrumentality relationship) would enhance his adherence to the belief, making him more resistant to subsequently received pressures to change.

2. Linking to Other Beliefs

A very popular area in this anchoring category of studies involves the linkage of the given beliefs to other beliefs in the person's cognitive system. The various balance theories are all relevant to this point. The general idea is that sensitizing the person to the fact that the given belief is logically related to many beliefs which he holds will make him adhere to it more strongly. Changing it will introduce a whole series of imbalances into his cognitive system, and these imbalances cause psychological discomfort. Much of the work so far has been confined to showing that this reasoning is indeed correct (Abelson and Rosenberg, 1958; Harary, 1959). However, some studies have actually manipulated these belief linkages (see Rosenberg and Hovland, 1960). McGuire's "Socratic effect" studies are also pertinent. They suggest that merely asking the person to rehearse the related beliefs which he already possesses makes more salient these linkages to the given belief, and thereby confers enhanced resistance to subsequent attacks—at least to the extent that such attacks will introduce inconsistencies into his belief system (McGuire, 1960a,b).

3. Linking to Valenced Sources and Reference Groups

A final class of anchoring effects considered here involves tying the given belief to positively valenced sources of one kind or another. The general assumption is that if the believer is made to see that his opinion is shared by others whom he values highly, the opinion will be more resistant to subsequent attacks. Many experiments have demonstrated the importance of this "source" variable in persuasion. Even anonymous individuals and groups have been shown to confer such resistance when the believer is made to recognize that they share his belief (Schachter and Hall, 1952; Bennett, 1955). The effect has also been demonstrated for positively valenced reference groups (Kelley and Volkhart, 1952; Kelley and Woodruff, 1956; Dittes and Kelley, 1956; Charters and Newcomb, 1958; Newcomb, 1961). Still other experimenters have demonstrated that tying the belief to highly regarded, specific individuals establishes the belief more firmly (Tannenbaum, 1956; Kelman and Hovland, 1953).

Each anchoring approach can be utilized to confer resistance in two ways. The believer can be provided with new information which connects the given belief with the other cognitions he already holds. Alternatively, work can be done within his already existing cognitive system by making more salient to him the linkages that already exist. For example, he might be questioned so as to call his attention to these linkages (as in the "Socratic effect" study cited above) or the social setting might be manipulated (as in the "salience of reference groups" studies cited above).

C. Inducing Resistant Cognitive States

It has been proposed that certain personality, motivational, or ideological states are correlated with resistance to social influence pressures. Hence, any treatment that induces such states in the believer should enhance his resistance to persuasion. One difficulty in applying this approach is that, despite very extensive work on the problem, few states have been discovered which are generally effective in predisposing the person to resist persuasion. Let us now examine a rather heterogeneous set of such variables.

1. Inducing Anxiety about the Issue

A good deal of research has been done on the use of fear-arousing appeals in persuasion usually with the notion that when we attach anxiety to a given issue, the person is subsequently inclined to avoid the topic. He should therefore avoid exposure to subsequent messages (including those attacking his position) on the issue and, consequently, should be less influenced by them. Nunnally and Bobren (1959) found that people do say they are less willing to receive further information on the topic after reading an anxiety-arousing message on it. On the other hand, Janis and Feshbach (1953) found that the greater the prior anxiety arousal, the *less* the resistance to a subsequent attack on the issue. Indeed, other studies (e.g., Berkowitz and Cottingham, 1960) have suggested that the effects of fear appeals are more complex than indicated by the original formulation.

2. Inducing Aggressiveness

We might also think that the person who has been made hostile to others would be more resistant to influence attempts. Contrary to such an expectation, Weiss and Fine (1956) have shown that the actual result of inducing aggressiveness is quite different: this treatment does increase the person's resistance to benevolent arguments but makes him *more* susceptible to misanthropic arguments. Nevertheless, since several studies do indicate that chronic hostility is associated (at least in males) with resistance to persuasion, this proposition apparently deserves further study (Lesser and Abelson, 1959; Linton and Graham, 1959; Janis and Rife, 1959; Janis and Field, 1959).

3. Raising Self-Esteem

Perhaps the most successful demonstrations of induced resistance to persuasion via personality restructuring are those in which the person's self-esteem is manipulated. A number of investigators have demonstrated that a prior success experience enhances the believer's resistance to subsequent social influence attempts (Kelman, 1950; Mausner, 1954; Samelson, 1957). Resistance is increased, even when the task on which the individual succeeds is quite different from the task employed in the influence attempt.

4. Ideological Preconditioning

The suggestion by some students of the "brainwashing" process that "ideological preconditioning" can induce resistance to influence attempts is also relevant here. This method involves giving the individual certain cognitive content that will increase his ideological autonomy. Among the contents that have been suggested are: pervasive ideologies, such as well-worked-out sets of religious beliefs that allow the person to counter the subsequent indoctrinator's ideology with his own; the belief that he has supporters as well as others dependent on his resisting (e.g., by inculcating ésprit-de-corps); the consciousness that he has secret resources of which the indoctrinator is unaware, etc. (U.S. Senate, 1956). Little if any experimental work has been done to test these notions. Such support as they have received comes from anecdotal reports. The success with which Westerners have resisted indoctrination attempts by the Chinese is greater for clergymen than for businessmen; for those who identify with their parents than for those who reject them; for Marines than for Army personnel, etc.

This technique of inducing cognitive states which produce resistance to persuasion calls for further study. There is a double problem involved here: identifying states that do indeed enhance resistance, and discovering ways of creating these states. The approach seems promising if pursued creatively, but to date confirmatory evidence is scant.

D. Prior Training in Resisting Persuasive Attempts

A final approach to conferring resistence to persuasion considered here involves giving the person some specific training that would enhance his ability to adhere to his belief when subsequently confronted with influence attempts. We shall mention briefly a number of such educational procedures that have been suggested and evaluated.

The most generic method involves general education. It has often been claimed that with better education the individual becomes more resistant to persuasion. However, empirical research does not consistently support such a proposition. Weitzenhoffer's (1953) review of the suggestibility literature shows there is no simple, negative relationship between intelligence and resistance to suggestion. There is some evidence that the more intelligent are more resistant to conformity pressures from peers (Crutchfield, 1955; Stukát, 1958); but they also seem to be, if anything, more susceptible to the mass-media kind of persuasion attempts (Hovland et al., 1949; Janis and Rife, 1959). Hence, it is by no means clear that any general-education manipulation (i.e., such as would increase scores on IQ tests) would have the effect of increasing resistance to persuasion.

Training more specifically tailored to reduce susceptibility to persuasion might be more successful. One type of such training has an aura of unhealthiness: namely, training that will enhance the selective avoidance or perceptual distortion of information that is at variance with one's beliefs. For selective avoidance to be effective, the believer must learn to recognize that the attacking message will be dissonant with his beliefs. Training to perceive the indexing characteristics of the message (Tannenbaum, 1955) would be an approach to this end. Perceptual distortion has also been shown to facilitate resistance to persuasion (Kendall and Wolf, 1949; Cooper and Dinerman, 1951; Kelley, 1957; Cantril, 1958). As with other defense mechanisms, facility in the use of such perceptual distortion can probably be acquired, although the training procedure would no doubt require considerable time and ingenuity. The effectiveness of this particular "clinical" approach remains in the realm of conjecture.

A presumably "healthier" type of specific pretraining involves enhancing the person's critical capacities so that he will be better able to recognize and discount persuasive attempts. A number of studies have shown that training in the critical evaluation of propaganda can increase the person's resistance to such material when he subsequently encounters these communications (Biddle, 1932; Collier, 1944; Allport and Lepkin, 1945; Citron and Harding, 1950). Also effective in this regard is providing the person with special instruction which urges him to be critical just before the attack on his beliefs. (Das *et al.*, 1955; Luchins, 1957). In these cases, the conferred resistance tends to be small. The work by McGuire stemming from inoculation theory, which is considered in the subsequent sections of this chapter, probes more deeply into the immunizing effectiveness of such prior training and warnings.

III. The Inoculation Approach

A. Use of Cultural Truisms

McGuire's series of experiments on inducing resistance to persuasion stems from a biological analogy, whence the term "inoculation theory." In the biological situation, the person is typically made resistant to some attacking virus by pre-exposure to a weakened dose of the virus. This mild dose stimulates his defenses so that he will be better able to overcome any massive viral attack to which he is later exposed, but is not so strong that this pre-exposure will itself cause the disease. Alternatively, biological resistance can be augmented by supportive therapy such as adequate rest, good diet, and vitamin supplements. Inoculation is likely to be superior to supportive therapy to the extent that the person has previously been brought up in a germ-free environment. It is a seeming paradox that individuals raised aseptically tend to appear vigorously healthy (even without supportive therapy) but are highly vulnerable when suddenly exposed to massive doses of the disease virus.

Since the experimenter wished to make heuristic use of the inoculation analogy in deriving hypotheses about producing resistance to persuasion, he chose to deal as far as possible with beliefs that had been maintained in a "germ-free" ideological environment, that is, beliefs that the person has seldom, if ever, heard attacked. Nearly all beliefs should be of this sort, according to the selective-avoidance postulate, which implies that a person avoids dissonant information wherever possible. While this has been widely accepted (Festinger, 1957; Klapper, 1949, 1960), the empirical evidence for it is not clear-cut (Steiner, 1962). Hence, to be more certain that the beliefs used in these experiments met the conditions of inoculation theory, "cultural truisms" were used as the beliefs to be made resistant to persuasive attacks. "Cultural truisms" are beliefs that are so widely shared within the person's social milieu that he would not have heard them attacked, and indeed, would doubt that an attack were possible. Beliefs maintained in so monolithic an ideological environment would approximate, as regards inoculation theory, the health status of an organism raised in a germ-free environment.

After much pretesting (which showed that cultural truisms were rarer in our college samples than had been expected), one area was finally found that abounded in almost unanimously accepted propositions, namely, health beliefs. Upwards of 75% of the student samples checked "15" on a 15-point scale to indicate their agreement with propositions like: "It's a good idea to brush your teeth after every meal if at all possible"; "Mental illness is not contagious"; "The effects of penicillin have been, almost without exception, of great benefit to mankind"; "Everyone should get a yearly chest X-ray to detect any signs of TB at an early stage." These truisms (which, as shown below, proved quite vulnerable when exposed to massive attacks without any prior "immunizing" treatment) were used, in the experiments described below, as the beliefs to be made resistant to persuasion by procedures derived by analogy from biological inoculation.

B. Basic Assumptions and Relevant Variables

1. Underlying Assumptions

McGuire's version of the inoculation theory assumes that pretreatments designed to make truisms resistant to subsequent persuasive attacks will be effective to the extent that they overcome two basic difficulties: one, the believer is unpracticed in defending his belief; and two, he is unmotivated to undertake the necessary practice. He is unpracticed because he has never been called upon to defend the truism. He is unmotivated to start practicing because he regards the belief as unassailable.

It follows that any prior treatment designed to improve the believer's defenses must motivate him to develop a defense of a truism whose validity he regards as obvious. Motivation can be supplied by making him aware of the vulnerability of the truism. That is, to be effective the prior defense of a truism presumably should be threatening rather than reassuring about the belief. An obvious way of threatening him is by pre-exposure to weakened forms of the attacking arguments.

It also follows that supplying motivation alone is inadequate for an effective defense. Because of the believer's lack of prior practice, he may not be able to bolster his belief sufficiently unless he is given careful guidance in developing defensive material; or, if he is required to develop such material on his own initiative, he must at least be given considerable time to do so.

From this background of assumptions, we derive a number of predictions about the relative immunizing effectiveness of various kinds of prior defenses. The three basic variables which are involved in most of these predictions are described first. The derivation of the specific predictions involving them is taken up in the later sections of this chapter which present the separate experiments.

2. The Defensive Variables

The first of these three variables is the amount of threat contained in the defenses. Two basic types of defenses were used which differed in amount of threat: "supportive" and "refutational." The supportive defense was nonthreatening; it consisted of giving the believer various arguments in support of the truism. The refutational defense was more threatening; instead of positively supporting the truism, it mentioned several arguments attacking the belief, and then proceeded to refute these attacking arguments. The experimenter reasoned that this pre-exposure would be threatening enough to be defense-stimulating, but not so strong as to overwhelm the truism.

These refutational defenses, considered in relation to the subsequent attacks, were one of two types. Either they mentioned and refuted the very arguments against the truism that were to be used in the subsequent attacks, or they mentioned and refuted arguments different from the ones to be used in the attacks. This refutational-same vs. refutational-different defensive variation is useful in determining whether any increased resistance to persuasion derives from the generalized motivational effect of the threatening mention of the arguments against the truism (as required by inoculation theory), or whether it stems from the useful defensive material provided directly by the refutations.

A second defensive variable that was manipulated in many of the experimenter's inoculation studies was the amount of unguided, active participation in the defense required of the believer. Two levels of this variable were generally used: a relatively passive condition, in which the believer read a defensive essay that had been prepared for him, and an active condition, in which the believer wrote such an essay. This variable was relevant to both of the assumed difficulties in immunizing cultural truisms: the believer's lack of practice and his lack of motivation.

A third variable manipulated in several of the experiments was the interval between the defense and attack. This time period ranged from a few minutes to a maximum of one week. Here the primary concern was the interaction between time and the other variables. The theoretical relevance of these three variables will be discussed later, along with the description of the experiments that tested the predictions in which they were involved.

A number of additional variables were manipulated to clarify certain theoretical ambiguities in one or another of the studies described below, but they are described later in the chapter with the experiment where they were employed.

IV. General Experimental Procedure

The basic procedures were quite similar from experiment to experiment in the series reported below. Hence, for economy of exposition the general methodological paradigm will be described at the outset. Then, in describing each individual experiment, its method will need to be described only in so far as it departs in important ways from this general paradigm.

The experiments involved two sessions, the first devoted to the defenses; the second, to the strong attacks and to measuring the resultant belief levels. The interval between the two sessions varied from a few minutes to 7 days. The subjects were usually college students enrolled in introductory psychology courses at large state universities who were fulfilling a course requirement that they participate in a certain number of hours of psychological experiments. The present studies were usually represented to them as studies of verbal skills. The issues being defended and attacked were the health truisms described above.

A. First (Defensive) Session

The subjects were told the experimenter was studying the relation between reading and writing skills in the two-session experiments. In the first 50-minute session the subject actually participated in several defensive conditions, e.g., he might receive an active-refutational, passive-refutational, active-supportive, and passive-supportive defense, each defense dealing with a different truism.

An active refutational defense consisted of a sheet of paper on which was listed a truism—e.g., "Everyone should brush his teeth after every meal if at all possible." Then would come a one-sentence argument against this truism—e.g., "Too frequent brushing tends to damage the gums and expose the vulnerable parts of the teeth to decay"—and the instructions to use the white space below to write a paragraph refuting this argument against the truism. Halfway down the page came another argument against the truism and instructions to refute it in the space following. The passive-refutational defense stated the truism and the two arguments against it in an introductory paragraph; then followed two further paragraphs, each refuting one of these arguments. The active and passive supportive defenses were analogous to the refutational in format, except that instead of arguments against the truism, they cited two arguments supporting it, and then (in the active condition) asked the subject to write paragraphs defending these supportive arguments, or (in the passive condition) presented two such defensive paragraphs for him to read. In the passive defenses, to substantiate the subterfuge that we were studying reading skills, the subject was asked to pick out and underline the crucial clause in each paragraph.

In some of the experiments, the subject filled out an opinionnaire on the truisms after completing these defenses, so we could measure the direct strengthening effects of the defenses prior to the attacks. More typically, no opinionnaire was administered until the end of the second session, and the direct strengthening effect was determined by including defense-only, no-attack conditions in the design.

B. SECOND (ATTACKING) SESSION

Immediately after (or 2 or 7 days after this defensive session) followed a 50-minute second session devoted to attacks on the truisms and administration of an opinionnaire to determine final belief levels on the truisms. The attacks all had the form of a three-paragraph essay (similar in format to the passive defenses). The first paragraph stated the truism, remarked that some informed people were beginning to question its validity, and mentioned two attacking arguments. Each of the next two paragraphs developed in detail one of these attacking arguments. For those conditions in which a refutational defense had been given, half were followed by an attack using the same arguments against the truism as had been refuted in the prior defense (constituting it a "refutational-same" defense); the other half were followed by attacks using quite different arguments against the truism from those that had been refuted in the defense (constituting a "refutational-different" defense). The designs typically had each subject furnish control data on a "defense-only" and a "neither-defense-nor-attack" truism. The specific truisms were, of course, rotated around the conditions from subject to subject.

After reading (and underlining the crucial clause in) the attacking messages, the subject filled out some personality tests (introduced to substantiate the claim that the experiment was investigating personality correlates of verbal skills). He then filled out the opinionnaire on the truisms, purportedly to determine if the subject's feelings about the topics had any effect on his ability to utilize his verbal skills in the reading and writing "tests." The opinionnaire consisted of four statements dealing with each truism. The subject was called upon to check off his agreement with the statement on a scale from one to 15. The direction of the statement was varied, so that sometimes 15 represented complete acceptance of the truism, and sometimes complete rejection. However, in the results reported below, to make reading easier, the appropriate responses are reversed so that the 15 score always represents complete acceptance of the truism and a one score, complete rejection of it.

After completing the opinionnaire, the subject replied to standardized questions probing his actual perception of the experiment. Finally, the true purpose of the experiment was revealed to him, and the various deceits used and the reasons for employing them were explained. Approximately 3 months later a follow-up letter was sent to him, reminding him that the argumentative material he had dealt with had been selected solely for experimental purposes and that the arguments were not necessarily true. More detailed information on the materials, designs, etc., are given in the original published reports of the experiments cited in the paragraphs that follow.

V. Supportive vs. Refutational Defenses

A series of experiments were carried out to test the hypothesis that defenses of truisms are effective to the extent that they contain threatening mention of arguments against the truism. These studies, in which the experimenter manipulated the extent to which the defenses mentioned arguments supporting the truism vs. arguments attacking the truism, are described in the present section. The first study showed that defenses which present arguments supporting the truism are less effective in conferring resistance to subsequent strong attack than are refutational-same defenses (which ignore arguments positively supporting the truism but do mention and refute the same arguments against the belief as are to be used in the subsequent attack). The second experiment demonstrated that a refutational defense is almost as effective when it refutes arguments against the truism which are different from those to be used in the later attack as when it refutes the very same arguments used in the attack.

A third study illustrated that, when combined with the threatening refutational defense, the supportive defense gains an efficacy that it lacks when used alone. In the fourth study, it was demonstrated that an extrinsic threat (forewarning of the impending attack) prior to the defenses, enhances their immunizing effectiveness, especially that of the otherwise not-threatening supportive defense. Conversely, a fifth study showed that a prior reassurance (feedback that one's peers also agree with the truism) decreases the effectiveness of the defenses. A sixth study revealed that the immunizing efficacy of the refutational defense derives at least as much from the threatening prior mention of the attacking arguments as from the reassuring earlier refutations of the attacking arguments which had been mentioned. Each of these studies is described in more detail, together with additional findings of interest, in the paragraphs below.

A. SUPPORTIVE VS. REFUTATIONAL-SAME STUDY

1. Experimental Conditions

In a first experiment (McGuire and Papageorgis, 1961), each of 130 students read a defensive essay on one truism and wrote a defensive essay on another in a regular meeting of his freshman English course. Two days later, he read messages attacking these two truisms and also a third, non-defended truism. On a fourth truism he received neither defense nor attack (the four specific truisms being rotated around the four conditions from student to student). He then filled out an opinionnaire measuring his beliefs on all four truisms.

For 66 of the students, each defensive essay was supportive, mentioning four arguments supporting the truism and then presenting a paragraph substantiating each argument (in the reading, passive condition), or then asking the student to write a substantiating paragraph for each argument (in the writing, active condition). For the other 64 students, each defensive essay was refutational, ignoring supportive arguments and mentioning four arguments against the truism and then presenting a paragraph refuting each (in the passive condition), or then calling upon the student to write a refuting paragraph against each argument (in the active condition). The passive-condition subjects were allowed 5 minutes to read each of the 1000-word essays; the active-condition subjects were allowed 10 minutes to write each essay. The attacks 2 days later consisted of 1000-word essays to be read, each mentioning four arguments against the belief and then presenting a paragraph substantiating each argument.

2. Immunizing Effectiveness

As Table I shows, the more threatening, refutational defense was clearly superior to the supportive defense in conferring resistance to the subsequent attacks. The attacks, when not preceded by a defense, reduced adherence to the truisms from 12.62 to 6.64 on the 15-point scale. When the refutational defense preceded the attacks, the mean belief score was reduced only to 10.33, which is significantly ($p < .001$) higher than in the attack-only condition. The supportive defenses were much less successful in inducing resistance. In the supportive defense conditions, the mean belief score after the attacks was 7.39, which is not only significantly ($p < .001$) lower than in the refutational-defense treatment, but is not even significantly higher than the no-defense, attack-only condition ($p = .16$). Hence the supportive defense is not only much less effective

TABLE I

MEAN BELIEF LEVELS AFTER ATTACKS[a] PRECEDED BY REFUTATIONAL–SAME
VS SUPPORTIVE DEFENSES[b,c]

Type of participation	Refutational defense then attack	Supportive defense then attack	Refute minus support
Passive reading	11.51 (35)[d]	7.47 (32)	+4.04
Reading and underlining	11.13 (31)	7.63 (32)	+3.50
Writing from outline	9.19 (31)	7.94 (32)	+1.25
Writing without guidance	9.46 (35)	6.53 (32)	+2.93
Weighted mean	10.33 (132)	7.39 (128)	+2.94

[a] Control levels: neither attack nor defense = 12.62 (N = 130); attack only (with no prior defense) = 6.64 (N = 130).

[b] 15.00 indicates complete adherence to the truism; 1.00 indicates complete disagreement.

[c] Data from McGuire and Papageorgis (1961).

[d] Numbers in parentheses give the number of cases on which cell means were based.

than the refutational in conferring resistance, but has not clearly been shown to be effective at all.

3. Direct Strengthening Effect

In this experiment, the subjects completed the opinionnaire not only at the end of the second session, but also at the end of the first session. Comparing each subject's two responses provides a measure of the direct strengthening effects of the various defenses (as opposed to their conferred resistance to the later attacks). In terms of this criterion, the supportive defenses apparently were superior to the refutational. Immediately after the supportive defenses, the mean belief score was 14.34; immediately after the refutational, it was 13.91 (p = .10 for the difference). Furthermore, while the refutational defense was superior to the supportive one in all four participation conditions as regards resistance conferral (see Table I), the supportive defense was superior in producing a direct strengthening effect. This type of reversal was found repeatedly in the present series of experiments: the defenses which left the beliefs seemingly strongest tended to be the defenses which conferred the least resistance to subsequent attacks. This reversal, called the "paper tiger" phenomenon, shows the peril of assuming the immunizing effectiveness of a defense to be a direct function of its apparent strengthening effect, and is in accord with the inoculation theory.

B. REFUTATIONAL-SAME VS. -DIFFERENT

1. Hypotheses

A later experiment by Papageorgis and McGuire (1961) compared the resistance-conferring efficacy of the refutational defense when the later attacks used arguments which differed from those mentioned and refuted in the defense, with their efficacy when the later attacks used the same arguments used in the defense. If, as implied by the inoculation theory, the refutational defense derives immunizing efficacy from the motivation-stimulating threatening mention of arguments against the truism, then its effectiveness should be general and manifested even against attacks using novel arguments. On the other hand, if the refutational defense gains its effectiveness solely from the refutation rather than the mention of the arguments, the resistance it confers should be more specific to attacks by the same arguments that had been refuted.

2. Procedure

The study designed to distinguish between these two explanations employed only refutational defenses, since the hypotheses did not concern the supportive defenses. Also, only passive (reading) defenses were employed, since the relevance of the active defenses (even of the refutational type) to the predictions is less clear; the amount of refutational material received was more under the subject's control than the experimenter's in the active condition. Alternative forms of the passive refutational defense were made up for each truism. Each form employed a different pair of arguments against the truism, the defensive message first mentioning and then refuting this pair in a 600-word essay. Correspondingly, there were two forms of the message attacking each truism, each form mentioning and then corroborating one of these pairs of attacking arguments. A crossover design was used so that each given pair of arguments refuted in a defense was followed by an attack using the same arguments for half the subjects, and by one using the different pair of arguments for the other half. A total of 73 summer school students served in the two sessions, defensive and attacking, which were separated by a one-week interval.

3. Results

Once again the attacks proved very damaging to the truisms when they were not preceded by a defense. In the attack-only condition, the mean belief level went down to 5.73 on the 15-point scale as compared to a mean of 13.23 in the neither-defense-nor-attack control condition, a drop significant at well above the .001 level. The refutational defenses did confer appreciable resistance to the attack: When the attack had been preceded by the refutational-same defense, the mean belief level was 9.25; after one preceded by the refutational-different defense, it was 8.70. Each of these means in the defense-and-attack conditions is significantly higher than the 5.73 mean in the attack-only condition, and they are not significantly different from one another. These outcomes tend to conform to inoculation theory, since the refutational defense confers resistance even to novel attacks. Indeed, the resistance to novel attacks that was produced is not significantly less than the resistance to attacks by the very same arguments that were refuted.

In a further attempt to identify the mechanisms underlying the resistance-conferral by the refutational defense, two additional variables were measured at the end of the second (attacking) session. One of these was a semantic-differential-type scale designed to measure the perceived quality and credibility of the arguments used in the attack. The attacks were seen as significantly ($p < .05$) less credible when preceded by a refutational defense (whether the defense was refutational-same or refutational-different) than when not preceded by any defense. A second post-attack test called upon the person to write down as many arguments as he could in support of the truism. The inoculation theory prediction was that the motivational stimulation from the threatening refutational defense would result in the believer's accumulating more supportive material for the truism during the week following the attack. However, although there was a slight tendency for the subjects who had received the refutational defense to think up more supportive arguments than those who had received no defense, the difference was not significant ($.20 > p > .10$).

C. COMBINATIONAL EFFECTS

1. Hypotheses and Method

A third experiment (McGuire, 1961b), like the second, used passive (reading) defenses only and compared the immunizing efficacy of combinations of supportive and refutational defenses with that of single defenses. In keeping with inoculation theory, the experimenter attributed the ineffectiveness of the supportive defense [found in McGuire and Papageorgis (1961) described above] to the believer's lack of motivation to assimilate its arguments; the supporting statements seemed to belabor the obvious. The refutational defense did supply some motivation by its threatening mention of arguments against the truism, but did not, in the case of the refutational-different defense, supply any specifically useful material to the unpracticed subject for acting on this induced motivation to bolster the truism. Hence, it was predicted that the supportive and refutational defenses used together would confer more resistance than the sum of their individual effects. It was further predicted that this "whole greater than the sum of its parts" effect would be more pronounced when the supportive defense was added to refutational-different than when added to refutational-same defenses.

One hundred sixty-two students enrolled in introductory college courses were used to test these predictions. They received supportive-only, refutational-only, or supportive-plus-refutational defenses on different truisms. In the cases of refutational defenses, half were refutational-same, and half, refutational-different. The attacking session followed immediately after the defensive.

2. Results

Both of the combination predictions were confirmed. When used alone, neither the refutational-different nor the supportive defenses conferred significant resistance to the immediate attacks. When used in combination, they produced considerable ($p < .01$) resistance. Also confirmed was the prediction that the combination with the supportive defense would be especially effective for the refutational-different defense; there was a significant interaction ($p < .01$) in the predicted direction between the refutational-only vs. refutational-plus-supportive variable and the -same vs. -different variable. The refutational-different defense profited more from the addition of the supportive defense as regards producing resistance to an immediate post-defense attack. These and other findings of the study under discussion are described more fully elsewhere (McGuire, 1961b).

D. ADDED THREATS AND REASSURANCES

1. Theory

According to the inoculation theory, prior defenses lose effectiveness in making truisms resistant to persuasion because the believer is over-confident and therefore unmotivated to assimilate the defenses adequately. This motivational deficit is particularily pronounced in the case of the supportive defense, while the refutational defense does contain an intrinsic threat—mention of attacking arguments—which arouses some motivation. If this theoretical analysis is correct, it follows that any extrinsic threat to the truism (e.g., a forewarning that it will be attacked), presented to the believer before the defense material, should increase his motivation to assimilate the material and hence enhance its immunizing effectiveness.

This extrinsic threat should be especially beneficial to the supportive defense which is particularly needful of such additional motivation. Conversely, a predefense reassurance that the truisms were indeed beyond controversy (e.g., by feedback that everyone in the believer's group agreed with them) should actually decrease the effectiveness of the defenses by further depressing the already inadequate motivation to assimilate these defenses. To test these derivations, two experiments were carried out, one manipulating extrinsic threats, the other, extrinsic reassurance.

2. Extrinsic Threat Manipulation

In the first of these two studies (McGuire and Papageorgis, 1962), each of the 96 subjects received supportive, refutational-same, and refutational-different defenses of three truisms and no defense of a fourth belief. All the defenses were of the passive (reading) type. Then the subjects were given four attacking messages, one aimed at each of the truisms. Finally, their opinions regarding each truism were measured.

For half the subjects the experiment was introduced in the usual way, as a verbal skills test dealing with health topics, and no mention was made of the fact that the truisms would be attacked in the later reading passages. The 48 subjects so instructed constituted the "no-forewarning" condition. The other 48 subjects, those in the "forewarning" condition, received a quite different rationale for the experiment. They were told the experimenter was measuring how persuasible they were by asking them to read attacks on four health truisms which they took for granted. Before they read the attacks, they also were informed, they would be allowed to read defenses of some of those beliefs.

3. Results

The forewarning of attack did indeed enhance the immunizing effectiveness of the defenses, as shown in Table II. It can be calculated from the scores in Table II that after the defenses and attacks in the forewarning condition, the mean belief level was 11.67, and in the no-forewarning condition it was only .10.93, a difference significant above the .05 level. Also as predicted, this enhancement due to the threatening forewarning is greater for the supportive than the refutational defense, the interaction being significant at the .05 level.

There are several possible explanations for these results, however. For example, the higher means in the forewarning conditions after defenses and attacks might not be due to the hypothesized enhancement of the defenses caused by the increased motivation which the threat produced, but rather could stem from a direct reduction in the impact of the attack due to its identification as such by the forewarning. The means in the

TABLE II
FINAL BELIEF LEVELS WITH AND WITHOUT FOREWARNING
BEFORE THE DEFENSES[a,b]

Foreknowledge of attack prior to defense	Attack-only (no prior defense)	Defense and attack conditions			Neither defense nor attack
		Supportive defense	Refut.-same defense	Refut.-diff. defense	
Yes	9.95	12.09	11.79	11.12	12.52
	(24)[c]	(48)	(48)	(48)	(24)
No	10.23	10.11	11.68	10.98	13.20
	(24)	(48)	(48)	(48)	(24)
Combined	10.09	11.10	11.73	11.05	12.86
	(48)	(96)	(96)	(96)	(48)

[a] 15.00 indicates complete adherence to the truism.
[b] Data from McGuire and Papageorgis (1962).
[c] Numbers in parentheses give the number of cases on which cell means were based.

attack-only control conditions shown in Table II rule out this alternative interpretation; when not preceded by a defense the attacks are at least as effective in the forewarning as in the non-forewarning condition. Further evidence along these lines is presented in the original publication.

4. Extrinsic Reassurance Manipulation

In the second of these two studies (Anderson, 1962), each of 96 subjects received a pattern of defenses and attacks similar to that in the forewarning study described above. However, in this study, instead of a threatening forewarning manipulation, there was a reassuring feedback prior to the defenses. At the beginning of the group-administered defensive session, all the subjects were asked to give their opinions on a series of health truisms, including the four crucial ones. By a subterfuge, 48 subjects were then given feedback which indicated that the other subjects had almost unanimously agreed that the four crucial beliefs were true beyond a doubt. These "high reassurance" subjects received no feedback on the "filler" truisms. The other 48 subjects (who constituted the "low reassurance" condition) received no feedback regarding the crucial truisms, although they did receive reassuring feedback regarding four filler truisms.

5. Results

The outcome of this study is shown in Table III. The final belief levels in the three defense-and-attack conditions combined was 10.63 in the reassurance condition and 11.53 in the no-reassurance condition, a difference significant at the .01 level. Hence, as predicted on the basis of

TABLE III

FINAL BELIEF LEVELS WITH AND WITHOUT REASSURING FEEDBACK
BEFORE THE DEFENSES[a,b]

Reassuring feedback of group agreement	Attack-only (no prior defense)	Defense and attack conditions			Neither defense nor attack
		Supportive defense	Refut.-same defense	Refut.-diff. defense	
Yes	10.20	9.58	11.52	10.80	12.40
	(24)[c]	(48)	(48)	(48)	(24)
No	10.74	11.06	12.12	11.41	12.68
	(24)	(48)	(48)	(48)	(24)
Combined	10.47	10.32	11.82	11.10	12.54
	(48)	(96)	(96)	(96)	(48)

[a] 15.00 indicates complete adherence to the truism.

[b] Data from Anderson (1962).

[c] Numbers in parentheses give the number of cases on which cell means were based.

inoculation theory, reassurance prior to the defenses actually lessens their immunizing effectiveness. That the effect is produced via the defenses (rather than through any direct effect of the reassurance manipulation upon the attacks) is shown by the fact that the difference between the high and low reassurance groups in the attack-only conditions is trivial.

The predicted interaction of reassurance and type of defense was not found in this study. It can be seen in Table III that the reassurance reduced the effectiveness of the supportive defense more than that of the refutational defenses. However, this trend is significantly only at the .20 level.

E. INDEPENDENT MANIPULATION OF THREAT AND REASSURANCE

1. Theory and Method

Yet another investigation sought to determine whether the immunizing efficacy of the refutational defense derives, as predicted from inoculation theory, from their threatening components. A final experiment (McGuire, 1963a) in this series utilized independent manipulation of the two components of the refutational defenses: namely, the threatening component (mention in the first paragraph of some arguments attacking the truism); and the reassuring component (refutations of these attacking arguments in the later paragraphs). To isolate the separate effects of these two components, they were manipulated orthogonally in the present experiment. Specifically, half of the refutational defenses were "high threat," mentioning four arguments attacking the truisms; and half were "low threat," mentioning two such arguments. Each of these types was further dichotomized so that half were "high reassurance" defenses, in which two of the mentioned attacking arguments were refuted; and half were "low reassurance" defenses, which refuted none of the mentioned arguments. The design is sketched in Table IVA.

TABLE IVA

NUMBER OF COUNTERARGUMENTS PRESENTED IN THE VARIOUS
REFUTATIONAL DEFENSE CONDITIONS

	Threat	
Reassurance	High threat	Low threat
High reassurance	4 mentioned	2 mentioned
	2 refuted	2 refuted
Low reassurance	4 mentioned	2 mentioned
	0 refuted	0 refuted

A total of 288 subjects served in this study, participating in a defensive and an attacking session separated by 2 days. All the defenses were of the "passive" type, requiring of the subject only that he read the prepared refutational-defense messages.

2. Results

The outcome, shown in Table IVB, indicates that both the threatening and the reassuring components of the refutational defenses contributed to

TABLE IVB

FINAL BELIEF LEVELS AFTER ATTACKS PRECEDED BY DEFENSES
INVOLVING VARYING NUMBERS OF COUNTERARGUMENTS[a,b]

	Threat		
Reassurance	High	Low	Overall
High	11.07	10.54	10.75
	(96)[c]	(144)	(240)
Low	10.97	9.75	10.23
	(96)	(144)	(240)
Overall	11.02	10.14	10.49
	(192)	(288)	(480)

[a] 15.00 indicates complete adherence to the truism.
[b] Data from McGuire (1963a).
[c] Numbers in parentheses give the number of cases on which cell means were based.

their resistance to attack. As regards reassurance, the superiority of high reassurance over low is significant at the .05 level ($F = 4.85$); in the case of the threat variable, the superiority of high threat over low is significant at the .01 level ($F = 13.52$).

These results confirm the inoculation theory prediction that the more threatening defense will be more effective in making truisms resistant to subsequent attacks. The theory did not rule out the possibility that other components of the refutational defense also would contribute to resistance to persuasion, any more than Boyle's law implies the invalidity of Charles's law. Hence, the finding that reassurance promotes resistance is not necessarily in conflict with inoculation theory. The experimenter's conjecture is that if the reassurance comes before the threat, the believer's confidence in the truisms is increased and his tendency not to heed the defenses is augmented. If, on the other hand, the reassurance comes after the threat has already stimulated the believer's motivation to assimilate the defense, then it will heighten resistance to attack. Further study should clarify this point.

VI. Effects of Active Participation in the Defense

A. THEORY

A second series of hypotheses derived from the inoculation notion dealt with the effects of requiring the believer to participate actively, without guidance, in the prior defense of the truisms. Our initial analysis of the resistance of cultural truisms to attack assumed that because these truisms had been maintained in an ideologically "germ-free" environment, there would be two deficits making it difficult to utilize prior defense to make them resistant to persuasion. First, there would be a practice deficit: since the believer would seldom if ever have been called upon to defend the truism, he would not find it easy to do so unless he was carefully guided in the defense. Second, there would be a motivational deficit: because the believer would be too confident of to the validity of these supposedly obvious and unassailable truisms, he would be little motivated to assimilate defensive material that was presented to him.

It follows that this "active participation in the defense" variable is relevant in opposite ways to both the practice and the motivational deficits of the truisms. With regard to the deficit in prior practice, the active (writing) defensive condition is more disadvantageous than the passive (reading) condition, since it imposes more demands upon the believer to summon up bolstering material from his inadequate cognitive repertory. He will tend to perform the writing task poorly and, consequently, the active defensive session tends to be unproductive and wasted. In contrast, the passive defense makes relatively little demand on the believer's prior preparation; he has only to read the presented defensive material. Hence, his lack of practice is no great handicap. In the case of the motivational deficit, on the other hand, the active condition is at less of a disadvantage than the passive, since the very poorness of the believer's performance at the essay-writing task should bring home to him how inadequately based is his confidence in the truism. This should motivate him to correct this state of affairs.

Since the theoretical analysis indicates that the two processes touched off by this active-passive manipulation have opposite effects on the dependent variable (conferred resistance), the experimenter might seem to be left in a sorry state for making predictions. Such is not the case, however. Predictions can be made regarding interaction effects between this activity variable and other variables which tend to intensify the advantages or disadvantages of active participation with respect to conferring resistance.

B. EFFECTS OF REQUIRING PARTICIPATION

1. Theory and Method

The first experiment designed to test the effect on conferred resistance of manipulating the amount of unguided, active participation in the defense varied this participation over four levels. The highest degree of unguided participation was called "unguided writing." It consisted of giving the subjects a sheet of paper headed by a statement of the truism and telling him that he had 20 minutes to write an essay defending the truism. Subjects were assigned either to a supportive-defense condition by being told that their essays should be restricted to presenting arguments positively supporting the truism, or to a refutational-defense condition by being told that their essays should mention and then refute possible arguments against the truism. They were told that their essays would be scored for argumentative skill and relevance, but were given no further guidance.

A slightly less demanding condition, called "guided writing" was the same as above, except that the sheets headed by the truisms also listed arguments that could be used in writing the essay. The people in the supportive-defense condition were given one-sentence synopses of each of four arguments supporting the truisms. Those in the refutational defense conditions were given four pairs of sentences, each pair consisting of a statement of an argument attacking the truism, and a statement suggesting a refutaton of that argument.

Still less demanding was the "reading and underlining condition." Here each subject received a mimeographed, defensive essay about 1000 words long to read. In the supportive condition the first paragraph mentioned four arguments supporting the truism, and then followed four paragraphs, each developing more fully one of the supporting arguments. In the refutational condition the first paragraph mentioned four arguments attacking the beliefs, and then followed four paragraphs, each refuting one of these attacking arguments. The subjects in this reading condition were instructed that they would have 5 minutes to read and to underline in each paragraph the shortest clause that contained the gist of the whole paragraph. They were told they would be scored on the basis of their accuracy at this task and their ability to answer a later series of reading comprehension questions.

The least demanding participation condition, called "passive reading," was the same as the reading and underlining condition, except that the underlining task was omitted so that the subject had simply to read the paragraph passively during the 5 minutes and prepare for the later reading comprehension questions.

In this experiment (McGuire and Papageorgis, 1961), each of the 130 subjects served in two defensive conditions in the first session: a writing defense on one truism and a reading defense on another. All the refutational defenses were of the refutational-same type. In the second session 2 days later, each received attacks on the two defended truisms and also an attack on a third, undefended truism (to yield an attack-only control score), and no attack on still a fourth truism (to yield a neither-defense-nor-attack control score). The four specific truisms were rotated around these four conditions from subject to subject. Beliefs were measured at the ends of both the first and second sessions.

While there are, as described above, both beneficial and detrimental effects to be expected from requiring active participation in the defense, it is possible under the experimental conditions obtaining here to make a main order prediction: the detrimental effects are likely to be dominant so that the active-participation requirement will probably have the net effect of interfering with the immunizing effectiveness of the defense. The reason is that the relative disadvantage of the active conditions (their being too demanding for the unpracticed subject) is likely to be fully operative, while their relative advantage (supplying motivation to take part seriously in the defense) is somewhat obviated by the moderate degree of such motivation established by the present conditions, even in the passive group. As the previously described series of experiments showed, the refutational defense, even in the passive condition, contains a motivation-stimulating threat to the belief. In addition, the reading-comprehension instructions also motivate these college student subjects to address themselves seriously to assimilating these defensive essays, even though the essays seem to belabor the obvious.

The above reasoning enables the experimenter to make predictions regarding both main effects and interactions in this study. Forced-compliance studies (Kelman, 1953; King and Janis, 1956; Brehm and Cohen, 1962) usually find that active participation in the defense of a belief opposing one's own views generally augments the amount of internalized attitude change. However, in the present case of defending already accepted truisms, the opposite is predicted: namely, the greater the active participation requirement, the less the conferred resistance to subsequent attacks.

The above considerations also give rise to the interaction prediction: the superiority of the passive over the active defense will be more pronounced with the refutational defense than with the supportive. As pointed out in the analysis of the experimental conditions, whatever advantage the active condition might offer—its motivation-inducing threat—is lost in the case of the refutational defense because here even the passive condition offers two sources of motivation to assimilate the defense: the mention of the threatening, attacking arguments which are to be refuted, and the achievement motivation to do well, produced by the announcement of the reading comprehension test.

2. Main Effect Results

The outcome of this experiment has already been presented in Table I, which shows the final belief scores in the eight defense-and-attack conditions (i.e., four levels of active participation for the supportive and for the refutational defenses) and in the attack-only and neither-defense-nor-attack control conditions. As Table I shows, the main effect prediction is confirmed; over the four levels of increasing participation there is a steady decline in immunizing effectiveness. With regard to the main manipulation of this variable, reading vs. writing, the superiority of the former is significant at the .001 level. (Also noteworthy is the finding of the same consistent trend over the four conditions in the direct strengthening effects of the defense, as shown by the mean belief levels at the end of the first session. The superiority of reading over writing in this regard reached the .05 level of significance, despite the low ceiling restraining any further increase in the pre-attack means.) This immunizing superiority of reading over writing is especially striking considering that the time allowed for the writing defense (20 minutes) was four times that allowed for the reading.

3. Interaction Result

The interaction prediction is also confirmed by the results. While the reading defense was superior to the writing for both supportive and refutational defenses, reading was only slightly superior to writing for the supportive defense (7.56 vs. 7.23) but considerably superior for the refutational defense (11.33 vs. 9.33). This interaction was significant at the .05 level. Several subsequent studies (McGuire, 1963a,c) confirmed both the main and the interaction effects reported here. However, they showed in addition that the sizable superiority of reading over writing for the refutational-same defense, which was demonstrated in this study, does not hold also for the refutational-different defense. Indeed, the superiority of reading over writing tends to be even less for the refutational-different defense than for the supportive defense. The next section discusses this lack of superiority with the refutational-different defense which can be derived from the inoculation theory.

C. ACTIVE AND PASSIVE COMBINATIONAL EFFECTS

1. Theory

In the case of refutational defenses, the inoculation theory has implications regarding the advisability of using double defenses, active plus passive (i.e., having the subject both read and write a refutational essay defending the truism), as compared with using just one of these. The implications follow from the same assumptions that were used to derive the previous predictions. The refutational-same defense presumably owes its efficacy to two factors. The first is its mild, motivating threat to the truism, due to its mentioning arguments attacking the truism and from demonstrating to the believer (especially in the active defense condition) how poorly prepared he is to defend the truism. The second immunizing source is the refutational material which is useful in resisting subsequent attacks that employ the same attacking arguments that had been refuted. This refutational material, however, is less useful against attacks employing novel arguments. Hence, the refutational-same defense derives its efficacy from both components, the threatening mention and the reassuring refutation of attacking arguments. But the refutational-different derives its efficacy mainly from the first component. From this now-familiar analysis, two interaction predictions follow.

The first prediction deals solely with the single defenses and involves an interaction between the active vs. passive variable and the refutational-same vs. -different variable. As discussed above, the active defense more effectively supplies the threatening motivational component and the passive better supplies the reassuring refutational content. Stringing together these various assumptions into a polysyllogism, we can derive the conclusion that for refutational-same defenses, the passive defense will be superior to the active, but for refutational-different defenses, the active will be superior to the passive.

The second prediction, dealing with an interaction between the single vs. double variable and the refutational-same vs. -different variable, is reached through reasoning very similar to the above. The attacking arguments are refuted less well in the single defense and, hence, the single defense supplies the motivation-inducing threatening component more effectively, while the double (active plus passive) defense more effectively supplies the reassuring refutational content. By again stringing together a polysyllogism of assumptions, we derive the following prediction: For refutational-same defenses, the double defense will be superior to the single, but for the refutational-different defense the single will be superior to the double.

2. Method

To test these two hypotheses within a single design, we used six refutational defense conditions: active-only, passive-only and active-plus-passive, each of these three being further dichotomized into refutational-same and refutational-different. (No supportive defenses were used in this study.) The second session, in which the usual attacking essays were presented, came 2 days later. There were also attack-only and neither-defense-nor-attack control conditions. A total of 168 college students served in both sessions, each furnishing data for four different conditions. Further details regarding the method can be found in McGuire (1961a).

When the double defenses (active plus passive) were used, the order in which they came was counterbalanced, so that half the subjects first wrote a refutational essay and then read an already prepared one; the other half read such an essay before they wrote their own. In the results reported below, both orders are combined, since the effect of order turned out to be trivial. It should be at least mentioned here, however, that this null effect of order is embarrassing to inoculation theory; on the basis of the same assumptions used throughout these studies, this theory yields a number of predictions regarding order effects. Yet in neither of the two studies designed to test order-effect predictions (McGuire, 1961a,b) were these predictions confirmed. The two studies cited discuss these embarrassing results more fully.

3. Results

The prediction regarding the single-defense condition was confirmed, at least in a weak, interaction reformulation. As seen in Table V, the passive defense is superior to the active for the refutational-same defense, but the reverse is true for the refutational-different defense. Considering the refutational-same and -different conditions separately, the superiority of the passive over active for the refutational-same defense is significant at the .08 level (two-tails), which tends to corroborate the result of the McGuire and Papageorgis (1961) study reported in the previous section; while the predicted reversal for the refutational-different defense, the superiority of the active over the passive, attains the .13 level of significance. Combining these two reverse trends, the predicted interaction is significant at the .02 level.

TABLE V

FINAL BELIEF LEVELS AFTER COMBINATIONS OF ACTIVE AND PASSIVE
REFUTATIONAL DEFENSES AND ATTACKS[a,b]

Type of attack	Participation in defense			
	Active only	Passive only	Active, then passive	Passive, then active
None	12.94 (48)[c]	12.75 (48)	12.57 (24)	13.37 (24)
Same counterarguments	10.66 (48)	11.47 (48)	12.15 (48)	12.18 (48)
Different counterarguments	11.42 (48)	10.62 (48)	10.92 (48)	10.71 (48)

[a] Control levels: neither-defense-nor-attack = 12.78 (N = 96); attack-only = 8.60 (N = 48).

[b] 15.00 indicates complete adherence to the truism.

[c] Numbers in parentheses give the number of cases on which cell means were based.

The second prediction regarding the single vs. double defense is also confirmed in its interaction formulation by the present study, as seen in Table V. For the refutational-same condition, the double defense is sizably superior to the single, the final means being 12.17 and 11.02, respectively, a difference significant at the .01 level. For the refutational-different defense, the double is only slightly superior to the single, the means being 10.82 and 11.06, respectively. This predicted interaction effect is significant at the .01 level.

VII. Persistence of the Induced Resistance

A. THEORY

1. Underlying Assumptions

The theoretical discussions in this chapter have continually assumed that the immunizing efficacy of the prior defenses derives from two mechanisms: from a threatening realization of the vulnerability of the belief, which, in the case of cultural truisms, supplies the much needed motivation to assimilate bolstering material; and from the actual presentation of such material. In the case of the active (essay-writing) defenses, the second mechanism is largely inoperative since little information is presented and the unpracticed believer is unable to summon up much defensive material from his own cognitive repertory. For the passive (essay-reading) defenses, however, the situation is more complex. The efficacy of the supportive defense derives primarily from the first mechanism; of the refutational-different, from the second; and of the refutational-same, from both.

Making additional assumptions about the different temporal trends of the two underlying mechanisms, this line of reasoning yields predictions about the persistence of the resistance conferred by the various kinds of defenses. The first of these assumed resistance-conferring mechanisms, the motivation-stimulating threat, may show a nonmonotonic time trend for the following reasons. Once the threat has motivated the previously overconfident believer to accumulate belief-bolstering material, he will still need time before he can act effectively on this motivation, since material relevant to these uncontroverted truisms is rather scarce in the ordinary, ideological environment. Hence, the believer will continue to accumulate additional material for a considerable time after being exposed to the threatening defense, resulting in a delayed-action effect as far as resistance to later attacks is concerned. On the other hand, as time passes and the threat recedes, the induced motivation to accumulate material will itself tend to decay. The result of these two tendencies is a nonmonotonic time trend (first rising, then falling) for induced resistance deriving from this first mechanism. Note that this time trend is the same as that for the typical biological inoculation; there too, a few days or weeks must pass after exposure to the weakened inoculation dose before the resistance builds up to its full strength, after which it tends to decay gradually. The parallel is not surprising since the analogy between the mechanisms in the two situations was our theoretical point of departure.

The second resistance-conferring mechanism, the actual communicating of belief-bolstering material in the defense, should show a much simpler relationship to time. Since the resistance conferred by this mechanism is a direct function of the retention of the bolstering material, we would expect its decay to follow the ordinary forgetting curve.

2. Prediction Regarding Actively Conferred Resistance

Since we hypothesize different persistence curves for the resistance conferred by the two underlying mechanisms, we can make distinctive predictions regarding the time trends of the resistance conferred by each type of defense, depending on the extent that each of the two mechanisms is assumed to be involved in that defense. The prediction is much the same for all types of active (essay-writing) defenses, whether supportive, refutational-same or -different. None of these variations presents appreciable amounts of useful belief-bolstering material in the active condition, and thus the second mechanism is inoperative from the start and does not contribute to the time trend. Such resistance as is conferred derives from the first (motivation-stimulating threat) mechanism, and hence the net time trend should be nonmonotonic. Most interesting, all three types of defense should show a delayed-action effect in the active condition, producing actually more resistance to attacks coming some time after the defense than to immediate attacks.

3. Predictions Regarding Passively Conferred Resistance

In the passive (essay-reading) condition, the predictions depend on the type of defense. What resistance is conferred by reading the supportive essay stems from the second mechanism (retention of the direct bolstering material it contains), so a simple decay function is predicted; the resistance conferred by the passive, supportive defense should decline progressively as the interval between the defense and attack increases. Since, as we have already seen, the passive refutational-different defense derives its efficacy almost entirely from the second (motivating-threat mechanism), we would expect its time trend to show the same nonmonotonic trend as would all three types of active defense. Since the efficacy of the passive refutational-same defense depends on both mechanisms we predict its time trend to be a composite of those of the two: namely, little decline at first, while the "forgetting" trend of the second mechanism is being largely offset by the delayed-action trend of the first mechanism, after which there is a much faster fall-off as both underlying trends are downward. Two studies that were designed to test these various time trend predictions are described in the sections following.

4. Selection of the Time Parameters

To test hypotheses about time trend differentials, especially when the functions are nonmonotonic or decay to a common asymtote (e.g., to zero in this case), it is necessary to set the time parameters at theoretically-strategic points in order that the predicted effects can be demonstrated. Selecting these strategic points presents a formidable methodological difficulty when, as in the present case, the theory is not well formed enough quantitatively to specify the exact time parameters. In anticipation of this problem, in the earlier studies reported above, the interval between defense and attack was deliberately set at different points from experiment to experiment. An examination (McGuire, 1962) of how these different settings appeared to affect the outcomes suggested that the critical persistence predictions could be tested by varying the intervals between defense and attack over the range of a few minutes to one week. Hence, in the studies reported below, these settings were selected as the range over which time was to vary.

B. PERSISTENCE OF PASSIVELY CONFERRED RESISTANCE

1. Method

The experiment designed to test the predictions about the differential decay rates of the resistance conferred by the three types of defense (supportive, refutational-same and refutational-different) under the passive (reading) conditions involved a mixed design in which each of the 160 subjects served in four conditions. Each subject received the defense of one truism several days before the attack (for 80 subjects, it was 2 days before; and for the other 80, 7 days before), and all received another defense a few minutes before the attack, so that the design included three different intervals between defense and attack. Equal numbers of subjects received supportive, refutational-same, and refutational-different defenses at all three intervals. Further details of the design, analyses, and other aspects of the procedure can be found in an earlier publication (McGuire, 1962).

2. Results

The persistence of the resistance conferred by the three types of passive defense is shown by the final belief scores contained in Table VI. As predicted, such small resistance as the supportive defense confers against immediate attacks has decayed ($p < .05$) almost completely within 2 days. At both the 2- and the 7-day intervals, the level to which the attack reduced the belief is approximately the same after a supportive defense as in the no-defense, attack-only condition.

For the refutational-same defense, however, the conferred resistance, as predicted, decays at a much slower rate. It is particularly in the early stages (again, as predicted) that the resistance produced by the refutational-same defense is more persistent. The interaction between the time (immediate vs. 2-day) variable and the supportive vs. refutational-same type of defense variable is significant at the .01 level. It can be seen that the direction of this interaction effect is in the opposite direction from that which would tend to result from a simple regression artifact.

The predicted nonmonotonic effect in the refutational-different condition is also confirmed. Resistance to attacks 2 days later is actually greater than to immediate attacks. This predicted delayed-action effect is significant at the .05 level. The predicted greater persistence during the first 2

TABLE VI

MEAN BELIEF LEVELS AFTER DEFENSES AND ATTACKS[a] SEPARATED BY
VARIOUS TIME INTERVALS, SHOWING THE PERSISTENCE OF THE
RESISTANCE TO PERSUASION CONFERRED BY THREE TYPES OF
PRIOR, PASSIVE BELIEF DEFENSES[b,c]

Interval between defense and attack	Defense-and-attack conditions		
	Supportive defense	Refutational-same defense	Refutational-different defense
Immediate	9.71	11.36	10.41
	(80)[d]	(80)	(80)
2 Days	8.51	11.08	11.45
	(40)	(40)	(40)
7 Days	8.82	9.49	9.68
	(40)	(40)	(40)

[a] Control levels: neither defense nor attack = 11.74 (N = 80); attack-only = 8.49 (N = 80).

[b] 15.00 indicates complete adherence to the truism.

[c] Data from McGuire (1962).

[d] Numbers in parentheses give the numbers of cases on which cell means were based.

days of the resistance conferred by the refutational-different over that conferred by the refutational-same defense is significant at the .05 level.

C. PERSISTENCE OF ACTIVELY CONFERRED RESISTANCE

1. Method

In a final experiment designed to test the relative persistence of actively and passively conferred resistance, the experimenter adopted the questionable economy of dropping out the 2-day interval condition. Each of the 72 subjects received an active and a passive defense (of two different truisms) one week prior to the attacks, and an active and passive defense of a third and fourth truism immediately prior to the attacks. The specific truisms were rotated around the defensive conditions from subject to subject. Then all four truisms were subjected to the usual attacks and the final belief levels were measured. Twenty-four of the subjects received supportive defenses, another 24, refutational-same, and a third 24, refutational-different defenses.

2. Results

The primary interest in this study was in the active conditions and the comparison between the active and passive. Thus, the 2-day condition, which is a crucial interval for some of the passive-defense effects that were demonstrated in the previous experiment, was omitted in this study. Even under these conditions, however, the distinctive effect in the passive condition was still apparent (see Table VII): the resistance conferred by the passive refutational-different defense showed significantly less of a decline over the week than that produced by the other two types of passive defenses, supportive and refutational-same. In fact, the slight increase in resistance conferred by the passive, refutational-different defense (not significant) suggests a delayed action effect even after one week, although, as the previous experiment showed (see Table VI) this effect is more apparent at the shorter, 2-day interval. For the active condition it

TABLE VII

MEAN BELIEF LEVELS AFTER DEFENSES AND ATTACKS SEPARATED BY
VARIOUS TIME INTERVALS, SHOWING THE PERSISTENCE OF
ACTIVELY AND PASSIVELY CONFERRED RESISTANCE[a,b]

Type of defensive material	Active defense		Passive defensive		All 4 combined
	Immediate attack	Attack one week later	Immediate attack	Attack one week later	
Supportive	8.30	9.89	9.72	9.47	9.34
	(24)[c]	(24)	(24)	(24)	(24)
Refutational-same	9.61	10.13	12.12	10.42	10.57
	(24)	(24)	(24)	(24)	(96)
Refutational-different	9.77	9.98	9.61	9.99	9.84
	(24)	(24)	(24)	(24)	(96)
All 3 Combined	9.22	10.00	10.48	9.96	9.91
	(72)	(72)	(72)	(72)	(288)

[a] 15.00 indicates complete adherence to the truism.

[b] Data from McGuire (1963b).

[c] Numbers in parentheses give the number of cases on which cell means were based.

was predicted that all three types of defense (supportive, refutational-same, and refutational-different) would show delayed action effects and, as seen in Table VII, just this was found. The greater resistance to attacks one week later than to immediate attacks for the three active types combined is significant at the .05 level. The design (as described above) used four different truisms for each of the three types of active defenses, and in nine of the twelve resulting comparisons there was the predicted delayed-action effect as regards conferred resistance.

The greater persistence of the actively-conferred resistance as compared to that produced by the passive defenses can be seen by inspecting the Table VII means. The belief level in the active condition has generally increased over the week, while it has weakened in the passive groups. This predicted interaction between time and activity is significant at the .01 level. Furthermore this interaction effect derives, as predicted, almost entirely from the supportive and the refutational-same types of defenses. As required by the theory, the resistance stemming from refutational-different defense is about equally persistent whether conferred actively or passively.

VIII. General Conclusion

The strategy used in this research program involved starting with relatively few assumptions and deriving from them a wide range of predictions. These were tested under a standardized set of conditions in experiments designed to be highly sensitive. The accumulating knowledge derived from the successive experiments clarified some of the parameters left undefined in the theory and thus allowed the experimenter to test progressively more elegant and complex derivations from the theory as he proceeded.

Space has not allowed a discussion of all the predictions and findings in this program. The positive was slightly accentuated by the experimenter's passing off with brief mention and references the failure to confirm the predicted order effects. Also omitted were results regarding cross-issue generalizations, effects of forewarnings, and effects of various kinds of prior commitments which were included in some of the studies reported. These findings were not described here because they were only peripherally related to inoculation theory.

The reader will note that all the studies reported here dealt with conferring resistance on a special type of belief, cultural truisms. The same inoculation theory which yielded these largely confirmed predictions regarding immunizing cultural truisms against persuasion might yield different hypotheses regarding the effects of the same defensive variables on making controverted beliefs resistant to persuasion. Hence, generalization from the above studies to the latter type of belief is not warranted. Further experiments will have to determine if inoculation theory will predict the immunizing efficacy of various types of defenses in the case of controversial beliefs as successfully as it has for truisms.

REFERENCES

Abelson, R. P., and Rosenberg, M. J. (1958). *Behav. Sci.* **3**, 1–13.
Allport, F., and Lepkin, M. (1945). *J. Abnorm. Soc. Psychol.* **40**, 3–36.
Anderson, L. R. (1962). M A. Thesis. University of Illinois, Urbana, Illinois.
Anderson, N. H. (1959). *J. Abnorm. Soc. Psychol.* **59**, 371–381.
Bennett, E. B. (1955). *Human Relat.* **8**, 251–273.
Berkowitz, L., and Cottingham, D. R. (1960). *J. Abnorm. Soc. Psychol.* **60**, 37–43.
Biddle, W. W. (1932). *Teach. Coll. Contrib Educ. No.* **531**.
Brehm, J. W. (1960). *In* "Attitude Organization and Change" (C. I. Hovland and M. J. Rosenberg, eds.), pp. 164–197. Yale Univ. Press, New Haven, Connecticut.

228   WILLIAM J. MCGUIRE

Brehm, J. W., and Cohen, A. R. (1962). "Explorations in Cognitive Dissonance." Wiley, New York.

Cantril, H. (1958). In "Readings in Social Psychology" (E. Maccoby, T. M. Newcomb, and E. Hartley, eds.), 3rd ed., pp. 291–300, Holt, New York.

Carlson, E. R. (1956). J. Abnorm. Soc. Psychol. 52, 256–61.

Charters, W. W., and Newcomb, T. M. (1958). In "Readings in Social Psychology" (E. Maccoby, T. M. Newcomb, and E. Hartley, eds.), 3rd ed., pp. 276–281. Hoit, New York.

Citron, A. F., and Harding, J. (1950). J. Abnorm. Soc. Psychol. 45, 310–328.

Cohen, A. R., Brehm, J. W., and Fleming, W. H. (1958). J. Abnorm. Soc. Psychol. 56, 276–278.

Cohen, A. R., Brehm, J. W., and Latané, B. (1959). J. Pers. 27, 63–73.

Collier, R. M. (1944). J. Social Psychol. 20, 3–17.

Cooper, E., and Dinerman, H. (1951). Public Opin. Quart. 15, 243–264.

Crutchfield, R. S. (1955). Am. Psychol. 10, 191–198.

Das, J. P., Rath, R., and Das, R. S. (1955). J. Abnorm. Soc. Psychol. 51, 624–628.

Deutsch, M., and Gerard, H. (1955). J. Abnorm. Soc. Psychol. 51, 629–636.

Dittes, J. E., and Kelley, H. H. (1956). J. Abnorm Soc. Psychol 53, 100–107.

Festinger, L. (1957. "A Theory of Cognitive Dissonance." Row, Peterson, Evanston, Illinois.

Fisher, S., Rubenstein, I., and Freeman, R. W. (1956). J. Abnorm. Soc. Psychol. 52, 200–207.

Harary, F. (1959). Behav. Sci. 4, 316–323.

Hicks, J. M., and Spaner, F. E. (1962). J. Abnorm. Soc. Psychol. 65, 112–120.

Hovland, C. I., and Mandell, W. (1957). J. Abnorm. Soc. Psychol. 47, 581–588.

Hovland, C. I., Lumsdaine, A. A., and Sheffield, F. (1949). "Experiments on Mass Communication." Princeton Univ. Press, Princeton, New Jersey.

Hovland, C. I., Campbell, E., and Brock, T. (1957). In "Order of Presentation in Persuasion" (C. I. Hovland, ed.), pp. 23–32. Yale Univ. Press, New Haven, Connecticut.

Janis, I. L., and Feshbach, S. (1953). J. Abnorm. Soc. Psychol. 48, 78–92.

Janis, I. L., and Field, P. B. (1959). In "Personality and Persuasibility" (I. L. Janis and C. I. Hovland, eds.), pp. 55–68. Yale Univ. Press, New Haven, Connecticut.

Janis, I. L., and Rife, D. (1959). In "Personality and Persuasibility" (I. L. Janis and C. I. Hovland, eds.), pp. 121–140. Yale Univ. Press, New Haven, Connecticut.

Kelley, H. H. (1957). In "Emerging Problems in Social Psychology" (M. Sherif and M. O. Wilson, eds.), pp. 229–248. Univ. of Oklahoma, Norman, Oklahoma.

Kelley, H. H., and Volkhart, E. H. (1952). Am. Sociol. Rev. 17, 453–465.

Kelley, H. H., and Woodruff, C. L. (1956). J. Abnorm. Soc. Psychol. 52, 67–74.

Kelman, H. C. (1950). J. Abnorm. Soc. Psychol. 45, 267–285.

Kelman, H. C. (1953). Human Relat. 6, 185–214.

Kelman, H., and Hovland, C. I. (1953). J. Abnorm. Soc. Psychol. 48, 327–335.

Kendall, P., and Wolf, K. M. (1949). In "Communications Research, 1948–1949" (P. F. Lazarsfeld and F. N. Stanton, eds.), pp. 152–179. Harpers, New York.

King, B. T., and Janis, I. L. (1956). Human Relat. 9, 177–186.

Klapper, J. T. (Aug., 1949) "Effects of the Mass Media." Bureau of Applied Social Research, Columbia Univ. (mimeo), New York.

Klapper, J. T. (1960). "Effects of Mass Communication," Free Press, Glencoe, Illinois.

Lana, R. E. (1959). Psychol. Bull. 56, 293–300.

Lewin, K. (1951). *In* "Field Theory in Social Science" (D. Cartwright, ed.). Harper, New York.

Lewin, K. (1958). *In* "Readings in Social Psychology" (E. Maccoby, T. Newcomb, and E. Hartley, eds.), 3rd ed., pp. 197–211. Holt, New York.

Lesser, G. S., and Abelson, R. P. (1959). *In* "Personality and Persuasibility" (I. L. Janis, and C. I. Hovland, eds.), pp. 187–206. Yale Univ. Press, New Haven, Connecticut.

Linton, H., and Graham, E. (1959). *In* "Personality and Persuasibility" (I. L. Janis and C. I. Hovland, eds.), pp. 69–101. Yale Univ. Press, New Haven, Connecticut.

Luchins, A. S. (1957). *In* "The Order of Presentation in Persuasion" (C. I. Hovland. ed.), pp. 33–61. Yale Univ. Press, New Haven, Connecticut.

McGuire, W. J. (1960a). *J. Abnorm. Soc. Psychol.* **60,** 345–353.

McGuire, W. J. (1960b). *J. Abnorm. Soc. Psychol.* **60,** 354–358.

McGuire, W. J. (1961a). *J. Abnorm. Soc. Psychol.* **63,** 326–332.

McGuire, W. J. (1961b). *Sociometry* **24,** 184–197.

McGuire, W. J. (1962). *J. Abnorm. Soc. Psychol.* **64,** 241–248.

McGuire, W. J. (1963a). Threat and reassurance as factors in conferring resistance to persuasion. (In preparation.)

McGuire, W. J. (1963b). Comparative persistence of actively and passively conferred resistance to persuasion. Unpublished manuscript.

McGuire, W. J. (1963c). Cross-issue generalization of conferred resistance to persuasion. Unpublished manuscript.

McGuire, W. J., and Papageorgis, D. (1961). *J. Abnorm. Soc. Psychol.* **62,** 327–337.

McGuire, W. J., and Papageorgis, D. (1962). *Public Opin. Quart.* **26,** 24–34.

Mausner, B. (1954). *J. Abnorm. Soc. Psychol.* **49,** 65–68.

Newcomb, T. M. (1961). "The Acquaintance Process." Holt, New York.

Nunnally, J., and Bobren, H. (1959). *J. Pers.* **27,** 38–46.

Papageorgis, D., and McGuire, W. J. (1961). *J. Abnorm. Soc. Psychol.* **62,** 475–481.

Raven, B. H., and Fishbein, M. (1961). *J. Abnorm. Soc. Psychol.* **63,** 411–416.

Rosenbaum, M. E., and Franc, D. E. (1960). *J Abnorm. Soc. Psychol* **61,** 15–20.

Rosenbaum, M. E., and Zimmerman, I. M. (1959). *Public Opin. Quart.* **23,** 247–254.

Rosenberg, M. J. (1956). *J. Abnorm. Soc. Psychol.* **53,** 367–372.

Rosenberg, M. J., and Hovland, C. I., eds. (1960). "Attitude Organization and Change." Yale Univ. Press, New Haven, Connecticut.

Samelson, F. (1957). *J. Abnorm. Soc. Psychol.* **55,** 181–187.

Schachter, S., and Hall, R. (1952). *Human Relat.* **5,** 397–406.

Smith, E. E. (1961). *Public Opin. Quart.* **25,** 626–639.

Steiner, I. D. (1962). *J. Abnorm. Soc. Psychol.* **65,** 266–267.

Stukát, K. G. (1958). *Acta Psychol. Gothoburgensia* **2.**

Tannenbaum, P. H. (1955). *Public Opin. Quart.* **19,** 292–302.

Tannenbaum, P. H. (1956). *Public Opin. Quart.* **20,** 413–425.

U.S. Senate, Committee on Government Operations. (1956). "The Interrogation, Indoctrination and Exploitation of American Military and Civilian Prisoners." U.S. Government Printing Office, Washington, D.C.

Weiss, W., and Fine, B. J. (1956). *J. Abnorm. Soc. Psychol.* **52,** 109–114.

Weitzenhoffer, A. M. (1953). "Hypnotism." Wiley, New York.

Zajonc, R. (1960). *J. Abnorm. Soc. Psychol.* **61,** 159–167.

SOCIAL MOTIVATION, DEPENDENCY, AND SUSCEPTIBILITY TO SOCIAL INFLUENCE[1]

Richard H. Walters and
Ross D. Parke

DEPARTMENT OF PSYCHOLOGY
UNIVERSITY OF WATERLOO
ONTARIO, CANADA

Numerous acquired drives have been postulated to account for complex social behavior, but only a few of these have received any detailed attention from developmental psychologists. The interest of child social

[1] The senior author gratefully acknowledges the financial support of the National Research Council of Canada (Grants No. APA-47 and APA-94), the Canadian National Health Grants Program (Public Health Research Grant 605-5-293), and the Defense Research Board of Canada (Grant No. 9401-24). This support provided the research, secretarial, and technical assistance without which this chapter could not have been written, as well as the equipment and supplies for a number of the studies to which reference is made.

psychologists has, in fact, focused on three general classes of behavior, achievement, aggression, and dependency, each of which is frequently presented as a "motivational system" (Child, 1954). The topic of aggression has been discussed in considerable detail by Bandura and Walters (1963a,b). In this chapter, the focus of attention is on classes of responses that have been linked, in the child-training and social-psychological literature, with the concept of a dependency drive. In Murray's (1938) need system, "succorance," roughly equivalent to dependency, and "nurturance" were presented as correlative. Since that time it has been generally assumed that adult nurturance is a critical factor in establishing dependency in children and in facilitating the socialization process in general (Bandura and Walters, 1959; Sears *et al.*, 1957).

In experimental social psychology, which has concerned itself primarily with the behavior of adults, conditions that facilitate social influence have received considerable attention. However, few attempts have been made to relate the findings of social psychologists to child-training procedures, in spite of the fact that the modification of children's behavior in the course of socialization is accomplished through social-influence processes. It has been generally assumed that dependency and susceptibility to social influence are in some way related (e.g., Schachter, 1959), but the basis of this relationship has never been systematically explored.

This chapter will examine critically a number of studies that have been interpreted as supporting the concept of a dependency or social drive. In most of these studies, the dependent variable has been some index of the extent to which social-influence procedures are successful in modifying the subjects' behavior. Consequently, in the course of evaluation, we have attempted to identify some mediating processes that may account for the apparent relationship between dependency and susceptibility to social influence. The primary concern, however, is to question traditional approaches to the problem of social motivation and to offer supporting evidence for an alternative approach that may help to bridge the gap between developmental theory and theories that have been evolved almost exclusively within the context of social-psychological research.

I. Problems of Social Motivation

A. The Theory of Acquired Social Drives

In spite of its critics, the belief that individuals acquire discriminable social drives or motives continues to dominate current theories of social behavior and development. These drives are said to be learned during the process of socialization and to energize and direct most adult human behavior. They supposedly originate as response systems that are established through their effectiveness in reducing unlearned, biologically based drives or that (if one wishes to avoid the snares of drive-reduction theory) terminate in the presentation of a primary reinforcer. In time these response systems acquire motivational properties of their own or, in Allport's (1937) terms, become functionally autonomous. By some alchemystical process the base metal of habits is transmuted into the glittering gold of drives or, to change the metaphor, into elusive motivating forces whose name is legion.

The theory of acquired social drives necessarily assumes that such drives have both energizing and directive properties, since they are manifested in specific forms of behavior—for example, an aggression drive in acts that produce pain or hurt for others and a dependency drive in acts that are capable of eliciting nurturant counter-responses. Learning theorists who have modified and extended Hull's basic system (1943) have not uniformly favored the dual-property drive construct and are now inclined to ascribe to drives only an energizing function (Brown, 1953, 1961; Spence, 1956). As Malmo (1958) pointed out, the generalized drive (D) of Hullian theory appears increasingly to play a role very similar to that of "arousal" or "activation" in neurophysiological approaches to behavior.

Psychologists who believe that social habits may become social drives have sometimes attempted to specify conditions that lead to this change in status. Sears and associates (1953) offered the theory that "conflict between expectancy of reward and expectancy of nonreward or punishment" is the differential factor that accounts for some, but not all, reinforced response sequences' (habits') acquiring motivational properties. This belief led to a search for curvilinear relationships between children's aggressive, dependent, and identification responses, on the one hand, and maternal punishment and frustration of these responses, on the other. The expectation was that children who were *moderately* frustrated and punished would show a greater incidence of the frustrated-and-punished behavior than children who had received either little or a great deal of frustration and punishment. Let us overlook the fact, for the present, that nonreward and punishment do not have identical effects and consider what kind of disciplinary actions may be implied by the description "moderate frustration and punishment." Presumably, parents who are moderately punitive and frustrative in respect to, let us say, dependency, allow dependency responses to be intermittently reinforced. Consequently, their children's dependency habits should be manifested more frequently under nonreward conditions than those of children whose parents reward dependency consistently or frustrate and punish dependency on all possible occasions. Moreover, parents who are moderately frustrative and punitive of dependency may give attention to a child only when he tries hard to gain this attention. This would be equivalent to reinforcing dependency responses on a variable-interval schedule and then only when the child is responding in an intense manner or at a high rate—a schedule that is especially likely to produce "aggressively dependent" children (Bandura and Walters, 1963b).

Thus, the evidence that Sears, Whiting, and their collaborators produced in support of the assumption of acquired social drives, i.e., curvilinear relationships between parental frustration and punishment and the incidence of frustrated and punished behavior in children, does not necessarily confirm their position. Their theorizing may reflect a confusion between habit and drive, which Brown trenchantly criticized. Brown (1953, p. 12) suggested that "the important motivating component of many of the supposed acquired drives for specific goal objects is actually a learned tendency to be discontented or to be distressed or anxious in the absence of these goal objects." According to this point of view, dependency, aggression, and other forms of social or antisocial behavior may be regarded as habits energized by conditioned emotional responses. Once this position is accepted, it is possible to seek relatively objective measures of emotional arousal that are independent of the behavior that the arousal or drive state is presumed to motivate.

The primary sources of drive that until recently received most emphasis in the literature were states or conditions of deprivation or distress, for example, hunger, thirst, and pain. It is therefore not surprising that most patterns of social behavior have also been depicted as originating from unpleasant, tense, or conflictful states. This manner of conceptualizing social phenomena is undoubtedly too narrow. Changes in theoretical orientation, reflected, for example, in White's (1959) paper on competence, have already fostered experimental studies in the areas of child, social, and clinical psychology in which arousal states are not induced by frustrating or threatening stimulation.

Probably many of the changes in socially significant behavior (for example, increased responsiveness to social reinforcers) that seem to occur under conditions of threat could be produced just as effectively by experimental manipulations that cannot parsimoniously be construed as danger signals. More effortful behavior seems to result as much from instructions to subjects that present the task to be accomplished as important, worthwhile, or rewarding, or by the introduction of nonthreatening novel situations (Berlyne, 1960, 1964), as from threat of failure or some other "anxiety"-producing condition. The shortcomings of Brown's theoretical analyses (1953, 1961) of socially significant behavior lie mainly in his emphasis on anxiety as the motivational component of "acquired drives." These shortcomings are, however, to be expected in view of the relative neglect, until recently, of "positive" sources of motivation. In fact, one of the tasks still confronting the social psychologist is to identify the social-stimulus variables that result in emotional arousal for different individuals and to trace the processes whereby these variables acquire their motivational effects. One should not assume in advance that all instances of social behavior—particularly "achievement-oriented" responses—are necessarily patterns of tension relief.

B. EMOTIONAL AROUSAL AND SOCIAL BEHAVIOR

The effects of emotional arousal on human performance have been the subject of a number of recent reviews (e.g., Bindra, 1959; Duffy, 1962). In many nonsocial tasks efficiency of performance appears initially to increase with increasing arousal and then to decline; however, the precise relationship between arousal and performance is also dependent on such factors as the complexity of the task and previously learned patterns of response inhibition and control. The criterion of efficiency cannot readily be applied to social behavior. Nevertheless, some of the changes in response characteristics that make for greater or lesser efficiency in nonsocial tasks probably exert considerable influence in determining the outcome of social-interaction processes.

In the first place, increased emotional arousal is frequently associated with an increase in overt activity. This effect has been neglected or minimized in discussions of a number of observational studies that have claimed to support specific-drive theories. A classic example is provided in the previously mentioned monograph by Sears et al. (1953). Curvilinear relationships were reported between maternal frustration and punishment for dependency and aggression and the incidence of dependency and aggression responses, respectively, in preschool children. A similar curvilinear relationship was found between maternal frustration and punishment and the activity level of children. There was, in fact, no consistent relationship between the *relative* incidence of dependency and aggression and the occurrence of maternal frustration and punishment for these kinds of responses. Thus, although the study of Sears et al. may be interpreted as indicating that inconsistent discipline (moderate reward and moderate frustration) increases the emotional responsiveness of a child, it provides no clear-cut evidence of any other motivational effect.

Secondly, emotional arousal may alter perceptual thresholds and modify the range and nature of cues to which an observer will respond (Bruner et al. 1955; Easterbrook, 1959; Kausler and Trapp, 1960; Smock, 1962). Most of the evidence for this effect comes from laboratory studies of vigilance and incidental learning; it is probable, however, that a similar effect occurs in social situations. Restriction of cues could result in the focusing of attention on precisely what someone else is doing, so providing a possible model with an increased opportunity of channeling a percipient's behavior in a specific direction. Moreover, an emotionally aroused person may attend more carefully to the actions of a reinforcing agent and thus learn more rapidly to identify the occasions on which reinforcements will be dispensed.

Thirdly, there is considerable evidence that emotional arousal results in increased intensity of responding. This latter effect is especially important for the high-magnitude theory of aggression proposed by Bandura and Walters (1963a,b). According to this theory, the social judgments involved in classifying activities as aggressive are considerably influenced by the intensity of the observed responses. For example, a child who gently pulls on his mother's skirts has traditionally been regarded as displaying dependency, whereas one who pulls in a violent manner is likely to be judged aggressive. It is little wonder that disruptive, socially disapproved, "negative attention-getting" behavior has posed a problem for child psychologists, who seem never quite certain to what drive system this behavior should be attributed.

Finally, an increasing level of emotional arousal necessarily involves a change in the internal cues to which a response will be made. These internal changes undoubtedly operate in conjunction with changes in environmental cues and accompanying cognitions to determine what specific habit patterns will be elicited. Let us suppose that a child is habitually shown affection and approval for running to his mother when an unfamiliar, emotionally arousing event occurs, but is shown little affection and approval for "proximity" responses when he is calm and relaxed. High-arousal cues will be associatively linked for this child with "dependency" habits, but low-arousal cues will be relatively more strongly linked with other patterns of response.

C. ASSESSING MOTIVATIONAL LEVELS

Exponents of activation and similar neurophysiological theories (e.g., Bindra, 1959; Duffy, 1951, 1957, 1962; Hebb, 1955; Malmo, 1959) have fostered the use of physiological indices of drive or arousal level. These indices have as yet been rarely employed in studies of social behavior in spite of the fact that they can provide an objective measure of motivational levels. Such measures may be utilized to assess the success of experimental manipulations and thus to clarify considerably experimental outcomes, especially when negative results are obtained. In studies of experimentally induced fear, anxiety, or threat, for example, the stimulus variables are usually only attenuated analogues of the anxiety-producing situations that occur in everyday life. Indeed, it is generally understood that the "ethical" psychologist will not subject children (or even adults) to situations producing potentially harmful effects that endure beyond the usually very brief testing session. Governed by these restraints, the manipulations may be so minimally effective that differences between experimental and control subjects are statistically nonsignificant. The addition of physiological measures may, in such cases, reveal the weakness of the experimental techniques and thus forestall the premature acceptance of a null hypothesis.

It is possible, of course, to question our subjects concerning their reactions to the experiment or to ask them to fill in questionnaires or inventories that supposedly reflect these reactions. Unfortunately, however, most paper-and-pencil tests of this kind are subject to response biases; moreover, standardized tests that have built-in safety devices against misrepresentation or biases are not always appropriate for use in specific experimental situations (Malmo, 1958). On the other hand, unstandardized ad hoc questionnaires may sometimes provide valuable supplementary data; Schachter (1959), for example, effectively employed such devices both for assessing subjects' reactions to experimental procedures and for identifying individual differences in responsivity that may be systematically related to prior social experiences. Ideally, perhaps, one should attempt to obtain self-reports as well as physiological measures, particularly in view of the marked differences that are found among individuals in the patterning of their physiological responses to stress.

It is not always practical to secure either extensive physiological measures of arousal or adequate self-reports of reactions to threat, especially when young children are employed as subjects. In the majority of studies of motivation reviewed in this chapter, it was simply assumed that the experimental manipulation had a drive-arousing effect. However, the possible advantages of social-psychological experiments in which physiological measures are employed or physiological responses are induced by drugs, and in which self-reports are also obtained, are evident from the research of Gerard (1963), as well as in some of the studies reviewed here.

An example of the usefulness of physiological measures for clarifying results is provided by McNulty and Walters (1962), who postulated that cognitive dissonance or the "existence of nonfitting relations among cognitions" (Festinger, 1957, p. 3) may be regarded as a set of response-produced cues that constitute a possible stimulus for emotional arousal. On the basis of their responses to an attitude-inventory concerning topics expected to elicit relatively strong expressions of opinion from adolescents, high school boys were assigned to one of four groups: high arousal with argument; high arousal without argument; low arousal with argument; low arousal without argument. Subjects under the high-arousal condition were told, after electrodes had been attached to their forearms, fingers, and neck, that the equipment was designed to test how well they thought and how emotionally stable they were. The remaining (low-arousal) subjects were informed that some physiological measures would be taken as a matter of interest, but that these had no relevance to the task they were going to perform.

All boys were then requested to discuss a topic with two trained adult confederates of the experimenter on whom dummy electrodes were placed; the topic was, of course, one on which the subject had previously expressed a strong opinion. With boys in the argument groups, the confederates expressed opinions that were contrary to those of the adolescents; with the no-argument subjects, the confederates maintained a neutral point of view. During the discussion, changes of opinion in the direction specified by the confederates were reinforced by the latter's verbal and gestural approval. Records of muscle tension throughout the interaction and self-reports of "anxiety" both before and after the discussion were secured from all subjects. The measures of behavioral change were based on attitude-inventory scores obtained immediately before and immediately after testing and the number of reasons given by subjects at each of these times in support of the attitude under discussion.

The physiological findings indicated that the aroused-argument subjects were reacting more emotionally than the other three groups during interaction with the confederates. It was consequently possible to carry out group comparisons based on differences in reactivity level as a supplement to the comparisons dictated by the original 2 × 2 factorial design. These comparisons indicated that the highly reactive group of subjects had changed their attitudes to a greater extent than subjects in each of the relatively nonreactive groups, and that the latter three groups did not significantly differ in the extent to which they exhibited attitude change. A significant difference between subjects in the arousal and nonarousal argument groups was of particular interest, since these two groups were treated in an identical manner by the confederates. This difference clearly justified the conclusion that the effectiveness of the social-influence procedures utilized in the study was a function of the emotional-arousal level of the subjects. In the absence of a physiological index of the success of the experimental manipulations, the crucial supplementary analysis on which this conclusion was based could not have been undertaken.

A few words should be said concerning the use of questionnaires such as the Manifest Anxiety Scale (MAS) (Taylor, 1953) as measures of drive or persisting emotional responsiveness (Spence, 1958). Perhaps "anxiety" as a personality variable has not been sufficiently sharply distinguished from the "situational anxiety" that is presumably assessed by physiological measures and also by subjects' self-reports of reactions to specific situations of threat or stress. There is some indication, for example, that persisting emotional responsiveness, as measured by the MAS, facilitates performance on simple learning tasks, but is associated with relatively poor performance on complex tasks in which the correct response has at the outset lower habit strength than other, competing responses (Spence *et al.*, 1956a,b). Spence (1958) attributed this phenomenon to the manner in which habit strength and drive interact in a multiplicative fashion to determine the excitatory potentials of correct and incorrect responses.

On the other hand, Malmo (1958), who has been mainly concerned with physiological-arousal indices, suggested that the difficulty of complex tasks may increase the drive or arousal level of subjects to the point at which learning is impaired. Thus, for him the varying performance of high-MAS and low-MAS subjects on tasks of different levels of complexity is consistent with the curvilinear relationship between arousal level and performance postulated by activation theorists. In advancing this argument, Malmo assumed that MAS scores and arousal indices were equivalent measures of drive. It is likely, however, that anxiety-questionnaire scores reflect the range of stimuli to which individuals will react as much as the intensity of their emotional responses. If this is the case, high-anxiety subjects may be relatively distractible and consequently make inappropriate responses in a complex learning situation. On the other hand, a situationally determined emotional response may be associated with the focusing of attention on relevant stimulus cues and may consequently foster successful task-oriented behavior.

In a recent study of avoidance learning (Parke and Walters, 1963) in which both anxiety-questionnaire scores and physiological measures were secured from subjects, the initial level of the subjects' performance appeared to be primarily influenced by persisting emotional responsiveness, whereas change in performance during the learning task seemed to be more closely associated with situational reactivity. Differential effects of this kind could be of considerable importance for understanding the influence of emotional arousal on behavior in social situations.

II. Dependency and Social Influence: Theoretical Considerations

A. DEFINITION OF DEPENDENCY

The term "dependency" has been employed both as a behavioral and as a motivational construct (Hartup, 1963). In the former capacity, it has referred to a set of interrelated and presumably substitutable responses such as asking for help or reassurance, seeking physical contact, and attracting the attention of others. Such responses have been regarded as sharing the characteristic of being capable of eliciting attending and ministering responses from others (Bandura and Walters, 1963b) or of being instrumental in obtaining social reinforcement (Hartup, 1963). Immediately, a semantic problem arises, for many of the responses that are instrumental in obtaining social reinforcement or gaining approval could readily be classified as "oriented toward achievement." Yet achievement-oriented behavior has at times been utilized as an index of independence, a construct traditionally structured as the obverse of dependency—or at least utilized to refer to a group of habits that are negatively related to dependency indices (Beller, 1959). This conceptual confusion is painfully apparent when one attempts to interpret experimental findings from studies in which changes in performance, supposedly motivated by a "need for achievement," have resulted from social reinforcement or the presentation of social models (Rosenthal *et al.*, 1963; Sampson, 1962).

One source of confusion is the judgmental process involved in classifying a response as dependent. Such categorization frequently involves reference to a cultural value system, so that behavior that is regarded as dependent within one cultural or subcultural framework (or for males, but not for females) is not so classified in another. Bandura and Walters (1963a,b) advocated a social-judgment approach to the problem of aggression on the grounds that behavior judged to be aggressive in one situation may not be so judged in another. This approach led to the conclusion that "a child does not learn aggressive habits nor does he acquire an aggressive drive; what he learns are potentially harm-producing responses which, if used in interpersonal transactions, are generally labeled (and usually censured) as aggression" (Cowan and Walters, 1963, pp. 550–551).[2] Analogously, it may be argued that although a child learns a variety of possibly interrelated responses—such as asking for help and soliciting approval—that may or may not be regarded as dependent, according to the circumstances in which they occur and the value system within which his behavior is judged, he does not, strictly speaking, acquire dependency habits or develop a dependency drive.

The value judgments involved in categorizing behavior as dependent frequently, though not always, concern the appropriateness of a response

[2] There are, of course, some kinds of responses that are usually judged to be aggressive in most or all societies. This consensus of judgments does not, however, indicate that there is some intrinsic characteristic of these kinds of responses that inevitably elicits the judgments. Even though deliberately killing a human being is usually regarded as aggressive, there are instances of this kind of response that would not be thus classified, for example, the mercy killing of Lenny in Steinbeck's "Of Mice and Men." In order for George to carry out the mercy killing, he needed only to have learned the component motor responses required for shooting Lenny and the cognitions involved in anticipating the consequences of his act.

for an agent having a known or assumed level of capacity for coping with a given situation. One must, in fact, make an initial distinction between behavior that reflects lack of some capacity and the occurrence of equivalent behavior under circumstances in which the individual's goals can be economically and readily attained without the mediation of others.

As a result of past social-learning experiences, some persons may tend to rely on others even when they are capable of carrying out activities efficiently and unaided. Others may avoid responses of these kinds even when this avoidance is uneconomical or prevents them from reaching their goals. Those who behave in the former manner are likely to be classified as dependent, whereas behavior of the latter kind tends to be regarded as indicative of "dependency anxiety" (Bandura and Walters, 1959) or of a "dependency deficit."

Distinctions have been made in the child-training literature between instrumental and emotional (Heathers, 1955) or between task-oriented and person-oriented (Bandura and Walters, 1963b) dependency behavior. These distinctions in part reflect another aspect of the social-judgment process. While it is culturally expected that an individual will continue to seek support, reassurance, guidance, and similar "dependency gratifications" from other persons during the course of his development, the precise manner in which he does so and the persons to whom these responses are primarily directed are subject to change. Judgments concerning dependency consequently involve not only the conditions under which the behavior in question is exhibited, but also the appropriateness of the person to whom it is directed in relation to the age and social status of the agent. Moreover, these judgments frequently involve an inference concerning the social consequences of behavior. For example, although psychopaths are frequently depicted as incapable of forming person-oriented dependency relationships, they are also described as possessing highly developed manipulatory skills that secure them dependency gratifications (Bandura and Walters, 1963b). The value system that governs descriptions of this kind includes expectations that members of society should not utilize others for gaining their own ends without consideration of the welfare of those whose interest and services they solicit.

An adequate theory of social behavior demands a thorough investigation of the process whereby social judgments are learned and of the stimulus conditions under which they are elicited. Social motives such as dependency and aggression are, in fact, quasi-evaluative labels reflecting social judgments that are made within particular cultural contexts. The labels, of course, have some objective reference, though often not well defined, to certain classes of behavior. The task of the social-learning theorist thus becomes twofold. In the first place, he must investigate the conditions under which the behavioral referents are acquired, modified, and maintained in the course of social learning. Secondly, he must determine how a child learns to make the social judgments that enable him to discriminate acceptable from nonacceptable responses, which are then classified, as (for example) dependent or nondependent, aggressive or nonaggressive, on the basis of their acceptability within the cultural system.

Positive, although far from perfect, relationships have been reported among classes of behavior customarily categorized as dependent, at least for younger children (Beller, 1955; Sears, 1963). Although these response categories are, in many respects, quite diverse, all appear to involve at least one common component, namely, orienting and attending to other persons. It is proposed that the apparent unitary nature of dependency behavior may be attributed to the relative strength and weakness of attending and orienting responses, which are presumably modifiable in accordance with well-established learning principles. In some contexts, these responses, together with accompanying instrumental acts, will be socially judged as dependent; in other contexts, they will not be so judged. In the remainder of this chapter, "dependency" is employed as a convenient label for referring to behavior that has customarily been classified in this way by developmental and social psychologists. Although we do not believe that dependency will ultimately prove a useful concept for ordering behavioral phenomena, its omission from further discussions of prior theory and research could result only in a plethora of unwarranted circumlocutions.[3]

B. DEPENDENCY AND BEHAVIOR MODIFICATION

Under circumstances in which they may or may not lack necessary skills, individuals differ in the extent to which they modify their behavior following exposure to social models or as a result of the presentation of

---

[3] Social and developmental psychologists sometimes assert that they are interested only in "socially significant variables"; and it is precisely because dependent, aggressive, achievement-oriented, and sex behavior are socially significant that they have received so much attention in the literature on socialization. However, the cultural value systems that direct attention to these kinds of behavior also influence the identification of the response patterns that are regarded as falling within one or other of these categories. Thus, attaching the label (for example) of dependency to a specific response pattern is a very different process from selecting a variable such as the tensile strength of steel, to which numerical values may be unambiguously attached. Strictly speaking, aggression, dependency, and other socially significant behavior patterns are not variables in the sense in which the term "variable" is used in the natural sciences. Perhaps it is time that social scientists stop pretending they are. The status of concepts like aggression and dependency does not, in fact, greatly differ from that of the more general evaluative labels—such as emotional disturbance and mental illness—that pervade the vocabulary of clinical psychologists (Bandura, 1964).

reinforcers, both positive and negative, by various social agents. This dimension of behavior may be called "social dependency" or "susceptibility to social influence." The proposed definition is both free of evaluative connotations and avoids reference to the intention of an agent. Consequently it escapes many of the classificatory problems that arise from the use of intentionality criteria in defining classes of social behavior (Bandura and Walters, 1963a,b). At the same time, the introduction of the term "social dependency" is intended to imply that evaluative judgments concerning dependency, which were discussed in the previous section, sometimes take into account the extent to which behavior is modified as a result of social influence.

Bandura and Walters (1963b) have described two major ways in which social influence may be exerted. One of these involves the presentation of real-life or symbolic models calculated to evoke imitative behavior. The other involves controlling reinforcements in a manner designed to elicit or maintain the behavior desired by socialization agents. These two methods of control do not operate entirely independently. Consequences to the model influence the extent to which the model's behavior will be imitated; moreover, imitative behavior is unlikely to persist if the consequences to the imitator are nonrewarding or adverse. Most of the experimental operations to be discussed in this chapter involve either the presentation of social models or the dispensing of social reinforcers.

Several investigators have reported a positive relationship between various measures of dependency and indices of susceptibility to social influence. Endsley (1960) found that children who sought praise frequently from their teachers performed better on a learning task, in which social reinforcers were dispensed for correct responses, than did children who sought praise relatively seldom. Similarly, Ferguson (1961) found that highly dependent children (in terms of Beller's scales) learned a simple discrimination task more readily than less dependent children when correct responses were verbally approved by the experimenter. Jakubczak and Walters (1959) assessed dependency by means of a semi-projective technique, and then tested high-dependent and low-dependent boys in the autokinetic-judgment situation. During the early stages of testing, the high-dependent boys matched the judgments of confederates of the experimenter to a greater extent than did low-dependent boys.

The evidence for a relationship between dependency and susceptibility to social influence is not confined to young children. Adolescents who are reluctant to accept help from others appear to respond relatively little to social reinforcement (Cairns, 1961). Dependency in adults, defined by means of responses on personality tests, has been shown to be associated with responsiveness to social reinforcement (Cairns and Lewis, 1962), compliance to verbal models (Cairns and Kaufman, 1962), and measures of group conformity (Mussen and Kagan, 1956).

The development of habits of orienting and attending to others may facilitate the social-influence process. In the first place, imitative learning is most likely when the attention of the observer is focused on the responses of the model; in fact, rather precise imitation will not occur unless the observer attends carefully. Secondly, attending to the actions of others ensures that the observer is aware of expressions of approval and disapproval and the manner in which these responses are associated with his own behavior. The strength of habits of attending to others may therefore be the variable that mediates the apparent relationship between what we have called social dependency and dependency behavior, as this has customarily been defined in the child-training literature.

This point of view differs considerably from those advanced by exponents of a social or dependency drive. It seeks to explain enhanced susceptibility to social influence in terms of both the strength of habits of orienting and attending and the influence of emotional arousal. The latter, as noted, may in itself serve to modify perceptual thresholds and the utilization of cues.

Conceptualizations of dependency as a specific motive have, generally speaking, been based on a questionable analogy to certain other forms of behavior. Just as the withholding, reduction, or restriction of food leads to food-seeking behavior motivated by a hunger drive, so the withholding, reduction, or restriction of social contact is assumed to arouse approval-seeking, help-seeking, or other dependent responses that are motivated by an affiliative, a dependency, or social drive. Relevant research studies have consequently involved the experimental isolation of subjects, the withdrawal of attention or approval by the experimenter, and comparisons of institutionalized and noninstitutionalized children on the assumption that institutionalized children have restricted social contacts. In the following section of this chapter, some of these studies will be re-examined in the light of the theoretical position offered above.

III. Dependency and Social Influence: Empirical Evidence

A. ISOLATION STUDIES

1. The Gewirtz-Baer Analysis of Dependency Behavior

Gewirtz (1957, 1961) utilized Skinner's (1953) concepts in learning-theory analyses of the effects of maternal deprivation on dependency behavior. These analyses defined social drive in terms of the experimental operations of social deprivation, nondeprivation, and social satiation, which were presumed to modify the effectiveness of social reinforcers.

Gewirtz's hypotheses were tested in two ingenious and methodologically influential experiments carried out by Gewirtz and Baer (1958a,b). In the initial study (1958a), 32 children (16 boys and 16 girls) were each tested twice—once after a 20-minute period of social isolation, and then again after being brought directly from the classroom. On each occasion the children were required to learn a simple two-choice discrimination task during which the experimenter dispensed reinforcers in the form of verbal approval for "correct" responses. In general, the children modified their responses more readily after isolation.

The second study (1958b) employed three experimental conditions: (a) isolation, again of 20 minutes' duration; (b) no deprivation; and (c) interaction. The interaction condition, consisting of 20 minutes of free-play activity in the presence of a responsive adult, was conceptualized as a satiation procedure. Children under the nondeprivation condition were tested immediately upon arrival at the experimental room and presumably had been exposed to a heterogeneous set of conditions involving varying degrees of social contact. Both boys and girls again served as subjects, but only one experimenter, a female, participated. Learning was most rapid following isolation, intermediate under the nonisolation condition, and slowest following social interaction.

Gewirtz and Baer (1958b) suggested the following interpretation of their findings. "In a special sense, then, it would appear that there exist for children social drives that respond to social reinforcer deprivation similarly as do many appetitive drives" (p. 170). Further support for this conceptualization was sought in an earlier study by Gewirtz (1954), in which children from whom adult attention had been withheld during an easel-painting session sought attention more frequently than those for whom adult attention was more readily available (Gewirtz et al., 1958).

There was a marked cross-sex effect both in the first of the Gewirtz and Baer isolation studies and in the attention-seeking study by Gewirtz. Increased "behavior for a social reinforcer" was found only when the experimenter was of the opposite sex from the subject. However, a similar effect was not present in the second of the Gewirtz and Baer experiments, which involved the testing by a female experimenter of subjects of both sexes. Moreover, a cross-sex effect has been found in social-reinforcement studies not involving low availability or deprivation of social stimuli (Stevenson, 1961, Stevenson and Knights, 1962b); consequently, such an effect appears unrelated to the drive state postulated by Gewirtz and Baer.

2. Two Reinterpretations of the Gewirtz-Baer Results

a. The arousal hypothesis. Walters and Karal (1960) offered the suggestion that the difference between deprived and nondeprived children in the Gewirtz and Baer experiments could be attributed to the emotionally arousing nature of the isolation procedure. Such an interpretation makes unnecessary the postulation of a specific social drive to account for the Gewirtz-Baer findings.

This suggestion was directly tested by Walters and Ray (1960) in a 2×2 factorial design involving both emotional-arousal and isolation manipulations. Arousal was induced by the use of a stranger as the experimenter's assistant and by an absence of information concerning the intentions of the experimenter. The isolation consisted of a 20-minute wait in a room adjoining that utilized for testing. Walters and Ray employed the same dependent variable as had Gewirtz and Baer and, like the latter experimenters, selected verbal approval as the reinforcer during the learning procedure. Their results indicated that the arousal variable, not the isolation procedure itself, was the crucial factor in facilitating learning. Further support for this position was obtained by Walters et al. (1960) in a study in which adolescent boys were exposed to stimulus situations similar to those used by Walters and Ray. Self-reports indicated that boys who had been led to believe that they were being tested for intelligence and emotional stability were emotionally aroused by the instructions they were given. The investigators found that these boys more readily changed their judgments in an autokinetic situation to accord with a fictitious set of norms supplied by the experimenter than did boys who were given relaxing instructions. Thus, observational learning appeared to be facilitated by emotional arousal, even in the absence of reinforcement to the observer for matching the "norms" supplied by the experimenter-model. In addition, when verbal reinforcements were subsequently delivered for specific autokinetic judgments, the aroused subjects were more readily influenced than those who were relatively relaxed.

A physiological index of emotional arousal was introduced by Walters and Parke (1964) in a study that partly replicated the procedures used by Walters and Ray, including the orthogonal manipulation of threat and isolation. Finger-temperatures were obtained while Grade IV children learned a two-choice discrimination task following exposure to one or other of the conditions employed in the earlier study. Subjects placed under the threat condition and subsequently isolated both exhibited greater emotionality— assessed from finger-temperature records—and learned faster than any other group of subjects. Possibly, isolation has a catalytic effect. A person in whom a state of anxiety or uncertainty has already been created may become increasingly apprehensive in the absence of stimuli capable of eliciting responses incompatible with the anxiety or uncertainty.

Since the Gewirtz-Baer interpretation of social-deprivation effects appeared to imply that the dispensing of reinforcers by a warm, nurturant adult was an essential part of their experiment, Walters and Parke used two kinds of reinforcement procedures. For half the children under each experimental condition, the experimenter interacted with the child in a friendly, reassuring manner while she verbally approved correct responses. For the remaining children, she dispensed material rewards (tokens, exchangeable later for a toy) through a screen which shielded her from the subject. There was no significant effect attributable to differences in the reinforcement procedure, either alone or in interaction with the other experimental variables. According to the social-deprivation hypothesis, it is the nature of the adult's approval or attentiveness as a specifically *social* reinforcer that accounts for the heightened susceptibility to social influence of previously isolated children. Failure to find any interaction effects involving isolation and type of reward suggests that this aspect of the hypothesis is mistaken. Consequently, the experimenters here have indirect support for the arousal interpretation, which demands only that the rewards be appropriate to the age, sex, and socioeconomic status of the recipients.

Additional evidence in favor of this arousal interpretation of isolation can be found in another study. On the basis of previous research (Levin and Baldwin, 1959; Paivio and Lambert, 1959) indicating that children whose anxiety is readily aroused by an audience tend to escape from an audience situation, Paivio (1963) predicted that children with high audience anxiety, assessed from the Children's Audience Sensitivity Inventory (Paivio *et al.*, 1961), would make shorter speeches following an emotionally arousing isolation experience than children whose audience anxiety was low. Confirmation of this prediction provided further support for the Walters-Karal arousal interpretation of isolation. Like Walters and Parke (1964), Paivio regards isolation as having a catalytic effect. "Any apprehension aroused in the subject by the experimenter's attitude or instructions may progressively increase during isolation, as in the phenomenon of incubation of fear" (p. 247). It is consequently unfortunate that Paivio did not indicate to his subjects, in advance of isolation, that they would later be required to make a speech. If he had done so, his results might have been more conclusive.

There is considerable evidence, then, that isolation may have an emotionally arousing effect that can influence responses in certain social situations. When the dependent variable is some measure of performance in a task in which reinforcers are dispensed for correct responses, increased arousal may foster greater attentiveness to the responses of the experimenter and therefore more efficient utilization of cues. If degree of susceptibility to social influence is regarded as a joint product of the strength of previously learned habits of attending to others and the current level of arousal of the subject, the isolation studies may be viewed as reflecting a pure arousal effect that produced differences among groups of children whose habits of attending to others were of approximately equivalent strength. The eliciting of such habits is, of course, contingent on the presence of stimulus conditions capable of eliciting socially dependent behavior.

b. *The frustration hypothesis.* Hartup (1958) tested the hypothesis that withdrawal of nurturance increases children's dependency behavior and thus facilitates the acquisition of responses that elicit adult approval. Girls and high-dependent boys from whom nurturance had been withdrawn learned simple cognitive tasks more rapidly than did children who experienced consistent nurturance. On the basis of this outcome, which will be discussed in a later section, and a somewhat similar finding by Rosenblith (1957), Hartup and Himeno (1959) predicted that social isolation would have *frustrative* effects and therefore lead to an increase in aggression. The children participated in two doll-play sessions, one of which was preceded by a 10-minute isolation period, the other by 10 minutes of interaction with the experimenter. The results were in accordance with prediction and led the authors to conclude that isolation has motivational effects other than the arousal of a social drive that motivates behavior "for" a social reinforcer.

The findings of Hartup and Himeno provide strong evidence against the social-drive hypothesis advanced by Gewirtz and Baer. Aggression, even in doll-play, can hardly be regarded as behavior aimed at eliciting positive social reinforcement. However, it is not necessary to conclude that isolation leads to two different kinds of effects, approval-seeking responses and aggression (Hartup and Himeno, 1959). With increased arousal, more intense or effortful behavior should be expected. The kind of behavior that is exhibited will, however, depend on the nature of the stimulus conditions and the relative strength of the component responses in the habit hierarchies associated with these conditions. Given a learning situation in which verbal approval is dispensed by an adult experimenter, one would expect attending responses to be relatively dominant. In contrast, a doll-play situation is not conducive to eliciting identifiably dependent behavior, but is likely to evoke a variety of acts that are classifiable as aggressive (Levin and Wardwell, 1962).

3. Age and Isolation Effects

If the theoretical position advanced above is correct, the effects of isolation should vary with the age of the subjects. Whereas for a young child even brief isolation may be a conditioned stimulus for emotional arousal, older subjects are more habituated to spending time alone and are unlikely to react to isolation in an emotional manner. Age changes in response to isolation are undoubtedly a function of a number of physiological and psychological changes that ordinarily occur as an individual matures.

Being alone is not usually a threatening state of affairs for an older child, adolescent, or adult who can take care of his everyday physical needs, and who, even if deprived of occupational or recreational activities, can spend his time in thought. In fact, for adults, lack of privacy or opportunity to be alone may be as emotionally arousing as the absence of company. This was particularly evident to Walters *et al.* (1963), who, in attempting to assess the responses of prisoners under solitary confinement, sought volunteers who would spend four days in isolation cells. A number of prisoners said that the confinement experience would not be entirely unpleasant. They remarked on the strain of spending hours in open-cage cells in the wings under the constant bombardment of cell-to-cell conversations and the unceasing output of announcements and other communications from the prisoners' radio.

For many older persons, then, isolation involves stress only when it is unduly prolonged or when there are threatening stimulus conditions present, particularly ones that cannot easily be handled alone. Consequently, some of the discrepant findings obtained from experimental studies of social isolation may be attributed to differences in the ages of the subjects and the precise conditions under which the isolation was imposed. In studies involving very young children (Gewirtz and Baer, 1958a; Hartup and Himeno, 1959), isolation effects undoubtedly occurred. These effects were also present to some degree in studies which utilized younger, grade-school subjects (Gewirtz and Baer, 1958b; Hops and Walters, 1963; Walters and Ray, 1960). In contrast, in the experiment by Walters *et al.* (1960), one hour's isolation had no effect on the social dependency of adolescent boys.

The negative findings of the latter study were possibly due largely to the briefness of the isolation procedure. Consequently, Walters and Henning (1962) utilized periods of 3 and 6 hours' isolation in examining the effects of isolation on the verbal behavior of adolescent boys. If isolation arouses a specific social drive, verbal communications, which are essentially social responses, would be expected to increase following a fairly long absence of opportunity to communicate (Walters and Karal, 1960). Moreover, if social drive enhances the effectiveness of social reinforcers (Gewirtz and Baer, 1958a), verbal behavior should be more readily modified through social reinforcement following an isolation period.

The findings of the Walters and Henning study were largely negative as far as isolation effects were concerned; in contrast, the nature of instructions to subjects had a marked effect on verbal behavior. Half the boys who were isolated and half a group of nonisolated controls were told that the task they were given (making up speeches) was an index of intelligence and emotional stability and that the experimenter was interested in how well they could perform. The remaining boys were simply instructed to carry out the task. In comparison to boys who were given "task-oriented" instructions, those given "ego-oriented" instructions were more verbally productive and the content of their speeches was more influenced by verbal reinforcements.

The overall results thus indicated that the variables under study could be influenced by instructions calculated to stimulate the subject to reach a high level of achievement. Although no direct measures of arousal effects were secured, one may infer that the "ego-oriented" instructions resulted in more effortful behavior and greater alertness to the verbal responses of the experimenter. Similar effects could apparently not be produced by an isolation procedure. Indeed, comparison of the verbal productivity of boys isolated for 3 hours and those isolated for 6 hours suggested that with somewhat prolonged isolation behavior becomes less effortful. Similar increasing "apathy" has been noted in college students who have experienced both reduced sensory stimulation and decreased social contact over a 24-hour period (Bexton et al., 1954).

The outcome of one study with adults may be interpreted as favoring the social-drive hypothesis. Walters and Quinn (1960) compared the effects of social isolation, sensory deprivation, and sensory deprivation accompanied by social isolation on the autokinetic responses of college students. Each experimental manipulation lasted only 30 minutes. Subjects under each of the "deprivation" conditions changed their responses in the direction specified both by contrary judgments and by differential reinforcements provided by the experimenter to a greater extent than did control subjects who experienced neither sensory deprivation nor social isolation. In this study, however, all subjects were given an impossible sorting task while being exposed to the experimental conditions. This task was designed to ensure that all subjects were similarly occupied during the whole of the 30-minute period. Under the control condition, the students were in social contact with the experimenter, who talked to them in a casual and friendly fashion, and they were, at the same time, not hampered by any restriction on their vision or hearing. Subjects in the three experimental groups were, in contrast, performing under conditions that were either unusual or, in the case of the socially isolated but not perceptually restricted subjects, that allowed them no friendly contact with the experimenter. It is thus possible that the significant antecedent variable, even in this experiment, was variation in degrees of stress (and consequently of emotional responsiveness) experienced by the four groups of students. This latter interpretation is certainly supported by subsequent studies that have examined the influence of threatening circumstances on performance in the autokinetic situation (Staples and Walters, 1961; Walters *et al.*, 1960).

The differential effects of experimentally induced isolation on subjects belonging to different age groups are thus, generally speaking, consistent with an interpretation of isolation as a potentially threatening stimulus condition. The precise effects of this threatening situation are nevertheless dependent on the prior experience of the isolated person and the circumstances under which isolation occurs (Walters and Henning, 1961).

4. Perceptual Isolation and Social Behavior

There have been many studies of the effects of perceptual isolation on the behavior of adults. However, the majority of these focused on changes in intellectual performance or perceptual functioning rather than on changes in social behavior. In most perceptual-isolation studies, moreover, the effects of social isolation and restriction of sensory input were inextricably confounded; consequently, the reported effects on social behavior are extremely difficult to interpret.

There is some evidence that prolonged perceptual isolation, involving a certain degree of social deprivation, is accompanied by autonomic reactivity indicative of emotional arousal (Davis, 1959; Mendelson *et al.*, 1960). Scott and co-workers (1959) reported both changes in alpha rhythms and increases in motor activity in isolated subjects. These subjects showed reduced thresholds for some kinds of sensory stimulation and possibly increased attention to some environmental events (Heron, 1961). They were also more influenced by symbolic social models (proponents of beliefs in psychical phenomena) than were nonisolated controls. These findings are consistent with the interpretation of isolation effects offered in this chapter.

A few experimenters, in addition to Walters and Quinn, have simultaneously investigated the effects of both sensory and social deprivation. Stevenson and Odom (1962) compared increases in rates of response under social reinforcement of three groups of children who played a marble-dropping game. Before testing, one group of children played in isolation with attractive toys for a 15-minute period, a second group was isolated for 15 minutes with no toys present, and a control group was tested without any previous manipulation. Both the isolation groups maintained their initial rates of response throughout a seven-minute testing period; the control group, on the other hand, showed a marked decrease in response. The absence of a significant difference between the two isolated groups was interpreted by the authors as supporting the hypothesis that increased effectiveness of social reinforcement following isolation is primarily due to deprivation of social stimuli, rather than to more general stimulus deprivation. However, in a subsequent, similar study, Hill and Stevenson (1964) found some support for the stimulus-deprivation hypothesis, although only for boys.

The stimulus-deprivation hypothesis is very difficult to evaluate at the present time. Studies with adult human subjects and animals suggest that novel, complex stimulation has an arousal effect, whereas stimulus deprivation, in initial phases, results in a decrease in arousal level (Berlyne, 1960; Bindra, 1959). Stevenson and Odom employed complex, battery-driven toys capable of evoking a high degree of interest or excitement in the majority of children. The similarity of results under their two isolation conditions may thus be attributable to arousal by two quite different types of stimulus situations. While the presence of toys may have detracted from the potency of isolation as an emotionally arousing experience, the toys themselves may have elicited compensatory excitement.

B. STUDIES OF NURTURANCE

1. Frustration as Nurturance-withdrawal

In many studies of the effects of frustration in nonsocial situations, the experimental operations have involved withholding of rewards previously dispensed for a response, removing some of the stimulus objects essential for the performance of an instrumental act, or eliciting responses incompatible with the frustrated behavior (Brown, 1961), while the dependent variable has been the strength of the response under investigation. The guiding hypothesis in most of these studies has been that *delay of reinforcement* increases the motivational level of the organism, and that, as a result, the frustrated organism responds in a more intense or energetic manner.

Severity of frustration has sometimes been defined in terms of the point in a response sequence at which blocking occurs, on the assumption that the nearer the organism is to the goal, the greater the frustration effect. Haner and Brown (1955) gave grade-school children the task of inserting 36 marbles in holes in a board and promised them a prize if they were successful on four trials. At the end of each trial, the experimenter sounded a buzzer, which the children turned off by depressing a plunger. On different trials, children were failed at varying distances from a goal, and a record was obtained of the amount of pressure they exerted on the plunger. Haner and Brown found that children who were near to completing a task when blocked made more intense responses than children who were farther from reaching their goal. The strength of reaction to blocking is, however, highly dependent on the extent to which the frustrated response sequence has been previously rewarded. In fact, blocking a weakly established habit appears to have little or no effect on subsequent responding (Holton, 1961; Penney, 1960).

Experimental operations involving delaying reinforcement for social responses have not always ensured that the blocked response is well established or that the subjects perceive the goal as readily attainable. Moreover, in a large proportion of studies, the withholding of reinforcers was confounded with the presentation of aversive stimuli in the form of insult or disparagement for failure. Discrepant results obtained in studies of dependency frustration may be largely due to such variations in experimental procedures.

For example, Hartup (1958) claimed that frustration of dependency behavior increased motivation and thus promoted faster learning. Cairns (1962), on the other hand, reported that children who had experienced dependency frustration failed to demonstrate any substantial amount of learning in a simple discrimination task. Children who had previously been reinforced for dependent responses learned this task relatively well. Although the tasks employed in these two studies were quite different, one would nevertheless not expect a reversal of findings if the experimental operations were otherwise comparable.

If the procedures are examined in more detail it can be seen that the studies differed in the extent to which the blocked response had been previously established. Cairns employed three groups of children. His frustrated children were first denied the opportunity of playing with attractive toys that they could obtain only with the help of the experimenter. They were then ignored by the experimenter for a 15-minute session. During this session one of the comparison groups received reinforcements for help-seeking responses. The other group also received reinforcements, but for these children reinforcement was not contingent upon the occurrence of help-seeking behavior. Under these circumstances, only those children who were rewarded for dependency showed any notable increase in learning in the discrimination task. In contrast to Cairns' procedures, the experimenter in Hartup's study first interacted in a nurturant manner with each of the two groups of children. One group of children was then frustrated through the *withdrawal* of the interest, approval, and affection that had been demonstrated in the immediately preceding period, while the remaining children were consistently nurtured.

The failure of Cairns' frustration procedure to yield an anticipated *increase* in responsiveness to social reinforcers may be largely due to the omission of prefrustration nurturance session of the kind employed by Hartup. There is, in fact, evidence that withholding of positive reinforcers produces marked increase in dependency behavior only in children whose past social-learning experiences have made them relatively high in dependency (Baer, 1962; Beller and Haeberle, 1961b). Hartup, in fact, found improved performance only in girls, who are generally rewarded for dependency to a greater extent than boys, and in high-dependent boys; the performance of low-dependent boys was not influenced by the withdrawal-of-nurturance procedure. If Cairns had first developed dependency habits within the frustration group and then withheld attention for help-seeking responses, his results may well have been consistent with Hartup's.

Erickson (1962) reported more effective verbal conditioning in children from whom adult attention and support had been withheld than in children with whom an adult had been continually communicating during a 15-minute "digit game." Improved learning following withholding of attention was apparent only when verbal approval was used as the reinforcer; when reinforcement consisted of marbles delivered by a dispenser, "deprived" and "satiated" groups of children did not greatly differ. Erickson's findings suggest that conditioning was successful *only* with subjects who had first been deprived of social interaction and then rewarded with verbal approval. This outcome might be regarded as supporting the social-drive hypothesis and as contrary to results reported by Walters and Parke (1964) concerning the relative efficacy of social and nonsocial reinforcements.

Erickson's marble-dispensing procedure was not, however, comparable to the manner in which material rewards were administered by Walters and Parke. The latter investigators explicitly set their subjects a discrimination-learning task and informed them that tokens, later exchangeable for toys, would be given for correct responses. In contrast, Erickson did not inform her subjects that the marbles signified a correct response or could be interpreted as rewards. Under the circumstances, it seems unlikely that the dropping of a marble was an adequate stimulus for the production of discrimination learning (Cairns, 1963; White, 1963).

Erickson's findings for verbally reinforced subjects are consistent with those reported by Hartup, since she first gave the "deprived" children her attention during practice on the verbal-conditioning task and then withdrew her attention while remaining in the room with the child. In other words, she first elicited and rewarded responses involving orienting toward and attending to the experimenter, and then withheld rewards for this kind of behavior. According to the point of view presented in this chapter, this method of "deprivation" should have an arousal effect; moreover, both the practice and testing sessions were well structured for eliciting habits of attending.

Rosenblith (1959, 1961) investigated the influence of withdrawal of attention on imitative behavior. In the first of two studies, she found that boys from whom a male adult model had withdrawn attention showed more imitative learning than did boys to whom the model had been continually attentive. The difference between these groups was not, however, statistically significant and both groups learned more than a control group who had been given further practice on the task instead of exposure to a model.

In the case of boys with a female leader and girls with a leader of either sex, withdrawal of attention did not enhance imitative behavior; in fact, girls learned more effectively through imitation when the model's attention was not withdrawn. A second somewhat similar study (Rosenblith, 1961) also brought conflicting results; the effect of withdrawal of attention was contingent upon the sex of the subject, the sex of the model, and the intelligence level of the child. In general, girls learned through imitation and exhibited more imitative responses in choosing pencils of varying colors when the model's attention was maintained; the same was true for boys when the model was a female. In contrast, withdrawal of attention enhanced imitative behavior in boys who were exposed to a model of the same sex as themselves.

In studies in which children are assigned to continuous nurturance and withdrawal-of-nurturance conditions, the withdrawal group is usually given a shorter nurturance period than the group that is continually nurtured. Thus, social dependency may be enhanced in one group on account of a longer reinforcement period, whereas in the other group, it may be enhanced by emotional arousal. Further studies in which possible increases in habit strength and arousal level are simultaneously investigated in a single, factorial design seem advisable in view of the results of Rosenblith's first study, in which both experimental groups showed more imitative learning than controls.

No convincing theoretical interpretation can be offered of the complex cross-sex effects reported by Rosenblith. In the case of certain forms of aggression, child observers seem to imitate more readily models for whom aggression is sex-appropriate (Bandura, 1962). It is difficult, however, to identify any characteristics of the color-matching or maze-solving responses investigated by Rosenblith that might elucidate her findings concerning the varying effects of nurturance and its withdrawal in relation to the sex of the model and the sex of the subject.

Stevenson and Hill (1963) investigated the relationship between frustration and responsiveness to social reinforcers. In a pretraining period the frustrated children were given difficult jigsaw puzzles that could not be completed within the time allowed; their failure was made explicit by a comment of the experimenter. The nonfrustrated children were given easy puzzles and the experimenter remarked on their success. In a subsequent marble-sorting task, half the frustrated and half the nonfrustrated children received supporting comments from the experimenter, while the remaining children were ignored. Nonfrustrated children who received no support responded at a higher rate than nonfrustrated, nonsupported children; in contrast, frustrated and subsequently supported children responded at a *lower* rate than frustrated children who received no support.

This study had many procedural differences from the experiments previously discussed. The "frustration" involved did not consist in the blocking of dependency responses, nor were rewards withheld or withdrawn. The experience of failure induced in the frustrated children, combined with the experimenter's disparaging remark, appears to be more of an aversive procedure than a frustration condition, as frustration has been defined in this section. Indeed, it is possible that the experimenter's verbalizations, as a result of the pretraining interaction, acquired some of the characteristics of a negative reinforcer. In this case, one might expect a reduction in the "frustrated" children's rate of responding in the "supportive" learning situation (Mandler and Kaplan, 1956), but an increase in rate of response, as a result of arousal, while the experimenter remained silent.

Although the experimental evidence is not entirely consistent, one may tentatively conclude that withholding of rewards increases susceptibility to social influence, *provided* that (1) dependency habits are already fairly strongly established in the frustrated persons' response repertories and (2) the testing situation is conducive to the manifestation of social dependency. The picture is, however, complicated by sex differences and, in imitation studies (Rosenblith, 1959, 1961), by interaction effects involving the sex of the subject and the sex of the model. Perhaps such phenomena will eventually be explained in terms of the differing experiences of boys and girls in their interactions with male and female agents during the socialization process.

2. Institutionalization

Investigations into the effects of maternal privation have indicated that institutionalization and other maternally-deprived children are sometimes socially nonresponsive and nondependent but at other times strive vigorously to gain the attention and interest of adults (e.g., Bowlby, 1952; Freud and Burlingham, 1944; Gewirtz, 1961; Goldfarb, 1943; Lowrey, 1940; Spitz, 1945; Yarrow, 1961). Such differences are undoubtedly due to varying past experiences involving differential amounts of reward, nonreward, and punishment for dependency behavior.

The possibility of modifying the social responsiveness of children through caretaking activities was demonstrated by Rheingold (1956), who nurtured a group of institutionalized children over an 8-week period. At the end of this period, the social behavior of the nurtured group was compared, in a standardized setting, with that of children who had remained in the usual institutional regime. The children in the experimental group were significantly more attentive and otherwise socially responsive both to the experimenter and to another female examiner than were the control children. Differences in social behavior had, however, largely disappeared when the children were retested one year later (Rheingold and Bayley, 1959), suggesting that the personalized care and attention provided by the institutional regime had been too inadequate to maintain the increased social responsiveness shown by the "mothered" children.

Rheingold's study employed infants who were only 5 to 7 months old when "mothering" began. Since all the children had been institutionalized for at least three months, for all practical purposes they may be regarded as having received roughly equivalent amounts of personalized care at the onset of the study. This experiment demonstrates that the dispensing of social reinforcers by adults increases the incidence of attending and orienting responses in children during the early infancy period. Presumably, most children who receive considerable personal care and attention during the first year of life develop fairly strong dependency habits.

The institutionalized children used in most other relevant experimental studies lived in their own or foster-homes during the infancy period and usually no information was provided concerning the nature of their experiences preceding institutionalization. Zigler (1961) remedied this defect in part by dividing institutionalized children into two groups, those relatively deprived of social contact and rewards prior to institutionalization and those who had come from relatively nurturant homes.

All children were tested for their persistence in a game under two conditions. In one, the experimenter intermittently encouraged and praised the child and indicated approval with nods and smiles, while in the other he remained attentive but otherwise nonresponsive. The more deprived children persisted longer in the game under both the support and nonsupport conditions than did the less deprived children. The children in this study were all feeble-minded; other studies by Zigler, Stevenson, and their co-workers (e.g., Zigler et al., 1958) nevertheless suggest that similar findings would have been obtained with subjects of average intelligence and that social deprivation provides "motivation to maintain interaction with an adult and to secure approval from him through compliance and persistence" (Zigler, 1961, p. 419). Although long-term low availability of adult attention and care is not directly comparable with the brief isolation procedure utilized by Gewirtz and Baer (1958a,b), the results have been interpreted as supporting Gewirtz's social-drive hypothesis.

There is, however, no evidence that length of institutionalization is consistently associated with the effectiveness of social reinforcement (Zigler and Williams, 1963). In fact, in one study (Stevenson and Knights, 1962a) girls who had returned to an institution following a summer vacation with families were found to be more responsive to social reinforcers immediately after their return to the institution than after 12 weeks of institutional residence. This finding suggests that institutionalization decreases the strength of habits of responding in ways that may result in social reinforcement and seems consistent with the findings reported by Rheingold (1956) and Rheingold and Bayley (1959).

There is, at present, no satisfactory explanation that accounts for the divergent findings from the many studies of the relationship between institutionalization and responsiveness to social reinforcers. Institutionalization is a highly complex variable and its effects, as Zigler (1963) suggested, are undoubtedly contaminated by the pre-institutional history of individual children. Moreover, variations in caretaking procedures from institution to institution also detract from the value of institutionalization as an experimental variable. The available evidence suggests that institutionalized children should have weaker dependency habits than noninstitutionalized children, although it is possible that in some institutions the more intense dependency responses performed by children may be differentially reinforced. On the other hand, the emotional responsiveness of institutionalized children to testing by a strange experimenter may be greater than that of children who are not in institutions. This differential responsiveness could perhaps in part account for some of the findings reported by Stevenson and Zigler.

Contradictory results in social-deprivation studies, in which susceptibility to social influence has been assessed in terms of social-reinforcer effectiveness, may also occur on account of variations in the manner in which the reinforcers are dispensed. Cairns, Gewirtz, Hartup, Walters and their co-workers have consistently paired reinforcers with some response of the subjects specified in advance by the experimenter. In contrast, Stevenson and Zigler have tended to favor *noncontingent* reinforcement procedures, in which "rewards" are intermittently dispensed on ratio or interval schedules for any one of two or more alternative responses and have used as their dependent variable the rate or persistence of responding with any of the possible alternatives. These latter procedures certainly do not provide conditions under which *specifiable* responses may be *learned*. Moreover, no general theory of behavior change seems yet capable of predicting the outcome of these manipulations. From a commonsense point of view, however, one may suspect that increased attention to the experimenter's reactions, which we have assumed to result from prior reinforcement of attending responses and from emotional arousal, may, under these conditions, slow down rates of responding within a relatively brief period of time and also limit the duration of the continued, indiscriminate production of responses.

3. Nurturance of Noninstitutionalized Children

In some of the studies already discussed, the antecedent variable was sometimes specified in terms of varying degrees of adult nurturance. Nurturance is a complex variable involving the positive reinforcement of the responses of orienting and attending to another person, the active eliciting of such behavior, and the conditioning of emotional-arousal responses to the presence and actions of the reinforcing agent. In child-training studies the occurrence of nurturant behavior has frequently been inferred from such parent characteristics as affectional demonstrativeness and warmth, assessed by interviews or similar techniques. These characteristics may, but need not, involve all three aspects of nurturance. They certainly involve many other facets of parent behavior as well (Bandura and Walters, 1963b).

Most of the available evidence suggests that parental nurturance is positively associated with the incidence of dependency behavior in children (Bandura, 1960; Bandura and Walters, 1959; Heathers, 1953; Levy, 1943; Sears et al., 1953, 1957). However, frequent and indiscriminately dispensed social reinforcements in the home may decrease their incentive value and thus reduce their effectiveness for producing behavioral change (Cairns, 1962).

Few experimental studies have employed controlled manipulations of adult behavior that parallel parental nurturance as this is manifested in familial settings. Bandura et al. (1963), in a comparative study of the status-envy, social-power, and secondary-reinforcement theories of imitative behavior, utilized groups, composed of two adults and a child subject, representing prototypes of the nuclear family. In the experimental condition, either the male or female provided the other adult with attractive toys and games, gave him juice and cookies, and promised him future rewards; under this condition, the child was left at a nearby table with unattractive toys and was essentially ignored. In another treatment, the child was the object of one adult's nurturance, while the second adult adopted the role of the deprived onlooker. Following the experimental manipulation, there was a test of imitative behavior in which both adults served as models in a discrimination-learning situation, and each exhibited a different set of unusual verbal and motor responses totally irrelevant to the successful completion of the task.

The children imitated the model who had dispensed the positive reinforcers during the nuclear-family situation to a greater extent than the adult who was the recipient of rewards. Moreover, this model preference was apparent even when the child himself had not received rewards. This latter result can be explained by the fact that conditions were provided under the adult-nurtured treatment for the classical conditioning of the child's orienting and attending responses to the behavior of the adult who dispensed reinforcers.

The role of nurturance in fostering imitative behavior was also investigated in a study by Bandura and Huston (1961). This experiment began with two fairly lengthy sessions in which a child experienced a highly nurturant rewarding interaction with an adult, who later served as a model. In a subsequent testing situation, similar to that employed by Bandura et al. (1963), children exhibited more responses imitative of the model than did children for whom the model had behaved in a distant, nonrewarding manner during pretesting sessions. The outcome of the studies by Bandura and his associates thus suggest that orienting and attending responses may be strengthened through both classical- and instrumental-conditioning procedures.

Nurturant parents often reward their children's approach responses, thus ensuring frequent parent-child interactions. These interactions provide opportunities for the parents to influence the social behavior of the child. Moreover, parental nurturance may facilitate the development of dependency behavior, as this was defined earlier, and thus increase the parents' effectiveness both as agents of reinforcers and as social models for the child.

IV. Schachter's Theory of Social Motivation: A Related Approach

A. AFFILIATION

Schachter (1959) investigated affiliative responses in anxiety-arousing circumstances on the assumption that avoidance of isolation is a function of anxiety about, or fear of, being alone when pain or danger threatens. On the basis of autobiographical data and observations of subjects in an exploratory investigation of experimentally induced isolation, Schachter postulated that anxiety is a frequent concomitant of isolation and that, consequently, affiliative tendencies should be increased under anxiety-inducing conditions (p. 12). His theoretical position thus has points in common with that advanced by the senior author (e.g., Walters and Henning, 1961), who suggested that isolation becomes emotionally arousing when (a) it is perceived as a source of danger; or (b) when it functions, in a catalytic manner, to heighten apprehension concerning some forthcoming event; or (c) when it provides an occasion for the recall of some earlier emotionally arousing experience. Moreover, both

Schachter and Walters have attempted to identify relationships between responses to isolation and other potentially arousing conditions, dependency training, and susceptibility to social influence.

In Schachter's experimental studies of anxiety and affiliation, undergraduates who were made anxious by a threat of shock chose to await the anticipated painful stimulation in the company of others rather than alone. This preference was exhibited even when communication during the waiting period was restricted, provided that the group members were presented as being all in the same predicament. Further analyses of data indicated that the relationship between anxiety and affiliative responses held only for subjects who were first-born and only children, but that later-born children did not exhibit affiliative tendencies when placed under stress.

Schachter related his birth-order effect to findings concerning dependency training. Field studies by Sears, Whiting, and their collaborators (Sears *et al.,* 1953, 1957; Whiting and Child, 1953) suggested to Schachter that early-born children experience more inconsistent nurturance than later-born children and that inconsistent nurturance leads to heightened dependency behavior. Moreover, a number of investigators (Haeberle, 1958; Rosenow and Whyte, 1931; Sletto, 1934; Sears, 1950) had directly examined the relationship between birth order and dependency and had reported relatively high dependency among first-born and only children. Schachter's position differs from that of earlier investigators mainly in its emphasis on the role of anxiety as the mediating process. In the first place, Schachter reported that early-born subjects were more anxious and frightened when faced with a standard anxiety-evoking situation than were later-born subjects and, secondly, that anxious, early-born subjects manifested more dependent responses in the form of seeking the company of others than did equally anxious, later-born children. An experiment by Ehrlich (1958), conducted as part of Schachter's project, confirmed a prediction that first-born and only children, who are supposedly relatively high in dependency, would change their judgments concerning the outcome of a case study in the direction of a fictitious group norm more readily than would later-born subjects.

After examining a number of alternative explanations of the apparent relationships between anxiety and affiliation, Schachter postulated the operation of needs for anxiety reduction and self-evaluation. Wrightsman (1960) demonstrated the occurrence of anxiety reduction in first-born subjects who were permitted to wait with others while anticipating that they would subsequently receive shock and the absence of this effect in the case of later-born subjects. In the same study, subjects waiting in "together" conditions, whether permitted to talk or not, exhibited a greater reduction in intraindividual variability in level of self-reported anxiety than did subjects who waited alone. This latter effect was not specific to first-born children, since the individual "together" groups were composed of both first-born and later-born children; however, as might be expected on the basis of Festinger's (1954) theory of social-comparison processes, the effect was pronounced only among groups composed of members whose initial level of anxiety was neither highly homogenous nor markedly heterogenous.

The affiliation studies certainly demonstrate a general relationship between emotional arousal, avoidance of isolation, and susceptibility to the influence of social models. It seems unnecessary, however, to postulate the operation of a general affiliative motive and also subsidiary needs for anxiety-reduction and self-evaluation in order to account for the findings. Indeed, considerable evidence supports a more parsimonious interpretation in terms of the association of habits of orienting toward and attending to others with stimulus conditions involving the anticipation of pain and its accompanying emotional-arousal cues.

Schachter's birth-order effect appears to hold up better for female than for male subjects when the stimulus conditions involve the anticipation of physical pain. This sex difference may be the outcome of the cultural expectation that males should demonstrate a certain degree of "stoicism" when faced with physical pain. Social-training procedures, fostered by this expectation, could hinder the formation of a strong association between the cognitive and emotional cues involved in the anticipation of physical pain and other-oriented habits. They could, in addition, weaken the intensity of the emotional responses of the majority of males to threats of physical pain. As a result, potential birth-order effects among males may be obscured under the threat-of-shock condition that was used in most of Schachter's experiments.

Moreover, the occurrence and precise nature of birth-order effects for male and female subjects are dependent not only on the nature of the stimulus situation but also on the classes of responses that are selected as indices of affiliation or susceptibility to social influence. Explanations of apparently conflicting findings are almost invariably presented in terms of the differential dependency, independence, or achievement training experienced by male and female children and the extent to which the experimental operations have had motivational effects on subjects of different sexes (Gerard and Rabbie, 1961; Rosenthal et al., 1963; Sampson, 1962; Staples and Walters, 1961). In other words, the interpretations that are offered explicitly or covertly assume that the phenomena to be explained are ultimately based on cue-habit associations similar to those already discussed in the analysis of dependency behavior. The authors suggest that orienting and attending responses are the essential, common components of most behavioral phenomena that have been classified as dependent or affiliative.

Further support for the suggested interpretation is provided in a study by Staples and Walters (1961), in which the dependent variable was the extent to which female subjects modified judgments in an autokinetic situation in response both to contrary judgments made by the experimenter and to selective verbal reinforcement of specified classes of responses. The testing procedure was, in fact, virtually identical with that used in the previously mentioned earlier studies by Walters and his associates (Walters and Quinn, 1960; Walters et al., 1960).

Staples and Walters reported that first-born female subjects, according to their self-reports, were more emotionally disturbed by the threat of receiving painful electric shocks for erroneous judgments than were later-born females, and that the first-born females were, in addition, more influenced by the responses of the experimenter. The study thus demonstrated relationships among birth order, emotional arousal, and susceptibility to social influence in a situation that did not involve affiliation, as defined in Schachter's experiment. Moreover, the relationships were demonstrated under conditions in which the effectiveness of the social-influence procedures could be successful only with subjects who gave careful attention to the contrary judgments supplied by the experimenter and to the discriminative stimuli provided by his verbal reinforcements. The effectiveness for first-born females of this social-influence procedure can be adequately accounted for in terms of their emotionally aroused condition and the relatively strongly developed association of this stimulus condition with habits of orienting and attending to others. Indeed, both the arousal condition itself and the cue-habit association may have operated concomitantly to enhance the effectiveness of the social-influence procedure.

There are undoubtedly some threatening circumstances under which affiliative responses are unlikely to receive positive reinforcement during the social-learning process, regardless of the sex or the birth-order of the child. Affiliative behavior should be relatively nondominant in the habit hierarchies of most persons under such conditions. Sarnoff and Zimbardo (1961) seem to have identified circumstances of this kind. In their experiment, "high fear" subjects were led to anticipate painful shocks under conditions similar to those employed in Schachter's experiments, while "high anxiety" subjects were led to believe that they would have to suck on a number of objects commonly associated with infantile oral behavior. In comparison to subjects under a "low fear" condition, the "high fear" subjects exhibited considerable affiliative behavior. In contrast, "high anxiety" subjects exhibited less affiliative behavior than did their controls.

In this study, "anxiety" was presumed to be aroused through the presentation of *objectively innocuous* stimuli; because of the inappropriateness of an emotional response to such stimuli, the emotionally aroused subjects sought to conceal their emotions and consequently preferred isolation to company. However, it is not necessary to postulate two distinct emotional states, "fear" and "anxiety," in order to account for these findings. The patterns of reward and punishment for emotional behavior differ according to the nature of the stimulus situation. Ridicule and other forms of social punishment are delivered to persons who display "irrational fears," but not, at least to the same extent, to those who seek to avoid objectively dangerous situations. The differential responses of the "high fear" and "high anxiety" subjects in the Sarnoff and Zimbardo experiment can thus be explained solely in terms of relative dominance of learned responses to two very different classes of stimulus situations and thus gives added support to an interpretation in terms of cue-habit associations.

A parallel explanation can be offered of Schachter's finding that affiliative behavior was manifested by highly anxious subjects only when they were told that the persons in whose company they were to await the anticipated shock were in the same predicament as themselves. Past experience may have led the subjects to believe that individuals who are not under threat are inclined to regard others' fears as exaggerated and are consequently likely to ridicule or despise the fearful person. In contrast, people who anticipate a traumatic event by which they are emotionally aroused are less likely to disparage others for exhibiting a similar fearful reaction. Differential responses to threat would therefore be expected even from first-born anxious subjects according to the consequences they anticipate for orienting toward available persons.

Zimbardo and Formica (1963) reinterpreted Schachter's birth-order effects in terms of self-esteem rather than dependency. They reported that first-born subjects are lower in self-esteem than later-borns, and that self-esteem and affiliative behavior following threat are negatively related. The authors proposed substituting self-esteem for dependency as a means of understanding birth-order effects on the grounds that the dependency explanation "though psychologically sound, . . . is not theoretically coordinated to the emotional comparison model" (p. 141). This represents a reversal of current trends, apparent in Schachter's (1959) exposition of affiliation, to bring into a meaningful relationship the findings of developmental and social psychologists.

It was suggested earlier that categorizing an individual as dependent is frequently based on judgments of the appropriateness of the circumstances under which he exhibits responses such as the seeking of help or approval. These classes of behavior may occur when the agent is capable of carrying out activities unaided. Everyone misjudges his capabilities occasionally and such events are of no particular interest to the social and personality psychologist. Consistent misjudgments are however, another matter; frequent underestimation of capacity is, in fact, one criterion by which persons are judged to be lacking in self-esteem. Habits of seeking help and approval under circumstances in which the agent is competent to act alone would not be maintained unless they are, at least intermittently, reinforced. One determinant of self-esteem is thus probably the reinforcement patterns that individuals have received for orienting and attending to others. Self-esteem, however, implies a self-reaction, which is undoubtedly related to the transmission of achievement standards by parents and other authority figures in the course of the socialization process (Bandura and Walters, 1963b).

A combination of high achievement standards with strongly established habits of depending on others appears to be highly conducive to the manifestation of low self-esteem. In child-training terms, the antecedent conditions of low self-esteem probably include a history of reward for orienting toward authority figures and negative reinforcement for self-reliance, together with frequent use by parents of symbolic models whom the child cannot hope to emulate and/or the presence in the home of a highly successful parent whose talents are better developed than those of the child. A somewhat similar set of antecedent child-training conditions was suggested by Lesser and Abelson (1959).

In contrast to Zimbardo and Formica, we favor an integration of findings from developmental and social psychology and consequently have presented self-esteem as an outcome of dependency training and the influence of social models. In other words, we prefer an interpretation of birth-order effects that is centered on antecedent-consequence sequences and feel that many social psychologists place too much emphasis on explanations in terms of contemporary causal relationships. In most of the circumstances under which susceptibility to social influence has been examined, an exemplary response is provided [or multiple examples, as in the Asch-type (1951) situation], or the subject is set a task and positively reinforced for correct responses. Under these circumstances, a combination of high-achievement standards and a history of reinforcement for attending and orienting toward others is likely to foster high social dependency. Indications that self-esteem and persuasibility are negatively related were provided by Cohen (1959) and Lesser and Abelson (1959). Moreover, subjects low in self-esteem were shown to match the responses of others to a greater extent than high self-esteem subjects (deCharms and Rosenbaum, 1960). In a later study, Rosenbaum et al. (1962) demonstrated that the relationship between self-esteem and matching behavior is apparent only if the model is competent and consequently is setting relatively high achievement standards. The analysis offered here, in terms of child-training variables, of the origins of low self-esteem and high susceptibility to social influence are consistent with these findings. The advantages of a child-training analysis of a demonstrated relationship between "personality variables" is that it is capable not only of revealing common antecedent conditions that can account for the relationship but also of fostering further research within the framework of well-established, social-learning principles.

B. EMOTIONAL-COMPARISON THEORY

Schachter discussed in some detail the role of needs for self-evaluation in social-influence processes. By extending Festinger's (1954) social-comparison theory, Schachter postulated that a drive exists in man to evaluate his emotions. When an objective, nonsocial means of evaluation is not available, a person supposedly evaluates the appropriateness of his emotional states through comparison with the emotional responses of others. Extending this chain of reasoning, Schachter and Singer (1962) hypothesized that if a person experiences a physiological-arousal state and has no appropriate explanation for his experience, he will describe his feelings in terms of the cognitions available to him. Within the context of an experiment reported by Schachter and Singer, this implied that an aroused and "uncertain" person would model his behavior after that of a confederate of the experimenter and report that he felt emotions that were appropriate to the behavior he manifested.

In the study by Schachter and Singer (details of which are provided in Schachter's chapter), college students received one of three treatments before being placed in a room with a confederate of the experimenter who behaved in an aggressive manner. In comparison to a placebo group, subjects who were injected with adrenaline and were not informed of its side-effects showed a considerable amount of aggressive behavior, whereas subjects who were injected with adrenaline and were informed of its side-effects showed very little imitative aggression. In another phase of the study, four treatments were employed, the three already described and one in which subjects were injected with adrenaline and deliberately misinformed of its side effects. In this phase the confederate exhibited age-inappropriate, euphoric behavior. Subjects who were misinformed or not informed concerning the true effects of adrenaline followed the confederate's example and behaved in an euphoric manner to a greater extent than did subjects who were given correct information concerning the drug. These results suggest that the influence of social models are most potent when the observers are emotionally aroused and cannot rationally attribute their feelings to stimuli other than the model's behavior.

Schachter and Singer interpreted their results as indicating that emotions are identified on the basis of available cognitions, but they were not explicit concerning the relationship between the imitative responses of the subjects and the nature of the cognitions involved. In fact, their interpretation took too little account of the sequencing of the phases of their experiment in which the subjects were required to give self-reports of their feelings only after exposure to the confederate. Identification of one's own emotions may be accomplished mainly through observing one's own actual or anticipated behavior and is certainly possible only as a result of social learning.

The aroused child who strikes out or screams is, on these and numerous similar occasions, told, "Don't be angry" and thus learns to identify emotional-arousal states that are accompanied by certain classes of potentially pain- or distress-producing responses as instances of the manifestation of anger. In other words, his emotional state is identified on the basis of his own observed behavior; *the agent calls himself angry because he has behaved or is behaving in a manner that is usually judged as aggressive or hostile.* Later in life, of course, a highly aroused person who contemplates, imagines, or anticipates aggressive actions that he may carry out will identify his emotion as anger, even though aggressive behavior does not actually occur. Although this point of view is not essentially different from Schachter's to the extent that it emphasizes cognitive factors, it regards these latter factors not as a component of the emotional state itself, but as cues that lead to a self-evaluative response. Our analysis also implies that the primary interest of the Schachter-and-Singer experiment lies in the enhancement of the influence of social models through a combination of arousal and information control and not in the subjects' self-reports of their reactions.

According to the theory advanced in this chapter, the injection of adrenaline should lead to increased activity and more careful attention to the behavior of others. It should therefore enhance the influence of social models. However, Schachter and Singer found subjects who were correctly informed of the effects of adrenaline imitated the model to a lesser extent than placebo subjects, and that misinformed subjects showed more imitative behavior than subjects who received no information. These results may be explicable in terms of learning factors. The informed subjects may have been positively reinforced, through confirmation of expectancies induced by the experimenter, for attending to their bodily symptoms. These reinforced responses may have interfered with attending responses directed towards the confederate. Misinformation, in contrast, may have had an almost diametrically opposite effect. Nonconfirmation of expectancies could have operated like an aversive stimulus to channel the subjects' attention away from his bodily states. Moreover, the uncertainty, which was in all probability generated by the discrepancy between the subjects' expected and actual bodily reactions may have become, through prior learning experiences, associated with the response of imitating others in the expectation they might be producing an appropriate response. A combination of past-learning experiences and current positive or negative reinforcements for attending to bodily reactions may thus account for the differential modeling effects that emerged in the Schachter and Singer study.

V. Modification of Attention through Social Learning

It is assumed throughout this chapter that the common component in dependency responses is orienting toward and attending to others, and that these responses can be influenced by reinforcement and modeling procedures. The essentially social responses with which this chapter is concerned may, in fact, be closely associated with the orienting response in animals to which Pavlov (1927) first drew attention.

The orientation reaction, a complex neurophysiological response with behavioral concomitants, is accompanied by modification of attention (Berlyne, 1960) and may well be the key to the understanding of many of the social phenomena that have been discussed in the preceding sections. Perhaps the origins of dependency behavior lie not in the mediation by nurturant adults of the child's biological needs, but in the selective reinforcement and modeling of orienting and attending responses in social situations. This is, of course, a highly speculative suggestion. Nevertheless, evidence has been provided that *attending* responses can be modified through social learning.

In a study designed to investigate "autistic" effects in perception (Murphy, 1947, 1956), Walters (1958) presented subjects with the task of locating a simple figure in a more complex colored figure in a test similar to the Gottschaldt Test. The simple figure could be located in one of two areas within the complex figure; these areas were of different colors. A training period followed in which, by means of a problem-solving device, some colors were associated with verbally mediated rewards and others with verbally mediated punishments (indications of failure). The Gottschaldt-like figures were then re-presented, and pretest-to-posttest changes in the subjects' responses were recorded. The results, with two separate groups of subjects, indicated an increase of responses to rewarded colors as a result of the conditioning procedure. Questionnaire data revealed that only a small minority of the subjects noticed the association between the reward and punishing responses of the experimenter and the colors employed in the training task. Not one of the subjects identified a meaningful connection between the training and testing procedures, even after they had been told that these were two parts of a single experiment. The results were interpreted as indicating that attention, "a complex of motor and neural adjustments," had been conditioned to specific aspects of stimuli through social reinforcements by the experimenter.

A later study (Walters *et al.*, 1964) is more directly relevant to the theoretical position that has been advanced in this chapter. Unmarried male undergraduate students were shown by a female experimenter a movie film including pictures of nude or semi-nude males and females, photographed in poses that were evidently designed to arouse erotic responses. The remaining pictures in the film consisted of fully clothed males and females depicted in typical advertisement poses and were regarded as "neutral" stimuli. The subjects were told that a moving spot of light on the film indicated the eye-movements of a previous subject. For approximately half the subjects the light roved over the bodies of the males and females portrayed in the film and most of the time appeared in the vicinity of the breast and genital region. For the remainder of the subjects the spot of light moved around the background of the picture, thus giving the subject the impression that the observer was not looking at the human bodies. Approximately half the subjects in each of the model-avoids and the model-attends groups were reinforced by hearing, on a sound strip, the experimenter's voice verbally approving the avoiding or attending behavior. Following exposure to the film, the subjects' own eye-movements were recorded as they observed a series of slides parallel to those exhibited on the film. The galvanic-skin responses of the subjects were secured throughout the experimental procedure.

Marked modeling effects were obtained to the sexually significant stimuli. The eye-movements of subjects in the model-attends group moved up and down the figure in the sexual pictures in a manner paralleling almost precisely the eye-movements of the film-mediated model, even to the concentration of attention on the more sexually significant parts of the figures. No modeling effects were obtained in the case of the neutral figures.

The galvanic-skin-response records suggested that the sexually significant stimuli had had an arousal effect, whereas this effect was largely absent in the case of the neutral stimuli. A combination of factors may account for the difference in the impact of the two classes of stimuli. The sexual pictures were not of a kind that are usually shown to students in the social setting of this study, especially with a female experimenter present. In addition, the content of most of the pictures could be expected to arouse doubts concerning the appropriateness of any response the subjects might give. Under conditions of uncertainty, persons, especially when emotionally aroused either by the nature of the situation or by the uncertainty itself, are especially likely to rely on the behavior of others for indications of how they should respond. The potency of social models for modifying the behavior of persons in whom uncertainty has been created is particularly evident in the studies by McNulty and Walters (1962) and Schachter and Singer (1962), which were described earlier.

Moreover, sexually significant stimuli may, on account of the curiosity of the subject or the novelty of their content, evoke exploratory, perceptual responses. If these responses are elicited in a social situation in some respects similar to those in which such responses have previously been censured, conflict may occur, accompanied by physiological arousal. The relationships between curiosity, novelty, arousal, conflict, orientation, and exploratory responses have been carefully discussed by Berlyne (1960); the study by Walters et al. (1964) merely indicates that once an orienting and attending response has been elicited, it can be influenced by social-training procedures.

The addition of reinforcement to the modeling technique did not greatly influence its efficacy, although reinforced subjects were, on the average, slightly more influenced by the model than those for whom reinforcements were omitted. The relative ineffectiveness of reinforcement under the conditions of this experiment may have been a by-product of the restriction of attention to salient cues that appears to accompany emotional arousal. Possibly, the attention of subjects was so concentrated on the visual aspects of the stimulus situation that the audibly presented reinforcements had very little effect. Support for this interpretation is provided by Berlyne's (1960) review of studies of both animal and human subjects that indicate that reliance on one sensory modality to the exclusion of another may accompany an increase in arousal.

A preliminary report by Cairns (1963) provides additional evidence in favor of our theoretical analysis of the relationship of dependency behavior to susceptibility to social influence. In one study 6-year-old children were first rewarded with toys for orienting and attending to a female experimenter and were then rewarded by the approval of a second female experimenter for "correct" responses in a discrimination task. Two control groups were employed. Children in one control group were reinforced with toys, but these reinforcements were not contingent upon the children's attending to the experimenter; for the second control group, the toys were placed just out of reach and no rewards were given during the training session. Only the children reinforced for orienting and attending responses showed any substantial amount of subsequent discrimination learning.

VI. Conclusion

The theme of this chapter is that reported relationships between such variables as social deprivation, dependency, self-esteem, and various measures of social influence can be largely understood in terms of (1) the eliciting and modification of orienting and attending responses, and (2) the behavioral effects of variations in emotional arousal. The emphasis on orienting and attending responses as a foundation for the development of dependency behavior receives both justification and support from Rheingold's (1961) observations on the exploratory behavior of human infants. We are inclined to agree with Rheingold that perceptual rather than physical contact may provide the basis of human sociability. Orienting and attending responses, which are largely mediated by the distance receptors,[4] are presumably modified by social-training procedures, such as those described by Bandura and Walters (1963b), so that they are eventually elicited in varying degrees of strength in different individuals and under different stimulus conditions. Variations in emotional arousal apparently have a complex effect on the behavior under discussion. In the first place, attending responses may be associatively linked, through prior reinforcement, with certain emotional-arousal cues. Secondly, arousal itself appears to modify perceptual responses in ways that could enhance or attenuate the influence of social agents.

To understand fully the nature of dependency behavior as a socially significant variable requires, in addition to the analysis presented in this chapter, an understanding of (a) the acquisition of social judgments involving the labeling of behavior as dependent, and (b) the conditions under which these judgments are evoked. Social-psychological theory is considerably hampered by the lack of any extensive exploration of the learning of social judgments. It also suffers from the virtual absence of psychological analyses of the social-judgment process that take into account both the nature of the stimulus conditions that elicit particular judgments and the manner in which these conditions become cues for evoking judgmental responses.

This chapter commenced with a discussion of the problem of acquired drives and, in particular, the status of the concept of a dependency motive. It is suggested that motives of this kind are not characteristics of human agents, but constructs by means of which human beings order social

[4] Rheingold emphasized the importance of visual contact with the environment, and we, too, have given primary attention to visual experiences. However, auditory experiences may play an equally important part in the development of social responsiveness. We are indebted to Dr. S. G. Laverty, of the Department of Psychiatry, Queen's University, Kingston, for pointing out the danger of placing too much emphasis on the role of visual perception.

phenomena and evaluate behavior in terms of its acceptability or nonacceptability within a given cultural context. In fact, motivational interpretations of behavior involve complicated evaluations having reference to complex stimulus events—for example, the social context of the act or the recent or more remote past of the agent—as well as to the consequences that an agent's behavior produces for others. It is therefore not surprising that evaluative judgments in terms of the intent or motive of the agent, rather than the consequences of the act, become relatively more frequent as a child grows older (Piaget, 1932) and increasingly conforms to the standards to which the child is exposed.

Nevertheless, response sequences are usually evaluated on account of their class membership and not as isolated acts. One may therefore seek common objective characteristics of response sequences that are customarily placed in a specific motivational category, as we have done in the case of dependency behavior, and attempt to trace the conditions under which these components are learned. We may, in addition, investigate the relationships between these response components and other behavioral phenomena. However, as students of social motivation, we shall not have completed our investigations until we have related our findings to the cultural context within which motives are defined.

REFERENCES

Allport, G. (1937). "Personality: A Psychological Interpretation." Holt, New York.

Asch, S. E. (1951). In "Groups, Leadership, and Men" (H. Guetzkow, ed.), pp. 177–190. Carnegie Press, Pittsburgh.

Baer, D. M. (1962). Child Develop. 33, 847–858.

Bandura, A. (1960). Relationship of family patterns to child behavior disorders. Progress Report U.S.P.H. Research Grant M-1734. Stanford Univ.

Bandura, A. (1962). In "Nebraska Symposium on Motivation" (M. R. Jones, ed.), pp. 211–269. Univ. of Nebraska Press, Lincoln, Nebraska.

Bandura, A. (1964). "Behavioristic Psychotherapy." Holt, Rinehart, & Winston, New York.

Bandura, A., and Huston, A. C. (1961). J. Abnorm. Soc. Psychol. 63, 311–318.

Bandura, A., and Walters, R. H. (1959). "Adolescent Aggression." Ronald, New York.

Bandura, A., and Walters, R. H. (1963a). In "Child Psychology," The 62nd Yearbook of the National Society for the Study of Education. Part I, pp. 364–415. The National Society for the Study of Education, Chicago.

Bandura, A., and Walters, R. H. (1963b). "Social Learning and Personality Development." Holt, Rinehart, & Winston, New York.

Bandura, A., Ross, D. and Ross, S. A. (1963). J. Abnorm. Soc. Psychol. 67, 527–534.

Beller, E. K. (1955). J. Genet. Psychol. 87, 25–35.

Beller, E. K. (1959). Trans. N.Y. Acad. Sci. [2] 21, 414–426.

Beller, E. K., and Haeberle, A. W. (1961a). Dependency and the frustration-aggression hypothesis. Unpublished manuscript, Child Develop. Center, New York City.

Beller, E. K., and Haeberle, A. W. (1961b). Dependency and the frustration-aggression hypothesis: II. Paper read at the Annual Meeting of the Eastern Psychol. Assoc., Philadelphia.

Berlyne, D. E. (1960). *"Conflict, Arousal, and Curiosity."* McGraw-Hill, New York.

Berlyne, D. E. (1964). *Ann. Rev. Psychol.* **15,** 115–142.

Bexton, W. H., Heron, W., and Scott, T. H. (1954). *Can. J. Psychol.* **8,** 70–76.

Bindra, D. (1959). "Motivation: A Systematic Reinterpretation." Ronald, New York.

Bowlby, J. (1952). "Maternal Care and Mental Health," WHO Mongr. Series No. 2. World Health Organization, Geneva.

Brown, J. S. (1953). *In* "Current Theory and Research in Motivation," pp. 1–21. Univ. of Nebraska Press, Lincoln, Nebraska.

Brown, J. S. (1961). "The Motivation of Behavior." McGraw-Hill, New York.

Bruner, J. S., Matter, J. and Papanek, M. L. (1955). *Psychol. Rev.* **62,** 1–10.

Cairns, R. B. (1961). *J. Pers.* **29,** 466–488.

Cairns, R. B. (1962). Antecedents of social reinforcer effectiveness. Unpublished manuscript, Univ. of Indiana.

Cairns, R. B. (1963). Antecedents of social reinforcer effectiveness. Paper read at the Biennial Meeting of the Soc. Res. Child Develop., Berkeley, California.

Cairns, R. B., and Kaufman, H. (1962). Prestige suggestibility and dependency inhibition. Unpublished manuscript, Univ. of Indiana.

Cairns, R. B., and Lewis, H. (1962). *J. Consulting Psychol.* **26,** 1–8.

Child, I. L. (1954). *In* "Handbook of Social Psychology" (G. Lindzey, ed.), Vol. 2, pp. 655–692. Addison-Wesley, Cambridge.

Cohen, A. R. (1959). *In* "Personality and Persuasibility" (C. I. Hovland and I. L. Janis, eds.) pp. 102–120. Yale Univ. Press, New Haven.

Cowan, P. A., and Walters, R. H. (1963). *Child Develop.* **34,** 543–552.

Davis, R. C. (1959). *J. Comp. Physiol. Psychol.* **52,** 309–314.

deCharms, R., and Rosenbaum, M. E. (1960). *J. Pers.* **28,** 492–502.

Duffy, E. (1951). *Psychol. Rev.* **58,** 30–40.

Duffy, E. (1957). *Psychol. Rev.* **64,** 265–275.

Duffy, E. (1962). "Activation and Behavior." Wiley, New York.

Easterbrook, J. A. (1959). *Psychol. Rev.* **66,** 183–201.

Ehrlich, D. (1958). Determinants of verbal commonality and influencibility. Unpublished doctoral thesis, Univ. of Minnesota.

Endsley, R. C. (1960). Dependency and performance by preschool children on a socially reinforced task. Unpublished M.A. thesis, State Univ. of Iowa.

Erickson, M. T. (1962). Effects of social deprivation and satiation on verbal conditioning in children. *J. Comp. Physiol. Psychol.* **55,** 953–957.

Ferguson, P. E. (1961). The influence of isolation, anxiety, and dependency on reinforcer effectiveness. Unpublished M.A. thesis, Univ. of Toronto.

Festinger, L. (1954). A theory of social comparison processes. *Human Relat.* **7,** 117–140.

Festinger, L. (1957). "A Theory of Cognitive Dissonance." Stanford Univ. Press, Stanford.

Freud, A., and Burlingham, D. T. (1944). "Infants without Families." International Universities, New York.

Gerard, H. B. (1963). Uncertainty as a drive in human behavior. Unpublished manuscript, Center for the Advanced Study of the Behavioral Sciences.

Gerard, H. B., and Rabbie, J. M. (1961). *J. Abnorm. Soc. Psychol.* **62,** 586–592.

Gewirtz, J. L. (1954). *Mongr. Soc. Res. Child Develop.* **19,** No. 2 (Serial No. 59).

Gewirtz, J. L. (1957). Social deprivation and dependency: A learning analysis. Paper presented at the Annual Meeting of the Amer. Psychol. Assoc., New York.

Gewirtz, J. L. (1961). In "Determinants in Infant Behavior," (B. M. Foss, ed.), pp. 213–283. Wiley, New York.

Gewirtz, J. L., and Baer, D. M. (1958a). J. Abnorm. Soc. Psychol. 56, 49–56.

Gewirtz, J. L., and Baer, D. M. (1958b). J. Abnorm. Soc. Psychol. 57, 165–172.

Gewirtz, J. L., Baer, D. M., and Roth, C. H. (1958). Child Develop. 29, 149–152.

Goldfarb, W. (1943). Am. J. Orthopsychiat. 13, 249–265.

Haeberle, A. (1958). Interactions of sex, birth order, and dependency with behavior problems and symptoms in emotionally disturbed preschool children. Paper read at Eastern Psychol. Assoc., Annual Meeting, Philadelphia.

Haner, C. F., and Brown, P. A. (1955). J. Abnorm. Soc. Psychol. 51, 204–206.

Hartup, W. W. (1958). Child Develop. 29, 191–201.

Hartup, W. W. (1963). In "Child Psychology," The 62nd Yearbook of the National Society for the Study of Education, Part I, pp. 333–363. The National Society for the Study of Education. Chicago.

Hartup, W. W., and Himeno, Y. (1959). J. Abnorm. Soc. Psychol. 59, 17–22.

Heathers, G. (1953). Child Develop. 24, 169–179.

Heathers, G. (1955). J. Genet. Psychol. 87, 277–291.

Hebb, D. O. (1955). Psychol. Rev. 62, 243–254.

Heron, W. (1961). In "Sensory Deprivation" (P. Solomon, P. E. Kubzansky, P. H. Leiderman, J. H. Mendelson, R. Trumbull, and D. Wexler, eds.), pp. 6–33. Harvard Univ. Press, Cambridge, Massachusetts.

Hill, K. T., and Stevenson, H. W. (1964). J. Abnorm. Soc. Psychol. in press.

Hill, W. F. (1960). Psychol. Rev. 67, 317–331.

Holton, R. B. (1961). Child Develop. 32, 107–116.

Hops, H., and Walters, R. H. (1963). Child Develop. 34, 553–562.

Hull, C. L. (1943). "Principles of Behavior." Appleton, New York.

Jakubczak, L. F., and Walters, R. H. (1959). J. Abnorm. Soc. Psychol. 59, 102–107.

Kausler, D. H., and Trapp, E. P. (1960). Psychol Rev. 67, 373–379.

Lesser, G. S., and Abelson, R. P. (1959). In "Personality and Persuasibility" (C. I. Hovland and I. L. Janis, eds.), pp. 187–206. Yale Univ. Press, New Haven.

Levin, H., and Baldwin, A. L. (1959). In "Nebraska Symposium on Motivation" (M. R. Jones, ed.), pp. 138–173. Univ. of Nebraska Press, Lincoln, Nebraska.

Levin, H., and Wardwell, E. (1962). Psychol. Bull. 59, 27–56.

Levy, D. M. (1943). "Maternal Overprotection." Columbia Univ. Press, New York.

Lowrey, L. G. (1940). Am. J. Orthopsychiat. 10, 576–586.

McNulty, J. A., and Walters, R. H. (1962). Can. J. Psychol. 16, 211–220.

Malmo, R. B. (1958). In "Nebraska Symposium on Motivation" (M. R. Jones, ed.), pp. 229–265. Univ. of Nebraska Press, Lincoln, Nebraska.

Malmo, R. B. (1959). Psychol. Rev. 66, 367–386.

Mandler, G., and Kaplan, W. K. (1956). Science 124, 582–583.

Mendelson, J., Kubzansky, P. H., Leiderman, P. H., Wexler, D., DuToit, C., and Solomon, P. (1960). A.M.A. Arch. Gen. Psychiat. 2, 147–155.

Murphy, G. (1947). "Personality: A Biosocial Approach to Origins and Structure." Harper, New York.

Murphy, G. (1956). Psychol. Rev. 63, 1–15.

Murray, H. A. (1938). "Explorations in Personality." Oxford Univ. Press, New York.

Mussen, P. H., and Kagan, J. (1956). J. Consulting Psychol. 20, 29–32.

Paivio, A. (1963). J. Abnorm. Soc. Psychol. 67, 247–253.

Paivio, A., and Lambert, W. E. (1959). *J. Pers.* **27,** 1-17.
Paivio, A., Baldwin, A. L., and Berger, S. M. (1961). *Child Develop.* **32,** 721–730.
Parke, R. D., and Walters, R. H. (1963). Alcoholism, avoidance learning, and emotionality. Unpublished manuscript, Univer. of Waterloo.
Pavlov, I. P. (1927). "Conditioned Reflexes." Oxford Univ. Press (Clarendon Press), London and New York.
Penney, R. K. (1960). *Can. J. Psychol.* **14,** 206–215.
Piaget, J. (1932). "The Moral Judgment of the Child." Kegan Paul, London.
Rheingold, H. L. (1956). *Mongr. Soc. Res. Child Develop.* **21,** No. 2 (Series No. 63).
Rheingold, H. L. (1961). *In* "Determinants of Infant Behavior" (B. M. Foss, ed.), pp. 143–171. Wiley, New York.
Rheingold, H. L., and Bayley, N. (1959). *Child Develop.* **30,** 363–372.
Rosenbaum, M. E., Horne, W. C., and Chalmers, D. K. (1962). *J. Pers.* **30,** 147–156.
Rosenblith, J. F. (1957). Attention-withdrawal in relation to the effects of children's learning by imitation. Unpublished doctoral thesis, Harvard Univer.
Rosenblith, J. F. (1959). *Child. Develop.* **30,** 69–80.
Rosenblith, J. F. (1961). *Child Develop.* **32,** 211–223.
Rosenow, C., and Whyte, A. H. (1931). *Am. J. Orthopsychiat.* **1,** 430–434.
Rosenthal, R., Persinger, G. W., Kline, Linda V., and Mulry, R. C. (1963). *J. Pers.* **31,** 313–335.
Sampson, E. E. (1962). *J. Abnorm. Soc. Psychol.* **64,** 155–159.
Sarnoff, I., and Zimbardo, P. G. (1961). *J. Abnorm. Soc. Psychol.* **62,** 356–363.
Schachter, S. (1959). "The Psychology of Affiliation." Stanford Univ. Press, Stanford.
Schachter, S., and Singer, J. E. (1962). *Psychol. Rev.* **69,** 379–399.
Schachter, S., and Wheeler, L. (1962). *J. Abnorm. Soc. Psychol.* **65,** 121–128.
Scott, T. H., Bexton, W. H., Heron, W., and Doane, B. K. (1959). *Can. J. Psychol.* **13,** 200–209.
Sears, R. R. (1950). *Am. Soc. Rev.* **15,** 397–401.
Sears, R. R. (1963). *In* "Nebraska Symposium on Motivation" (M. R. Jones, ed.), pp. 25–64. Univ. of Nebraska Press, Lincoln, Nebraska.
Sears, R. R., Whiting, J. W. M., Nowlis, V., and Sears, P. S. (1953). *Genet. Psychol. Monogr.* **47,** 135–234.
Sears, R. R., Maccoby, E. E., and Levin, H. (1957). "Patterns of Child Rearing." Harper, New York.
Skinner, B. F. (1953). *"Science and Human Behavior."* Macmillan, New York.
Sletto, R. F. (1934). *Am. J. Sociol.* **39,** 657–659.
Smock, C. D. (1962). Effects of motivational factors on perceptual-cognitive efficiency of children who vary in intellectual level. Cooperative Research Project No. 790. Purdue Univ.
Spence, K. W. (1956). "Behavior Theory and Conditioning." Yale Univ. Press, New Haven, Connecticut.
Spence, K. W. (1958). *Am. Psychologist* **13,** 131–141.
Spence, K. W., Farber, I. E., and McFann, H. H. (1956a). *J. Exptl. Psychol.* **52,** 296–305.
Spence, K. W., Taylor, J. A., and Ketchel, R. (1956b). *J. Exptl. Psychol.* **52,** 306–310.
Spitz, R. A. (1945). *Psychoanal. Study Child* **1,** 53–74.
Staples, F. R., and Walters, R. H. (1961). *J. Abnorm. Soc. Psychol.* **62,** 716–719.
Stevenson, H. W. (1961). *J. Abnorm. Soc. Psychol.* **63,** 147–154.
Stevenson, H. W., and Hill, K. T. (1963). Frustration and social reinforcement. Unpublished manuscript, Univer. of Minnesota, 1963.

Stevenson, H. W., and Knights, R. M. (1962a). *Am. J. Mental Deficiency* **66,** 589–594.

Stevenson, H. W., and Knights, R. M. (1962b). *Am. J. Mental Deficiency* **66,** 866–871.

Stevenson, H. W., and Odom, R. D. (1962). *J. Abnorm. Soc. Psychol.* **65,** 429–431.

Taylor, J. A. (1953). *J. Abnorm. Soc. Psychol.* **48,** 285–290.

Walters, R. H. (1958). *J. Abnorm. Soc. Psychol.* **57,** 197–201.

Walters, R. H., and Henning, G. B. (1961). *Aerospace Med.* **32,** 431–434.

Walters, R. H., and Henning, G. B. (1962). *Can. J. Psychol.* **16,** 202–210.

Walters, R. H., and Karal, P. (1960). *J. Pers.* **28,** 89–107.

Walters, R. H., and Parke, R D. (1964). *J. Exptl. Child Psychol.,* in press.

Walters, R. H., and Quinn, M. J. (1960). *J. Pers.* **28,** 210–219.

Walters, R. H., and Ray, E. (1960). *J. Pers.* **28,** 358–367.

Walters, R. H., Marshall, W. E., and Shooter, J. R. (1960). *J. Pers.* **28,** 518–529.

Walters, R. H., Callagan, J. E., and Newman, A. F. (1963). *Am. J. Psychiat.* **119,** 771–773.

Walters, R. H., Bowen, N. V., and Parke, R. D. (1964). *Percept. Motor Skills.* **18,** 469–483.

White, R. W. (1959) *Psychol. Rev.* **66,** 297–333.

White, S. H. (1963). *In* "Child Psychology." The 62nd Yearbook of the National Society for the Study of Education, pp. 196–235. The National Society for the Study of Education, Chicago, Illinois.

Whiting, J. W. M., and Child, I. L. (1953). "Child Training and Personality." Yale Univ. Press, New Haven, Connecticut.

Wrightsman, L. S., Jr. (1960). *J. Abnorm. Soc. Psychol.* **61,** 216–222.

Yarrow, L. F. (1961). *Psychol. Bull.* **58,** 459–490.

Zigler, E. (1961). *J. Abnorm. Soc. Psychol.* **62,** 413–421.

Zigler, E. (1963). *Am. J. Orthopsychiat.* **33,** 614–623.

Zigler, E., and Williams, J. (1963). *J. Abnorm. Soc. Psychol.* **66,** 197–205.

Zigler, E., Hodgden, L., and Stevenson, H. W. (1958). *J. Pers.* **26,** 106–122.

Zimbardo, P. G., and Formica, R. (1963). *J. Pers.* **31,** 141–162.

SOCIABILITY AND SOCIAL ORGANIZATION IN MONKEYS AND APES

William A. Mason*

DELTA REGIONAL PRIMATE RESEARCH CENTER
TULANE UNIVERSITY
NEW ORLEANS, LOUISIANA

The social psychology of monkeys and apes is fundamentally a branch of comparative psychology. As such, its objectives and methods are more directly influenced by biological—and especially evolutionary—considerations than is the study of human social behavior. Many disciplines outside psychology have had a strong traditional interest in primate social behavior, and some of the most important, recent contributions to the field were made by anthropologists, sociologists, and zoologists. Although there are exceptions, the psychologist generally favored an experimental approach and worked with small groups of animals in a laboratory setting, while other scientists were more concerned with collecting descriptive data on natural populations. Clearly, both approaches have their ad-

* Present address: International Center for Medical Research and Training, Universidad del Valle, Cali, Colombia.

vantages and limitations, and each is complemented and strengthened by the other.

The study of primate behavior is now in a period of vigorous growth which is but one aspect of a widespread acceleration of research on the general biology of the primates (see, e.g., "The Relatives of Man," *Ann. N.Y. Acad. Sci.* **102,** (1962). We are moving rapidly toward a separate field of primatology, embracing a diversity of contributing disciplines. An inevitable outcome of this broad-spectrum expansion of primate research will be a closer relationship between primate behavioral studies and problems of general biology. This is desirable on general scientific grounds, of course, but more particularly because the full contribution of the nonhuman primates to an understanding of the behavior of man requires an evolutionary-biological perspective.

One of the first systematic attempts to encompass the facts of primate social behavior in a biological framework was Zuckerman's "The Social Life of Monkeys and Apes" (1932). In this highly influential work, Zuckerman concluded that monkeys and apes, in contrast to the majority of mammals, were sexually active at all seasons of the year. He reasoned that sexual attraction was a major source of primate sociability and group cohesion. Sexual attraction, together with dominance or social rank, were regarded as primary determinants of the organization of primate groups.

Zuckerman's thesis was consistent with his own observations, particularly of baboon groups, and provided an important stimulus and focal point for discussions of primate societies (see, e.g., Chance, 1955, 1961; Sahlins, 1959). Recent data make it clear, however, that the dual factors of sexuality and dominance cannot constitute a sufficient basis for primate gregariousness and social organization.

For the macaque monkeys and possibly other primates, breeding is largely confined to certain periods of the year, yet there are no corresponding seasonal variations in group cohesiveness (Altmann, 1962b; Koford, 1963a). Furthermore, specific and relatively stable preferences may exist between like-sexed animals of similar or disparate ages which are unlikely to be based on sexual attraction. Even in adult, heterosexual pairs in which an affinity begins with a sexual liason, the relationship may persist into the female's pregnancy, long after copulation has ceased (Altmann, 1962b).

Similarly, it is unlikely that dominance can be regarded as the primary source of primate social organization. While it may be true that social structure is most highly differentiated and distinct among primates characterized by sharply defined dominance relationships (e.g., baboons and macaques), it is a mistake to view dominance as the keystone of social organization. A number of different primates, of which the howling monkey is a well-known example, live in organized groups occupying a definite and limited range. Such groups are characterized by stable membership and by a high degree of inter-individual coordination in feeding, in progressions, and in response to external threat. Yet there is little evidence of intragroup fighting or sharply defined dominance relationships (Carpenter, 1934; Collias and Southwick, 1952).

In some primate groups one or more animals may serve a special function in group coordination and control. Although these individuals are often dominant in the sense that they are physically superior to other group members and have priority of access to the good things of life, this is by no means their most interesting social characteristic. Consider the following description of the mountain gorilla:

> The focal point of each group is the leader who is without exception, the dominant silverbacked male. The entire daily routine—the time of rising, the direction and distance of travel, the location and duration of rest periods, and finally the time of nest building—is largely determined by the leader. Every independent animal in the group, except occasionally subordinate males, appears to be constantly aware of the location and activity of the leader either directly or through the behavior of animals in his vicinity. Cues reflecting a changed pattern of activity are rapidly transmitted through the group and the subsequent behavior of the members is patterned after that of the leader (Schaller, 1963).

It should be noted, moreover, that in spite of the prominent role of the silverbacked male in controlling and coordinating group activity, he is tolerant toward other group members and his assertions of dominance are infrequent and usually subtle and indirect.

Thus, recent evidence clearly indicates that the origins of primate sociability and the sources of order in the societies of monkeys and apes are highly complex problems which we are still far from resolving. They are central problems, however, and encompass most of the important questions which students of primate social behavior were concerned with in the past and will investigate in the future. While the day is still remote when these questions can be adequately treated systematically and in detail, something is to be gained from the attempt to do so now. This chapter is written in that spirit.

I. Expressions of Primate Sociability and Social Organization: General Considerations

There is little profit in attempting formal definitions of sociability and social organization. Baldly stated, the experimenter is concerned with two related questions: (1) What factors cause primates to remain in groups, to be attracted to one another? (2) What determines the specific patterns of social relationship and interaction within a group, and between one group and another?

Neither gregariousness nor social organization are simple, unitary characteristics. Both are complex phenomena comprising a number of different aspects of social behavior. In general, of course, one could say that gregariousness is high in groups in which the members remain close together, are distressed by solitude, show frequent, nonaggressive forms of body contact, rarely compete, act in concert in response to external threat, and are capable of displaying mutual aid. However, these various characteristics cannot be assumed to be highly intercorrelated, and the chief concern is with describing specific manifestations of gregariousness, suggesting wherever possible the conditions that influence their development and expression.

The phenomena of social organization present a similar problem. A group would be considered highly organized if (1) major social interchanges (sex, grooming, aggression) followed regular and specific interindividual channels; (2) if there was a consistent, spatial arrangement of individuals during feeding, progressions, and rest periods; and (3) if group members regularly responded differentially to external threat. Other characteristics indicative of a high degree of social organization could be given. Again, however, intercorrelations between different measures might be low, and there is less concern with establishing levels of social organization for different primate groups than with describing specific aspects of social organization and the conditions that produce them.

Finally, it should be emphasized that gregariousness and social organization are interdependent. Obviously, in the absence of gregarious dispositions, there could be no social organization. Furthermore, the particular patterns of affinities and interactions that define various clusters or subgroups within a group are plainly an important facet of social organization. On the other hand, there are aspects of social organization—territorialty, the frequency and specific modes of intra-group communication, the number, age, and sex distributions of the individuals comprising a group, the permeability of group boundaries, and the character of relations with alien groups—which can be considered without regard to the sources and patterns of sociability within the troop.

II. Sources of Primate Sociability

A. FILIAL ATTACHMENTS

The beginning of primate sociability is the infant's tie to the mother. Although a close relationship to the mother is essential for survival in most mammals, this is especially true of primates. Unlike many mammalian young that can be left in a den or nest until old enough to go with the mother when she forages for food, the baby monkey or ape must accompany its mother everywhere from the very beginning. The nonhuman primates are basically quadrupeds, and it is essential that the infant be able to maintain bodily contact with the mother while receiving only occasional maternal assistance. This is accomplished, of course, by the clinging and grasping reactions which are vigorous and well formed at birth in both monkeys and apes (although less so in the latter).

The strength and tenacity of these primitive, infantile social responses have been known for many years (e.g. Wallace, 1869), but their role in psychological development is just beginning to be understood. Tinklepaugh and Hartman (1932) recognized the importance of tactile stimulation in the motivations of the young primate and described contact-seeking as the dominant drive of the newborn macaque. Foley (1934, 1935) concurred in this view and provided many illustrations of the strength of contact-seeking behaviors in a young, hand-raised rhesus monkey. These reports clearly indicated that contact-stimulation was a variable of great potential importance, but systematic data on its role in early psychological development were lacking until Harlow and his associates at the University of Wisconsin ran their well-known experiments.

The early experiments in this series used a variety of artificial mothers to compare the effectiveness of different maternal attributes in producing filial attachment in rhesus monkeys. The principal variables investigated were lactation, movement, form of the surrogate object, and contact stimulation, presented singly and in different combinations (Harlow, 1960; Harlow and Zimmermann, 1958). Each of these factors was found to influence the strength of filial attachment, measured by duration of contact with the surrogate objects, but contact-stimulation produced the most dramatic and persistent effects. To demonstrate the range of these effects required the use of situations in which the monkey was either confronted with fear stimuli, subjected to the stress of a strange environment, or required to perform an instrumental response in order to achieve contact with the surrogate.

The results of these tests are familiar and will only be summarized briefly. The cloth surrogate was shown to be an effective incentive for lever-pressing, for the solution of simple, mechanical puzzles, and for performance in a runway; and its effectiveness was most evident in situations in which the monkey was frightened or upset. The Wisconsin researchers found that the absence of the artificial mother provoked distress, that it was sought in stressful situations, and that its presence in such situations reduced distress.

The most interesting social attribute of the cloth, artificial mother was its ability to mitigate distress reactions—to provide "emotional security." This attribute corresponds closely, of course, to an important function of the natural mother. The experimental demonstration of this characteristic is significant because it relates an important aspect of the phenomenon of filial attachment to a potentially definable class of stimulus parameters, thereby creating the opportunity for analytic study of the mechanisms involved in the formation of early social bonds.

It is possible, however, that no single mechanism will account for the infant primate's tie to its natural mother. Many types of stimulation may be discerned which can reasonably be expected to contribute to the infant-mother bond, although their mode of operation is as yet imperfectly understood. Enough is known, nevertheless, to provide some preliminary suggestions.

One of the first efforts to account for the development of an attachment in the young primate was made more than 20 years ago by T. L. McCulloch (1939). McCulloch described a series of experiments in which he rewarded the learned behavior of young chimpanzees by presenting claspable objects as incentives. He showed that a sack, paper toweling, or clinging to the experimenter could be used as rewards for performance on discrimination and delayed-response tasks, but emphasized that these conditions were effective only when the chimpanzees were excited or disturbed. He reasoned that disturbing stimuli lowered the threshold for clasping and led to increased activity. When this activity resulted in contact with an appropriate object, clasping occurred, which brought about a cessation of activity. The reinforcing effects of clasping were thus believed to reside in its inhibitory action (McCulloch, 1939).

In a number of experiments with young chimpanzees, the experimenter has recently confirmed McCulloch's finding that clinging is associated with a high level of excitement or emotional arousal. To manipulate arousal, physical restraint, strange surroundings, noise, social deprivation, and a stimulant drug (Dexidrene) were used. All of these conditions sharply increased the likelihood that clinging would occur. The effect was demonstrated when the object of clinging was another chimpanzee, a human companion, or an inanimate object (Mason, in press).

Evidence was also found that the act of clinging has definite, inhibitory effects. One experiment, for example, demonstrated that neonatal chimpanzees vocalized less to shock when they were held in the ventroventral attitude characteristic of the position on the mother than when they rested on a bare surface (Mason and Berkson, 1962). Thus, the data suggest that clinging is most likely to occur under high arousal and that clinging causes arousal reduction. This thesis is consistent with the observation that clinging and contact with the mother are most frequent under stress conditions—during inter- or intra-group fights, upon entering a strange territory, or when predators are present—and with the finding that clinging increases sharply following a period of enforced separation of mother and infant (Jensen and Tolman, 1962; Lashley and Watson, 1913; Seay, Hansen & Harlow, 1962; Tinklepaugh and Hartman, 1932).

Mason suggested elsewhere that arousal reduction may play an important part in the formation of filial attachments (in press). If this view is correct, one would expect an attachment to be more strongly manifested in infants whose level of arousal is high (and arousal reduction correspondingly great). Consistent with this is the finding that infant rhesus monkeys whose artificial mothers stimulated them with an aversive air blast spent more time in contact than did monkeys raised with nonaversive surrogates (Rosenblum and Harlow, 1963).

Clinging is only one aspect of the complex, infant-mother relationship. Even if the proposed reinforcing mechanism for clinging should be correct, other factors, possibly associated with different mechanisms, may be involved. However, what little is known about these additional factors suggests that the reinforcing mechanisms may be similar to those proposed for clinging. Consider sucking. The Wisconsin studies showed that a stronger attachment (measured by contact duration) is produced when contact-stimulation and sucking are combined than when either of these variables is presented alone. Bridger's findings with human neonates suggested that sucking, like clinging, reduces arousal (Harlow, 1960; Bridger, 1962).

Specific forms of stimulation provided by the mother may also be arousal reducing. Grooming, a conspicuous feature of maternal, primate behavior, apparently produces this type of calming (Altmann, 1962b; Jay, 1962; Mason, in press). A similar tranquilizing effect may result from the rhythmic stimulation provided by the mother as she goes about her normal activities. Rocking, which is widely used of course to pacify human babies appears to have similar consequences for infant chimpanzees (Allesch, 1921). Early in life, rhesus monkeys prefer a rocking, artificial mother over a stationary one (Harlow, 1960), and it is worth noting that chimpanzees and macaques raised alone usually develop stereotyped self-rocking or other repetitive activities which are especially prominent when they are upset (Berkson, Mason, and Saxon, 1963; Mason, 1960a). Possibly, these acts serve to mitigate emotional distress.

Whatever the role of arousal reduction in the formation of filial attachment, it is clear that the mother comes to occupy a central place in the emotional life of the young primate. She is sought when danger threatens, and her presence is a source of comfort and emotional security. It is these effects above all that characterize the filial attachment.

Thus viewed, the filial attachment serves a homeostatic function by modulating excessive arousal effects. One would therefore expect the tie to the mother to be most evident in stressful situations, and this has been seen to be the case. On the other hand, there is no question that the trend of development is away from the mother and toward increasing interaction with other group members. How does the attachment to the mother and the motivations and response systems that produced this bond affect relations with other animals?

B. Implications of Filial Attachment for Subsequent Social Relations

Even a preliminary statement of the relation between early social attachments and subsequent sociability requires information on three factors: (1) Developmental changes in the strength of the infantile response tendencies and motivations that produce filial attachment; (2) the effects of short-term motivational changes, e.g., fear, on the strength of these behaviors; (3) the basis of transfer or generalization.

Generally speaking, one would expect the degree of transfer to be greater the younger the subject, the more intense its state of emotional arousal at the time of testing, and the greater the physical and behavioral similarity between the test stimulus and the original object of the attachment. While the available evidence is consistent with this generalization, it is largely circumstantial, and in some instances hardly more than anecdotal.

Age changes have received the most attention. In nature, of course, social development is characterized by a gradual reduction in the frequency of clinging and sucking and in the amount of time spent with the mother, and by a corresponding growth in the frequency of interactions with peers. Although the rate at which these changes occur is influenced by the mother, the trend appears to be minimally dependent on experience and occurs in monkeys given as little as 3 minutes a day for social interaction—as well as in animals receiving more extensive social experience (Hansen, 1962; Mason, 1963; Rosenblum, 1961).

Even though the strength of clinging and similar infantile contact-seeking behaviors wanes as development proceeds, there are many indications that these responses persist long after the young primate ceases to be nutritionally dependent on the mother. Field studies describe small, stable subgroups consisting of a mother, a suckling infant, and an older youngster, presumably a sibling (Carpenter, 1934; Goodall, in press, Southwick, Beg, and Siddiqi, in press; and long-term observations of free-ranging macaques suggest that some affinity between a mother and her offspring may persist into maturity (Altmann, 1962b; Imanishi, 1960; Koford, 1963b). Moreover, under conditions of intense, emotional arousal, behavior may exhibit the same form as in the early phases of the relationship. For example, Hamilton (1914) observed that a female macaque and her daughter, rejoined after more than a year's separation, immediately ". . . rushed into an embrace."

Thus, there appears to be no definite point at which the young primate ceases to show some affinity for the mother. Furthermore, there is convincing evidence that the same motivations that produced the tie to the mother continue to operate in the weanling and may result in the formation of attachments to other individuals. This phenomenon has been observed in both monkeys and apes and it occurs in nature as well as in captivity.

Such an attachment may occasionally be inferred from a close follower-leader association. For example, an adult, silverbacked, male gorilla and a large infant left the main group and apparently remained together for nearly a month when the adult was found dead and the infant was captured (cited in Schaller, 1963). Often there is a definite suggestion that the older animal functions as a mother substitute. Carpenter (1934) observed a young howling monkey alternately following and being carried by an adult male which it nestled against during rest periods. Likewise, young baboons and macaques may have an adult "foster parent" of either sex that carries, grooms, and protects them and is sought in moments of distress (Bolwig, 1959; Haddow, 1952; Itani, 1959; Koford, 1963a). In captivity the preadolescent primate commonly forms an emotional tie which has many attributes of a filial attachment to a cagemate or to its human caretaker (Bolwig, 1959; Jacobsen, Jacobsen, and Yoshioka, 1932; Mason, in press; Watson, 1914).

These relationships reflect, at least in part, a transfer from previous experience. The most pertinent data come from studies of animals given no opportunity to form social attachments during infancy. For example, rhesus monkeys provided cloth surrogates for the first time when several months old eventually spent considerable time in contact with the object while in the living-cage, but derived no security from its presence in a strange situation (Harlow, 1960). Similarly, chimpanzees raised in social isolation until 21 months of age played together freely, but did not cling or show other evidence of filial-like attachment to peers, even after hundreds of hours of group living. Wild-born animals of the same age quickly form strong, mutual attachments (Mason, Davenport, and Menzel, in press). Early experience with the mother may also be reflected in the contrasting reactions to white rats of wild-born and socially deprived adolescent macaques (Mason and Green, 1962). Compared to deprived monkeys, wild-born animals living with white rats made more contacts with them and more frequently selected them when they were offered as incentives.

Inasmuch as the socially deprived monkeys lacked experience with peers as well as with the mother, whereas the wild-born animals had both types of experience, it cannot be concluded that the attachment to the mother alone accounted for the difference between groups. On the other hand, the responses of the wild-born monkeys typically consisted of simple forms of contact (clasping, holding, resting against) such as often occur between infant and mother. The importance of early attachments is further indicated by the differential reactions of African and surrogate-reared chimpanzees to social stimuli. Exposed to the stress of a novel environment, surrogate-reared chimpanzees cling to familiar, inanimate objects (e.g., rag mop or stuffed toy), but tend to avoid such contact with people. In comparable circumstances African-born animals ignore inanimate objects, but cling readily to other chimpanzees or to people (Mason, in press).

The range of acceptable mother substitutes apparently narrows as the animal grows older, and by early adolescence (i.e., about 2 and 6 years in rhesus monkey and chimpanzee, respectively) the mother-reared animal continues to cling to conspecifics, but generally refuses to do so with people, even after many months in captivity.

This evidence, while admittedly incomplete, warrants an attempt to characterize the parts played by infantile, contact-seeking responses and the attachment to the mother in subsequent social relations. Infantile social responses (especially clinging, according to present evidence) have a major role in the development of the attachment to the mother. These behaviors and the motivations associated with them become less prominent with advancing age, but there is no indication that they disappear entirely. On the contrary, under conditions of intense emotional arousal some responses (e.g., clinging) may occur in essentially infantile form in fully mature animals. More often, however, similar functions appear to be served in the adult by a variety of simple, contactual behaviors—grasping, huddling, pushing, leaning against, or draping an arm around a companion—which may be derived from infantile social responses. The experience with the mother probably has an important, selective effect on the type of objects toward which such behaviors are directed. In the natural habitat the growing primate is usually surrounded from infancy by individuals whose appearance and reactions to him are similar to those of the mother (see below), thus providing seemingly optimal conditions for the generalization or extension of filial attachments.

Although little is known of phyletic differences, sufficient data exist to suggest that the rate at which infantile responses and motivations recede varies in different species, both absolutely and relative to rate of physical growth. The great apes are characterized by slow growth rates compared to the monkeys, of course, but they also seem to show more marked retention of infantile characteristics into later stages of development. Intrageneric differences are also found. Thus, the stump-tail macaque, unlike the closely related rhesus monkey, remains docile and will cling to people into the fourth year of life (Kling and Orbach, 1963).

When such differences have been firmly established and are based on a broader sampling of species, fresh opportunities will be created for correlating the gregarious traits of childhood with later aspects of sociability and social organization.

C. Other Sources of Primate Sociability

1. Novelty and Social Activities

As dependence on the mother becomes less intense, new motivations and activities appear which draw the young primate into contact with other animals. The initial impetus is probably an attraction to mildly novel stimuli which are provided at first by the physical environment and later by other animals. Simple forms of exploration and play predominate in the beginning and are soon augmented by more specialized patterns of social interaction. These activities and the social relations they generate constitute additional sources of primate sociability.

Experimental studies have demonstrated that play, grooming, and being groomed have definite rewarding effects for young chimpanzees, and the same is doubtless true for other primates (Falk, 1958; Mason, Hollis & Sharpe, 1962). Under some conditions the effectiveness of a highly preferred social activity may equal or surpass that of food (Mason, Saxon, and Sharpe, 1963). It has also been shown, however, that the preference for different social activities varies with motivational factors, tentatively identified with changes in arousal level. Low or moderate levels of arousal predispose the young chimpanzee toward play, and playing apparently serves to increase arousal; high levels of arousal, on the other hand, are associated with avoidance of play and enhanced preference for clinging or being groomed, both of which appear to be arousal-reducing (Mason, in press).

This analysis helps to account for moment-to-moment variations in social activity and suggests that the social environment is a rich and structured source of reinforcers. Thus, apart from the more direct, adaptive consequences of such activities as sex-play, wrestling, and grooming in preparing the animal for later social adjustments, these behaviors probably serve to strengthen gregariousness and lead to the development of specific affinities between animals whose activity patterns are complementary (Nowlis, 1941). Presumably, some such process accounts for the formation of subgroups of like-sexed animals of similar age, a common occurrence among free-ranging primates (Altmann, 1962a; Carpenter, 1934; Chance, 1956; Nolte, 1955; Reynolds, 1963; Washburn and DeVore, 1961).

2. Sexual Attraction

Sexual attraction has been accorded a special place in discussions of primate sociability. However, in view of recent demonstrations of marked seasonal variation in the reproductive activities of macaques and the suggestion of similar differences among other Old World monkeys, the importance of sexual attraction should be reconsidered. It now appears that in these primates "primary" sexual activity, i.e., copulations resulting in ejaculations and pregnancy, "cannot be responsible for the maintenance of group cohesion throughout the year" (Lancaster and Lee, in press). Nevertheless, sexual behavior must certainly be included among the many potential sources of gregariousness.

However, the problem should not be tied too closely to adult sexuality. Sexual presentation, mounting, and thrusting are unequivocally present in all young primates and are particularly prominent in young baboons and macaques. Peripheral stimulation from the genitalia during sex play presumably is rewarding and contributes to development of basic sex skills which are lacking in the inexperienced animal (Mason, 1960b; see also Sheffield, Wulff & Backer, 1951).

Hormonal factors are important in mature animals, most evidently in female, who displays a definite period of estrus or enhanced sexual excitability as part of her menstrual cycle. In some forms (baboons, some macaques, chimpanzees) estrus is associated with a pronounced swelling in the pudendal region, which probably helps the male to detect the female's sexual condition. At this time there is strong mutual attraction between the sexes. Approach and sexual overtures may be made by male or female. There is frequently an increase in mutual grooming, and in some species (baboons, macaques, langurs, howling monkeys) the female may form a close, temporary alliance with a single male. The animals remain together, sometimes at a distance from the main group, and the female may be permitted certain liberties—such as feeding from the same source as the male —which she would not ordinarily be accorded. The female may consort successively with several males in the course of a single estrus period see, e.g., (Tokuda, 1962). Rotating mateships are not characteristic of all primates. In chimpanzees the receptive female may mate with several males in turn, whereas in gibbons, marmosets, and hamadryas baboons, copulation occurs principally with one partner (Carpenter, 1940; Goodall, in press; Kummer and Kurt, 1963; Stellar, 1960).

Perhaps the most important question concerning the effects of mating behavior on sociability is whether any persistent affinity arises between the mating pair as the result of satisfactory, sexual relations. If such an effect exists, it is probably not strong. However, reports that females seem consistently to prefer specific males suggest that abiding affinities may develop during sexual activities. A similar conclusion can be drawn from the observation that male and female may continue to associate closely after copulation has ceased (Altmann, 1962b; Carpenter, 1942; Imanishi, 1960; Jay, in press; Washburn and DeVore, 1961; Yerkes and Elder, 1936).

3. Attraction of Older to Younger Animals

Another important source of sociability is the attraction of older animals to the young. The strength of the mother's attraction to her offspring, characteristic of most mammals, has always been recognized. It is now clear that in primate societies a similar but less intense reaction often occurs in nonparturient females, and even in males. In chimpanzees and in both Old and New World monkeys, the presence of an infant evokes excitement and curiosity in many members of the group. Females seem especially attracted, and juveniles and adults may crowd around the mother seeking to touch or hold the infant.

Males vary considerably, both within and across species, in their responses to young. However, contrary to the earlier supposition that males are characteristically hostile and aggressive toward young animals, present evidence indicates that they are more often attentive and protective (Altmann, 1962a; Washburn and DeVore, 1961). Males have been observed to transport young for short distances among gorillas (Schaller, 1963), chimpanzees (Nissen, 1931), in various species of African arboreal monkeys (Booth, 1962), and in howling monkeys (Carpenter, 1934).

More elaborate forms of infant care by males have been observed infrequently, but do occur. The male marmoset characteristically carries the infants at all times except during nursing and cleaning, when they are transferred to the mother (Stellar, 1960). Male "adoptions" of weanling infants have been reported for baboons (Bolwig, 1959) and described in detail for the Japanese macaque (Itani, 1959). The motivation for this behavior is obscure. Itani (1959) found that male "adoptions" occurred principally in the season when new infants were arriving and that it was displayed by prime males high in the social hierarchy. A rating of the "personality" characteristics of these animals led to the conclusion that they were high in sociability, low in aggressiveness, and strongly oriented toward the central part of the group which includes the most dominant males and females.

III. Social Organization

A. SOCIAL STRUCTURE

Insofar as the various sources of sociability described above lead to the development of specific, interindividual preferences and create differential patterns of interaction among the various members of the group, they can also be regarded as sources of social structure. Of the various possible combinations of individuals, those most commonly described for primate societies consist of clusters of (1) adult males, (2) adult and juvenile females and young, and (3) juvenile males. Male-female associations comprise a fourth subgroup which is most conspicuous during breeding periods. Each subgroup is characterized by spatial proximity among its members and by more frequent intercourse within than between subgroups. The cumulative reinforcing effects of these social interchanges are presumably important factors in the formation and maintenance of subgroups.

On the other hand, present knowledge of social reinforcers is clearly insufficient to explain the substantial differences among species in the presence and distinctiveness of subgroupings. Clusters of adult or subadult males, for example, are unusual in hamadryas baboons, gibbons and (probably) marmosets. In the hamadryas baboon, the minimal social unit is a single, adult male and anywhere from one to nine females and their offspring. Subadult males may be loosely associated with such a group, but often live outside it (Kummer and Kurt, 1963). In gibbons and marmosets, the basic unit is an adult pair and their immature offspring (Carpenter, 1940; Stellar, 1960).

Species also differ in the consistency of the spatial arrangement of group members. In some forms, notably baboons and macaques, the location of individuals may follow a definite pattern. This is most evident in Japanese macaques in which animals are arranged within a series of concentric circles, the centermost containing the most dominant males and the dominant females and their infants, and the periphery consisting of subadult and low status adult males (Imanishi, 1960; Tokuda, 1962). In the majority of primates, however, the distribution of animals in space follows no definite pattern, or a pattern may be apparent only in special circumstances—during progressions, for example, or when the group is attacked. Species also vary in the fluidity or permeability of group boundaries. In chimpanzees, gorillas, and redtail monkeys, groups meet without conflict and may merge temporarily, whereas in rhesus monkeys, howlers, and gibbons, intergroup relations are often antagonistic (Southwick, 1962).

DeVore (1963) pointed out that social structure is generally more rigid in terrestrial primates than in arboreal forms. He noted the close correlation between ecological adaptation, morphology, and the behavior of the species. In the most thoroughly studied ground-living monkeys, the baboons and macaques, there is pronounced sexual dimorphisim associated with adaptation of the male for defense of the group. These monkeys tend toward larger and more compact groups and show more sex behavior, fighting, and dominance-related activities than do arboreal monkeys.

Life on the ground is more hazardous than life in the trees, and one can appreciate how the contrasting patterns of social organization of terrestrial and arboreal primates might contribute to species survival. However, as yet there is no satisfactory explanation of the psychological basis of these differences.

Maslow (1935, 1940) made the first and virtually the only explicit attempt to account for species differences in social organization. He made extensive use of success in competition for food in his investigations, and his theoretical statements understandably stressed dominance as a central dimension for comparative analysis. Maslow found that species differed markedly in qualitative expressions of dominance and he believed that these differences were correlated with other aspects of social behavior. The Old World monkeys, particularly the baboons and macaques, were characterized as vicious and brutal in their dominance interactions. In these forms sexual behavior was closely linked to status, with the masculine role assumed by the dominant animal, regardless of its sex (Maslow, 1936). Dominance was said to be less conspicuous in chimpanzees and New World monkeys, and in the last group, social interactions of any kind were relatively infrequent (Maslow, 1935, 1940).

B. DOMINANCE

1. Conditions Affecting Dominance Relations

Subsequent, experimental investigations of dominance have continued to use food-getting success as a measure of social rank. In the vast majority of these studies the rhesus monkey served as subject. The results indicate that in experienced animals dominance is established quickly, often in the absence of fighting, and once established is highly stable (Maroney, Warren, and Sinha, 1959; Miller and Murphy, 1956). Attempts to alter dominance status by manipulating food deprivation and food quality, and by administering tranquilizing drugs and sex hormones, were largely unsuccessful (Leary & Slye, 1959; Leary and Stynes, 1959; Mirsky, 1955; Warren and Maroney, 1958). Changes in dominance status were produced, however, by certain types of brain damage. The effects of experimental lesions in the amygdaloid complex, the hippocampus, and the cingulate gyrus were summarized by Mirsky (1960). Each lesion decreased fear reactions to humans, but only the amygdala lesion influenced dominance scores, and the effect was a reduction in dominance. Mirsky suggested that

. . . all these lesions have the effect of destroying or weakening previously learned connections between complex social stimuli and socio-emotional responses. The loss or forgetting of learned responses to the human being is manifested in the following way: the operated animal responds directly and simply to the offer of food by accepting it readily. This would account for the apparent increase in fearlessness in the individual-cage situation. The amygdala lesion produces more of such impairment or "forgetting" than do the other limbic lesions, and this is reflected in the group-cage situation. The animal's cage mates, which are unimpaired, seem to sense its uncertainty and hesitation and, according to their own pattern of social responses (their own aggressiveness), may attack and then dominate a previously dominant animal.

This interpretation was tested by providing three, dominant, amygdalectomized monkeys with postoperative success experience with small animals. Instead of the characteristic loss in dominance when returned to its original group, each operate retained its former position or gained in rank. Other observations are consistent with the suggestion that social learning plays a critical part in the dominance relations. Monkeys lacking social experience show unstable dominance with frequent reversals in rank (Mason, 1961); children of high status mothers are more likely to be dominant than the children of low status mothers (Imanishi, 1960; Koford, 1963b); and a low status animal presented as a conditioned stimulus for shock to a dominant partner gains in social rank (Miller, Murphy, and Mirsky, 1955).

As the result of experimental investigations, a substantial amount of information has been collected on the variables influencing dominance in rhesus monkeys. Scant attention has been given, however, to the tasks of describing the effects of dominance on social organization and of accounting for species differences in the expression of dominance.

2. Dominance and Social Relationships

With regard to the effects of dominance on social organization, field studies suggest that the laboratory definition of dominance as "priority of access" is too narrow and fails to encompass other important social characteristics associated with high status. It is for this reason, perhaps, that some field workers refer to highly dominant males as leaders (Imanishi, 1960; Goodall, in press; Jay, in press; Koford, 1963a; Schaller, 1963). Leadership in the sense of initiating progressions and determining the line of march may, in fact, be one of the attributes of such an individual. Often, however, he has other important functions. Dominant males quell intra-group fights; they are the primary source of protection for females and young; they are attractive to all members of the group and may be sought by the fully estrus females; and they may significantly influence the size of the group's range. Unless the concept of dominance is expanded and refined to take these attributes into account, theory and research in this area are certain to be limited and distorted (Schneirla, 1952).

3. Emotion Arousal and Dominance

One of the most difficult problems is to reconcile the finding that dominance is based on fear-aggression with the observation that the dominant animal is often sought or followed by the other members of the group. Chance's (1955) hypothesized "attraction toward the aggressor" would account for this paradoxical situation. The difficulty, however, is that the most common reaction to direct aggression is flight. Nevertheless, it may be possible to explain the attraction to the dominant animal by placing Chance's hypothesis within a somewhat broader conceptual framework. Investigations with inanimate objects have shown that whether a primate ignores, approaches, or avoids a given stimulus depends on its physical properties (size, complexity, movement characteristics) and on the amount of previous exposure to the stimulus or to similar objects (Butler, 1958; Menzel, in press; Welker, 1961). Objects which produce avoidance in the beginning may, after a series of exposures, elicit strong approach. It is important to note that the moderately novel stimulus is generally more attractive than the familiar one. Thus, on a continuum of emotional arousal there appears to be an intermediate range between extreme "fear" and "disinterest" when attraction is maximal (Hebb, 1955).

Applying this line of reasoning to social stimuli, one would expect that the animal that generates mild fear for whatever reason—because of its size or its general comportment (e.g., chest thumping, branch shaking, loud vocalizations, rushing, chasing, all of which are characteristic of dominant males in various species)—will become the object of ambivalent reactions. According to this view, a dominant animal that is frequently and openly aggressive will be less attractive than one that merely threatens aggression. It is true that serious, full-blown attacks by dominant animals appear to be infrequent, whereas threats and aggressive "displays" are a fairly common occurrence. Chance's (1955) observation that attraction to an aggressor appeared after a delay is consistent with the present hypothesis, since approach would not be expected until the initially high level of emotional arousal had dissipated somewhat.

The present thesis also explains the attraction to a dominant animal in the absence of overt aggression, as apparently occurs in the young male langur. According to Jay (in press):

> The male infant has no contact with adult males until he is approximately ten months old. At this time the infant first approaches the adult in a highly specialized manner. The infant runs, squealing tensely, to the moving adult and veers away just before it touches him. Gradually the infant appears to gain confidence and touches the male's hindquarters. Within a week after this the infant approaches and mounts by pulling himself up over the adult's hindquarters. . . . In a few weeks another element is added and the infant runs around to face and embrace the adult.

Although this is a highly specialized pattern seen only in the young male langur, the basic sequence is remarkably similar to that described by Menzel (in press) for the reaction of rhesus monkeys and chimpanzees to novel inanimate objects.

Species differences in the intensity of dominance behavior are clearly indicated by field reports. The picture they provide is generally consistent with Maslow's original characterization, except that in no species is severe fighting frequent or widespread.

In considering the origin of these species differences, dominance should probably not be regarded as a unitary motive or trait, but rather as a reflection of more general factors. It is difficult to characterize such factors on the basis of present evidence. However, the finding that fearfulness, combativeness, and sexual behavior are all relatively prominent in species showing sharply defined dominance gradients suggests that dominance is associated with a tendency toward more extreme overt reactions to environmental stimuli, as has been shown for rhesus monkeys in comparison with gibbons (Bernstein, Schusterman, and Sharpe, 1963).

Psychology has thoroughly explored the possibility of human personality types and the majority of psychologists have apparently abandoned any serious hope that a workable scheme will be discovered. Nevertheless, the heuristic value of a typological approach is considerable, particularly in the early stages of research. In view of the rapid accumulation of data on the contrasting social organizations of different primates, the next few years will almost certainly see a revival of interest in phyletically oriented psychological typologies, similar to that first attempted by the Yerkeses (1929) for the anthropoid apes.

C. COMMUNICATION

No one doubts that communication plays an essential part in coordinating and controlling the activities of organized primate groups. In fact it has been suggested that a society be defined as ". . . an aggregation of socially intercommunicating individuals that are bounded by frontiers of far less frequent communication" (Altmann, 1962a).

Nevertheless, in spite of the recent upsurge of interest in primate communication, we are still far from a detailed understanding of the problem. Any discriminable individual act can, in principle, serve a communicative function. In practice, however, attention has centered on those responses which characteristically occur in a social context and seem likely to produce some effect on other individuals.

1. Normative Studies

The two main approaches to primate social behavior—the normative and the experimental—are evident in the study of communication, although the boundaries between these approaches have already become blurred. The normative study of primate communication has two primary objectives. Each of these will be considered in turn.

The first objective is to describe the elements of communication. Logically, this presupposes information about the responses that possess or lack communicative value, but the patterns are often selected for study on the basis of presumed rather than demonstrated functions. The task of description is usually accomplished by verbal characterizations, supplemented by drawings, motion pictures, or sound spectrographs. Descriptive accounts of at least a few of the probable elements of communication have been presented for lemurs, several varieties of monkeys, and the anthropoid apes. These accounts indicate that the nonhuman primates possess a potential "vocabulary" of considerable size (Marler, in press).

The second objective of normative studies is to determine the communicative function that such responses serve. In many cases this information is suggested by the use of such terms as "warning calls," "threat displays," or "pacificatory gestures." While these interpretations assume a reliable interindividual correlation between the initial response or signal and the reaction it evokes, the precise nature of this relationship can seldom be inferred from the existing data. Only a few investigators have attempted to treat natural forms of communication in quantitative terms (Altmann, 1962b). One difficulty is the enormous investment in time required to secure sufficient data to establish firmly the communicative value of a specific response. Altmann's data, probably the most complete available, were derived from over 18 months' intensive study of a single island population of rhesus monkeys under unusually favorable observational conditions (Altmann, 1962b).

There is another difficulty for the naturalistic approach. The behavior singled out by the investigator as the signal is often embedded in a complex matrix in which the general features of the situation, and the history of both parties in the communicative act—as well as their motivational states —may be influential variables. Furthermore, primate signals almost always occur in clusters: "In most situations it is not a single signal that passes from one animal to another, but a whole complex of them, visual, auditory, tactile, and sometimes olfactory. There can be little doubt that the structure of individual signals is very much affected by this incorporation in a whole matrix of other signals" (Marler, in press).

Thus, while the need for additional naturalistic studies is great, it is clear that further progress also requires the simplification of real life situations that is best accomplished in a laboratory setting.

2. Experimental Studies

Experimental studies of communication have thus far been directed toward two questions: The first concerns the determinants of signaling behavior. As Andrew (1962) remarked ". . . calls are not given by

Primates in order, for example, to warn fellows of impending danger, in a way a man might cry 'Look out.' " Although there is a distinct possibility that some responses may be used instrumentally as the result of social learning, the basic form of most signals is almost certainly unlearned. However, the situations in which they occur, their frequency of occurrence, and the details of patterning are probably much affected by experience. The responses that appear most prominently in communication often occur in the contexts of aggression, sexual behavior, and the relations between mother and young. Often they have strong emotional overtones. There have been several recent investigations of situational or stimulus determinants of these behaviors.

Inanimate objects have long been known to be effective elicitors of affective-social responses. It was shown with young laboratory-reared rhesus monkeys that the complexity and/or animal likeness of such inanimate objects is an important dimension whose effectiveness varies with age (Bernstein and Mason, 1962). Other experiments investigated the effects of social isolation and the size, proximity, intensity, familiarity, and direction of movement of stimuli. Wherever specific affective-social responses were recorded, differential effects were usually obtained.

It is clear, therefore, that the factors involved in the evocation of affective-social responses are not limited to social stimuli, nor do the traditional drives (e.g., aggression, sex) offer much help in explaining these phenomena. Preliminary efforts to conceptualize casual factors in the elicitation of affective-social responses found it necessary to assume a central, intensive dimension, variously characterized as level of arousal (Mason, in press), effective stimulus intensity (Menzel, in press), or degree of stimulus contrast (Andrew, 1962).

A second question considered in experimental investigations of communicative behavior concerns the development and maintenance of signalling behavior. Many traditional problems of primate social psychology—cooperation, food-sharing social facilitation, imitation, observational learning—were indirectly concerned with interindividual transmission of information. However, the major purpose of most experiments was to demonstrate that nonhuman primates are capable of successful performance on tasks believed to be important in the social affairs of man, and relatively little attention was given to specifying the factors that contribute to such performance. These studies served a useful function by illustrating the scope and importance of communication in primate social relations, but they provide little insight into the communicative process itself. Although recent communication experiments are also demonstrational in character, they provide methods which are suitable for systematic investigations.

Psychologists readily see communication in terms of the constructs and procedures of contemporary learning experiments. This learning perspective is plainly evident in two recent series of experiments on primate communication. One (Mason and Hollis, 1962) employed a test situation closely analogous to the Wisconsin General Test Apparatus, except that a social stimulus was substituted for the conventional stimulus object. Two monkeys faced each other, with four pairs of food carts mounted on a table between them. Each pair of carts was connected by an expandable rack so that movement of one cart simultaneously extended the other in the opposite direction. One monkey, the operator, had access to the four handles which controlled the carts, but the carts were shielded so that he could not see the location of the food. His partner was able to see the food but could obtain the reward only if the operator selected the appropriate handle. Thus, the rewards of neither animal could exceed chance unless the partner served as a discriminative stimulus to the operator indicating the location of food.

Young laboratory-reared rhesus monkeys tested in this situation eventually achieved a high level of performance, but the effect of training was specific to the role in which the animal was originally trained. When operator-informant roles were reversed, no evidence was found of transfer to the complementary role. Transfer of training was also tested in trained operator monkeys by introducing new monkey informants and by placing inanimate stimuli behind the rewarded food carts before each trial. There was clear evidence of positive transfer to each of these conditions, but performance with monkey informants was markedly superior to that with inanimate stimuli. It was also shown that operator-monkeys were capable of discriminating between two informants, only one of which could be "correct" on any trial, and that they would learn to defer a well-trained response to the food carts until they had first performed a lever response which revealed the informant.

This testing situation provides an unequivocal measure of successful performance and lends itself to analytic study of the factors influencing such performance. Its major limitations are its remoteness from natural forms of communication (monkeys do not ordinarily communicate face-to-face about the location of food) and the relatively meager data it has thus far provided on how the information is transmitted. Both of these limitations were largely overcome in a second series of experiments by Miller and his associates.

The general approach may be illustrated in an experiment by Mirsky, Miller, Murphy (1958). Monkeys were trained to perform an avoidance response upon presentation of a stimulus monkey, and this response was then extinguished. Subsequently, when the subjects saw the stimulus animal receiving shock, the showed a dramatic recovery of the extinguished, conditioned response. This experiment showed that one monkey's responses to a painful stimulus conveyed information to another monkey, which caused it to recover an extinguished response. However, it did not obviate the possibility that the noise and commotion attendant upon shock to the stimulus animal provided an aversive condition which was not specifically social.

Subsequent experiments by Miller and co-workers (1959a,b), again using a conditioning technique, permitted a more precise determination of the effective elements in the communication of affect. Monkeys were conditioned to perform an avoidance response upon presentation of a life-sized, colored slide of a nonfearful monkey, and the response was then extinguished. When the monkeys were later shown slides of the same stimulus animal in fear or pain postures, the avoidance response was reinstated, in spite of the fact that the subject received no painful stimuli. Moreover, photographs of the stimulus animal showing fear were more effective than pictures of the same animal in nonfearful poses. This is remarkable when it is recalled that the original conditioned stimulus was a picture of a nonfearful monkey. Similar results were obtained when the test stimulus consisted of only the facial expressions of calm and fearful monkeys.

Recently a new procedure for the investigation of communication of affect was introduced (Miller, Banks, and Ogawa, 1962). Monkeys were conditioned to avoid shock by pressing a bar after presentation of a light. Following acquisition of the avoidance response, two animals were placed facing each other and the bar was removed from one animal and the light from the other. Thus, to avoid the shock the animals had to communicate in some fashion. Successful performance was obtained but the mode of communication could not be determined. A refinement of this technique was recently reported, however, using a closed-circuit television system which limits expressive behaviors to one modality (Miller, Banks, and Ogawa, 1963). The results indicated that televised images of facial expression are a sufficient basis for the communication of affect. Furthermore, the fact that the monkeys performed at a high level from the beginning of the social tests suggested that the animals were responding to social cues acquired at some earlier period in their development.

There is little if any direct evidence that early social experience is important in the acquisition of communicative skills. Some suggestive indications of the role played by early experience are provided, however, by the deficiencies and aberrations observed in the social relations of laboratory-reared rhesus monkeys (Mason, 1960a). Along the same lines, it should also be noted that when these monkeys were housed and tested in pairs, they performed more efficiently on tests of communication than did animals maintained individually except during testing (Mason and Hollis, 1962).

Field studies provide many illustrations of the varied role of communication in the daily activities of an organized group. Progressions, the recognition and response to predators, the stability of relations within the group, and even the acquisition of food habits (Kawamura, 1959) are influenced by the transmission of information among the members of the troops. Doubtless many of these phenomena are based on forms of learning which can be accommodated by the traditional paradigms. Certainly group living provides many opportunities for such learning. On the other hand, there is always a possibility that under natural conditions the acquisition of cue functions may be greatly facilitated by innate predispositions. Certain stimulus configurations—an abrupt increase in size (Schiff, Caviness and Gibson, 1962), staring and perhaps certain gestures, facial expressions, and sounds (Mowbray and Cadell, 1962)—may be associated with primitive approach-withdrawal tendencies which are strengthened and refined by social experience.

IV. Relevance to Human Social Behavior

Everybody knows that man belongs in the order primates, together with apes, monkeys, and a variety of more obscure creatures, including the lemurs and tarsiers. Nevertheless, the differences between man's behavior and that of other primates are impressive, and there is good reason to ask how studies of monkeys and apes might contribute to human social psychology.

An attempt to answer this question requires that the primates be considered in evolutionary perspective. The record of paleontology, as well as systematic comparisons of the structural and functional characteristics of living primates, suggests that the living members of this order may be arranged in a linear series which *approximates* the actual sequence of primate evolution (Clark, 1959).

If this is true, it means that data from the existing primates can be used to establish probable trends or dimensions of systematic variation in primate evolution. For such an enterprise to succeed, however, information must be collected on the widest possible range of species, for there is little question that the behavior of the living primates includes specializations whose nature and number can be properly assessed only within a broad, comparative framework. As yet this framework is incomplete, but it is growing rapidly, and even now a few broad trends can be discerned.

One of the most firmly established of these trends holds special promise for the problem of primate social behavior. As is well known, compared to apes, monkeys are relatively mature at birth and grow rapidly, while the apes are similarly precocious compared to man. Slower growth rates increase the duration of social dependence and bring about changes in the relation between mother-infant, particularly in the opportunities for social learning. Of greater significance is the possibility that associated with the trend toward increasing prolongation of growth rates, there is a tendency for juvenile traits to be retained into later stages of development. Thus, social dependence, docility, playfulness, a strong impulse toward investigatory activities, lack of aggression, and the variable and incomplete character of many instinctive patterns are prominent traits in all young primates. By adolescence they seem to have largely disappeared in the normally socialized macaque, while they continue to be prominent in the behavior of the adolescent chimpanzee.

In man, as in all primates, these traits seem to recede with advancing age, but they are retained longer, well into reproductive maturity. Consider, for example, the nature and amount of rough-and-tumble play that occurs among human parents and children. Although such activities also occur between chimpanzee parent and child, they are relatively limited in variety and frequency. In the majority of monkeys, parental play is rare, if not altogether absent.

Thus it is possible that many of man's distinctive psychological traits arise from a common source, namely the tendency to retain infantile or juvenile characters into adulthood. This is conjecture, of course, and the evolutionary trends that culminated in man cannot yet be described with confidence. The possibility that behavioral studies of the nonhuman primates may contribute to the solution of this evolutionary question adds an exciting dimension to primate research.

V. Conclusions

1. The living primates have evolved as gregarious animals and much of their behavior is specifically adapted to life in groups.

2. Many factors can be discerned which might contribute to gregariousness. Some of these have been the subject of experimental investigations. The sources of the infant's tie to the mother have been the most thoroughly studied, and the data are consistent with the hypothesis that arousal reduction is an important reinforcing mechanism in the formation of filial attachment.

3. There are also indications that the affinity for the mother persists into early adolescence and probably beyond. Moreover, it seems that the factors that produced this bond are functioning during the post-weaning period, providing a basis for the formation of new attachments. Describing the development of infantile social responses, particularly the effects of

early attachment on later social relations, is a major task for the future. Contact-seeking appears to be a primitive reaction to stress in primates of all ages. It is a reasonable hypothesis that this tendency has its roots in the social responses of infancy.

4. Other sources of sociability become manifest during later periods of development. There is good evidence that social play, grooming, sexual behavior, and the activities centering around the care of the young are highly rewarding for many members of the group, although the relative preference for these activities varies with age, sex, and short-term motivational changes. Presumably, in natural groups, animals prefer companions whose activity patterns are congruent with their own, thus contributing to the formation of the clusters or subgroups that are a conspicuous feature of many primate societies.

5. These subgroups are an important facet of social organization. However, it seems unlikely that the variations in interindividual preference involved in the formation of subgroups can account for interspecies differences in social organization.

6. In general, social organization appears to be more rigid in the terrestrial baboons and macaques than among primates favoring an arboreal habitat. As compared to arboreal monkeys and to the forest-dwelling great apes, the baboons and macaques are distinguished by relatively impermeable group boundaries, by the prominence of sexual behavior and aggression, and by the intimate association of these activities with the expression of dominance. DeVore (1963) suggested that these traits, together with certain morphological characteristics, are adaptations for life on the open ground where predation poses a serious threat.

7. Analysis of the behavior of individual animals should help to clarify the problem of interspecies differences in social organization. For example, there are data suggesting that dominance is most pronounced in those groups showing a general tendency toward more direct or extreme overt reactions to environmental stimuli. As yet, however, there are no systematic studies relating species differences in individual responsiveness to characteristics of social organization.

8. It is widely recognized that communication is intimately involved in the coordination and control of activities within organized groups. In the past five years there was a substantial increase in descriptive accounts of the "expressive" behaviors (vocalizations, postures, facial expressions) which presumably serve as signals in primate communication. The factors eliciting these responses and the reactions they evoke in other animals were less thoroughly studied. There is a suggestion that the form of these responses and their relation to some motivational state are less sensitive to individual experience than their effectiveness as social signals. This is not

to say, of course, that the signal is unlearned and the response to it is acquired, for in either case there is doubtless a complex interaction between innate predispositions and experience.

9. Students of primate behavior note a discrepancy between intellectual achievement as revealed by laboratory investigation and the apparent requirements of the natural environment. Experiments on primate communication established the relevance and importance of discrimination-learning ability to social interaction. Possibly a major selective pressure during the evolution of primate discrimination-learning capabilities has been the need to adjust to a complex social milieu which places a premium on the ability to identify individual status characteristics and to respond appropriately to changes in companions of mood, motivation or intent.

10. The living primates approximate a linear evolutionary sequence, raising the possibility that comparative study of the living primates will contribute to an understanding of the evolutionary trends that culminated in man.

ACKNOWLEDGMENTS

The first draft of this chapter was written at the Yerkes Laboratories of Primate Biology. Portions of the section on communication appeared in the *Annual Review of Psychology*. Support was provided by a Public Health Service Special Fellowship and by Research Grant MH-5636 from the National Institute of Mental Health.

REFERENCES

Allesch, G. J. von (1921). *Sitzber. Preuss. Akad. Wiss. Berlin* pp. 672–685.
Altmann, S. A. (1962a). *In* "The Roots of Behavior" (E. L. Bliss, ed.) pp. 277–285, Harper (Hoeber), New York.
Altmann, S. A. (1962b). *Ann. N.Y. Acad. Sci.* **102,** 338–435.
Andrew, R. J. (1962). *Ann. N.Y. Acad. Sci.* **102,** 296–315.
Berkson, G., Mason, W. A., and Saxon, S. V. (1963). *J. Comp. Physiol. Psychol.* **56,** 786–792.
Bernstein, I. S., Schusterman, R. J., and Sharpe, L. G. (1963). *J. Comp. Physiol. Psychol.* **56,** 914–916.
Bernstein, S., and Mason, W. A. (1962). *J. Genet. Psychol.* **101,** 279–298.
Bolwig, N. (1959). *Behaviour* **14,** 136–163.
Booth, C. (1962). *Ann. N.Y. Acad. Sci.* **102,** 477–487.
Bridger, W. H. (1962). *Recent Advan. Biol. Psychiat.* **4,** 95–107.
Butler, R. A. (1958). *J. Indiv. Psychol.* **14,** 111–120.
Carpenter, C. R. (1934). *Comp. Psychol. Monogr.* **10,** 1–168.
Carpenter, C. R. (1940). *Comp. Psychol. Monogr.* **16,** 1–212.
Carpenter, C. R. (1942). *Biol. Symp.* **8,** 177–204.
Chance, M. R. A. (1955). *Man* **176,** 1–4.
Chance, M. R. A. (1956). *Brit. J. Anim. Behav.* **4,** 1–13.
Chance, M. R. A. (1961). *In* "Social Life of Early Man" (S. L. Washburn, ed.), Viking Fund publication in *Anthropology, No.* **31.**
Clark, W. E. L. (1959). "The Antecedents of Man." Edinburgh Uni. Edinburgh.

Collias, N., and Southwick, C. (1952). *Proc. Am. Phil. Soc.* **96,** 143–156.
DeVore, I. (1963). *In* "Classification and Human Evolution" (S. L. Washburn, ed.), Viking Fund publication in *Anthropology No.* **37.**
Falk, J. L. (1958). *J. Exptl. Anal. Behav.* **1,** 83–85.
Foley, J. P., Jr. (1934). *J. Genet. Psychol.* **45,** 39–105.
Foley, J. P., Jr. (1935). *J. Genet. Psychol.* **47,** 73–97.
Goodall, J. (in press). *In* "Primate Behavior: Field Studies of Monkeys and Apes" (I. DeVore, ed).
Haddow, A. J. (1952). *Proc. Zool. Soc. London* **122,** 297–394.
Hamilton, G. V. (1914). *J. Anim. Behav.* **4,** 295–318.
Hansen, E W. (1962). The Development of Maternal and Infant Behavior in the Rhesus Monkey. Unpublished dissertation, Univ. of Wisconsin, Madison, Wisconsin.
Harlow, H. F. (1960). *Am. J. Orthopsychiat.* **30,** 676–684.
Harlow, H. F., and Zimmermann, R. R. (1958). *Proc. Am. Phil. Soc.* **5,** 501–509.
Hebb, D. O. (1955). *Psychol Rev.* **62,** 243–254.
Imanishi, K. (1960). *Current Anthropol.* **1,** 393–407.
Itani, J. (1959). *Primates* **2,** 61–93.
Jacobsen, C. F., Jacobsen, M. M., and Yoshioka, J. G. (1932). *Comp. Psychol. Monogr.* **9,** 1–94.
Jay, P. C. (1962). *Ann. N.Y. Acad. Sci.* **102,** 181–514.
Jay, P. C. (in press). *In* "Primate Behavior: Field Studies of Monkeys and Apes" (I. DeVore, ed.).
Jensen, G. D., and Tolman, C. W. (1962). *J. Comp. Physiol. Psychol.* **55,** 131–136.
Kawamura, S. (1959). *Primates* **2,** 43–60.
Kling, A., and Orbach, J. (1963). *Science* **139,** 45–46.
Koford, C. B. (1963a): *In* "Primate Social Behavior" C. H. Southwick, ed.) pp. 136–152. Van Nostrand, Princeton, New Jersey.
Koford, C. B. (1963b). *Science* **141,** 356–357.
Kummer, R. H., and Kurt, H. (1963). *Folia Primat.* **1,** 4–19.
Lancaster, J. B., and Lee, R. B. (in press). *In* "Primate Behavior: Field Studies of Monkeys and Apes" (I. DeVore, ed.)
Lashley, K. S., and Watson, J. B. (1913). *J. Anim. Behav.* **3,** 114–139.
Leary, R. W., and Slye, D. (1959). *J. Psychol.* **48,** 227–235.
Leary, R. W., and Stynes, A. J. (1959). *Arch. Gen. Psychiat.* **1,** 499–505.
McCulloch, T. L. (1939). *J. Psychol.* **7,** 305–316.
Marler, P. (in press). *In* "Primate Behavior: Field Studies of Monkeys and Apes" (I. DeVore, ed.).
Maroney, R. J., Warren, J. M., and Sinha, M. M. (1959). *J. Social Psychol.* **50,** 285–293.
Maslow, A. H. (1935). *J. Indiv. Psychol.* **1,** 47–59.
Maslow, A. H. (1936). *J. Genet. Psychol.* **48,** 310–338.
Maslow, A. H. (1940). *J. Social Psychol.* **11,** 313–324.
Mason, W. A. (1960a). *J. Comp. Physiol. Psychol.* **53,** 582–589.
Mason, W. A. (1960b). *J. Abnorm. Soc. Psychol.* **60,** 100–104.
Mason, W. A. (1961). *J. Comp. Physiol. Psychol.* **54,** 694–699.
Mason, W. A. (1963). *Percept. Motor Skills* **16,** 263–270.
Mason, W. A. (in press). *In* "Behavior of Nonhuman Primates" (A. M. Schrier and H. F. Harlow, eds.). Academic Press, New York.
Mason, W. A., and Berkson, G. (1962). *Science* **137,** 127–128.

Mason, W. A., Davenport, R. K., Jr., and Menzel, E. W., Jr. (in press). *In* "Early Experience and Behavior" (G. Newton, ed.). Thomas, Springfield, Illinois.

Mason, W. A., and Green, P. H. (1962). *J. Comp. Physiol. Psychol.* **55,** 363–368.

Mason, W. A., and Hollis, J. H. (1962). *Anim. Behav.* **10,** 211–221.

Mason, W. A., Hollis, J. H., and Sharpe, L. G. (1962). *J Comp. Physiol. Psychol.* **55,** 1105–1110.

Mason, W. A., Saxon, S. V., and Sharpe, L. G. (1963). *Psychol. Record* **13,** 341–345.

Menzel, E. W., Jr. (in press). *Psychol. Forschung.*

Miller, R. E., Banks, J. H., and Ogawa, N. (1962). *J. Abnorm. Soc. Psychol.* **64,** 343–348.

Miller, R. E., Banks, J. H., and Ogawa, N. (1963). *J. Abnorm. Soc. Psychol.* **67,** 24–30.

Miller, R. E., and Murphy, J. V. (1956). *J. Social Psychol.* **44,** 249–255.

Miller, R. E., Murphy, J. V., and Mirsky, I. A. (1955). *J. Comp. Physiol. Psychol.* **48,** 392–396.

Miller, R. E., Murphy, J. V., and Mirsky, I. A. (1959a). *J. Clin. Psychol.* **15,** 155–158.

Miller, R. E., Murphy, J. V., and Mirsky, I. A. (1959b). *Arch. Gen. Psychiat.* **1,** 480–488.

Mirsky, A. F. (1955). *J. Comp. Physiol. Psychol.* **48,** 327–335.

Mirsky, A. F. (1960). *Ann. N.Y. Acad. Sci.* **85,** 785–794.

Mirsky, I. A., Miller, R. E., and Murphy, J. V. (1958). *J. Am. Psychoanal. Assoc.* **6,** 433–441.

Mowbray, J. B., and Cadell, T. E. (1962). *J. Comp. Physiol. Psychol.* **55,** 350–357.

Nissen, H. W. (1931). *Comp. Psychol. Monogr.* **8,** 1–122.

Nolte, A. (1955). *Z. Tierpsychol.* **12,** 77–87.

Nowlis, V. (1941). *Comp. Psychol. Monogr.* **17,** 1–57.

Reynolds, V. (1963). *Folia Primat.* **1,** 95–102.

Rosenblum, L. A. (1961). The Development of Social Behavior in the Rhesus Monkey. Unpublished Ph.D. dissertation, Univ. Wisconsin, Madison, Wisconsin.

Rosenblum, L. A., and Harlow, H. F. (1963). *Psychol. Rept.* **12,** 83–85.

Sahlins, M. D. (1959). *Human Biol.* **31,** 54–73.

Schaller, G. B. (1963). "The Mountain Gorilla: Ecology and Behavior." Univ. Chicago, Chicago, Illinois.

Schiff, W., Caviness, J. A., and Gibson, J. J. (1962). *Science* **136,** 982–983.

Schneirla, T. C. (1952). *Psychol. Bull.* **49,** 559–597.

Seay, B., Hansen, E. W., and Harlow, H. F. (1962). *J. Child. Psychol. Psychiat.* **3,** 123–132.

Sheffield, F. D., Wulff, J. J., and Backer, R. (1951). *J. Comp. Physiol. Psychol.* **44,** 3–8.

Southwick, C. H. (1962). *Ann. N.Y. Acad. Sci.* **102,** 436–453.

Southwick, C. H., Beg, M. A., and Siddiqi, M. R. (in press). *In* "Primate Behavior: Field Studies of Monkeys and Apes" (I. DeVore, ed.).

Stellar, E. (1960). *J. Comp. Physiol. Psychol.* **53,** 1–10.

Tinklepaugh, O. L., and Hartman, C. G. (1932). *J. Genet. Psychol.* **40,** 257–286.

Tokuda, K. (1962). *Primates* **3,** 1–40.

Wallace, A. R. (1869). "The Malay Archipelago." Macmillan, London. (Reprinted, Dover, New York, 1962.)

Warren, J. M., and Maroney, R. J. (1958). *J. Social Psychol.* **48,** 223–233.

Washburn, S. L., and DeVore, I. (1961). *Sci. Am.* **204,** 62–71.

Watson, J. B. (1914). "Behavior, an Introduction to Comparative Psychology." Holt, New York.

Welker, W. I. (1961). *In* "Functions of Varied Experience" (D. W. Fiske and S. R. Maddi, eds.). Dorsey, Illinois.

Yerkes, R. M., and Elder, J. H. (1936). *Comp. Psychol. Monogr.* **13**, 1–39.

Yerkes, R. M., and Yerkes, A. W. (1929). "The Great Apes." Yale, New Haven, Connecticut.

Zuckerman, S. (1932). "The Social Life of Monkeys and Apes." Kegan, Paul, London.

AUTHOR INDEX

Numbers in italics indicate the pages on which the complete references are listed.

A

Abelson, R. P., 29, *41, 46,* 196, 198, *227, 229,* 265, *274*
Ahmed, M., 24, *48*
Akuto, H., 39, *46*
Allesch, G. J. von, 283, *302*
Allport, F., 200, *227*
Allport, G. W., 5, 14, 23, 33, *41, 43,* 233, *272*
Altmann, S. A., 278, 283, 284, 287, 288, 289, 294, 295, *302*
Ambler, E., 71, *79*
Anastasi, A., 3, *41*
Anderson, G. L., *41*
Anderson, H. H., *41*
Anderson, L. R., 170, 186, *188,* 212, 213, *227*
Anderson, N. H., 194, *227*
Andrew, R. J., 295, 296, *302*
Ansari, A., 31, *42*
Archer, W. K., 28, 39, *46*
Argyle, M., 122, 143, *147,* 151, 187, *188*
Arkoff, A., 88, 93, 97, *110*
Arrowood, A. J., 96, 97, *109*
Asch, S. E., 265, *272*
Atkins, J., 9, *48*
Avigdor-Coryell, R., 25, *42*
Ax, A. F., 70, *79*

B

Backer, R., 288, *304*
Baer, D. M., 245, 249, 254, 257, *272, 274*
Bagby, J. W., 13, *42*
Baldwin, A. L., 247, *274, 275*
Bales, R. F., 142, *146*
Bandura, A., 232, 234, 236, 240, 241, 242, 243, 255, 259, 260, 265, 271, *272*

Banks, J. H., 298, *304*
Banton, M., 30, *42*
Baron, R., 41, *42*
Barrett, D., 117, 118, *146*
Bartlett, F. C., 6, 13, 14, *42*
Bass, A. R., 171, 186, *188, 190*
Bass, B. M., 150, 152, *188*
Bastide, R., 7, *42*
Bavelas, A., 112, 114, 117, 118, *146*
Bayley, N., 257, 258, *275*
Becker, H. S., 77, *79*
Beg, M. A., 284, *304*
Beller, E. K., 240, 242, 254, *272, 273*
Bennett, E. B., 194, 197, *227*
Bennis, W. G., 121, 131, 132, *146*
Berger, S. M., 247, *275*
Berghe, P. L. van den, 7, 31, *42*
Bergius, R., 10, *47*
Berkowitz, L., 139, 141, *146,* 153, 185, *188,* 198, *227*
Berkson, G., 282, 283, *302, 303*
Berlyne, D. E., 234, 252, 268, 270, *273*
Bernstein, I. S., 294, *302*
Bernstein, S., 296, *302*
Bexton, W. H., 250, 251, *273, 275*
Biddle, W. W., 200, *227*
Bieri, J., 154, *188*
Biesheuvel, S., 32, *42*
Bindra, D., 235, 236, 252, *273*
Bjerstedt, A., 3, *42*
Blaisdell, F. J., *188*
Bobren, H., 198, *229*
Bock, R. D., 34, *44*
Bogardus, E. S., 31, *42*
Bolwig, N., 285, 289, *302*
Bond, J. R., 99, 100, *109*
Bonte, M., 14, *42*
Booth, C., 289, *302*
Borgatta, E. F., 83, 85, *109*
Borgatta, M. L., 82, 83, 85, *109*
Bowen, N. V., 269, 270, *276*

SUBJECT INDEX

A

Acquired drive, 231–234, 271
Action quantization, 113, 118
Activation, *see* Arousal
Affiliation (also Gregariousness, Sociability), 260–264, 279, 280, 284, 287–289, 292, 293, 300, 301
Aggression, as response, 198, 233–236, 240–242, 248, 255, 266, 267, 280, 289, 292, 293, 296, 300, 301
as drive, 232, 233, 240
Altruism, 100, 101, 108
Anticipation, *see* Expectation
Anxiety, 234, 236, 238, 239, 241, 246, 247, 260–264
reduction of, 261
(*see also* Arousal, Emotion)
Arousal (also Activation), 50–53, 56, 62–65, 68–71, 73, 76, 79, 233–239, 245–249, 252, 254–256, 261, 263, 266, 267, 269–271, 282–284, 287, 289, 296
reduction of, 261, 282, 283, 287, 300
(*see also* Emotion)
Ascendance, *see* Dominance
Attitude, 2, 5, 7, 8, 12, 24, 25, 27, 32, 33, 40, 41, 191–227, 238
Authoritarianism, 141–143, 187
Autonomy, *see* Independence

B

Birth order, 261–265

C

Categorization, 5–11, 13, 16, 18–22, 25, 27, 40, 41, 236, 240, 242
availability of category in (also Codability), 13, 14, 19, 21, 37
content of category, 20–22, 25

Centrality, 114–116, 120–122, 125–127, 130–132, 137, 141, 144
Clasping, *see* Contact-seeking
Codability, *see* Categorization, availability
Cognition, 2–4, 7, 9, 13, 17–19, 29, 37–39, 50, 51, 53, 196–199, 215, 236, 240n, 262
consistency theories of, 29, 30, 196
Compliance, *see* Conformity
Conflict, interorganismic, 84, 85, 90, 91, 104–106, 270, 290–292, 294
Conformity (also Compliance), 34, 195, 199, 218, 244
Connotative meaning, 11, 25–28, 39, 40
Contact-seeking (also Clasping), 281–284, 286, 301
Coordination, 84, 85, 99, 106, 107, 161, 279, 296, 301
Culture, 2–5, 10, 12–20, 22, 26, 27, 33, 34, 36–38, 40, 262
and beliefs, 2, 33, 41
and discriminations, 5, 13, 21, 22
limits on influence of, 15–19, 26–28, 33, 39, 40
and perception, 12–15, 18, 22, 24, 25, 28–30, 41

D

Decision making, 83–85, 118, 194, 195
Dependency, as drive, 232, 233, 239, 240, 244, 271
as response, 233–236, 239–243, 248, 249, 253, 254, 256, 258, 259, 261–265, 268, 270, 271, 300
training, 261, 265
Deprivation, 234, 244–247, 249–252, 254, 256–258, 271, 291
Discipline, 235
Dissonance, state of, 199, 200, 237
(*see also* Cognition, consistency theories)